D1721188

European Yearbook of International Economic Law

EYIEL Monographs - Studies in European and International Economic Law

Volume 3

Series editors
Marc Bungenberg, Saarbrücken, Germany
Christoph Herrmann, Passau, Germany
Markus Krajewski, Erlangen, Germany
Jörg Philipp Terhechte, Lüneburg, Germany
Andreas R. Ziegler, Lausanne, Switzerland

EYIEL Monographs is a subseries of the European Yearbook of International Economic Law (EYIEL). It contains scholarly works in the fields of European and international economic law, in particular WTO law, international investment law, international monetary law, law of regional economic integration, external trade law of the EU and EU internal market law. The series does not include edited volumes. EYIEL Monographs are peer-reviewed by the series editors and external reviewers.

More information about this series at http://www.springer.com/series/15744

David Sifonios

Environmental Process and Production Methods (PPMs) in WTO Law

 Springer

David Sifonios
University of Lausanne
Lausanne, Switzerland

ISSN 2364-8392   ISSN 2364-8406   (electronic)
European Yearbook of International Economic Law
EYIEL Monographs - Studies in European and International Economic Law
ISBN 978-3-319-65725-7   ISBN 978-3-319-65726-4   (eBook)
DOI 10.1007/978-3-319-65726-4

Library of Congress Control Number: 2017951620

© Springer International Publishing AG 2018
This work is subject to copyright. All rights are reserved by the Publisher, whether the whole or part of the material is concerned, specifically the rights of translation, reprinting, reuse of illustrations, recitation, broadcasting, reproduction on microfilms or in any other physical way, and transmission or information storage and retrieval, electronic adaptation, computer software, or by similar or dissimilar methodology now known or hereafter developed.
The use of general descriptive names, registered names, trademarks, service marks, etc. in this publication does not imply, even in the absence of a specific statement, that such names are exempt from the relevant protective laws and regulations and therefore free for general use.
The publisher, the authors and the editors are safe to assume that the advice and information in this book are believed to be true and accurate at the date of publication. Neither the publisher nor the authors or the editors give a warranty, express or implied, with respect to the material contained herein or for any errors or omissions that may have been made. The publisher remains neutral with regard to jurisdictional claims in published maps and institutional affiliations.

Printed on acid-free paper

This Springer imprint is published by Springer Nature
The registered company is Springer International Publishing AG
The registered company address is: Gewerbestrasse 11, 6330 Cham, Switzerland

Preface

The last decades have shown that we live in a world of rapidly changing environmental challenges. Pressure on the environment and natural resources has increased dramatically, threatening biodiversity and the future availability of resources; the rise of greenhouse gases in the atmosphere requires global efforts to mitigate climate change; the reduction of the environmental footprint of energy consumption calls for the massive development of renewable energy; etc.

Trade instruments have commonly been seen as possible means to achieve environmental objectives, especially when the source of the environmental problem is located abroad, in a country that does not necessarily participate in international efforts to pursue such objectives.

At the same time, the use of trade instruments to achieve environmental goals has often been met with strong political opposition, due in part to the complexity of the different and competing interests at stake. These tensions and difficulties are reflected in the relevant WTO case law, which has significantly evolved and is particularly complex. At the beginning of the 1990s, the *US – Tuna* reports expressed the view that PPM measures could not be justified under the GATT. A few years later, the *US – Shrimp* reports eventually upheld an environmental PPM measure, which showed that such measures are not illegal per se under WTO law. Yet many issues remained unresolved after this case, when it comes to the conditions under which environmental PPM measures are justifiable. Since then, WTO case law has developed considerably and has significantly influenced the issue of process-based measures. It has, however, also added to the complexity of the PPM case law, and to a certain impression that as PPM case law has developed, so has its somewhat confusing character.

The PPM debate is thus an extraordinary field for academic research. The main idea at the origin of this book was to analyse how the multilateral trading system could address the huge challenges of reconciling the different views and interests at stake when it comes to PPM measures, through the application of the WTO agreements in their current version. To this end, my research has focused on three main issues: why PPM measures are so controversial, what is the current status of

PPM measures in WTO law *de lege lata* and how legitimate and illegitimate PPM measures could be distinguished *de lege ferenda*.

Many people have supported me through my doctoral research, and I express my appreciation to all of them.

First, I am most grateful to my supervisor, Professor Andreas Ziegler, for his much appreciated trust, support and encouragement. My appreciation also goes to Professor Michael Hahn, Werner Zdouc and Serge Pannatier, for their constructive and thoughtful comments on my research.

A warm word of thanks goes to my friends and colleagues, who have shared through the years part of the journey towards the completion of this book. I am also very grateful to Anoula, André and Johan, who have always been there to support me in my academic activities and in my life.

Finally, my deepest gratitude goes to Sandra, for her continuous loving support, her infinite patience and her availability to discuss many of the challenging legal issues of my research. The achievement of this book owes a great deal to her.

Lausanne, Switzerland   David Sifonios

Contents

Chapter 1
Introduction

Environmental policies aimed at managing the environmental impact of products are often based on a life-cycle analysis, which takes into consideration the production, consumption and disposal phases of a product's life.[1] States may seek to adopt product standards or disposal requirements that reduce environmental effects but also to regulate the production methods of the goods sold in their internal market, including imported products. Certain production methods may indeed result in important environmental harm. For instance, natural resource exploitation may result in extensive environmental damages, such as incidental catch of non-target species in fish trawling, destruction of primary forests to harvest tropical timber or the use of certain farming methods (slash and burn, extensive use of chemicals, etc.). Another significant impact of goods' production is greenhouse gas emissions, which affect the global climate regardless of the precise location of the emission sources. In other words, the interdependence of ecosystems implies that the environmental impact of the production methods of product in one particular country can have effects in other countries.[2]

---

[1] See e.g. Appleton (1997a), pp. 12 f. (pointing out in particular that life-cycle labelling schemes may be voluntary or mandatory. Such mandatory labelling requirements are a form of import ban on products which are ineligible for the label); OECD (1997a), p. 9 ('[l]ife-cycle approaches have been recognised as valuable tools for governments, industry and consumers in understanding the complex environmental effects of products from the "craddle to the grave", and in reducing environmental burdens caused by products during their life cycle'); OECD (1995), p. 26 ('[l]ife-cycle approaches are a central feature of product-related environmental policies').

[2] Perrez (2000), pp. 167 f. ('[t]herefore, today, one has to accept that the use of one resource entails indirect or direct use of another resource [. . .]. [B]ecause the use of one resource mostly involves the use of another resource, most of the states have at least an indirect interest in the use of most of the resources of this globe'); Sands (2012), p. 12 ('[m]any environmental resources and their environmental components are ecologically shared. The use by one state of natural resources within its territory will invariably have consequences for the use of natural resources and their environmental components in another state').

© Springer International Publishing AG 2018
D. Sifonios, *Environmental Process and Production Methods (PPMs) in WTO Law*,
European Yearbook of International Economic Law 3,
DOI 10.1007/978-3-319-65726-4_1

From an environmental policy viewpoint, sources of environmental harm may be problematic regardless of their domestic or foreign location. However, when a particular source is located beyond the jurisdiction of a state, measures aimed at addressing it may give rise to issues of state sovereignty.[3] If a state decides to address environmental harm caused by practices in other countries by way of trade restrictions, its efforts may also conflict with international trade rules.[4]

This issue has given rise to a particular intense controversy in WTO law, in the context of which such trade measures are referred to as process and production methods (PPMs).

The main source of the debates on PPM measures is the product-process distinction applied by the GATT 1947 Panels in the two *US – Tuna* reports. These two Panels expressed a very restricted view concerning the legality of PPM measures. These disputes arose at the beginning of the 1990s and concerned a US embargo on Mexican tuna that was caught in a manner that resulted in incidental killings of dolphins.[5] This measure was challenged by Mexico in the *US – Tuna I* case. The United States also enacted a secondary embargo applying to all third countries that did not prohibit imports of tuna from Mexico. The European Communities challenged the secondary embargo, in the *US – Tuna II* case.[6]

Both Panels rejected the possibility to justify a PPM measure conditioning market access to the adoption of particular environmental policies by the exporting Members. They were of the opinion that two physically identical or similar products had to be considered as 'like' regardless of differences in their production processes and that PPM measures could in any case not comply with the national treatment obligation.[7] Moreover, they found that these measures could not be justified under Article XX, at least when they aimed at the protection of environmental resources beyond the jurisdiction of the importing state, because they perceived that allowing such measures would entail risks of jeopardising the functioning of the GATT.[8] In their view, if such practices were allowed, the GATT could 'no longer serve as a multilateral framework for trade among contracting parties'[9] and would 'provide legal security only in respect of trade between a limited number of contracting parties with identical regulations'.[10]

In brief, under the product-process distinction applied by the *US – Tuna* Panels, PPM measures violated Article III and could not be justified under Article XX. It was thus often assumed in trade circles following the *US – Tuna* cases that PPM

[3]See *infra*, Chap. 5.

[4]See the detailed analysis of WTO law *infra*, Chaps. 6–8.

[5]*US – Tuna I*, Panel Report; *US – Tuna II*, Panel Report.

[6]*US – Tuna II*, Panel Report.

[7]See *infra*, 6.3.1.2.2 and *US – Tuna I*, Panel Report, para. 5.8 ff.

[8]See *infra*, 7.1.2.1.1.

[9]*US – Tuna I*, Panel Report, para. 5.26.

[10]*US – Tuna I*, Panel Report, para. 5.27.

measures were prohibited under the GATT.[11] These reports have given rise to intense criticism, both from a legal viewpoint and as regards the consequences of this approach for state sovereignty and the ability of GATT Members to pursue environmental objectives.[12]

One year after the *US – Tuna* case, a major institutional change occurred, namely the creation of the WTO in 1995. The text of the GATT was not modified during the Uruguay round of negotiations. However, the WTO Agreement itself introduced important elements that have influenced the interpretation of the GATT. More precisely, the drafters of the GATT 1947 indicated in its Preamble that one of the objectives of the General Agreement was developing the 'full use of the resources of the world'. By contrast, the Preamble of the Marrakesh Agreement establishing the WTO refers to the objective of allowing the 'optimal use of the world's resources in accordance with the objective of sustainable development'. The WTO Agreement Preamble thus indicates that developing trade is not the sole purpose of the WTO. Sustainable development suggests that trade, the environment and development should be mutually supportive.[13]

Another major change introduced at that time was the creation of the Dispute Settlement Body, which represents a quasi-judicial organ. An Appellate Body has been instituted, to which panel reports can be appealed. Moreover, reports of panels and of the Appellate Body are automatically adopted in the absence of a negative consensus among WTO Members,[14] whereas a positive consensus was necessary under the GATT 1947.[15] Reports of WTO adjudicating bodies do not formally amount to binding precedents. They have nevertheless a considerable practical influence since WTO adjudicating bodies tend to systematically rely on past reports.[16] In practice, the Appellate Body has also adopted much more legally subtle reasoning than GATT 1947 panels.[17]

---

[11]See e.g. GATT Secretariat (1992) ('[i]n principle, it is not possible under GATT's rules to make access to one's own market dependent on the domestic environmental policies or practices of the exporting country'). See also Hudec (2000), p. 189, with further references; Charnovitz (2002), pp. 76 f., with further references; Schoenbaum (1997), pp. 288 and 290; Okubo (1999), pp. 618 ff.; Marceau (2002), p. 807; Joshi (2004), p. 79; Pauwelyn (2004), p. 585.

[12]See e.g. Jackson (1997), p. 238; Hudec (2000), pp. 187 ff.; Charnovitz (2002), p. 60; Howse and Regan (2000), pp. 249 ff.; Vranes (2009), p. 322. See also Matsushita et al. (2015), pp. 722 ff.

[13]See e.g. the Johannesburg Plan of Implementation of the World Summit on Sustainable Development, which refers to the efforts to 'promote the integration of the three components of sustainable development—economic development, social development and environmental protection—as interdependent and mutually reinforcing pillars' (para. 2).

[14]See Articles 16 and 17 of the Understanding on Rules and Procedures Governing the Settlement of Disputes.

[15]See e.g. Davey (1987), pp. 85 ff.; Luff (2004), p. 772.

[16]See Matsushita et al. (2015), p. 75; *Japan – Alcohol II*, Appellate Body Report, para. 108; *US – Shrimp 21.5*, Appellate Body Report, para. 109.

[17]See in particular the analysis of the GATT *US – Tuna* cases and the WTO *US – Shrimp* cases in Chaps. 6 and 7 below.

This greater legal sensitivity, and the influence of the objective of sustainable development on the interpretation of the GATT, was particularly apparent in the *US – Shrimp* Appellate Body report.[18] This dispute concerned a US import prohibition of shrimp caught in a manner that harmed sea turtles. The United States basically required shrimp-producing countries that exported shrimp products to the United States to adopt regulations mandating the use of fishing methods that did not harm sea turtles. Four Asian shrimp exporting countries challenged this measure.[19] The Panel applied a similar reasoning as that of the *US – Tuna* Panels. But the Panel report was overturned by the Appellate Body, which rejected that PPM measures could be prohibited because they required the adoption by the exporting country of environmental policies prescribed by the importing state.

Because of certain minor irregularities in the contested measure, the Appellate Body still found the measure to be inconsistent with the GATT. The United States made the changes required by the Appellate Body. When Malaysia challenged these implementation measures, the Appellate Body eventually upheld the United States measure.[20] This report had far-reaching consequences since it concerned a PPM measure that had no impact on the physical characteristics of the final product and that had been unilaterally imposed by a WTO Member. It has shown that if certain conditions are met, PPM measures can comply with the GATT. In other words, the Appellate Body implicitly rejected the product-process distinction in its *US – Shrimp* report.

Many issues remain unsettled, however, when it comes to the circumstances in which a PPM measure may comply with GATT provisions. On the other hand, the issue of PPM measures has remained intensely debated, for several reasons.

First, the PPM issue is controversial because the WTO agreements contain very few specific rules applying to PPM measures. No GATT provisions specifically discipline PPM measures. The way GATT rules should be interpreted when it comes to PPM measures has thus been highly debated. The Agreement on Technical Barriers to Trade (TBT Agreement) refers to PPMs since it applies to technical regulations, which are defined as a document that lays down product characteristics 'or their related process and production methods'. It is, however, usually considered that this definition only covers PPM measures that leave a physical trace on the final product (so-called product-related PPMs (pr-PPMs), or incorporated PPMs), such as the use of pesticides in agriculture, which are still present in the end product.[21] By contrast, the widely shared view is that the TBT Agreement does not apply to PPM measures that do not have any impact on the physical characteristics of the

---

[18]See e.g. Matsushita et al. (2015), p. 732, stating that the *US – Shrimp* case is 'a well-reasoned decision of great importance for the trade and environment controversy'. See also Ziegler and Sifonios (2017) for a discussion of the influence that the concept of sustainable development, and its underlying vision of the future, has had on the WTO case law.

[19]*US – Shrimp*, Panel Report; *US – Shrimp*, Appellate Body Report.

[20]*US – Shrimp 21.5*, Appellate Body Report.

[21]See e.g. Appleton (1997a), p. 122, with further references; Appleton (2009), p. 139; Conrad (2011), pp. 378 ff.; Cooreman (2017), pp. 24 f. See also *infra*, 8.1.

product (so-called non-product-related (npr-PPMs), or unincorporated PPMs), which are thus only covered by the GATT.[22] The Agreement on the Application of Sanitary and Phytosanitary Measures (SPS Agreement) also refers to process and production methods.[23] But it is generally considered in this context as well that the SPS Agreement only applies to product-related PPM measures.[24]

Another fundamental aspect that explains why PPM measures have given rise to such intense controversy is that their use affects a very broad range of competing interests. As it will be explained in details below, PPM measures can be a useful and necessary tool to achieve international and global environmental protection.[25] At the same time, they are viewed suspiciously by free traders because of their possible use to achieve protectionist objectives and because they can significantly increase obstacles to trade, thereby jeopardising trade liberalisation.[26] On the other hand, they may be viewed by some as conflicting with the principle that states have the sovereign right to exploit their natural resources and regulate the activities occurring within their territory. PPM measures have given rise to particular strong opposition when they are unilaterally imposed by an industrialised country against a developing state, which often have different economic and environmental priorities and different financial and technical means.[27]

Institutional aspects also explain the extent of the PPM controversy in WTO law. The GATT is a trade agreement. But many trade disputes may have consequences on non-trade issues such as environmental protection. Certain critics argue that non-trade issues have often been largely ignored within this trade institution that the WTO represents.[28] Yet in the absence of any international institutions comparable to the WTO in the field of international environmental law, and because the WTO has a rather unique and efficient dispute settlement system, disputes relating to trade and the environment are often brought in practice to WTO adjudicating bodies, which must then address potentially sensitive non-trade issues.

These different circumstances explain in part why the PPM issue has continued to generate intense debate, even after the *US – Shrimp* case.

In recent years, the PPM issue has in particular been discussed in the climate change context.[29] Both the United States and certain countries of the European Union have contemplated at some point the idea of introducing CO_2 emission

---

[22]See *infra*, 8.1.

[23]See the definition of SPS measures in Annex A of the SPS Agreement.

[24]See e.g. Conrad (2011), pp. 420 f.

[25]See *infra*, Chap. 3.

[26]See *infra*, 2.1.

[27]See *infra*, 2.1.

[28]See e.g. Guzman (2004), p. 304 *et passim*. Guzman argues for the introduction of non-trade issues into the mandate of the WTO. For a critique of this proposal, see McGinnis and Movsesian (2004).

[29]See e.g. Holzer's book on Carbon-Related Border Adjustment and WTO law (2014). See also Green (2005); Pauwelyn (2007); Bhagwati and Mavroidis (2007); Regan (2009); Appleton (2009); Condon (2009); Hufbauer et al. (2009).

regulation both for domestic and imported products.[30] Such trade restrictions would constitute a form of unincorporated PPM measure. The precise conditions under which they could comply with the GATT remain unsettled. In any event, if such measures were adopted, they would undoubtedly be controversial, in particular if they are applied by industrialised countries against developing countries.

In order to understand the complexity of the PPM issue, this work examines in the next chapters the traditional arguments against and in favour of PPM measures. Chapter 2 looks at the main arguments that have traditionally been invoked against the use of PPM measures. Chapter 3 introduces certain elements of economic theory and explains that a prohibition of PPM measures could result in important risks of global inaction in the management of international environmental problems. Chapter 4 analyses the principle of international environmental law regarding the rights and duties of states in relation to natural resource exploitation and conservation. Chapter 5 examines the international law rules on extraterritoriality and non-intervention, which are sometimes invoked as an argument against the use of PPM measures.

The following chapters analyse then in detail the relevant provisions of the WTO agreements. Chapter 6 deals with GATT national treatment obligation (Article III). Chapter 7 explores the general exceptions provision (Article XX). These chapters show that while the product-process distinction was based on rigid dichotomies between permissible and impermissible measures, case law has evolved towards a more flexible system, which allows the adoption of PPM measures in certain circumstances, even though the exact conditions under which PPM standards are justifiable are not entirely clear yet. Chapter 8 looks at the relevant provisions of the TBT Agreement. Chapter 9 concludes by an overall critical assessment of case law *de lege lata* and *de lege ferenda*.

To conclude this introduction, a few comments should be made on aspects that are not examined in this book.

First, while this study analyses the GATT and the TBT Agreement, it does not review the Agreement on the Application of Sanitary and Phytosanitary Measures (SPS Agreement). The SPS Agreement applies to certain types of PPM measures[31] but only those that are applied to protect animal or plant life or health *within the territory* of the WTO Member enacting that measure.[32] Hence, the prevailing view is that the SPS Agreement applies only to measures that carry diseases or harmful substances to the territories of the importing Member, i.e. to measures based on product-related PPMs.[33] Such kind of SPS measures based on product-related

---

[30]See e.g. Bhagwati and Mavroidis (2007) or Pauwelyn (2007).

[31]See Annex A of the SPS Agreement which reads in relevant part '[s]anitary or phytosanitary measures include all relevant laws, decrees, regulations, requirements and procedures including, *inter alia*, end product criteria; process and production methods; . . .'.

[32]See the definition of 'sanitary or phytosanitary measure' in Annex A of the SPS Agreement, paragraph 1 (a) to (d).

[33]See e.g. Conrad (2011), pp. 420 f.

PPMs has not given rise to significant debates in academic writings to date, perhaps because risks of protectionist abuses are perceived to be less intense when animal or plant life or health within the importing country's territory are at stake. The more controversial non-product-related PPM measures taken to protect animal or plant life or health in foreign countries are subject to the GATT[34] and are examined in detail in Chaps. 6 and 7 below.

Second, this book does not examine PPM measures that would not be based on environmental objectives but on social goals, such as the protection of human rights or labour conditions prevailing during the manufacturing process of imported products.[35] Environmental PPM measures may be analysed in the light of various objective characteristics, such as the existence of transboundary externalities,[36] global public goods[37] or international acknowledgement of the legitimacy of a particular objective in a multilateral environmental agreement,[38] which may play a role in their analysis under the GATT.[39] Moreover, Article XX contains at least two explicit exceptions applying to environmental measures, i.e. sub-paragraphs (b) and (g). When it comes to labour conditions, it may be more difficult to rely on objective criteria to differentiate between justifiable and unjustifiable restrictive trade measures, apart from cases of severe violations of core human rights. In order to justify a social PPM measure, Article XX(a), which protects public morals, could be invoked.[40] This provision has never been invoked to date to justify a 'social PPM' measure, and it was applied in only one case brought to DSB, the *EC – Seal Products* case. This case concerned an import ban on seal products justified on the basis of the cruelty of the way seals are killed, which represents a form of non-product-related PPM measure. It does not seem excluded that Article XX(a) could be invoked to justify a trade measure based on differences in human rights protection or on labour standards, provided that it may be shown that the conditions prevailing in the producing country violate public morals. If differences in labour conditions that amount to core human rights violations would probably comply with this condition, it remains unknown if less severe differences would also justify a trade restrictive measure, and in that case what criteria could be used to draw the line between admissible and inadmissible measures. Hence, differences between environmental and social PPM measures seem sufficiently important to justify that the former be addressed separately. That being said, certain results of this study can probably also be applied *mutatis mutandis* to PPM measures that are based on social objectives.

---

[34]See e.g. Conrad (2011), p. 421.

[35]On this issue, see e.g. Charnovitz (1998); Howse (1999); Guzman (2003); Nadakavukaren Schefer (2010); Conrad (2011).

[36]See *infra*, 3.2.1.

[37]See *infra*, 3.2.2.

[38]See *infra*, Chap. 4.

[39]See *infra*, 7.1.2.2.2.

[40]On the possibilities to invoke Article XX(a) for instance against products made by child labour, see e.g. Charnovitz (1998), Howse (1999).

Chapter 2
Main Arguments Against the Use of PPM Measures

The legality of PPM measures has been one of the most controversial issues in WTO law.[1] If these instruments have given rise to intense debates, it is because strong arguments against their use and against their prohibition coexist.

Arguments against the use of PPM measures are summarised in this chapter. They are mainly twofold: first, it has been maintained that PPM measures interfere with the producing country's sovereignty, which may in particular have different economic means and priorities (Sect. 2.1). Second, it may be perceived that process standards are incompatible with the world trading system and may threaten its proper functioning (Sect. 2.2).

2.1 Sovereignty, Extraterritoriality and the Interests of Developing Countries

Various arguments relating to sovereignty have been invoked against the use of PPM measures.

First, it has been maintained that PPM measures interfere with the exporting country's sovereign right under international law to regulate activities occurring

---

[1]See e.g., on the one hand, Hudec (2000), p. 188 (stating that the *US – Tuna* reports, which basically outlawed PPM measures under the GATT 1947, were 'greeted by a storm of protest from environmental organizations and other allied groups') and, on the other hand, Bhagwati (2004), p. 157 (stating about the *US – Shrimp* report, which eventually upheld a non-product-related PPM measure, that it 'left many observers in the developing countries outraged' and that it was a 'dangerous' decision because it opened up a 'Pandora's box'). See also Charnovitz (2002), p. 59 (stating that PPMs are the subject of one of the 'most knotty controversies' in the trade and environment debate. He also asserts on p. 61 that the *US – Shrimp* case demonstrated 'the cloud of suspicion surrounding the application of PPMs').

© Springer International Publishing AG 2018

D. Sifonios, *Environmental Process and Production Methods (PPMs) in WTO Law*,
European Yearbook of International Economic Law 3,
DOI 10.1007/978-3-319-65726-4_2

within its jurisdiction (territoriality principle) or, in other words, that PPM trade restrictions must be viewed as *extraterritorial measures*.[2] This argument is based on the view that process-based import restrictions prescribe the adoption of a conduct abroad.[3] The regulated activity can either occur in the jurisdiction of another state, which has the exclusive right to regulate activities in its territory under international law, or in areas beyond any jurisdiction such as the high seas, in which states have the exclusive right to regulate the activities of their nationals.[4] Producers that do not comply with this requirement cannot access the importing country's market because of a conduct that occurred beyond the jurisdiction of the importing country. In this view, customary international law rules on extraterritorial jurisdiction imply that the importing country needs to rely on a recognised jurisdictional basis so as to have the right to regulate foreign conduct.[5] These arguments are further analysed in Chap. 5 below.

Second, certain countries have supported the view that PPM measures represent a form of *interference in internal affairs*, which violate the international law principle of non-intervention. Under customary international law, states are indeed prohibited from coercing another state into adopting a policy that this state has the sovereign right to choose.[6] Under this view, economic coercion induced by PPM measures should be treated as a violation of the customary international law principle of non-intervention.[7] It will be, however, shown below that economic coercion has generally not been recognised in customary international law as a violation of the principle of non-intervention.[8]

Third, when it comes to natural resource management, international law acknowledges the principle of *permanent sovereignty over natural resources*, which implies *inter alia* that states have the exclusive right to exploit their natural resources pursuant to their own environmental and developmental policies.[9] Many

---

[2]Bagwell et al. (2002), p. 76; Horn and Mavroidis (2008), p. 1125 *et passim*; Jansen and Lugard (1999), p. 533 and n. 6 p. 535; Schoenbaum (1997), pp. 279 f. See also Jackson (1992), p. 1244 who argues that '[p]ossibly these exceptions should be limited to the situation where governments are protecting matters that occur within their territorial jurisdiction'; *US – Tuna II*, para. 5.17. See also *infra*, Chap. 5.

[3]This view has not remained uncontested. See *infra*, Chap. 5.

[4]See e.g. Brownlie (2012), pp. 456 ff.

[5]This view has not remained uncontested. See *infra*, Chap. 5.

[6]Declaration on Principles of International Law Concerning Friendly Relations and Cooperation Amongst States in Accordance with the Charter of the United Nations, UNGA Res. 2131, UN, GAOR, 20th Sess., UN Doc A/6220 (1965), Chap. 1 (b) ('[n]o state may use or encourage the use of economic, political, or any other type of measures to coerce another state in order to obtain from it the subordination of the exercise of its sovereign rights or to secure from it advantages of any kind').

[7]Gathii (2000), pp. 2029 f. See also the arguments of the complainants in the *US – Shrimp* case, Panel Report, para. 3.6, 3.41, 3.104 and particularly 3.157.

[8]See *infra*, Chap. 5.

[9]UNGA Res. 2635, UN GAOR, 25th Sess., UN Doc. A/8028 (1970); Principle 2 of the Rio Declaration. See also *infra*, Chap. 4.

developing states have thus opposed the use of PPM measures because they were perceived as conflicting with these countries' right to choose their environmental and developmental policies according to their own priorities. However, it will be shown below that the evolution of international environmental law implies that permanent sovereignty over natural resources is not an unfettered principle and is restricted by various international environmental duties and principles.[10]

Arguments relating to sovereignty have often been invoked by developing countries, as a defence against attempts of industrialised states to impose their high environmental standards.[11] For instance, the Group of 77 (G-77) declared in 2000 its rejection of all attempts to use environmental, labour standards or human rights as reasons for restricting market access for developing countries.[12]

The main problem with PPM measures adopted by countries with large markets against smaller and poorer nations is that a significant difference may exist in their priorities, as reflected in their economic, developmental and environmental policies. Imposing higher environment standards implies costs on exporting countries that may not correspond to their social and economic preferences.[13] The objective of developing countries is generally economic development, education, reduction of poverty or improvement of basic infrastructure. Usually, they are first and foremost concerned with national programmes that provide direct and immediate benefits to their citizens and not global problems that pose uncertain and distant risks to their environment.[14] On the other hand, developed countries can more easily afford the 'luxury' of focusing on these distant risks because basic needs are secured.[15] Adoption of PPM measures by developed countries against developing nations thus tends to reflect a 'Northern-biased agenda'.[16]

Another objection of developing countries against the imposition of high environmental standards by developed states is that global environmental problems that the international community has to face nowadays are the result of more than 150 years of pollution mainly caused by industrial development of northern countries. Requiring the same environmental standards for southern states may seem thus unfair not only because these countries also have the right to develop, which may imply an increase in their global environmental impact, but also because developed nations are largely responsible for current global environmental threats

---

[10]See *infra*, Chap. 4.

[11]See e.g. *US – Tuna I* (United States v. Mexico) and *US – Shrimp* (United States v. India, Malaysia, Thailand and Pakistan). See also Charnovitz (2002), pp. 62 f.

[12]Declaration of the South Summit from the Group of 77, 12–14 April 2000, para. 21, p. 7 ('[w]hile recognizing the value of environmental protection, labour standards [...] and protection of all universally recognized human rights and fundamental freedoms, [...] we reject all attempts to use these issues as conditionalities for restricting market access or aid and technology flows to developing countries').

[13]Bierman (2001), p. 433.

[14]Esty (1994), p. 185.

[15]*Ibid.*, p. 184.

[16]Bierman (2001), p. 433.

because of their past pollution and because of their resource-intensive consumption patterns.[17]

It could also be noted that the imposition of PPM measures is an effective tool only for large markets, often against countries with smaller markets.[18] When trade restrictions are used to impose values on others, it could be seen as a signal that values of economically strong nations are morally superior to those of economically poor ones (eco-imperialism).[19] Developing nations are particularly attached to their exclusive right to exploit their natural resources,[20] for obvious historical reasons. These attempts may even be seen as 'potential subterfuge designed to maintain the economic dominance of the industrialized world'.[21]

In brief, from a north-south perspective, allowing the adoption of PPM measures by rich developed countries against poor developing nations may seem unjust for historical reasons on the one hand and because the priorities and means of states to address global environmental threats differ quite significantly.[22] These concerns have led in particular to the development of the principle of common but differentiated responsibilities, which has been included in various multilateral environmental agreements, as it will be shown in Chap. 4 below.

2.2 Incompatibility with the World Trading System

The other main traditional argument invoked against the use of PPM measures is that they conflict with trade interests and the functioning of the world trading system. The various arguments that have been invoked in this field may be classified into two main categories. First, it has been contended that PPM measures implied risks of jeopardising the multilateral trading system through unrestrained proliferation of obstacles to trade. Second, PPM measures may be viewed as conflicting with comparative advantages, on which the principle of trade liberalisation is based.

The first argument was particularly apparent in the two unadopted *US – Tuna* GATT Panel reports, at the beginning of the 1990s. In these reports, the Panels expressed the view that if the GATT allowed an importing Member to adopt trade measures to force other Members to change their environmental policies within their own jurisdiction, the GATT could 'no longer serve as a multilateral framework for trade among contracting parties'.[23] One of their main concerns was that

---

[17]Esty (1994), pp. 185 ff.; Jackson (1992), p. 1230.

[18]OECD (1997b), p. 33.

[19]Bhagwati (1993), p. 174; Bhagwati (2004), p. 155.

[20]See *infra*, Chap. 4.

[21]Esty (1994), p. 182.

[22]See e.g. Bhagwati (1993), pp. 186 f.

[23]*US – Tuna II*, Panel Report, para. 5.26; *US –Tuna I*, Panel Report, para. 5.28.

accepting such a rule could mean that the GATT would provide legal security only between Members with *identical* internal regulations.[24] As a consequence, the *US – Tuna* Panels basically held that PPM measures could not be justified under the GATT.

Even though these two reports remained unadopted, their reasoning has had a significant influence among trade circles. It has been often assumed following these reports that PPM measures were prohibited under the GATT.[25] The *US – Tuna* Panels mainly based their exclusion of PPM measures on the risks of incompatibility of unilaterally imposed environmental standards. They apparently feared that there might be conflicting requirements when several importing countries decide to impose their internal standards to a particular producing state, which would eventually threaten trade relations. This argument has also been expressed by scholars who argued that allowing the regulation of PPMs by the importing country would be like opening a 'Pandora's box' and would represent a 'slippery slope', by which trade rules would allow regulations that represent significant non-tariff barriers to trade[26] and that may be a form of 'green protectionism'.[27] It has indeed been contended that protectionist objectives can quite easily be disguised behind environmental pretexts.[28]

This 'slippery slope' argument has been invoked in particular in response to specific types of PPM measures, such as those based on *moral* preferences. It has been argued that such measures could result in a 'proliferation of trade restrictions without any disciplines or restraint'[29] because moral preferences may vary among countries and cannot be controlled by an international tribunal, for instance by using a scientific test.

Likewise, it has often been maintained that allowing *unilateral* PPM measures, as opposed to trade measures provided for in an MEA, implied important risks of 'slippery slope'. For instance, the GATT Secretariat has maintained in 1992 that a prohibition of PPM measures 'protects relations from degenerating into anarchy

---

[24]*US –Tuna I*, Panel Report, para. 5.28.

[25]See e.g. GATT Secretariat (1992) ('[i]n principle, it is not possible under GATT's rules to make access to one's own market dependent on the domestic environmental policies or practices of the exporting country'). See also Hudec (2000), p. 189, with further references; Charnovitz (2002), pp. 76 f., with further references; Schoenbaum (1997), pp. 288 and 290; Okubo (1999), p. 618 ff.; Marceau (2002), p. 807; Joshi (2004), p. 79; Pauwelyn (2004), p. 585.

[26]Bhagwati (2004), pp. 154 f. (stating that the fear of allowing PPMs measures 'was that an open-ended grant of exception on values-related PPMs could lead to a slippery slope and a flood of exclusions that could not be challenged'); GATT Secretariat (1992) ('[i]f the door were opened to use trade policies unilaterally to offset the competitiveness effects of different environmental standards, or to attempt to force other countries to adopt domestically-favoured practices and policies, the trading system would start down a very slippery slope'); Jackson (1992), pp. 1241 f.

[27]Cosbey (2002), pp. 13 f.; Petersmann (1996), p. 50 *et passim*.

[28]Jackson (1992), p. 1235 ('[e]nvironmental policies can be so easily used as an excuse for protectionism').

[29]Bhagwati (1993), p. 171. See also GATT Secretariat (1992), explaining that the rationale for the exclusion of PPMs is 'that to do otherwise would invite a flood of import restrictions'.

through unilateral actions in pursuit of unilaterally-defined objectives, however they may appear. If the goal is to influence environmental policies and practices in other countries, the option which is most consistent with orderly international relations is inter-governmental cooperation leading to a multilateral agreement.'[30] However, as it will be shown in Chap. 3 below, the prohibition of unilateral trade measures could lead to important risks of international inaction in the field of environmental protection.

More fundamentally, as already mentioned, PPM measures may be seen as conflicting with the objective of trade liberalisation, based on the theory of comparative advantages. Countries specialise in the areas in which they are the most efficient comparatively to others, which allows states not to waste resources producing goods that other countries are able to produce more efficiently.[31] Economic theory posits that differences in internal regulations of factors of production, including environmental regulations, contribute to determining comparative advantages of states.[32] In that respect, it has been claimed that allowing a state to impose through PPM measures its own environmental standards on its trading partners could defeat the basic goals of comparative advantages[33] and thus reduce GATT efficiency.[34]

However, this view has not remained uncontested. Some have pointed out that certain differences in internal environmental regulations should not be regarded as the basis of legitimate advantages, such as cases in which the same externality is caused by the producers of the importing and exporting countries.[35] For instance, greenhouse gases emitted in both countries have the same effect on the global climate. If only the importing country internalises these externalities, the producers of the exporting country do have a cost advantage, which trade rules should, however, not encourage in all circumstances. Not all differences in internal regulations may thus necessarily be considered as comparative advantages protected by the GATT.[36]

---

[30]GATT Secretariat (1992).

[31]Jackson (1992), p. 1231.

[32]See Bhagwati (1993), p. 167; Jackson (1992), p. 1231; Jackson (1997), pp. 236 f.

[33]Jackson (1997), p. 237.

[34]See e.g. Trebilcock and Giri (2004), p. 57. It has also been argued that certain differences in internal regulations represent merely cost advantages, which are not relevant for the achievement of efficiency, for instance when two countries produce the same externality but only one of them internalises these costs (see Howse and Regan 2000, p. 281).

[35]See Howse and Regan (2000), p. 281. They argue that this cost advantage would be derived to mere legal facts, while foreign producers would produce the same externality on a shared resource as domestic producers. See also Chang (1995), pp. 2131 ff.

[36]For further details, see *infra*, 7.1.2.2.

2.3   The Influence of These Arguments in the PPM Debate

These different arguments against the use of PPM measures were viewed by certain free traders and GATT officials, in particular at the beginning of the 1990s, as reasons to favour a pure and simple prohibition of PPM measures,[37] in order to exclude any risks of jeopardising the multilateral trading system or any risks of protectionist abuses disguised by environmental pretexts.[38]

However, the hard stance taken by the *US – Tuna* Panels, which resulted in a prohibition of PPM measures, gave rise to strong opposition against the GATT from environmentalists and part of the civil society. Free trade critics used the expression of 'GATTzilla' to describe what was perceived as a trading system that threatened environmental protection and state sovereignty.[39] It was perceived by some that the GATT restricted unduly their Members' regulatory autonomy and entailed risks of preventing governmental action to address global environmental issues.[40] A prohibition of trade sanctions based on environmental objectives would indeed give rise to important risks of cooperation failures and of international inaction in the field of environmental protection, as it will be shown below.[41] It will also be seen that international environmental law shows that states may have an internationally recognised interest in environmental practices abroad.[42]

From a legal perspective, the prohibition of PPM measures also gave rise to critical comments. Certain arguments against PPM measures are based on customary international law (extraterritorial jurisdiction, non-intervention, permanent sovereignty over natural resources). These arguments are critically assessed from a legal viewpoint in Chaps. 4 and 5 below. Others are based on GATT/WTO law itself, which is extensively examined in Chaps. 6–8.

At this stage, it should at least be noted that the very strict approach regarding the legality of PPM measures advocated by the *US – Tuna* Panels and the GATT Secretariat at the beginning of the 1990s has not been endorsed by the Appellate Body in the *US – Shrimp* case.[43] Since it is mainly the widespread use of PPM measures that gives rise to significant risks for the multilateral trading system, it remains possible to adopt disciplines that condition their use. They would reduce the risks for the multilateral trading system, without preventing any state action through trade restrictions to protect the environment. It is basically what the Appellate Body did in this report, in which it eventually upheld a unilateral

---

[37] See GATT Secretariat (1992) (explaining that the rationale for the exclusion of PPMs is 'that to do otherwise would invite a flood of import restrictions'); Jackson (1992), pp. 1241 f.

[38] See *US – Tuna I*, Panel Report, para. 5.28; *US – Tuna II*, Panel Report, para. 5.26.

[39] Esty (1994), pp. 35 ff.

[40] Strauss (1998), p. 771.

[41] See *infra*, Chap. 3.

[42] See *infra*, Chap. 4.

[43] See in particular *infra*, 7.1.2.1.

npr-PPM measure,[44] after the United States had made a series of changes requested in the initial report. This evolution shows that the Appellate Body has refused to apply strict approaches, which certainly avoided risks of 'slippery slope' but would have resulted in undue restriction of states' sovereignty and to intense opposition to the GATT. If the current approach is thus much more balanced than the one that prevailed in trade circles at the end of the GATT 1947 era, the precise legal disciplines applicable to PPM measures remain unsettled. These aspects are examined in details in Chaps. 6–8.

---

[44]See *US – Shrimp 21.5*, Appellate Body Report.

Chapter 3
Market Failures, Cooperation Failures and the Management of Resources of Common Interest

The previous chapter has described the main reasons why PPM measures are criticised. But if these measures are so controversial, it is also because convincing arguments exist that process standards applied to imports are a useful and necessary instrument to achieving effective protection of global ecosystems, under certain circumstances.[1] This chapter aims at examining the role and importance of PPM measures in environmental policies addressing global environmental issues, in the light of economic theory.

3.1 Market Failures and the Need for State Intervention in the Environmental Field

The need for state intervention in the form of environmental regulation can be explained through the economic model of market failures. This model shows that regulating pollution or natural resource consumption maximises utility and is therefore desirable. Since significant environmental impact of any product is caused by its production, the regulation of production processes plays an important role in achieving environmental protection.

Liberal markets are based on the interplay between supply and demand. For each commodity or service in the market, prices and quantities produced are determined

---

[1] Shortly after the adoption of the first *US – Shrimp* report, strong demonstration took place in Seattle to denounce this decision which was viewed as impeding the ability of WTO Members to protect the environment through their import policies (even though the decision was probably not understood in depth by protesters, since developing countries also opposed that decision and its core findings, which were viewed as giving too much leeway to WTO Members to adopt trade-related environmental measures).

© Springer International Publishing AG 2018

D. Sifonios, *Environmental Process and Production Methods (PPMs) in WTO Law*,
European Yearbook of International Economic Law 3,
DOI 10.1007/978-3-319-65726-4_3

by the intersection of the demand and supply curves.[2] This intersection at which equilibrium occurs corresponds to the point at which the marginal cost equals the marginal benefit. Economic theory describes the situation in which equilibrium occurs for each and every good and service on the market as a *general equilibrium*.[3] It occurs in a perfectly competitive market in which buyers' private marginal benefit, social marginal benefit, sellers' private marginal cost and social marginal cost all equal the market price.[4] The general equilibrium is an abstraction, which is unlikely to be realised in the real world,[5] because the condition to achieve general equilibrium is that all markets are perfectly competitive.[6]

In practice, inevitable distortions exist, and they prevent the achievement of general equilibrium. In particular, unregulated markets fail to produce an optimal allocation of production factors because a difference exists between private and social benefits and costs of an activity.[7] This is referred to as *market failures*, which may justify state intervention in order to improve economic efficiency.[8]

In the environmental field, two types of market failures are relevant: negative and positive externalities. In a typical exchange on the market, the parties capture all the benefits and pay all the costs. But sometimes some of these costs or benefits may spill over onto other parties than those involved in the particular transaction.[9] These are called negative externality (external cost) and positive externality (external benefit, also called public goods).[10]

3.1.1 Negative Externalities

A negative externality occurs when a difference exists between the social and private costs of a transaction. Social efficiency would suppose that the agents in a transaction would bear all its costs—including environmental costs—and enjoy all its benefits. But sometimes firms or individuals do not have to pay for the

---

[2]See generally e.g. Stiglitz and Walsh (2006), pp. 67 ff.

[3]See e.g. Cooter and Ulen (2008), p. 43. See also Stiglitz and Walsh (2006), p. 215.

[4]See e.g. Pugel (2009), p. 180.

[5]See e.g. Bowles (2004), pp. 215; Cooter and Ulen (2008), p. 43; Pugel (2009), p. 181.

[6]See e.g. Cooter and Ulen (2008), p. 43.

[7]Economists also refer to the possibility of 'government failure' when government policies distort otherwise economically efficient markets. See Pugel (2009), p. 182.

[8]See e.g. Stiglitz and Walsh (2006), p. 242. It should be pointed out however that this does not necessarily mean that state intervention by way of *trade measures* is an efficient form of intervention. See *infra*, 3.4. See also e.g. Pauwelyn (2004), p. 579.

[9]See e.g. Cooter and Ulen (2008), p. 44; Stiglitz and Walsh (2006), p. 252.

[10]See e.g. Pugel (2009), p. 269 ('[a]n externality exists when somebody's activity brings direct costs or benefits to anybody who is not part of the marketplace decision to undertake the activity').

environmental costs caused by a particular transaction, such as pollution. The costs caused by the degradation of air, water or soil quality are borne instead by society as a whole, while the agents involved in the transaction enjoy all the benefits.

When some costs are externalised, the market leads to an inefficient allocation of goods because the generator of the externality does not take into account the social costs involved.[11] When the costs can be externalised, the level of production of an individual agent (where its marginal costs equal its marginal benefits) will be higher than the level that social efficiency would require (where the social marginal costs equal the social marginal benefits). Operating along the private marginal cost curve will result in higher output and lower price than operating along the social marginal cost curve.[12]

Since a rational individual will ignore the externalities it produces, government intervention is required to *internalise* that external cost, i.e. to make the parties to a transaction pay for all its costs.[13] Internalisation occurs through policies that induce agents to operate along the social marginal cost curve.[14] In the case of pollution, this is achieved through the so-called polluter-pays principle.[15] Certain international instruments recognise the need to internalise all environmental externalities.[16] In that respect, the internalisation of environmental negative externalities is a fundamental aspect of environmental policy.[17]

Many environmental externalities are produced during the production phase, and their internalisation requires the regulation of process and production methods. Besides pollution caused during production processes, other production activities may involve external costs on the environment that the producer does not have to pay, such as bycatch in fisheries,[18] the destruction of rich ecosystems to obtain new areas of land exploitable for agricultural purposes (forest fires to create 'slash and burn' fields, destruction of mangroves for aquaculture, etc.) or what has been

---

[11]Externalisation of environmental benefits will typically lead to suboptimal provision. This type of market failures is referred to as public good, as it is explained in the next subsection.

[12]See e.g. Cooter and Ulen (2008), p. 44; Stiglitz and Walsh (2006), p. 252.

[13]See e.g. Cooter and Ulen (2008), p. 45; Stiglitz and Walsh (2006), p. 252.

[14]See e.g. Cooter and Ulen (2008), p. 45.

[15]See *infra*, Chap. 4.

[16]*Idem*.

[17]See Rao (2002), p. 48 ('[t]he existence of uncompensated and unsustainable environmental externalities is often the single most important reason for policy intervention, whether at global or state level, and whether the interventions are sought through market mechanisms, through regulatory mechanisms, or through a combination of both').

[18]In 1994, the FAO estimated that approximately 27% of fish caught in the world were discarded (representing 27 million tons). In 2005, another study of the FAO using different methods of calculation estimated that 8% of fish caught annually is discarded (representing 7.3 million tons). See Kellerher (2005). These bycatches represent a significant cost for the environment, which trawlers (and especially shrimp trawlers which represent 50% of all world bycatch) do not have to pay.

referred to as 'appropriation externalities' entailed by exploitation of common or shared resources.[19]

3.1.2   Public Goods

If economic activities can cause negative environmental externalities, nature itself freely provides benefits to individuals, which are positive externalities, also referred to as public goods. They include clean air, pristine environments, a stable climate or biodiversity.[20] Certain public goods are provided by the state, such as national defence, fire protection, roads, health or education.

Public goods imply a difference in a transaction between the private and social benefits enjoyed. An individual agent is unable to retain all the benefits of the production of a public good while incurring all the costs. Public goods, first, are characterised by their *non-rivalrous consumption*, or jointness of supply, which means that the marginal cost of providing a public good to an additional person is zero.[21] For instance, the benefits of a stable climate for one individual do not reduce the benefits available to the others. Second, public goods are *non-excludable*, which means that it is impossible or prohibitively costly to exclude non-paying beneficiaries from enjoying the benefits of the good, for instance by fencing.[22] For example, it is impossible to provide different benefits to different countries or individuals depending on the costs they have incurred to mitigate climate change.

When the costs for a private agent to supply a public good exceed the private benefits of that agent, even though the social benefits would still outweigh these costs, the market will result in undersupply of that public good. A private supplier cannot exclude users that did not pay their share of the costs. This means that the most rational choice for an individual will be not to pay the costs. This ability to 'free ride' on the efforts of others to provide a non-excludable good[23] has the consequence that no private profit-maximising firm will be willing to provide the good, leading to a suboptimal result. [24]

---

[19]In the case of exploitation of common or shared resources, such as fisheries, each time someone appropriates some of that resource, it reduces the yield others could receive from fishing, thereby creating an externality. See Ostrom et al. (1994), pp. 10 f.

[20]See Rao (2000), pp. 167 f.; Rao (2002), p. 51.

[21]See e.g. Cooter and Ulen (2008), p. 108; Hardin (1982), p. 17; Ostrom et al. (1994), p. 6; Perrez (2000), pp. 193 ff.; Vogler (2000), pp. 2 ff.

[22]See e.g. Nordhaus (2006), p. 88; Stiglitz and Walsh (2006), p. 254; Cooter and Ulen (2008), p. 108; Hardin (1982), p. 17; Ostrom et al. (1994), p. 6; Perrez (2000), pp. 193 ff.; Vogler (2000), pp. 2 ff.

[23]See *infra*, the 'free rider problem' (Sect. 3.4.2).

[24]See e.g. Cooter and Ulen (2008), p. 109; Stiglitz and Walsh (2006), p. 255.

According to economic theory, state intervention is required in order to supply public goods to a socially optimal level.[25] It may provide the public good indirectly through subsidies (basic science research, clean energies) or directly assume the costs through tax revenues (national defence or protection of endangered species or biodiversity).

3.2 Market Failures Affecting the International Environment

As the previous section has shown, environmental policy often deals with the regulation of production processes. Each country defines its applicable laws, which means that some national systems provide larger environmental protection than others, depending on internal political choices.

This may not be problematic as far as the domestic environment of each state is concerned. However, more and more environmental issues cannot be seen as domestic issues anymore because of the interdependence of ecosystems that transcend territorial boundaries. In that respect, the use of one resource within a state often has consequences for the use of natural resources in another state.[26] For instance, increasing the emissions of greenhouse gases affects the global climate, wherever these gases were emitted.

Both externalities (Sect. 3.2.1) and public goods (Sect. 3.2.2) give rise to specific difficulties at the international level.

3.2.1 Transboundary Externalities

Negative externalities may not only affect the environment of the states in which they originate from, but they can also spill over territorial boundaries and affect other countries. The most obvious case of *physical transborder spillovers* is air pollution (for instance, when sulphur dioxide (SO_2) is emitted in one country and results in acid rain in another) or water pollution (for instance, contamination of a shared lake or watercourse affecting neighbouring countries).[27] Externalities may

---

[25]See e.g. Cooter and Ulen (2008), p. 46; Stiglitz and Walsh (2006), p. 255.

[26]Perrez (2000), pp. 167 f. ('[t]herefore, today, one has to accept that the use of one resource entails indirect or direct use of another resource [...]. [B]ecause the use of one resource mostly involves the use of another resource, most of the states have at least an indirect interest in the use of most of the resources of this globe'); Sands (2012), p. 12 ('[m]any environmental resources and their environmental components are ecologically shared. The use by one state of natural resources within its territory will invariably have consequences for the use of natural resources and their environmental components in another state').

[27]Pugel (2009), pp. 278 ff.; Stiglitz and Walsh (2006), p. 414.

not only concern two or several neighbouring countries. Economic activities anywhere in the world can impose external costs on the whole world, such as climate change, degradation of the ozone layer, species extinction or depletion of common resources such as fish stocks.[28]

Apart from physical spillovers, the environmental practices in one state can also have *non-physical effects* in another. Environmental damages caused affect both use and non-use value of environmental goods derived from citizens domestically.[29] The former refers to goods that are directly 'consumed' and the value of which is established by the market or to goods that are used indirectly, such as the services rendered by ecosystems, like carbon sinks or waste assimilation. The latter captures cases in which people put monetary values on natural resources that are independent of any present or future use that these people may have of these resources.[30] The exploitation of natural resources such as fish or timber in a foreign country beyond the maximum sustainable yield can deprive an importing country of the future use of these resources and reduce their use value. On the other hand, the destruction of habitats, environmental exploitation abroad or internal pollution can cause the extinction of endangered species or the destruction of pristine environments, which affect people domestically (non-use value).[31] The importing country's citizens can also simply value the existence and preservation of environmental goods. Environmental degradation or pollution can reduce this existence value, which is part of non-use value, and thus affect people domestically, through non-physical international externalities.[32]

Another category of non-physical externalities is *'moral' externalities*. In that case, people in one country are affected simply by knowing that something perceived as morally negative occurs abroad.[33] In this category falls in particular all animal welfare concerns. People in one country may feel offended by knowing that products they buy at home have caused animals to suffer abroad. Examples include the use of leghold traps, battery cages in poultry farming or the use of cruel methods to kill seals.[34]

In the international trade context, it might also be referred to a further type of externalities, i.e. *competitive externalities*. They are only indirectly related to environmental externalities. When environmental standards are lower abroad than domestically, a state may fear to lose jobs because states with lower standards have a competitive advantage compared to them. They may thus engage in a 'race to the

---

[28]See Pugel (2009), p. 281.

[29]See Steward (1992), pp. 1329 ff. See also Chang (1995), p. 2166.

[30]See Freeman (2003), pp. 137 ff. See also Chang (1995), pp. 18 ff.

[31]*Ibid.*

[32]See Steward (1992), pp. 1329 ff.; Chang (1995), p. 2166 ff.; Perrez (2000), p. 207. The destruction of these resources would cause 'preservation externalities'.

[33]See Perrez (2000), p. 207.

[34]The WTO *EC – Seal Products* case precisely concerned a European import ban imposed as a reaction to the cruel methods used in seal hunting on the public moral exception.

bottom' that may be detrimental to both states to avoid the effects of competitive externalities.[35]

Externalities have been described as 'one of the most important core dilemmas or policy problems of the relationship between trade and environmental policies' because environmental regulation seeking internalisation of externalities may in certain ways clash with basic trade liberalisation rules.[36] As this chapter will show, traditional solutions for addressing market failures in the international context may imply the use of import restrictions.

3.2.2   Global Public Goods

The issue of proving the socially optimal level of public goods that transcend national boundaries may also be particularly problematic. The issue of the adequate provision of public goods can arise at the local, national and international levels, depending on who benefits from the supply of that good.[37] Global public goods are those the impacts of which are indivisibly spread across the entire globe.[38] As a result, no country can be prevented from enjoying the benefits of a global public good, and a country's enjoyment of that good does not reduce the amount available to others.[39] Examples include a stable climate, conservation of fish stocks of the high seas, efforts to combat AIDS or attempts to get rid of nuclear weapons.[40]

This characteristic of global public goods results in a tremendous challenge in providing their socially optimal level. When the benefits are global, each state must decide whether to invest in costly measures that will produce benefits that it will not be able to capture entirely.[41] Their position is the same as an individual supplier of a local public good at the domestic level, which means that global public goods are likely to be under-supplied. Like all public goods, markets fail because of the inability of private agents to retain all the benefits of providing a public good.

The main problem is a lack of economic and political mechanism to resolve this type of market failure. At the national level, the state has the power to enforce its regulation in order to provide public goods. At the international level, however, only a supranational entity such as an international organisation with similar enforcement powers could ensure that each state pays its appropriate share of the costs.[42] Each state must consent to the creation of an international organisation to

---

[35]See Steward (1993), pp. 2039 ff.; 2059; Perrez (2000), p. 207.

[36]See Jackson (1992), p. 1231.

[37]See e.g. Nordhaus (2006), p. 92.

[38]See e.g. Samuelson and Nordhaus (2005), p. 370.

[39]See Barrett (2007), p. 1.

[40]See e.g. Nordhaus (2006), p. 92.

[41]See e.g. Samuelson and Nordhaus (2005), p. 371.

[42]See Sandler (1997), pp. 12 ff.

which some part of its sovereignty would be transferred or to international obligations to participate in international efforts to provide a global public good. International relations have shown that states are often extremely reluctant to accept this.

Other characteristics of public goods can also influence the difficulty to achieve the optimal provision of global public goods. The costs and benefits of the provision of a public good can be unequally distributed. In the case of climate change, the costs of reducing CO_2 emissions would largely be borne by northern countries, while many models predict that it is southern countries that would suffer the most. The stronger these asymmetries are, the harder it will be to obtain the consent of a majority or of all states to take costly measures to achieve that goal.[43] Scientific uncertainty may increase these difficulties to reach a global consensus.

Similarly, the number of nations concerned may also be a difficulty: it is obviously easier to achieve an agreement with a limited number of neighbouring countries than to reach a global consensus on the appropriate level of provision of a public good that impacts the entire globe.

The distribution of costs and benefits of a global public good may vary not only through space but also through time, between the present and future generations.[44] The present generation may be reluctant to bear important costs to provide a global public good that will be enjoyed by a generation that is not born yet (e.g., climate change). It may have a tendency to enjoy the benefits of a global public good without paying for costs that will mainly be borne by future generations (e.g., loss of biodiversity, overfishing, etc.).

Finally, the optimal provision of a global public good may be particularly difficult to achieve when it depends on the aggregate efforts of all states to achieve a particular result (summation good).[45] Risks of cooperation failures are likely to abound when summation goods are at stake, in particular because of the free rider problem,[46] as it will be shown below.

Climate change mitigation efforts gather most of these difficulties. It is a global issue, regarding a summation good, with various distributions of costs and benefits across countries and some scientific uncertainty, with possible important asymmetries in the costs and benefits of reducing greenhouse gas accumulation in the atmosphere. Besides, climate change is a typical example of an issue that concerns future generations as well because stock externalities are at stake.[47]

---

[43]*Ibid.*

[44]See Sandler (1997), p. 212.

[45]'Summation goods' are not the only type of global public goods. Their provision can depend on the development of a cutting-edge technology ('best-shot') or on the efforts of least successful states to achieve a particular result, such as the efforts to eradicate a disease ('weakest link'). See Barrett (2007), pp. 22 ff.; Sandler (1997), pp. 46 ff.; Kaul et al. (1999), pp. 486 ff.

[46]See Barrett (2007), pp. 74 ff.

[47]See Nordhaus (2006), pp. 90 f. The impact of stock externalities depends on the slow accumulation of variables forming over time a stock that may have positive consequences, such as knowledge, or negative consequences, such as climate change caused by the accumulation of greenhouse gases in the atmosphere.

Many activities result in the slow accumulation of greenhouse gases in the atmosphere over time, creating a stock that has negative consequences, i.e. global warming. Depreciation of this stock may take time and result in long-lasting and severe consequences. But these consequences may fall far in the future and affect especially future generations.[48] Introducing benefits of future generations into policy decisions and international negotiations is one more difficulty in achieving an appropriate supply of global public goods. In brief, asymmetries exist not only with respect to states' contribution to global greenhouse gas emissions, national priorities or financial and technical means to reduce greenhouse gas emissions but also as regards the distribution of benefits of climate change mitigation through space and time.

3.3 Private Goods, Public Goods and Common Pool Resources

Public goods have been examined above as one type of market failure, requiring state intervention. On the basis of their characteristics, it is also possible to distinguish them from other types of goods, in particular private good and common pool resources. Each of these types gives rise to different kinds of challenges when it comes to their efficient management and is subject to different kinds of property rights.

Two characteristics are used to distinguish private goods, public goods and common pool resources. First, they can be excludable or non-excludable, depending on how easy or costly it is to exclude users from consuming them, whether they are provided by nature or by economic agents. While it may be easy to exclude users from enjoying certain specific goods, for instance, by fencing, others are *non-excludable* because it is impossible or too costly to exclude only certain users. It is impossible, for instance, to exclude certain persons from enjoying the benefits of a stable climate or to supply a different amount of protection against nuclear attacks.[49]

The second attribute used to distinguish types of goods is whether one person's use precludes another's. The consumption of certain goods by one individual reduces the amount available to others, such as eating an orange. On the other hand, clean air breathed by an individual does not diminish the quantity of clean air available to others.[50] This condition is referred to as non-rivalrous consumption[51] or jointness of supply.[52]

---

[48] See Sandler (1997); Nordhaus (2006), p. 91.

[49] See e.g. Cooter and Ulen (2008), p. 108; Hardin (1982), p. 17; Ostrom et al. (1994), p. 6; Perrez (2000), pp. 193 ff.; Vogler (2000), pp. 2 ff.

[50] *Ibid.*

[51] See Cooter and Ulen (2008), p. 45.

[52] See Hardin (1982), p. 17; Vogler (2000), p. 4.

On the basis of these two characteristics, it is possible to distinguish different types of goods.[53] Private goods are those that are excludable and that have a rivalrous consumption. Public goods are non-excludable and have a non-rivalrous consumption. Among non-excludable goods, some of them do have a rivalrous consumption, such as fisheries or shared watercourses, which are called *common-pool resources*. While it is prohibitively costly to fence the entire ocean (non-excludability), extracting fish reduces the amount available to others (rivalrous consumption). Common pool resources can be shared between two or several neighbouring countries. They can also be shared by all states, such as resources of the high seas.

When it comes to property rights, natural resources can be subject to private or common property. Among the latter, the applicable regime can be that of *res communis*, i.e. common property resources collectively owned by a community, such as natural resources of states' exclusive economic zone or local common resources managed collectively by a local community. The applicable property regime can also be that of *res nullius*, i.e. open access resources that belong to all and can become the object of private appropriation by anyone.[54, 55] Many of the most precious natural ecosystems are owned in common with open access, such as oceans, the atmosphere, groundwater or fisheries.[56] Open access may cause significant problem for the sustainable management of the natural resources concerned.[57]

Environmental goods' characteristics of non-excludability and non-rivalry, as well as the types of property rights applicable to them (open access), have important consequences on the risks of environmental harm and on the difficulties in achieving international cooperation to ensure their conservation, as the next sections will show.

In the context of the PPM debate, the terms 'global commons' are often used to describe resources of common interest, including the atmosphere, fisheries in the high seas or biodiversity.[58] But theses terms are usually not defined and, in the view of the present author, are rather vague. The 'global commons' could refer to common pool resources shared between all states (high seas, ozone layer) or to global public goods, such as biodiversity. The applicable property rights are quite different in these two cases since resources that allow the existence of the global

---

[53]See generally Hardin (1982), pp. 17 ff.; Ostrom (1990), 1982, pp. 30 ff.; Ostrom et al. (1994), pp. 6 ff.; Perrez (2000), pp. 193 f.; Rao (2002), p. 50.

[54]See Common and Stagl (2005), p. 338; Vogler (2000), p. 4; Rao (2002), p. 47.

[55]With the exception of the deep seabed, which is subject to the particular property rights regime entailed by the concept of 'common heritage of mankind'.

[56]See Sandler (1997), p. 12.

[57]See *infra*, the 'tragedy of the commons' (3.4.4).

[58]See e.g. OECD (1997b), p. 15 (referring to environmental effects to 'global commons' or to 'environmental resources which are shared by all countries', including depletion of the ozone layer, climate change, biodiversity or endangered species); Condon (2004), p. 141 (suggesting that the 'global commons' include the ozone layer, climate change, biodiversity and endangered species).

public good that biodiversity represents are mainly located within individual states, which means that their proper management gives rise to different issues. Harm caused to common pool resources is also in principle easier to identify. It usually consists in negative physical externalities, while detection of harm caused to a global positive externality is more difficult since it depends on a larger variety of factors (harm caused to ecosystems as a whole, exploitation beyond the maximum stainable yield, destruction of habitats, etc.).

It will also be argued below that the PPM measures addressing harm caused to common pool resources or loss in a global public good give rise to certain distinct issues and require separate analysis.[59] It is argued here that it is thus more appropriate to distinguish clearly the 'global commons', which should refer to common pool resources shared by all states (high seas, atmosphere, the ozone layer, etc.), and 'global public goods', which encompass global positive externalities.

3.4 State Intervention to Address International Environmental Issues

It has been explained that states are reluctant to transfer some part of their sovereignty to a supranational entity. However, in many situations, it is in the interests of all states (or at least of a majority of them) to cooperate to achieve optimal outcomes. Cooperation is indeed the most efficient way to address these issues since it enables intervention at the source (Sect. 3.4.1).

However, if no international organisation has the power to enforce international obligations, all states have an incentive not to cooperate because of the free rider problem (Sect. 3.4.2), which may result in cooperation failures because of the 'prisoner's dilemma' (Sect. 3.4.3) and may ultimately lead to the 'tragedy of the commons' (Sect. 3.4.4). When cooperation fails, trade measures may play a role in the solutions to resolve collective action problems (Sect. 3.4.5).

3.4.1 The Intervention at the Source Principle

The existence of negative environmental externalities is viewed in economic theory as a reason justifying government intervention to correct a market failure.[60] Numerous different instruments can be used to internalise environmental externalities, such as enacting a regulation to reduce pollution (command and control),

---

[59]See *infra*, 7.3.4.2.
[60]See Cooter and Ulen (2008), p. 45; Stiglitz and Walsh (2006), p. 252.

taxing pollution, adopting a marketable permit system, changing the allocation of property rights, etc.[61]

In terms of efficiency, the first-best solutions are measures addressing the source of the problem, which means that a state should be able to address specifically the distortions that make private costs and benefits differ from social costs and benefits[62] ('specificity rule'[63] or 'intervention at source principle'[64]).

But in cases of market failures affecting international environmental issues, the harmed state cannot directly intervene to tax or restrict the harmful activities abroad (internalisation of externalities through a Pigouvian tax), and neither has any supranational entity the authority to enforce property rights (in application of the Coase theorem), even though both approaches could potentially increase global welfare, by achieving an optimal level of pollution or natural resource exploitation (amount of pollution or natural resource exploitation that brings the greatest net gain to the world as a whole).[65]

Since no state can directly intervene beyond its jurisdiction, the second-best solution in these situations is international cooperation, by which a country may negotiate with the foreign states concerned an internalisation of the environmental externalities at issue.[66] If an international agreement is concluded, then each party to the agreement will take measures addressing the source of the problem within its territory.

If negotiations fail, it means that a state negatively affected by an externality originating from a foreign country will not be able to address directly the source of the problem. In that case, the next-best solution to restrict pollution-creating activities in that foreign country is to adopt international trade policies that seek to influence these activities.[67] Such measures are only third-best options since they do not address the source of the problem, and their efficiency is thus not

---

[61]See e.g. Petersmann (1996), pp. 11 ff.; Stiglitz and Walsh (2006), pp. 407 ff.; Pugel (2009), pp. 182 ff. Two main economic theories are usually opposed here: the tax-or-subsidy approach (Pigouvian tax) and the property rights approach (based on the Coase theorem). The idea is to achieve the optimal level of pollution, i.e. the amount of pollution that brings the greatest net gain to the world as a whole. If the government chooses to adopt a Pigouvian tax, it should know the marginal costs and benefits of pollution. In the property rights approach, the Coase theorem posits that absent transaction costs, parties will negotiate till they reach the optimal level of pollution, irrespective of how property rights are assigned but provided that property rights can be enforced. See e.g. Pugel (2009), pp. 278 ff.

[62]See Pugel (2009), p. 272 ('[t]he specificity rule says to intervene at the source of the problem. It is usually more efficient to use the policy tool that is specific to the distortion that makes private costs and benefits differ from social costs and benefits').

[63]Pugel (2009), pp. 183 f.

[64]Petersmann (1996), p. 47, with further references.

[65]See Pugel (2009), pp. 278 ff.

[66]See Charnovitz (2002), p. 73 (noting that multilateral cooperation is a first-best option, even though it may not always be available); Pauwelyn (2004), p. 579 (noting that negotiating higher or common standards with other countries is preferable to using trade restrictions).

[67]See Pugel (2009), p. 281.

guaranteed.[68] These reasons show that achieving cooperation is preferable not only because unilateral measures are negatively perceived[69] but also because it can guarantee greater efficiency of environmental protection measures.

Since trade measures give rise to many criticisms (see Chap. 4) and may even not be efficient, should they not be banned? Such a ban would in fact entail important risks of cooperation failures because of the free rider problem.

3.4.2   The Free Rider Problem

Individuals can obtain two main types of benefits from the environment. First, certain *private* benefits can be gained by appropriation of natural resources, such as the extraction of resources in common fisheries or watercourses, the exploitation of common areas such as grazing lands or the use of sink capacities of ecosystems like the atmosphere or watercourses to get rid of polluting substances.

When the environment is used that way, the benefits are entirely enjoyed by the individuals concerned, who do not have to pay for the environmental costs of their activities, whereas all persons exploiting that resource share the externalities that have been generated. This results in a difference between the social and private marginal cost curves, which leads to socially suboptimal outcomes, in the form of over-exploitation of natural resources or sink capacities of ecosystems.

On the long run, each user has an interest in the conservation of the exploited resources. However, the *common* benefits of conserving an (open access) common pool resource or a global public good are non-excludable.

Non-excludability means that states can enjoy the benefits of these goods whether or not they pay for their costs. Economists posit that rational agents try to maximise their individual utility, which means that the most rational choice in this case is to let others pay the costs of environmental protection and enjoy 'freely' all the benefits, without having incurred any cost. In the case of climate change, because 1 tonne of CO_2 has the same effect on the global climate wherever it is emitted, states have incentives to let other states reduce their GHG emissions and enjoy 'freely' the benefits of a more stable global climate without having paid any of the costs of climate change mitigation.

---

[68]The efficiency of trade measures to pursue environmental objectives will in particular depend on the extent to which the exporting country is dependent on the importing country's market and on whether the exporting country can easily transfer its products to other exports markets. The respective size of the countries involved is also a fundamental element determining the effectiveness of a trade measure (those adopted by the US or the EU have much more importance for exporting countries due to the size of these markets). See Petersmann (1996), p. 15. Discussing the issue of efficiency of process-based measure, see also Chang (1995), pp. 2184 ff.

[69]See *infra*, 7.3.4.1.1.

This is referred to as the 'free rider problem' and may lead to the underproduction of a public good or to the excessive use of a shared resource.[70] It arises whenever benefits of a group effort fall on every agent in the group regardless of how much each individual agent does or does not contribute.[71]

Free riding is one of the biggest problems and challenges that the international community must face as far as shared resource conservation and protection of the global environment is concerned.[72] It is relevant both between individual agents within a particular country at the national level and between states themselves at the international level.[73] At the domestic level, when voluntary participation to the costs of providing a public good is insufficient, the state can force its citizens to pay an appropriate share of the costs, through the collection of taxes. But at the international level, no supranational entity can in principle force states to cooperate, which makes free riding especially problematic.[74] The lack of world government implies that states must participate voluntarily to the provision of global public goods.[75]

But because it is impossible to exclude states that refuse to cooperate in the provision of a global public good from enjoying its benefits, a state undertaking efforts to address a global environmental threat may in fact have adopted costly measures domestically, without eventually being able to achieve the environmental goal pursued, if other states continue their environmentally harmful practices. As a result, a risk exists that the states having adopted costly environmental regulations succeed only in harming their economies without yielding any environmental result.[76] To overcome the free rider problem, states must find a way to ensure the cooperation of the other states concerned.

3.4.3   The Prisoner's Dilemma

The possibility to free ride because of the non-excludability of public goods represents a major obstacle of international cooperation. It results in *incentives not to cooperate* in the protection of common pool resources or global public goods. In many cases, every state would be better off if global pollution or natural resource

---

[70]See generally Cooter and Ulen (2008), pp. 46, 109 ff.; Stiglitz and Walsh (2006), pp. 255; Pugel (2009), pp. 201, 283; Hardin (1968), p. 1244; Perrez (2000), p. 194.

[71]See Pugel (2009), p. 201.

[72]See Barrett (2007), p. 291.

[73]For instance, in the case of fisheries, individual fishermen will try to free ride on the efforts of stock conservation of others in national waters; in the high seas, in which states have jurisdiction to regulate the activities of their nationals, each state has incentives to let other countries restrain the fishing activity of their nationals without restricting theirs.

[74]See Barrett (2007), p. 83.

[75]*Ibid.*

[76]See Barrett (2007), p. 318; Chang (1995), p. 2177.

exploitation were reduced to the socially optimal level. For instance, every country has in principle an interest in mitigating the effects of climate change by reducing greenhouse gas emissions. But on the other hand, if states cannot ensure that other countries, especially major polluters or exploiters, will also restrict their pollution or common pool resource exploitation, they incur the risk of adopting costly measures in vain.

Therefore, economic theory postulates that the most rational choice for a state is not to take any of these costly measures. If other countries do reduce their emissions and mitigate climate change, the non-cooperating countries will be able to free ride on the others' efforts. If instead other countries do not reduce their emissions, it will have to face the consequences of climate change, but at least without having paid in vain for costly emission reduction measures. In other words, regardless of the behaviour adopted by other states, a state will individually be better off if it does not cooperate (dominant strategy), even though all states would be better off if all had cooperated.[77]

This situation is a typical example of what game theory calls the 'prisoner's dilemma',[78] which results in collective action problems and risks of cooperation failures. Game theory examines the strategy that a person adopts when her optimal choice of action depends on what another actor chooses.[79] The prisoner's dilemma model explains that the lack of possibility between two players to make credible commitments to cooperate leads to non-cooperation (or non-enforcement of a prior agreement) even though both players would be better off had they all cooperated.[80]

The main challenge is that to achieve a Pareto optimum, both actors must change their behaviour. If only one player changes its behaviour, he will be worse off and no individual player has therefore any incentive to change it if the other player does not. This is characterised as a Nash equilibrium.[81]

---

[77]See e.g. Common and Stagl (2005), pp. 498 ff.; Samuelson and Nordhaus (2005), pp. 214 ff.

[78]In brief, in the classical example two prisoners are questioned about an offense in which both are involved, even though the prosecution does not have substantial proof against any of them, save a possible confession of one of the prisoner. Therefore prosecutors try to induce confession by keeping each of them in separated cells and telling them that one of them would not be condemned should he confess the offense and the other would not (this one would get 5 years of jail), 3 years if both of them would confess whereas the prisoners know that they would not get more than one year if none of them should confess. By cooperation, both players could achieve the best result (1 year instead of three). But without any mean to verify that the other prisoner will comply with a promise to cooperate, the most rational choice of each player will be to defect (i.e. confess), because the cooperating actor would get seven years if the other one did not hold his promise. In short, the dominant strategy for each player is always to defect, whether the other player cooperates or not. The result is a Pareto-suboptimal solution since each player could achieve a better solution by cooperating.

[79]See Cooter and Ulen (2008), p. 38.

[80]On credible commitments, see e.g. Barrett (2007), p. 66; Stiglitz and Walsh (2006), p. 327.

[81]Named after John Nash, winner of the Nobel Prize in Economics. See e.g. Cooter and Ulen (2008), p. 40; Samuelson and Nordhaus (2005), pp. 214 f.; Stiglitz and Walsh (2006), pp. 313 f.

Whenever a particular public good is supplied by adding the contribution of every state in the world (summation good), collective action problems in the form of the prisoner's dilemma are likely to abound.[82]

3.4.4 The Tragedy of the Commons

In brief, it has been shown that, on the one hand, in open access commons, anyone can appropriate all the benefits of private exploitation or use and externalise its costs, which results in levels of exploitation superior to the social optimum. On the other hand, individuals—or states in international matters—have incentive not to cooperate in the conservation of the global commons, despite the risks of over-exploitation.

The production of excessive environmental externalities, combined with strong incentives not to cooperate in environmental protection, can lead to dramatic consequences, i.e. the eventual destruction of the resource, which will damage all its users. This is what Garett Hardin has famously described as the 'tragedy of the commons'.[83] The classical example used by Hardin was the common pastures used as grazing land, which could be used freely by all herders. The rational choice of each individual herder was to add as much as possible new animals on common pastures to maximise its payoff. But individually, the rational behaviours of each herder led to a globally irrational one because over-exploitation caused by the fact that the degradation costs implied by adding an animal could be externalised on all users led to the eventual destruction of the common resource.

The same reasoning as that applied in the classical example of common pastures may apply to a wide variety of cases in which agents do not take account of the effects of their action on the well-being of others,[84] such as financing of common projects, traffic congestion, teamwork or the management of global commons and shared natural resources, such as climate change, protection of the ozone layer, biodiversity, fisheries or water and air quality.[85]

Economists usually explain the problem of the tragedy of the commons by a lack of property rights. The real cause of the 'tragedy' is open access because, in that case, no one has an incentive to restrict production to a socially optimal level, as it is not possible to exclude free riders.[86] Common pool resources subject to a common

---

[82]Kaul et al. (1999), p. 487.

[83]Hardin (1968), p. 1243.

[84]See e.g. Bowles (2004), p. 27.

[85]See Perrez (2000), p. 195.

[86]See Common and Stagl (2005), p. 339; Ostrom (1990), p. 23; Sandler (1997), p. 11 ('[c]ommon ownership, *when coupled with open access*, would also lead to wasteful exploitation in which a user ignores the effects of his or her action on others. Open access to the commonly owned resources is a crucial ingredient of waste and inefficiency'. Original emphasis).

property regime and managed collectively have existed successfully for centuries in certain parts of the world. It allowed an allocation of use rights and mechanisms for restricting access to outsiders (making the resource excludable).[87]

These solutions are easier to implement for local commons. As for the 'global commons', such as use of the atmosphere as a common sink or the fisheries of the high seas, allocating and enforcing property rights is costly. Property rights could theoretically be created through the allocation of marketable permits. But the political and practical problems to achieve such a result are considerable. It does not resolve either the problem of the provision of global public goods, such as biodiversity. In all these cases, the challenge of the free rider problem remains and the risk of 'tragedy' is real because of the collective action problems.

3.4.5 Solutions to Collective Action Problems

The prisoner's dilemma is an important tool for understanding how cooperation may fail or be successful, especially in international relations.[88] In particular, it shows that individually rational behaviours can lead to globally irrational ones, such as suboptimal global welfare and severe environmental damages. It has been described as 'the most difficult of all international cooperation problems', as evidenced in particular in the case of climate change.[89]

In the basic prisoner's dilemma game, each player makes only one decision. When a game is played many times (repeated games), the nature of the game changes.[90] A common strategy when a game is played an indefinite number of times is tit-for-tat: a player will cooperate until the other player defects and then defect until the other player cooperates.[91] To promote international cooperation in case of repeated games, economists have suggested various strategies, such as improving communication and transparency, building trust and reputation, creating institutions to ensure cooperation (such as the WTO, which ensures the enforcement of international trade agreements), providing side payments, sharing costs differently, etc.[92]

---

[87] See generally, Ostrom (1990); Sandler (1997), pp. 11 f. ('[c]ommon property institutions have developed that succeed in managing resources, provided that the owners can limit exploitation to those within the group who abide by the rules'). See also World Bank (1992), p. 69.

[88] See Kaul et al. (1999), pp. 7 f.

[89] Barrett (2003), p. 83.

[90] See e.g. Stiglitz and Walsh (2006), pp. 319 ff.

[91] See the theory developed by Axelrod (1984).

[92] See e.g. Cooter and Ulen (2008), p. 41; Stiglitz and Walsh (2006), pp. 319 ff.; Stern (2007), pp. 510 f. (with further references).

It should, however, not be overlooked that real behaviour is more varied than game theory presupposes.[93] For instance, it tends to focus on self-interest very narrowly defined and might ignore perspectives of responsibility and ethical standards.[94]

Another theoretical way to resolve the prisoner's dilemma is to introduce a 'fine' that removes that dilemma.[95] If the defecting player must pay compensation to the cooperating player superior to the gain that each would receive if they cooperated, then the dominant strategy is cooperation, and the agreement between the two players becomes self-enforcing.[96] The problem as far as interstate relations is concerned is that this agreement must be binding. In the absence of any third party such as a world government that could enforce it, states cannot make credible commitments that they will abide by the agreement. As a result, the dominant strategy is still defection, when transnational externalities are concerned.[97]

The remaining possibility to change the incentives to cooperate and deter free riding is adopting trade restrictions or trade sanctions against non-cooperating countries, as a way to make the agreement self-enforcing.[98] In order for collective action to be successful, all participants must receive a net benefit to motivate the participants because nations are assumed to behave so as to further their own interests, not the good of the world.[99] Trade measures may in fact be the only way for a country to influence the policies of foreign states.[100] The possibility to sanction free riding or non-compliance with the obligations of a treaty removes the incentives to free ride or to defect. Individual gains from such behaviour may be compensated by sanctions, while global participation may achieve Pareto improvements for all countries, including the free riders and defectors. Trade measures can assure that signatory states abide by the rules of a treaty.[101] Economists have shown that the success of any MEAs depends crucially on credible enforcement rules in the form of sanctions.[102] In fact, the credible *threat* to impose sanctions can be

---

[93]See Barrett (2003), p. 83.

[94]See Stern (2007), p. 512.

[95]See Barrett (2007), pp. 62 ff.

[96]*Ibid.*

[97]*Ibid.*

[98]See Barrett (2007), p. 314.

[99]See Sandler (1997), pp. 14 ff., in particular p. 22.

[100]See e.g. Pugel (2009), p. 274 ('[i]f one nation must act alone, trade barriers could be an appropriate second-best solution. [. . .] if our nation suffered from transborder pollution [. . .] from foreign production [. . .], the only way in which our nation can discourage the foreign pollution is by taxing imports of the products made by a polluting process').

[101]See Barrett (1997), pp. 345–361, in particular pp. 345 and 359.

[102]See Böhringer (2002), p. 294 ('[t]he success of any IEA [international environmental agreement] depends crucially on the incentive-compatible specification of credible enforcement rules (sanctions), which include the magnitude and duration time of punishment, the frequency of compliance monitoring and the discounting of time by governments').

enough to ensure full cooperation in international efforts to address global environmental problems.[103]

Trade measures are thus one possible instrument to address the free rider and defector problems, even though they are no panacea.[104] They may often not be the best policy option, in particular because they may be inefficient if the producing country does not change its production practices and chooses not to export anymore the targeted products to the regulating country. On the other hand, they impose a cost both on the exporting and importing countries. The threat of trade sanctions is not necessarily efficient in deterring free riding, if a state cannot make the threat credible, in particular because the costs for the state taking the trade sanction are greater than the possible gains.[105] If countries are worse off by adopting a trade sanction, they will not use it, and the threat to use the 'stick' will be incredible.[106] Trade measures are credible when the level of participation is high. But increasing that level could mean that it risks never being reached or that the commitments of the treaty would be reduced in order to achieve broad participation. As a consequence, no significant environmental result would ensue.[107] Practical difficulties also exist. If it may be relatively easy to ban products such as chemicals that harm the ozone layer (CFC), a tax on greenhouse gases emitted during the production process is difficult to evaluate and control.

Despite these imperfections, trade measures are often the only available instrument to address the major challenge of international environmental protection, namely the free rider problem.

3.5   Consequences for the PPM Issue

The preceding sections have shown that environmental policies often concern the internalisation of externalities or measures aimed at the provision of public goods. When the source of the environmental harm concerned is located abroad, a state has no possibilities to intervene directly at the source of the problem. International cooperation is then necessary to address directly the source of the problem. But cooperation requires consent of the country in which the activities concerned occur.

---

[103]See Barrett (1997), pp. 345–361, in particular pp. 345 and 359. Barrett has analysed the case of international efforts to protect the ozone layer and the provisions of the Montreal Protocol. He concludes that 'the credible threat to impose trade sanctions may be capable of sustaining full cooperation in the supply of a public good' and that 'if the threat to impose sanctions were not allowed by the rules of the game, supply of the public good would be Pareto-inefficient'.

[104]See e.g. Bhagwati and Mavroidis (2007), who analyse the possibility to use trade measures against countries which refuse to sign the Kyoto Protocol. While they consider that such measures could comply with WTO rules, they argue that politically such measures should be avoided.

[105]See Barrett (2007), pp. 317 ff.

[106]*Ibid.*, p. 82.

[107]*Ibid.*, p. 100.

This country may not be willing to cooperate for a variety of reasons, such as differing environmental priorities or simply because the externalisation of the environmental costs at issue may be quite profitable. It can also accept to sign an international agreement but then fail to comply with the international obligations provided therein.

In such cases, in which international cooperation cannot provide efficient results, the sole possibility for the state concerned by the environmental impact of foreign activities, in the absence of any supranational entity with enforcement powers, is to adopt trade restrictions against the products produced in the countries in which the activities at stake occur.

In a way, to forbid the use of trade leverage would give a 'right' to free-riding countries to harm the environment[108] and implies conversely the risk that shared resources could not be protected.[109] Indeed, states would have no incentive to agree to pay the costs of protection knowing that others will not and that these efforts would thus yield no environmental results. In other words, prohibiting trade measures would not only prevent states from addressing environmentally harmful practices abroad; it would also encourage them to refrain from adopting similar regulation for domestic activities. In such circumstances, the rational choice is not to adopt the environmental regulation at stake. The fact that states cannot be coerced to participate in international efforts to provide a global public good has been referred to as the 'Westphalian dilemma': as far as the optimal provision of global public goods is concerned, the system of states' sovereignty based on the 1648 Treaty of Westphalia is a major political hurdle, so that 'the requirement of unanimity is in reality a recipe for inaction'.[110]

On the other hand, many modern environmental problems demand coordinated international action and depend on the aggregate efforts of the international community, such as the protection of the ozone layer, fight against climate change, conservation of biodiversity and fish stocks, etc. Scientific evidence has shown that environmental catastrophes could happen if current practices remain unchanged. For instance, the GIEC reports show that climate change is likely to have very diverse effects, such as melting of the polar ice caps; changes in the acidity of oceans, which will affect marine ecosystems; intensification of hurricanes or heat waves; etc.[111] Overfishing could rapidly lead to many species' extinction, while fish

---

[108]See Chang (1995), p. 2150.

[109]See Barrett (2007), p. 323 ('where the environment is transboundary, and where trade restrictions can be used to correct them, a prohibition on their use may mean that the shared environment cannot be safeguarded'); Parker (1999), p. 122 ('to forbid use of trade leverage is to forbid the preservation of the commons. To require all trade leverage to be authorized or obligated by a pre-existing agreement will have the same effect because recalcitrant countries will know that they can do as they wish by simply refusing to sign the agreement').

[110]Nordhaus (2006), pp. 92 f.

[111]See e.g. Intergovernmental Panel on Climate Change (IPCC), *Climate Change 2014: Synthesis Report*, Geneva 2014, p. 53.

provides more than 1.5 billion people worldwide with almost 20 per cent of their average per capita intake of animal protein.[112]

In brief, despite the many criticisms addressed to PPM trade measures, they remain useful and sometimes necessary instruments of international environmental policy and may be crucial in addressing the free rider problem, the suboptimal supply of global public goods or the protection of the global commons.

The focus should not be on forbidding trade measures but rather on the circumstances under which trade measures to address environmental harm occurring abroad should be authorised. For instance, the imposition of most domestic environmental regulations of a state to imported products would appear to be based mainly on competitiveness concerns and would not be accepted under trade rules. The objective is thus to determine when the importing state has a sufficiently close interest in the environmental situation at stake to impose a restrictive trade measure. This issue will be further examined below.[113]

Moreover, there are often diverging opinions between countries on the necessity of internalising an externality,[114] on the urgency of intervention or on the allocation of the financial costs of internalisation. Such difficulties should lead not to a prohibition of PPM measures but rather to a discussion on the criteria that could be used to determine in which cases an importing state may impose its view through the application of a PPM trade measure.

---

[112]Fish provide also 3 billion people with at least 15 per cent of such protein. See FAO, *The State of World Fisheries and Aquaculture*, Rome 2010.

[113]See *infra*, 7.1.2.2.

[114]For instance, the United States and the European Communities did not agree, in the WTO *EC – Hormone* case, on whether hormone-treated beef represented an externality and whether that externality had to be internalised. As Pauwelyn (2004), p. 579, has pointed out, the fundamental issue in this case was whether there was a need for the government to intervene at all or whether the market could deal with the problem.

Chapter 4
Principles of International Environmental Law Regarding the Regulation of Production Methods Affecting Resources of Common Interest

International environmental law is part of the general background underlying the PPM debate. Various arguments in favour or against the use of PPM measures are based on international environmental law. On the one hand, countries opposing the use of PPM measures often invoke the principle of permanent sovereignty over natural resources. On the other hand, other concepts, such as that of 'common concern', show that foreign states may have an interest in the management of a particular country's natural resources.

Furthermore, the Vienna Convention of the Law of Treaties provides that there shall be taken into account, together with the context, any relevant rules of international law applicable in the relations between the parties.[1] There are many rules of international law that may potentially be applicable to the question of the legality of a PPM measure in the relations between the parties. In particular, international treaties applicable between the parties, such as multilateral environmental agreements, could be covered.[2]

More importantly still, the WTO Agreement Preamble mentions sustainable development as an objective of the WTO. The Appellate Body has adopted the view that this objective of sustainable development brings 'texture and shading' to the interpretation of the covered agreements,[3] which means that the international environmental law background has an influence on the interpretation of the relevant provisions of the GATT.

Many of the concepts and principles mentioned in this chapter are based on the Rio Declaration on Environment and Development and to a lesser extent on

---

[1] See Article 31(3)(c) of the Vienna Convention on the Law of Treaties. For further developments on the rules of customary international law on treaty interpretation in the practice of the Appellate Body, see *infra*, 9.2.

[2] See Marceau (1999), p. 132.

[3] *US – Shrimp*, Appellate Body Report, para. 153 f. See also Ziegler and Sifonios (2017) discussing the influence that the concept of sustainable development has had on WTO case law.

© Springer International Publishing AG 2018
D. Sifonios, *Environmental Process and Production Methods (PPMs) in WTO Law*,
European Yearbook of International Economic Law 3,
DOI 10.1007/978-3-319-65726-4_4

Agenda 21.[4] Both these instruments are non-binding. Nevertheless, it has been suggested that the Rio Declaration represents at present 'the most significant universally endorsed statement of general rights and obligations of states affecting the environment'.[5] It contains in part a restatement of existing customary law on transboundary matters, an endorsement of new or developing principles of law and partly a statement of policies and ideals set out in more detail in Agenda 21,[6] which is a programme of action applicable to many fields of international environmental protection.[7]

Despite their non-binding nature, Agenda 21 and the Rio Declaration may be relevant to the interpretation of other international treaties and instruments.[8] They also illustrate international acknowledgment of the legitimacy of certain environmental objectives or plans of action, the implementation of which by way of trade measures might possibly be contested before the WTO.

This chapter examines the content and implications of the concepts of sustainable development (Sect. 4.1) and permanent sovereignty over natural resources (Sect. 4.2) for the PPM issue.

Another principle that is sometimes discussed in the context of environmental trade measures in a large sense is the precautionary principle. This principle has influenced in particular the rules of the Agreement on the Application of Sanitary and Phytosanitary Measures (SPS Agreement).[9] Environmental PPM measures are often based on scientifically documented environmental harm, for which the principles described in this chapter may be important and which constitutes the focus of this study. The precautionary principle remains relevant in cases in which there is no scientific evidence of environmental harm but in which risks of damages to life or health or the environment exist. Yet for the purposes of this study, the precautionary principle will not be examined in further detail.

---

[4]Some of the principles of the Stockholm Declaration are also mentioned in this Chapter. It was adopted as a result of the United Nations Conference on the Human Environment, held in Stockholm in 1972, which was the first intergovernmental conference focusing on environmental issues. Principle 21, which is examined in this Chapter, is the key normative concept of the Stockholm Declaration and was drawn from existing treaty and customary law. Other principles of the Declaration are more policy-oriented. The Stockholm Declaration has been one of the bases of the Rio Declaration, adopted 20 years later. See e.g. Birnie et al. (2009), pp. 48 f.

[5]Birnie et al. (2009), p. 112.

[6]*Ibid.*

[7]See e.g. Birnie et al. (2009), p. 52.

[8]*Ibid.*

[9]See the sixth paragraph of the Preamble and Article 3.3 of the SPS Agreement, which recognise that the level of protection of human, animal or plant life or health chosen by a WTO Member may be higher than that of international standards, guidelines and recommendations (see also *EC – Hormones*, Appellate Body Report, para. 120 f. and in particular para. 124). See also Article 5.7 of the SPS Agreement, which states that when scientific evidence is insufficient, a Member may provisionally adopt SPS measures on the basis of available pertinent information.

4.1   Principles Relating to Sustainable Development

The concept of sustainable development is the result of reflexion processes conducted in the United Nations since the 1972 Stockholm Declaration.[10] The 1987 Report of the World Commission on Environment and Development, which is entitled *Our Common Future* and is often referred to as the Bruntland Report, gave this concept international recognition. It defines sustainable development in the following way:

> Sustainable development is development that meets the needs of the present generation without compromising the ability of future generations to meet their own needs.
>   It contains within it two key concepts:
>
> • The concepts of needs, in particular the essential needs of the world's poor, to which overriding priority should be given; and
> • The idea of limitations imposed by the state of technology and social organization on the environment's ability to meet present and future needs.[11]

As such, no legally binding instrument contains a generally agreed definition of sustainable development. The definition given in the Bruntland Report is, however, so frequently quoted that it has acquired a quasi-official status.[12] It is also generally recognised that the concept of sustainable development has influenced the content of the international agreements adopted in the 1992 UN Conference on Environment and Development held in Rio de Janeiro, i.e. the Rio Declaration, Agenda 21, the UN Framework Convention on Climate Change (UNFCCC), the Convention on Biodiversity (CBD) and the Statement of Principles on Forests.[13]

As such, the precise legal meaning and implications of the concept of sustainable development remain unsettled.[14] It is sometimes viewed rather as an 'overarching framework'[15] or a 'metaprinciple', which influences other legal rules or principles, in particular when they threaten to overlap and conflict with each other.[16]

It is nevertheless generally recognised that one of the main bases of sustainable development is the principle of *integration* of economic, social and environmental policies. It is mentioned in particular in Principle 4 of the Rio Declaration, which states: 'in order to achieve sustainable development, environmental protection shall constitute an integral part of the development process and cannot be considered in isolation from it'.

---

[10]See e.g. Principles 8 and 13 of the Stockholm Declaration. Bürgenmeier (2005), p. 38; French (2010), p. 52.

[11]World Commission on Environment and Development (1987), p. 43.

[12]See e.g. Barstow Magraw and Hawke (2007), p. 618.

[13]See Birnie et al. (2009), p. 123; Barstow Magraw and Hawke (2007), p. 616.

[14]See e.g. French (2010), p. 58; Barstow Magraw and Hawke (2007), p. 614.

[15]Barstow Magraw and Hawke (2007), p. 614.

[16]Lowe (1999), pp. 30 f.

The integration principle has also been endorsed in the 2002 Johannesburg Plan of Implementation, which refers to the need to promote 'the integration of the three components of sustainable development—economic development, social development and environmental protection—as interdependent and mutually reinforcing pillars'.

Other elements are generally considered to be part of sustainable development, in particular intergenerational equity,[17] intragenerational equity (common but differentiated responsibilities),[18] sustainable use[19] and cooperation.[20] Some of these principles or concepts may be relevant in the PPM debate and could influence the interpretation of the relevant GATT provisions. They are examined below.

4.1.1   The Elimination of Unsustainable Production and Consumption Practices

In order to achieve sustainable development, the Rio Declaration has referred to the need to adopt a comprehensive approach embracing the different activities resulting in environmental degradation. More particularly, Principle 8 of the Rio Declaration states:

> To achieve sustainable development and a higher quality of life for all people, states should reduce and eliminate unsustainable patterns of production and consumption and promote appropriate demographic policies.[21]

One of the primary concerns of the signatories of the Rio Declaration was obviously the existing imbalance in global consumption patterns and the environmental consequences of industrialised countries' consumption. Agenda 21 similarly refers to the need to address the 'excessive demand and unsustainable lifestyles among the richer segments [of humanity], which place immense stress on the

---

[17]See Principle 3 of the Rio Declaration: '[t]he right to development must be fulfilled so as to equitably meet developmental and environmental needs of present and future generations'. See also Birnie et al. (2009), pp. 119 ff.; French (2010), pp. 60 f.

[18]Intragenerational equity is not mentioned in the Rio Declaration but has been taken into account in specific MEAs such as the UNFCCC, through the concept of common but differentiated responsibilities. See Birnie et al. (2009), pp. 122 ff.; French (2010), pp. 60 f.

[19]See Birnie et al. (2009), pp. 119 and 190 ff.; French (2010), pp. 59 f.

[20]See French (2010), p. 61.

[21]See also Agenda 21, Chapter 4, para. 4.3: 'the major cause of the continued deterioration of the global environment is the unsustainable pattern of consumption and production, particularly in industrialised countries, which is a matter of grave concern'. Agenda 21 also states that the priority for developing countries, on the other hand, is to adopt appropriate demographic policies, since the growth in world population will result in growing impact on the environment and natural resources consumption. The WSSD Plan of Implementation also declares that '[f]undamental changes in the way societies produce and consume are indispensable for achieving global sustainable development' (WSSD Plan of Implementation, para. 14, p. 7).

environment', while 'the poorer segments (. . .) are unable to meet food, health care, shelter and educational needs'.[22] This concern is not directly related to the regulation of PPM measures.

But another important concern is promoting 'patterns of consumption and production that reduce environmental stress'[23] and 'the efficient use of [natural] resources consistent with the goal of minimizing depletion and reducing pollution'.[24] While minimising depletion and reducing pollution as means to reduce environmental stress can be achieved in part by reducing 'excessive demand and unsustainable lifestyles', it obviously also requires some kind of regulation of production practices, since many environmental externalities are caused during the production process, in the form of damage to natural resources (appropriation externalities, bycatch, over-exploitation, etc.), which can increase risks of depletion, or in the form of pollution.

The WSSD Plan of Implementation thus explicitly refers to the *polluter-pays principle* as an instrument that can be used to promote sustainable patterns of production and consumption.[25] Originally an economic principle, the polluter-pays principle gained its first notable international support in the Rio Declaration, which states at Principle 16:

National authorities should endeavour to promote the internalization of environmental costs and the use of economic instruments, taking into account the approach that the polluter should, in principle, bear the cost of pollution, with due regard to the public interest and without distorting international trade and investment.

The legal content and scope of the polluter-pays principle are still uncertain. It has been argued that the terms used seem to indicate that the polluter-pays principle lacks the normative character of a rule of law[26] and remains rather an economic principle.[27] As a result, the polluter-pays principle is usually not viewed as a generally applicable rule of customary international law,[28] although some consider the polluter-pays principle to be a general principle of law.[29] It seems clear, however, that states or courts are not bound by international law to 'make the

---

[22]Agenda 21, Chap. 4, para. 4.5.

[23]Agenda 21, Chap. 4, para. 4.7.

[24]Agenda 21, Chap. 4, para. 4.5.

[25]WSSD Plan of Implementation, para. 15(b), p. 7.

[26]See Birnie et al. (2009), pp. 322 f., with references to case law.

[27]See Kiss and Beurier (2010), p. 164.

[28]See Sands (2012), p. 229. He adds that the conclusion is different in relation to the EC, the UNECE or the OECD.

[29]See Daillier et al. (2009), p. 1443. Some international instruments describe the polluter-pays principle as a general principle of international law, such as the Preambles of the 1990 International Convention on Oil Pollution Preparedness, Response and Cooperation, the 1992 Convention on the Transboundary Effects of Industrial Accidents and the 2003 Kiev Draft Protocol on Civil Liability and Compensation for Damages Caused by the Transboundary Effects of Industrial Accidents on Transboundary Waters.

polluters pay'.[30] Rather, the polluter-pays principle is generally viewed as an 'international guideline'.[31]

This does not mean that the polluter-pays principle may not have any influence on environmental and economic policies. Soft law principles laid down in instruments of international environmental law suggest standards that states should pursue.[32] They indicate in particular the consensus of the international community on the path to be taken to tackle environmental issues and point to the general approach that states should adopt to achieve that objective.[33] Besides, the diverse functions of the polluter-pays principle[34] combine economic, social and environmental objectives, thereby making it a valuable instrument in achieving sustainable development.[35]

In brief, Principle 16 of the Rio Declaration does not indicate that states have a duty to make the polluters pay, but it shows that a state's effort to internalise the environmental costs of the products sold on its territory is an objective that has been recognised as legitimate by the international community.

On the other hand, as Agenda 21 explicitly states, developed countries should 'take the lead' in achieving sustainable consumption patterns.[36] This objective cannot logically be achieved without any regard to the overall environmental impact of the products consumed, including the impact caused by the production methods used. In other words, the world's largest consumers of natural resources have a greater responsibility in the elimination of unsustainable production and consumption patterns. Developed countries, which consume a majority of the world's natural resources, should ensure that the products sold on their markets promote sustainable production methods, such as fishery practices.[37] Because the largest markets are also the largest importers, achieving the objective embodied in Principle 8 of the Rio Declaration could imply that process standards should be applied to imported products as well because domestic restrictions on production are in principle insufficient to achieve significant results in the protection of the global environment.

In brief, international environmental law contemplates the possibility to regulate environmentally harmful production processes as an instrument to achieve sustainable development. In particular, the importance of the internalisation of

---

[30]See Birnie et al. (2009), p. 323.

[31]See Cassese (2005), p. 491. In the same vein, for Birnie and Boyle the polluter-pays principle is a 'guiding principle' (Birnie et al. 2009, p. 323).

[32]Ibid.

[33]Ibid.

[34]The Polluter-Pays Principle has been described as having 'internalizing, redistributive, preventive and curative' functions (Schwartz 2010, p. 256; de Sadeleer 2002, p. 34).

[35]See Schwartz (2010), p. 256.

[36]Agenda 21, Chap. 4, para. 4.8.

[37]See e.g. CIEL et al. (1999), pp. 24 f.

environmental externalities and of the elimination of unsustainable environmental practices has been recognised.

4.1.2 Sustainable Use

The principle of sustainable use of natural resources is an important part of sustainable development.[38] The main idea underlying sustainable use is that sustainable development involves limitations on the utilisation of natural resources.[39]

The Rio Declaration does not refer explicitly to sustainable use. Since then, the 2002 ILA New Delhi Declaration of Principles of International Law relating to Sustainable Development refers to the duty of states to ensure sustainable use of natural resources. It provides that 'states are under a duty to manage natural resources, including natural resources solely *within their own jurisdiction,* in a rational, sustainable and safe way'.[40] This principle indicates a move beyond the simple principle of prevention of transboundary harm, by limiting states' absolute freedom to use their own resources.[41]

The New Delhi Declaration indicates a direction in which international environmental law seems to evolve.[42] However, it is still uncertain whether it imposes a generally applicable obligation on states.[43] First, the definition of what is sustainable will depend on the circumstances of each case. As Judge Weeramantry has asserted in relation to sustainable development, '[w]hether development is sustainable by reason of its impact on the environment will be a question to be answered in the context of the particular situation involved'.[44] It may be difficult to adopt a definition of sustainable use that can be generally applicable to the wide array of environmental issues that may arise in the context of natural resource exploitation.

Even more importantly, the legally binding nature of the principle of sustainable use depends much on the specific sector to which it is applied and to the commitments made in specific treaties. Many MEAs contain provisions relating to the rate of exploitation of specific natural resources, in particular in the field of fishery management. Different terms are used, each referring to the same idea, namely that the use and exploitation of natural resources should be sustainable.

For instance, the Law of the Sea Convention provides that states should take conservation measures designed to maintain or restore populations of fish at levels

---

[38]See e.g. Sands (2012), p. 207.

[39]See Birnie et al. (2009), p. 199; Sands (2012), p. 210.

[40]Emphasis added.

[41]See French (2010), pp. 59 f.

[42]See French (2010), p. 60.

[43]See e.g. Birnie et al. (2009), p. 199; French (2010), p. 60; Lowe (1999), p. 29.

[44]Gabcikovo-Nagymaros, Separate Opinion of Judge Weeramantry, *ICJ Reports 1997*, p. 89.

that can produce the 'maximum sustainable yield'.[45] The World Charter for Nature states that ecosystems and land, marine and atmospheric resources shall be managed to achieve and maintain 'optimal sustainable productivity'.[46] The Convention on Biodiversity refers extensively throughout its provisions to the objective of conservation and sustainable use of biological diversity. It defines sustainable use as 'the use of components of biological diversity in a way and at a rate that does not lead to the long-term decline of biological diversity, thereby maintaining its potential to meet the needs and aspirations of present and future generations'.[47]

The principle of sustainable use may have acquired a normative content in certain specific sectors, such as the management of fisheries or water resources. But generally, states retain a large autonomy in the application of this principle in the absence of specific treaty commitments.[48]

In any event, the principle of sustainable use shows that states may have in certain fields a recognised interest in other states' natural resource management and in particular in the intensity of natural resource exploitation.

4.1.3 The Principle of Common but Differentiated Responsibilities

As mentioned above, the principle of intragenerational equity is generally regarded as one element of sustainable development. Even though the Rio Convention does not refer by name to this principle, it refers in Principle 5 to the 'essential task of eradicating poverty as an indispensable requirement for sustainable development'. The special needs of developing countries are further recognised in many multilateral environmental agreements, such as the Ozone and Climate Change Conventions, through provisions pertaining to financial assistance, transfers of technologies and the principle of common but differentiated responsibilities.[49]

Basically, the principle of common but differentiated responsibilities acknowledges the common interest, concern and responsibility of all states in the management of global environmental problems. But the protection of global environmental problems entails important costs and burdens, in particular in relation to pollution reduction, which needs to be allocated between states.[50] When it comes to allocating the burdens and costs of reducing global pollution, or to allocating increasingly

---

[45] 1982 UNCLOS, Art. 61(3).

[46] World Charter for Nature, para. 4.

[47] Convention on Biodiversity, Art. 2.

[48] See e.g. Birnie et al. (2009), pp. 200 f.; French (2010), p. 60.

[49] See Birnie et al. (2009), p. 122.

[50] See Shelton (2007), p. 652.

scarce natural resources,[51] questions of equity arise.[52] In practice, states contribute to a very different extent in causing environmental damages and have very different technical and financial means to take costly measures aimed at the prevention of environmental harm, depending on their level of development.[53]

In these circumstances, imposing 'equal obligations on subjects of law that are unequal in relevant ways may be perceived as unjust if they exacerbate inequalities or impose unfair burdens on those least able to bear them'.[54] In the field of climate change negotiations, it can be argued that demanding the same efforts to limit CO_2 emissions to countries with very different development levels seems unfair. The common but differentiated responsibilities principle thus recognises that the costs of international environmental protection need to be allocated in a 'fair' manner among states.[55] It can be viewed as the flipside of the principle of common concern[56] and is related to the principle of equity and distributive justice.[57] Differential treatment contradicts the traditional application of the principle of states' sovereign equality, which would imply similar obligations for each state.[58]

Initially, the Bruntland Report laid the foundation of the principle of common but differentiated responsibilities.[59] It was then included in the Rio Declaration, in particular through Principle 7, which reads:

> States shall cooperate in a spirit of global partnership to conserve, protect and restore the health and integrity of the Earth's ecosystem. In view of the different contributions to global environmental degradation, states have common but differentiated responsibilities. The developed countries acknowledge the responsibility that they bear in the international pursuit to sustainable development in view of the pressures their societies place on the global environment and of the technologies and financial resources they command.

---

[51]*Ibid.*

[52]See Birnie et al. (2009), p. 132.

[53]See Perrez (2000), p. 295; Sands (2012), p. 233.

[54]Shelton (2007), p. 647.

[55]See Perrez (2000), p. 297. What actually represents a fair allocation of burdens and costs of global environmental protection is certainly controversial, as is for instance shown by the view held by the US Senate in 1997 that any international treaty in the field of climate change that would require emissions reductions only for developed countries but not for developing countries would be discriminatory and unfair (see Shelton 2007, p. 640).

[56]See Brunnée (2007), p. 566.

[57]See Machado Filho (2008), pp. 93 ff.; Perrez (2000), p. 295 (arguing that 'the principle of common but differentiated responsibilities is a direct consequence of the application of the principle of common concern in connection with broader general principles of international law, namely the principle of equity and fairness, the principle of international solidarity, and the principle of partnership among nations and peoples'); Sands (2012), p. 233.

[58]See Cullet (1999), p. 549. See also Shelton (2007), p. 645, who explains that 'for most of its history, international law regulated bilateral and reciprocal relations and allocated rights and responsibilities on the basis of sovereignty and legal equality among states. Strictly legal, that is, formal equality demands rules of identical treatment, to ensure full respect for the sovereignty of each state regardless of size or wealth.'

[59]See Honkonen (2009), p. 70.

Principle 7 highlights the need for all states to participate in international efforts to address global environmental problems.[60] Besides, it requires an examination of the particular needs and interests of developing countries. Many MEAs contain provisions referring to the special needs of developed countries,[61] such as the recognition that economic development and eradication of poverty are the 'first and overriding priorities' of developing countries.[62]

The Rio Declaration recognises as well the 'special situations and needs of developing countries' and the necessity to address these interests.[63] Taking the particular needs of developing countries into account may require an improvement of capacity building and transfers of technologies.[64] But it may also imply that applicable standards should reflect the particular circumstances that prevail in different countries and that they may thus vary accordingly.[65]

The principle of common but differentiated responsibilities is mentioned in many multilateral environmental agreements.[66] Treaty regimes may thus provide for differing lengths in the implementation periods, less stringent commitments or special technical and financial support, as well as technology transfers.[67] In some MEAs, the obligation of developing countries to comply with their obligations depends on the implementation of developed states' commitments to provide financial assistance and technology transfers.[68]

---

[60]See Sands (2012), p. 233.

[61]See e.g. Principle 23 of the Stockholm Declaration, which recognises the need to consider 'the applicability of standards which are valid for the most advanced countries but which may be inappropriate and of unwarranted social cost for the developing countries'. See also Principle 6 of the Rio Declaration: '[t]he special situation and needs of developing countries, particularly the least developed and those most environmentally vulnerable, shall be given special priority. International actions in the field of environment and development should also address the interests and needs of all countries.'

[62]See Art. 4(7) of the UNFCCC; Preamble and Art. 20(4) of the Biodiversity Convention.

[63]Principle 6: '[t]he special situation and needs of developing countries, particularly the least developed and those most environmentally vulnerable, shall be given special priority. International actions in the field of environment and development should also address the interests and needs of all countries.'

[64]Principle 9: 'States should cooperate to strengthen endogenous capacity-building for sustainable development by improving scientific understanding through exchanges of scientific and technological knowledge, and by enhancing the development, adaptation, diffusion and transfer of technologies, including new and innovative technologies.'

[65]Principle 11: '[e]nvironmental standards, management objectives and priorities should reflect the environmental and development context to which they apply. Standards applied by some countries may be inappropriate and of unwarranted economic and social cost to other countries, in particular developing countries.' This principle was mentioned already in the Stockholm Declaration, Principle 23 and was reaffirmed in the WSSD Plan of Implementation, para. 15(a), p. 7.

[66]For instance, the UNFCCC (Art. 3 and 4); CBD (Preamble and Art. 20); WSSD Plan of Implementation, para. 2, 14, 20, 38, 39 and 81.

[67]See Birnie et al. (2009), pp. 133 ff.; Perrez (2000), p. 296; Sands (2012), pp. 235 f.

[68]Art. 4(7) of the UNFCCC; Art. 20(4) of the Biodiversity Convention.

It should also be noted that the principle of common but differentiated responsibilities does not apply universally to all environmental risks.[69] Sometimes it is essential to have common international standards for effective international regulation, for instance in international regimes dealing with nuclear safety,[70] pollution from ships,[71] trade in endangered species[72] or protection of Antarctica.[73]

One controversial question is whether the principle of common but differentiated responsibilities implies that states have a duty to provide preferential treatment. Despite the existence of Principle 7 of the Rio Declaration, its binding nature remains disputed.[74] The fear of developed countries of the broad-ranging long-term consequences of recognising the principle of common but differentiated responsibilities as a compulsory part of international environmental law may explain part of this result.[75] Despite its 'near universal acceptance', due to the widespread ratification of the Climate Change, Biodiversity and Ozone Conventions,[76] states' attitude to this principle is rather ambivalent. Some have pointed out that whether it is a legal principle or just a political guideline is still open to debate.[77] It seems that the principle of common but differentiated responsibilities is not merely soft law but that it has not yet crystallised into custom either.[78] It still lacks the *opinio iuris* necessary for the establishment of customary international law.[79] The principle has been described as an 'emerging principle of international law'[80] or as a 'framework principle',[81] requiring further clarification in the conclusion of more specific agreements, protocols or annexes.[82]

It has been suggested that even though the common but differentiated responsibilities principle does not impose *per se* binding obligations, 'it provides a general

---

[69] See Birnie et al. (2009), p. 136; Machado Filho (2008), p. 126.

[70] 1994 Convention on Nuclear Safety.

[71] 1973 International Convention for the Prevention of Pollution from Ships.

[72] 1973 Convention on International Trade in Endangered Species of Wild Fauna and Flora.

[73] 1991 Protocol on Environmental Protection to the Antarctic Treaty.

[74] See Cullet (2010), p. 178; Honkonen (2009), pp. 297 ff., in particular p. 301 ('[i]t is most likely too early to classify the CBDR as a customary principle of international environmental law'); Machado Filho (2008), p. 134 ('it would be extremely premature to state that such principle has been crystallised as customary law'); French (2010), p. 61 (stating that a settled *opinio juris* on this issue is still lacking).

[75] See Cullet (2010), p. 178.

[76] As pointed out by Birnie et al. (2009), p. 132. Cullet (2010), p. 178, noted that the CBDR principle is part of all major treaties addressing global environmental issues.

[77] See French (2000), p. 38.

[78] See Beyerlin (2007), p. 444; Machado Filho (2008), pp. 136 f.; Rajamani (2006), p. 160; Birnie et al. (2009), p. 135 (noting that the CBDR is 'far from being merely soft law').

[79] See e.g. Honkonen (2009), p. 302.

[80] See Brown Weiss (2000), p. 350.

[81] See Birnie et al. (2009), p. 135.

[82] See e.g. Birnie et al. (2009), p. 17.

orientation and direction towards which states should orientate their conduct'.[83] Yet the common but differentiated responsibilities principle does not provide a 'common formula' or a single remedy generally applicable. The general orientation that should be followed by states and the coordinated actions that should be established must be determined in the light of the specific objectives of each conventional instrument to which the principle applies.[84]

Another important aspect of the common but differentiated responsibilities principle, in the context of PPM measures, is that one of the basic ideas behind this principle is that some countries should contribute more than others to the provision of global public goods.[85] This may in turn influence the legitimacy of PPM trade measures, when developed states want to impose high environmental standards to developing nations that contributed less to the global environmental threat concerned and that do not have the same technical and financial means. This does not mean, however, that the common but differentiated responsibilities principle would render such measures illegal since it cannot be viewed as a rule of customary international law. It could, however, be one of the relevant elements to consider in the analysis of specific environmental trade measures. In any event, the precise legal consequences of this principle should be examined in the light of the specific commitments made in potentially applicable MEAs.

4.1.4   Cooperation

Although the principle of cooperation is not an obligation specific to sustainable development, the Rio Convention acknowledges that it is a necessary component of the achievement of sustainable development. Principle 7 provides that 'states shall cooperate in a spirit of global partnership to conserve, protect and restore the health and integrity of the Earth's ecosystems'. The Preamble similarly refers to the 'goal of establishing a new and equitable global partnership through the creation of new levels of cooperation among states'.

It is also clear that protection of global ecosystems imposes international cooperation.[86] This obligation is thus reflected in both the Stockholm and Rio Declarations.[87] The international legal order of cooperation is, however, superimposed on the traditional law of coexistence,[88] which comprises the principle of permanent sovereignty over natural resources. In other words, the general duty to cooperate

---

[83]Machado Filho (2008), p. 135.

[84]See Machado Filho (2008), pp. 135 f.

[85]See Stone (2004), p. 299.

[86]See Daillier et al. (2009), pp. 1455 f. ('[l]a coopération internationale pour la sauvegarde et la préservation de l'environnement est une nécessité, imposée par la globalité de l'écosystème').

[87]See Stockholm Principle 24 and Rio Principle 7.

[88]See Perrez (2000), p. 256.

coexists with the principle of state sovereignty, insofar as no state may unilaterally impose its will on others.[89]

General international law also implies a duty to cooperate. The importance of cooperation has considerably evolved throughout the twentieth century. Whereas international law has traditionally been seen as a limited set of rules designed to assure the peaceful coexistence of equally sovereign states (international law of coexistence), the growing interdependencies among states in a large variety of fields have transformed international law into a law of cooperation.[90] The UN Charter illustrates this evolution since cooperation is one of the fundamental objectives of the United Nations.[91] UN Charter Article 1 provides that 'international cooperation in solving international problems of an economic, social, cultural, or humanitarian character' is one of the major purposes of the United Nations. It may have the nature of a general custom, in part in the light of the considerable number of international treaties aimed at establishing and reinforcing cooperation among states.[92]

The legal content of that general duty to negotiate establishes a non-specific obligation to act cooperatively but is too vague to require states to act in a specific way or to adopt specific measures.[93] It simply indicates that states have to try and find through dialogue a solution compatible with the interests of others and to contribute to the solution of common problems, without specifying the concrete form or means of this contribution.[94]

Besides that general duty to negotiate, some concrete and more precise forms of cooperation obligations exist.[95] In particular, the prevention of transboundary harm implies notification and consultation obligations in relation to transboundary risks.[96] Achieving conservation and equitable use of shared resources also implies

---

[89]See Dupuy (2000), p. 23.

[90]See Friedman (1964); Dupuy (1998), p. 278; Dupuy (2000), p. 23; Perrez (2000), pp. 255 ff.

[91]See Dupuy (2000), p. 23 (in his view, cooperation is 'the alpha and the omega of United Nations, but also of general international law'); Perrez (2000), pp. 257 f. and 266 ff.

[92]See Dupuy (2000), pp. 22 f. He adds 'today's international law is conceived of, if not always practiced as, the international law of cooperation'. See also Perrez (2000), p. 271, with further references.

[93]See e.g. Daillier et al. (2009), p. 1456 ('en l'absence d'un traité imposant aux Parties des obligations spécifiques, il s'agit là probablement davantage de directives générales que d'obligations de comportement juridiquement sanctionnables'); French (2010), p. 61 ('it is equally apparent that the precise ambit of a duty to co-operate remains vague'); Prost (2005), p. 175 ('[i]l est généralement admis que si une obligation doit être déduite de ces textes fondamentaux du droit international de l'environnement, c'est une obligation très générale de coopérer, qui se traduit par un devoir de consultation et d'information des Etats intéressés, bien plus que par une obligation de négocier des accords internationaux'); Perrez (2000), p. 261.

[94]See Dupuy (2000), p. 24; Perrez (2000), p. 261.

[95]See Sands (2012), pp. 203 f.

[96]See e.g. Art. 4 of the 2001 ILC Articles on Prevention of Transboundary Harm from Hazardous Activities ('states concerned shall cooperate in good faith and, as necessary, seek the assistance of one or more competent international organizations in preventing significant transboundary harm or

cooperation. The relevant UN Resolutions provide for a duty to cooperate on the basis of a system of information and prior consultation.[97] On the other hand, achieving sustainable development, protecting issues of common concern and giving effect to the principle of common but differentiated responsibilities all require cooperation between states.[98]

Not surprisingly, most multilateral environmental agreements contain a duty to negotiate, which may be translated in more specific commitments,[99] depending on the context in which the treaty applies. These concrete kinds of cooperation obligations may take different forms and imply varying degrees of restriction on state sovereignty, from mere information exchange obligations to obligations to provide financial and technical assistance or obligations to implement common measures and establish common institutions.[100] For instance, the climate change regime instituted by the United Nations implies cooperation obligations in these three fields.[101]

If cooperation in addressing global environmental issues is a general obligation, the details and concrete implications of that duty depend on the specific provisions of the applicable treaties. In any event, the general principle is that states must take into account interests of others and contribute to the solution of common problems.[102]

In the context of the interrelation between trade and the environment, an important issue that has arisen is the extent to which the principle of cooperation restricts the possibilities of states to act unilaterally.

There have been international attempts mainly by developing countries to give the duty to cooperate a more legally binding content, through the limitations of unilateral action by way of trade measures to protect the environment. For developing countries, an important part of their future development may depend on their ability to increase their exports, through an open multilateral trading system. Unilateral actions have been seen as an obstacle to achieving this objective. For instance, Agenda 21 states:

> Protectionist pressures and unilateral policy actions continue to endanger the functioning of an open multilateral trading system, affecting particularly the export interests of developing countries.[103]

Similarly, Principe 12 of the Rio Convention provides:

---

at any event in minimizing the risk thereof'). See also Principle 19 of the Rio Declaration; Birnie et al. (2009), pp. 177 ff.

[97] See Resolution 3129 XXVIII; Art. 3 of the 197 Charter of Economic Rights and Duties of States.

[98] See the detailed analysis of Perrez (2000), pp. 283–303.

[99] See Sands (2012), p. 204.

[100] See Perrez (2000), pp. 262 ff.

[101] See the detailed analysis of Perrez (2000), pp. 317–330.

[102] See Perrez (2000), p. 330.

[103] Agenda 21, para. 2.8.

Unilateral actions to deal with environmental challenges outside the jurisdiction of the importing country should be avoided. Environmental measures addressing transboundary or global environmental problems should, as far as possible, be based on an international consensus.

This principle has also been mentioned and developed in paragraph 39 of Agenda 21. It basically means that multilateral solutions are to be preferred, for various reasons, such as the possibility to guarantee intervention at the source. Agenda 21 indeed recognises that 'environmental policies should deal with the root causes of environmental degradation'.[104] If unilateral measures 'should be avoided' and be based 'as far as possible on international consensus', unilateral measures are not prohibited per se.[105] Agenda 21 thus states that 'domestic measures targeted to achieve certain environmental objectives may need trade measures to render them effective'.[106] Yet Agenda 21 encourages states, in such a case, to enact non-discriminatory and transparent measures and to 'give consideration to the special conditions and development requirements of developing countries as they move towards agreed environmental objectives'.[107]

When it comes to the possibility to adopt unilateral measures, one controversial issue is how to determine if a particular country has attempted 'as far as possible' to achieve international consensus. Neither the Rio Declaration nor Agenda 21 provides further indications. This issue had to be examined by the Panel and the Appellate Body in the *US – Shrimp* case and still remains controversial in WTO law, as it will be shown below.[108]

4.1.5 Conclusion

Even though they may not have the status of binding international obligations, the different principles that form part of the concept of sustainable development may all have an influence on the examination of PPM measures under the GATT. The need to eliminate unsustainable patterns of consumption and production and to internalise environmental externalities illustrates that the regulation of PPMs may be a necessary instrument to achieve sustainable development, which means that, from a general viewpoint, the GATT should not, in the light of the objective of sustainable development of the WTO, be interpreted so as to extensively restrict the ability of WTO Members to adopt PPM measures. On the other hand, the principle of common but differentiated responsibilities may require developed states to take the particular interests of developing countries into account in the design and

---

[104] Agenda 21, para. 39.3(d).
[105] See Sands (2012), p. 807.
[106] Agenda 21, para. 39.3(d).
[107] *Idem.*
[108] See *infra*, 7.3.4.

implementation of a PPM scheme. Finally, the principle of cooperation encourages states to favour multilateral solutions, even though unilateralism is not prohibited per se.

4.2 The Principle of Permanent Sovereignty Over Natural Resources

4.2.1 Significance and Content

It has been seen that the concept of sustainable development contemplates the possibility for states to adopt measures addressing the environmental impact of protection methods. But other principles of international law are also frequently invoked to oppose the use of PPM measures, namely the right of the exporting country to regulate the activities occurring in its territory and to exploit its natural resources. This issue relates in part to the law of prescriptive jurisdiction, which will be examined in the next chapter. But it also concerns aspects of international environmental law, through the principle of permanent sovereignty over natural resources.

This principle is mentioned in many international instruments, such as the Rio Convention, which states in Principle 2:

States have, in accordance with the Charter of the United Nations and the principles of international law, the sovereign right to exploit their own resources pursuant to their own environmental and developmental policies.

When it comes to the content of this principle, certain states have historically defended at first an absolute application of sovereignty over natural resources. At the end of the nineteenth century, General Attorney Harmon claimed that the United States' 'full sovereignty over its national territory' enabled this country to extract as much water as it seemed fit from the Rio Grande, regardless of the needs and interests of downstream states, in that case Mexico.[109] However, the absolute sovereignty over water within a state's territory, which characterised what is called the 'Harmon doctrine', has been dismissed by modern commentators and has not been confirmed by international practice.[110]

The contemporary form of the principle of sovereignty over natural resources has emerged in the 1950s, during the process of decolonisation.[111] At that time, the main objective of newly independent states was to establish control over their

---

[109]See 21 *Ops. Atty. Gen.* (1895) 274, p. 283.

[110]See e.g. Birnie et al. (2009), pp. 540 f.; Tomuschat (1993), pp. 294 f.; Kiss and Beurier (2010), n° 213, p. 215.

[111]For a detailed presentation of the origins of the concept of permanent sovereignty over natural resources, see Perrez (2000), pp. 72 ff.

natural resources, in particular oil and minerals, which were often exploited by foreign companies.[112] Developing countries wished to secure the legality of nationalisation of foreign enterprises, which wanted to keep exploiting natural resources on the basis of the rights acquired during the colonial period.[113]

Several resolutions of the UN General Assembly adopted after 1952 have mentioned the principle of sovereignty over natural resources,[114] and they culminated in the adoption of Resolution 1803 (XVII) by the UN General Assembly in 1962, entitled 'permanent sovereignty over natural resources'. The Resolution declares:

> The right of peoples and nations to permanent sovereignty over natural wealth and resources must be exercised in the interest of their national development and of the well-being of the people of the state concerned.

> The exploration, development and disposition of such resources, as well as the import of the foreign capital required for these purposes, should be in conformity with the rules and conditions which the peoples and nations freely consider to be necessary or desirable with regard to the authorization, restriction or prohibition of such activities.[115]

Interestingly, Resolution 1803 does not make any distinction between living and non-living resources and does not refer to any duty of conservation.[116] Its exclusive focus is on property rights over national natural resources. This general right reflects the right of every state to choose freely the socio-economic system that best suits its development potential.[117]

The precise legal status of the principle is still debated.[118] If some have contended that Resolution 1803 is not binding,[119] others are of the view that it reflects an international legal right.[120] Two international arbitral tribunals have accepted that the principle of permanent sovereignty over natural resources reflects customary international law.[121]

---

[112]See Birnie et al. (2009), p. 191; Sands (2012), p. 191.

[113]See Perrez (1996), p. 1192.

[114]See UNGA Res. 523 (VI) of 12 January 1952; Res. 626 (VII) of 21 December 1952; Res. 1314 (XIII) of 12 December 1958; Res. 1515 (XV) of 15 December 1960.

[115]Paragraphs 1 and 2 of Resolution 1803 (XVII). The Preamble mentions, *inter alia*, the 'sovereign right of every state to dispose of its wealth and its resources', 'the inalienable right of all states freely to dispose of their natural wealth and resources in accordance with their national interests' and the fact that 'any measure in this respect must be based on the recognition of the inalienable right of all states freely to dispose of their natural wealth and resources in accordance with their natural interests'.

[116]See Birnie et al. (2009), p. 191.

[117]See Schrijver (2007), p. 341.

[118]See e.g. Perrez (1996), p. 1193 with further references.

[119]See Birnie et al. (2009), p. 191.

[120]See Sands (2012), p. 192.

[121]See Texaco Overseas Petroleum Co. and California Asiatic Oil Co. v. Libya, 53 ILR (1977) 389, para. 87; Kuwait v. American Independent Oil Co., 21 ILM (1982) 976.

This principle has been confirmed in other United Nations General Assembly resolutions[122] and has also been mentioned in many multilateral environmental agreements, such as the Basel Convention,[123] the Biodiversity Convention[124] or the Climate Change Convention.[125]

The principle of permanent sovereignty thus certainly remains the cornerstone of states' rights and duties over natural resources within their territory.[126] Certain exporting countries thus sometimes invoke this principle to resist international attempts to impose obligations restricting this sovereignty.[127] In this context, developing countries often argue that the adoption of trade barriers by developed states to induce developing countries to enact high environmental standards that may conflict with their economic and developmental priorities[128] is a form of 'eco-imperialism'.[129]

4.2.2 Limits to the Principle of Permanent Sovereignty Over Natural Resources

However, from a legal viewpoint, the principle of permanent sovereignty over natural resources is not absolute: other principles of international environmental law restricting sovereignty have developed. In a way, sovereignty over natural resources and environmental protection are 'objectives pulling in opposing directions'.[130] While the former has historically sought to establish the right of states to

---

[122]See Resolutions 3201 and 3281 (which recognise that 'each state enjoys a sovereign right to nationalize, in which case appropriate compensation should be determined according to its own law and by its own courts').

[123]The Preamble of the Basel Convention recognises that 'any state has the sovereign right to ban the entry or disposal of foreign hazardous wastes and other wastes in its territory'.

[124]Art. 15(1) of the CBD recognises that 'the sovereign rights of states over their natural resources, the authority to determine access to genetic resources rests with the national governments and is subject to national legislation'.

[125]The Preamble of the UNFCCC recalls that 'states have, in accordance with the Charter of the United Nations and the principles of international law, the sovereign right to exploit their own resources pursuant to their own environmental and developmental policies, and the responsibility to ensure that activities within their jurisdiction or control do not cause damage to the environment of other States or of areas beyond the limits of national jurisdiction'. See also Art. 1 of the 1994 International Tropical Timber Agreement ('[r]ecognising the sovereignty of members over their natural resources, ...'). See also Principle 21 of the Stockholm Declaration and Principle 2 of the Rio Declaration, commented *infra*, Sect. 4.2.2.1.

[126]See e.g. Birnie et al. (2009), p. 192; Schrijver (2007), p. 250.

[127]See Perrez (2000), pp. 69 ff. and 95 ff.

[128]See Perrez (2000), p. 95.

[129]See e.g. Esty (1994), pp. 181 f. and 185 ff.

[130]Sands (2012), p. 190.

exploit freely their natural resources, the latter requires the development of inter-national obligations restricting this absolute freedom.

Various principles of international environmental law have emerged in this field and entail limits to permanent sovereignty over natural resources. First, this principle applies only with respect to resources located within national jurisdiction and to environmental externalities affecting the domestic environment only. States have, however, a duty to prevent transboundary harm (Sect. 4.2.2.1). The principle of equitable use imposes a limit on the exploitation of shared resources (Sect. 4.2.2.2). Finally, the concept of common concern indicates that foreign states may have an interest in the environmental policies of a particular country affecting a recognised international environmental objective (Sect. 4.2.2.3).

4.2.2.1   Prevention of Transboundary Harm

The principle of permanent sovereignty over natural resources is first limited by the obligation to prevent transboundary harm. After the adoption of the principle of permanent sovereignty over natural resources in the 1950s and 1960s, new instruments of international environmental law have confirmed permanent sovereignty but in parallel have systematically emphasised the corollary duty that states must not cause damage to the environment of other states or to the global commons, which can be described as a reformulation of the maxim *sic utere tuo ut alienum non laedas.*[131]

Principle 21 of the Stockholm Declaration stated in 1972 as follows:

> States have, in accordance with the Charter of the United Nations and the principles of international law, the sovereign right to exploit their own resources pursuant to their own environmental policies, and the responsibility to ensure that activities within their jurisdiction or control do not cause damage to the environment of other states or of areas beyond the limits of national jurisdiction.

Twenty years later, this principle was integrated in Principle 2 of the Rio Declaration, which reaffirmed the responsibility not to cause damage to the environment of other states or of areas beyond the limits of national jurisdiction and declared that states have the sovereign right to exploit their own resources pursuant to their own environmental and development policies.[132]

---

[131] Use your own property so as not to injure that of another (principle of good neighbourliness). Birnie et al. (2009), p. 137; Perrez (1996), p. 1201; Tomuschat (1993), p. 296; Schrijver (2007), p. 243.

[132] Principle 2 of the Rio Declaration states that 'states have, in accordance with the Charter of the United Nations and the principles of international law, the sovereign right to exploit their own resources pursuant to their own environmental and developmental policies, and the responsibility to ensure that activities within their jurisdiction or control do not cause damage to the environment of other states or of areas beyond the limits of national'. See also Perrez (1996), p. 1203 with further references.

The obligation not to harm the environment of other states or the global commons has been recognised by international tribunals before the Stockholm Convention, in particular in the Trail Smelter,[133] Corfu Channel[134] and Lac Lanoux[135] cases. More recently, the ICJ held in its *Advisory Opinion on the Legality of the Threat or Use of Nuclear Weapons* as follows:

> The existence of the general obligation of states to ensure that activities within their jurisdiction and control respect the environment of other states or of areas beyond national control is now part of the corpus of international law relating to the environment.[136]

It is now generally accepted that this principle is a customary international law rule.[137] The duty not to cause transboundary harm and not to damage areas beyond states' jurisdiction constrains the sovereign right of states to exploit their natural resources[138]; it balances rights and responsibilities.[139]

However, its exact scope and implications are still uncertain, in particular because not all instances of transboundary damages are unlawful.[140] Restriction is limited to serious consequences, which means that transfrontier damage must reach a certain level of harm.[141] The Stockholm and Rio Declarations do not indicate all the elements necessary to determine if a state has violated its obligation, in particular because it does not specify what an environmental damage is, which damages are prohibited and what the consequences are of the violation of the principle of transboundary harm prevention.[142] More detailed rules are required in order to prevent and curb transboundary pollution in an effective manner.[143] In any event, the more intense is the environmental harm caused, the less persuasive is the polluting state's invocation of its right to freely use its natural resources.[144]

In the context of the PPM debate, the principle of transboundary harm prevention shows that an exporting state cannot legitimately invoke permanent sovereignty over its natural resources to oppose PPM measures addressing activities that

---

[133]Trail Smelter Case (United States v. Canada), 3 R.I.A.A 1905, 1911. The Arbitral Tribunal held that 'under the principles of international law, as well as of the law of the United States, no state has the right to use or permit the use of its territory in such a manner as to cause injury by fumes in or to the territory of another or the properties or persons therein, when the case is of serious consequence and the injury is established by clear and convincing evidence'. *Idem* at 1965.

[134]*Corfu Channel Case*, ICJ Reports (1949) 1.

[135]*Lac Lanoux Arbitration*, 24 ILR (1957) 101.

[136]*Legality of the Threat or Use of Nuclear Weapons, advisory Opinion*, ICJ Report (1996), p. 226, para. 29.

[137]See e.g. Birnie et al. (2009), p. 143; Perrez (1996), p. 1200; Sands (2012), p. 196.

[138]See Perrez (1996), p. 1202; Tomuschat (1993), p. 296; Sands (2012), pp. 195 and 200.

[139]See Perrez (1996), p. 1201.

[140]See Schrijver (2007), p. 243; Kiss and Beurier (2010), p. 131.

[141]See Perrez (1996), p. 1199.

[142]See Sands (2012), p. 196.

[143]See Tomuschat (1993), p. 295.

[144]See Perrez (1996), p. 1202.

result in significant transboundary effects or that have a negative impact on the environment of the importing country or of areas beyond any jurisdiction.

4.2.2.2 Equitable Use

Certain obligations of international environmental law limit the principle of permanent sovereignty over natural resources in cases of shared resources. Natural living or mineral resources are not always confined within the territory of one state but may extend across several countries (common pool resources). When resources are shared between two or several countries, controversies may arise in relation to their management, exploitation and conservation. The most obvious examples are international watercourses, atmospheric resources, fisheries or migratory animals. As it has been mentioned before, historically the 'Harmon doctrine' claimed at the end of the nineteenth century that sovereignty was not restricted by the fact that certain natural resources could be shared with other states.[145] This doctrine has not been confirmed by later practice or in treaty law. International environmental law has rather developed principles applicable to shared resources, which restrict to some extent state sovereignty over natural resources, through bilateral or multilateral treaties dealing with specific resources.[146]

In the 1970s, efforts were carried out to formulate generally applicable standards in relation to the use of shared resources. The UN General Assembly adopted the Charter of Economic Rights and Duties of States, which includes a provision stating as follows:

> In the exploitation of natural resources shared by two or more countries, each state must co-operate on the basis of a system of information and prior consultations in order to achieve optimum use of such resources without causing damage to the legitimate interests of others.[147]

The General Assembly also adopted a resolution mandating the General Council of UNEP to establish international standards for the conservation and harmonious exploitation of shared resources, in order in particular to develop effective cooperation between countries on the basis of a system of information and prior consultation.[148] An intergovernmental working group of experts established 'Draft Principles of Conduct in the Field of the Environment for the Guidance of States in the Conservation and Harmonious Utilization of Natural Resources Shared by Two or More States', which were adopted by the UNEP General Council in 1978. These principles provide in particular for an obligation to cooperate to protect the

---

[145]See *supra*, Sect. 4.2.1.

[146]See Brownlie (1979), pp. 289 ff.

[147]UNGA Resolution 3281 (XXIX) adopted on 12 December 1974.

[148]See UNGA Resolution 3129 (XXVIII) on Co-operation in the field of the Environment concerning Natural Resources Shared by Two or More States, adopted on 13th December 1973.

environment.[149] They refer to an obligation to conduct environmental impact assessment before engaging in any activity that may create a risk of significantly affecting the environment of another state.[150] They indicate as well that states sharing resources should exchange information, consult and notify neighbouring states in relation to activities that are expected to affect significantly the environment of other states.[151] The Draft Principles also refer to the concept of equitable utilisation, stating that states should cooperate 'with a view to controlling, preventing, reducing or eliminating adverse environmental effects which may result from the utilization of such resources'.[152]

The concept of equitable utilisation has been developed, in particular, in the context of international watercourses and was applied, for instance, in the *Gabcikovo-Nagymaros* case, in which Czechoslovakia denied Hungary of its right to an equitable and reasonable share of the natural resources of the Danube.[153] It has also been applied by the ICJ in the context of fisheries beyond the exclusive economic zone.[154]

This principle requires a balancing of the interests of the states engaged in the exploitation of shared resources.[155] The relevant interests and circumstances depend on the applicable international instruments and on the context of each cases in which equitable use is applied.[156] It has been included, for instance, in the Montreal Protocol,[157] the Climate Change Convention[158] and the Convention on Biological Diversity.[159]

It should be pointed out that equitable utilisation addresses environmental problems from the viewpoint of countries exploiting the resources and may be ill-suited when it comes to achieving common interests or the protection of

---

[149]Principles 1 and 2.

[150]Principle 4.

[151]Principle 6.

[152]Principle 1.

[153]*Gabcikovo-Nagymaros Project (Hungary/Sloavakia)*, Judgement, ICJ Reports (1997) 7, at 56. For a comment of this case, see, e.g., Sands (2012), pp. 313 ff.

[154]*Icelandic Fisheries* cases, United Kingdom v. Iceland, Merits, ICJ Reports (1974) 3, at 31 and Federal Republic of Germany v. Iceland, Merits, ICJ Reports (1974) 175, at 199.

[155]See Birnie et al. (2009), p. 202.

[156]See Birnie et al. (2009), p. 202; Sands (2012), p. 215.

[157]The Preamble of the Montreal Protocol refers to the objective to 'protect the ozone layer by taking precautionary measures to control equitably total global emissions of substances that deplete it (. . .)'.

[158]Art. 4(2)(a) of the UNFCCC refers to 'the need for equitable and appropriate contributions by each of these Parties to the global effort regarding' the objective of mitigation of climate change, by limiting its anthropogenic emissions of greenhouse gases.

[159]Art. 1 of the CBD provides that '[t]he objective of this Convention, to be pursued in accordance with its relevant provisions, are the conservation of biological diversity, the sustainable use of its components and the fair and equitable sharing of the benefits arising out of the utilization of genetic resources (. . .)'.

common areas, which may involve other interests to be taken into account.[160] However, other principles of international environmental law are applicable when it comes to the conservation of natural resources in the light of common interest of states, such as the concept of common concern.

In any event, the concept of equitable utilisation implies certain restrictions to the principle of permanent sovereignty over natural resources in case of shared resources.

4.2.2.3   Common Concern

At the end of the 1980s, the international community started to realise that the increase in the amount of greenhouse gases in the atmosphere could lead to adverse changes in the world climate. At the same time, states began to negotiate an international agreement addressing the conservation of world biological diversity. During the negotiations, it was suggested that the world climate and biodiversity should be viewed as 'common heritage of humankind'. This proposal was rejected in part because it would have implied important restrictions on the states' sovereignty over natural resources since common heritage as it is applied in particular to the resources of the deep seabed implies a common property regime.

Because of these controversial consequences, no agreement was reached on the use of the concept of 'common heritage'. Some political compromise was achieved by referring instead to climate change and biological diversity as 'common concern of humankind',[161] which are now widely accepted principles in the light of the large number of signatories of the UNFCCC and CBD.[162] This concept had not been previously employed in international law,[163] but this terminology was not entirely novel. In the middle of the twentieth century, certain international instruments relating in particular to the management of fisheries had affirmed that conservation and rational exploitation of fish stocks were of common concern to the signatories.[164] Other treaties referred to the 'common interest',[165] or the 'interest of all mankind'.[166]

---

[160]See Birnie et al. (2009), p. 202.

[161]The very first paragraph of Preamble of the UNFCCC acknowledges that 'change in the Earth's climate and its adverse effects are a common concern of humankind'. The Preamble of the CBD affirms that 'conservation of biological diversity is a common concern of humankind'.

[162]See Bierman (2001), p. 431; Bowman (2010), p. 504.

[163]See Birnie et al. (2009), p. 129.

[164]See e.g. the Preamble of the 1959 North-East Atlantic Fisheries Convention, which reads 'to ensure the conservation of the fish stocks and the rational exploitation of the fisheries of the North-East Atlantic Ocean and adjacent waters, which are of common concern to them (. . .)'.

[165]Preamble of the 1946 International Convention for the Regulation of Whaling ('. . .it is in the common interest to achieve the optimum level of whale stocks as rapidly as possible without causing widespread economic and nutritional distress').

[166]Preamble of the 1959 Antarctic Treaty ('it is in the interest of all mankind that Antarctica shall continue forever to be used exclusively for peaceful purposes. . .').

While these phrases did not carry special legal connotation but rather the recognition of some shared motivations,[167] the use of the concept of 'common concern' in relation to climate change and biodiversity conservation seems to indicate a different status, insofar as international governance relating to these concerns may prove essential for the survival of mankind.[168] Some have, however, described the concept of common concern as a political term[169] or an ultra soft law concept[170] and have wondered if it could have any legal content.[171] It is true that both the Climate Change and Biodiversity Conventions reaffirm the principle of permanent sovereignty over natural resources.[172] 'Common concern' does not 'internationalise' natural resources property as 'common heritage' does.[173]

There is no doubt that the present legal implications and material content of the concept 'common concern' is still not precisely elaborated.[174] But many recognise that this concept does have some legal consequences[175] and that it does influence states' interactions.[176]

As such, common concern does not imply specific rules for the conduct of states,[177] which need to be established in particular through appropriate institutional forum in which negotiations can take place.[178] But what the recognition that a matter amounts to 'common concern' does indicate is that each state has a

---

[167]See Bowman (2010), p. 501.

[168]See Biermann (1996), p. 431.

[169]See Baslar (1998), pp. 289 and 314.

[170]*Ibid.*, p. 314; Kirgis (1990), p. 525.

[171]See Atapattu (2006), p. 120 (who is of the view that common concern 'does not seem to carry any legal implications'); Birnie et al. (2009), p. 130 (who do not deny any legal content but wonder what it can be knowing that common concern is neither common property, nor common heritage and that it entails a reaffirmation of the sovereignty over natural resources).

[172]See the Preambles of the UNFCCC and of the CBD.

[173]The concept of 'common heritage of mankind' applies to the moon and resources of the deep seabed, under the 1979 Agreement Governing the Activities of States on the Moon and Other Celestial Bodies and the 1982 United States Convention on the Law of the Sea. Legally, the concept of common heritage is a narrow concept relating to property rights in the form of common ownership. Resources which have been recognised as 'common heritage of mankind' are subject to the principle of non-appropriation, which means that no state can exercise sovereignty or sovereign rights to appropriate any of its part. Moreover, resources must be conserved and exploited to the benefit of all countries, by contrast to living resources of the high seas. The emergence of this concept can be seen as efforts by newly independent states in the 1960s and 70s to reshape international law to reflect developing countries concerns. For further details, see e.g. Baslar (1998); Brownlie (1979), pp. 297 ff.; Brunnée (2007), pp. 562 ff.

[174]See e.g. Biermann (1996), pp. 426, 431 *et passim*; Birnie et al. (2009), p. 129.

[175]See Brunnée (2007), p. 566; Kirgis (1990), p. 526; Bowman (2010), p. 503.

[176]See Brunée (2006), p. 309 ('[b]ut precision does not equal influence — even open-textures common concern concepts, irrespective of their binding force at customary law, play significant roles in framing states' interaction, notably within treaty-based regimes').

[177]See Brunnée (2007), p. 566.

[178]See Bowman (2010), p. 503.

legitimate interest in the conservation of resources of global significance and a common responsibility to participate in their conservation.[179] Giving the status of 'common concern' to particular issues places them on the international agenda and arguably removes them from states' reserved domain.[180] One of the most obvious consequences is that all states have a very general *obligation to cooperate* in the management of common concern issues.[181]

Another consequence is that sovereignty is not absolute or unlimited in relation to the exploitation or use of natural resources of common concern but is qualified by the duty to have regard to the recognised interests of the community of states as a whole.[182] These two obligations may be seen as duties owed *erga omnes*,[183] which means that all states 'would have concomitant legal interests and could demand others to adjust conduct accordingly'.[184]

It may, however, be difficult to evaluate the precise nature of this restriction of permanent sovereignty. The extent to which exploitation or use of natural resources of common concern should be limited and the nature of state obligation to enact effective conservation measures depend on the specific obligations laid down in relevant treaties.

---

[179]See Birnie et al. (2009), p. 130; Kirgis (1990), p. 527; Kiss (1996), p. 2 (common concern of humankind implies that 'the whole humanity is entitled to express its concern'); Honkonen (2009), p. 68; Bowman (2010), p. 503. See also UN CSD, Report of the Expert Group Meeting on Identification of Principles of International Law for Sustainable Development, Prepared by the Division for Sustainable Development for the Commission on Sustainable Development Fourth Session (1996), para. 82 ('[t]he foundation of the concept [of common concern] is the recognition of a legitimate interest of the international community to concern itself with certain issues and values which, by their nature, affect the community as a whole').

[180]See Birnie et al. (2009), p. 131; Murase (1995), pp. 312 f. n. 47; Cottier and Matteotti-Berkutova (2009), p. 29; Bowman (2010), p. 503.

[181]See Atapattu (2006), p. 120; Birnie et al. (2009), pp. 132 f. and 662 (in relation to natural living resources); Bowman (2010), p. 503; UN CSD, Report of the Expert Group, para. 88 (the concept of common concern of humankind can 'be viewed as a specific manifestation of the overarching duty to cooperate, which constitutes the very anchor of international law'). See also Principle 7 of the Rio Declaration. See, however, Murase (1995), pp. 312 f., n. 47, who asserts that the concept of common concern 'cannot be construed as conferring states any substantive obligation nor procedural standing for the enforcement of the rules incorporated in the relevant instruments'. This general obligation must thus be specified in particular treaty commitments. See Perrez (2000), pp. 259 ff.

[182]See Birnie et al. (2009), p. 130 (pointing out that 'sovereignty is not unlimited or absolute'); Brunnée (2007), p. 566 (expressing that CCM indicates that 'states' freedom of action may be subject to limits'); Bowman (2010), p. 503 (who maintains that sovereignty is 'conditioned by the need to have regard to the recognised interests of the community at large'); UN CSD, Report of the Expert Group, para. 83 ('[t]he concept of the common concern of humankind might signal that the protection of the global environment can no longer be considered to be solely within the competence of individual sovereign nations. The concept could imply the right and duty of the international community, and thus of each state, to act in a manner which reflects this concern').

[183]See e.g. Birnie et al. (2009), p. 131; Kirgis (1990), p. 527; Brunnée (2007), p. 566; Bowman (2010), p. 503.

[184]See Brunnée (2007), p. 566.

In any event, common concern means that, in the fields covered by this concept, states may not always invoke legitimately the principle of permanent sovereignty over natural resources as an absolute defence against international efforts to change the domestic practices of that state, which threaten issues of common concern. In such a situation, the rest of the international community may wish to take certain measures in reaction to this conduct, in particular the adoption of trade restrictions,[185] the legality of which depends on customary rules on jurisdiction and on applicable international trade rules.

It must be pointed out, however, that the concept of common concern is also closely related to equity considerations, in particular because states contribute unevenly in the creation of global environmental problems and do not have the same technical and financial means to address them. These aspects are incorporated in the principle of common but differentiated responsibilities, which is analysed above.[186]

4.2.3 Conclusion

Permanent sovereignty over natural resources implies that, in principle, states have the right to choose their own environmental and developmental policies related to natural resources located in their territory. International environmental protection efforts may thus collide with permanent sovereignty over natural resources in certain circumstances.

Nevertheless, various principles of international law impose limits to the possibilities of states to freely exploit their natural resources, in particular when such exploitation results in transboundary harm or affect shared resources. In such cases, the responsible state cannot legitimately invoke permanent sovereignty over natural resources to justify its activities.

In the absence of transboundary effects, the environmental policies of a state may also affect environmental interests recognised as 'common concern', such as biodiversity conservation, which has been described as a global public good in the previous chapter. It has also been shown that the principle of sustainable use, which requires limitations on the exploitation rate of natural resources, is one of the core elements of sustainable development. The concept of common concern, or the principle of sustainable use, may not entail precise limitations on the principle of permanent sovereignty over natural resources as such, in the absence of specific treaty commitments. However, such concepts do show, in the context of the PPM debate, that the importing state may have a legitimate interest in the environmental

---

[185]The question whether the rest of the international community of states can take countermeasures in reaction to the violation of international obligations in this case will not be examined here.

[186]See Birnie et al. (2009), pp. 130 and 132 ff.; Brunnée (2007), pp. 566 f.; Bowman (2010), pp. 503 f.

policies of the exporting state, even in the absence of transboundary physical effects. Examining whether the domestic environmental policies of the exporting state contravene basic principles of international environmental law could represent an objective element to take into account in the assessment of the legitimacy of trade measures adopted by the importing country in reaction to these foreign policies. The violation of principles of international environmental law does not necessarily legally entitle the importing state to take countermeasures. But they show, in the context of the GATT general exceptions provision, that the environmental objective of the importing state has been internationally recognised as legitimate and thus that the importing state may have a sufficient interest to justify a restrictive trade measure.[187]

---

[187]For further details, see *infra*, 7.1.2.2.

Chapter 5
The Customary International Law Rules on Prescriptive Jurisdiction

The last chapter has shown that even though international obligations related to environmental protection are emerging, the principle of permanent sovereignty over natural resources retains considerable importance in international environmental law and entails *inter alia* the right to choose economic and developmental policies.

Exporting countries that must comply with a PPM measure taken by an importing country may tend to view such regulation as interference in their own sovereignty. On the other hand, the importing country could consider that the adoption of PPM measures is possible on the basis of its own sovereignty over import policies. Hence, PPM trade measures can be seen as instances in which a competition exists between two sovereign states on the right to set applicable rules on certain production activities.

This issue of jurisdiction allocation between the importing and exporting countries must be examined in two stages: it is first necessary to analyse the applicable rules of public international law before focusing on the commitments made by WTO Members in the GATT and the extent to which they agreed on a different regulatory regime in this field. The analysis of the rules of public international law in the context of measures enacted by WTO Members is justified on the basis of Article 31(3)(c) of the Vienna Convention of the Law of Treaties, which provides that there shall be taken into account, together with the context, any relevant rules of international law applicable in the relations between the parties. This extends to

© Springer International Publishing AG 2018
D. Sifonios, *Environmental Process and Production Methods (PPMs) in WTO Law*,
European Yearbook of International Economic Law 3,
DOI 10.1007/978-3-319-65726-4_5

general principles such as good faith[1] or the principle of non-intervention[2] or to the rules of customary international law on prescriptive jurisdiction.[3]

This chapter analyses two aspects of the principles of international law related to prescriptive jurisdiction: the rules on extraterritorial jurisdiction (Sect. 5.1) and the principle of non-interference in internal affairs (Sect. 5.2). Chapter 7 examines the extent to which WTO Members have contracted out of their original sovereignty through commitments made in the GATT.[4]

5.1   Trade Measures and the Rules on Extraterritorial Jurisdiction

5.1.1   Prescriptive Jurisdiction

The rules on prescriptive jurisdiction refer to the capacity to make law, whether by legislative, executive or judicial action (prescriptive of legislative jurisdiction), and to the capacity to ensure compliance with such law, either by executive action or through a judicial decision (enforcement jurisdiction).[5]

Most of the times, states adopt norms that govern persons, activities, things or legal interests on a domestic level. But states may also adopt laws that govern matters that are not exclusively domestic[6] and that are applicable to situations occurring beyond the territory of the regulating state.[7] The term 'extraterritorial jurisdiction' is often used to refer to cases in which a state adopts norms regulating situations presenting significant links with different legal orders,[8] which can lead to clashes of jurisdictional authority among states.[9]

---

[1]The Appellate Body has often referred to this principle, in particular in the context of the chapeau of Article XX, which has been interpreted as an expression of the principle of good faith. See *infra*, 7.3.1.

[2]For instance, in the *US – Shrimp* case, the plaintiffs claimed that the United States measure violated the principle of non-interference in internal affairs, recognised by the UN Charter (Panel Report, para. 3.6, 3.12 and 3.157).

[3]See Bartels (2002), p. 365; Schoenbaum (1997), p. 279; Jansen and Lugard (1999), p. 533, n. 6; Bagwell et al. (2002), p. 76; Horn and Mavroidis (2008), pp. 1125 f. *et passim*.

[4]See in particular *infra*, 7.1.2.

[5]See e.g. Brownlie (2012), p. 456; Shaw (2014), p. 469; Restatement of the Law, Third, The Foreign Relations of the United States (1987), p. 232.

[6]See Ryngaert (2015), p. 6; Mann (1964), p. 14.

[7]See Stern (1992), p. 243.

[8]See Ryngaert (2015), p. 7, with further references. He points out that this terminology is not accurate since it usually also refers to cases in which the regulating state can rely on the territoriality principle. He argues that the term 'extraterritorial jurisdiction' should only be used to refer to the personality, protective and universality principles of jurisdiction, which have no territorial nexus whatsoever with the regulating state.

[9]See Qureshi and Ziegler (2011), p. 83.

Many academic writings have been devoted to the issue of jurisdiction.[10] One of the only clear rules in this field is that enforcement jurisdiction is only territorial: states are prohibited to enforce any rule or decision beyond their national territory, failing a permissive rule to the contrary.[11] They are, however, not barred in principle from enforcing extraterritorial jurisdiction within their national boundaries (indirect enforcement jurisdiction).[12]

When it comes to prescriptive jurisdiction, states are not prohibited per se to enact rules addressing situations occurring abroad. However, international law is still unclear on the boundaries of this right. The definition of extraterritorial jurisdiction is still subject to debate.[13] According to the *Restatement*, prescriptive jurisdiction is a state's power to 'make its law applicable to the activities, relations, or status or persons, or the interests of persons in things'.[14] Stern has suggested that a rule amounts to extraterritorial application when it applies to situations occurring beyond the territory of the regulating state.[15] In her view, extraterritorial application of a domestic rule is forbidden by international law when it is *meant to regulate* a situation that has no *reasonable connection* with the state that has adopted that rule.[16] It has been contended that the definitions of extraterritorial jurisdiction are

---

[10]See e.g. Ryngaert (2015); Mann (1964); Akehurst (1972/1973); Mann (1984); Brownlie (2012), pp. 456 f. (chapter 21); Shaw (2014), pp. 469 f. (chapter 12), with further references. In the context of WTO law and PPMs see Cooreman (2017), pp. 83 ff.

[11]*S.S. Lotus case*, Permanent Court of International Justice, 1927, (ser. A) No. 10, pp. 18 f. ('the first and foremost restriction imposed by international law upon a state is that—failing the existence of a permissive rule to the contrary—it may not exercise its power in any form in the territory of another state. In this sense jurisdiction is certainly territorial; it cannot be exercised by a state outside its territory except by virtue of a permissive rule derived from international custom or from a convention').

[12]*S.S. Lotus case*, Permanent Court of International Justice, 1927, p. 19 ('[i]t does not, however, follow that international law prohibits a state from exercising jurisdiction in its own territory, in respect of any case which relates to acts which have taken place abroad, and in which it cannot rely on some permissive rule of international law').

[13]See Akehurst (1972/1973), p. 145; Nollkaemper (1998), p. 188; Bartels (2002), p. 365, in particular n. 56; Qureshi and Ziegler (2011), p. 83 ('there is by no means a universally conception of what constitutes extra-territorial exercise of jurisdiction').

[14]Restatement of the Law, Third, Foreign Relations of the United States (1987), p. 232 ('[u]nder international law, a state is subject to limitation on (a) jurisdiction to prescribe, i.e. to make its law applicable to the activities, relations or status of persons, or their interests of persons in things, whether by legislation, by executive act or order, by administrative rule or legislation, or by a determination of a court').

[15]Stern (1998), p. 198 ('[u]ne norme est d'application extraterritoriale lorsqu'elle s'applique à des situations juridiques se déroulant hors du territoire de l'Etat qui l'a émise').

[16]Stern (1998), p. 199 ('[l]'application extraterritoriale du droit est donc interdite lorsqu'elle n'est pas raisonnable et prend les formes suivantes: [...] adoption par le législateur d'une norme destinée à régir une situation n'ayant aucun rattachement raisonnable avec l'Etat qui adopte cette norme'). See also alternative definitions mentioned by Bartels (2002), p. 365, n. 56.

sufficiently flexible to argue that certain extraterritorial environmental policies require a justification under the rules on extraterritorial jurisdiction.[17]

But since these situations occur in a foreign jurisdiction, international law must provide rules to determine the limits of the possibilities to claim extraterritorial jurisdiction and to deal with conflicts of jurisdiction between different states. Two systems could apply in this respect: either states are allowed to regulate any situation as long as no rule of international law forbids it or states are prohibited to exercise jurisdiction, unless it can rely on a permissive rule of international law.[18]

The *first* approach was applied by the Permanent Court of International Justice in the *Lotus* case. The Court held that international law did not contain, as it stood at the time of the dispute, any 'general prohibition to states to extend the application of their laws and the jurisdiction of their courts to persons, property and acts outside their territory'. It further stated:

> Far from laying down a general prohibition to the effect that states may not extend the application of their laws and the jurisdiction of their courts to persons, property and acts outside their territory, [international law] leaves them in this respect a wide measure of discretion which is only limited in certain cases by prohibitive rules; as regards other cases, every state remains free to adopt the principles which it regards as best and most suitable. (. . .) In these circumstances, all that can be required of a state is that it should not overstep the limits which international law places upon its jurisdiction.[19]

It has been contended that the 'minimalist' vision of international law applied in the *Lotus* case seemed 'increasingly less tenable', given in particular the broad range of economical, political and social matters addressed now by international law.[20] Thus, the *second* approach is often presented as reflecting the current state customary international law.[21] In this view, a state that wants to exercise its prescriptive jurisdiction with respect to activities occurring abroad or towards persons who are not present on its territory must be able to justify its regulation on the basis of a recognised jurisdictional basis, such as nationality.

Whether the prohibitive rule system applied in the *Lotus* case does not represent customary international law as it stands at present is still debated: if the *Lotus* rule has been widely criticised, there are in fact divergent views on the subject.[22] Others seem to have interpreted the *Lotus* rule in a way compatible with the permissive rule approach. Stern has indeed understood the *Lotus* rule as meaning that prescriptive

---

[17]See Nollkaemper (1998), p. 188.

[18]See Ryngaert (2015), p. 29.

[19]*S.S. Lotus case*, Permanent Court of International Justice, 1927, p. 19.

[20]Sands (2001), p. 548. See also Ryngaert (2015), p. 34, with further references.

[21]See Mann (1964), pp. 10 f.; Stern (1986), pp. 19 ff.; Bartels (2002), p. 368 n. 65 with further references (noting that the *Lotus* rule 'has been almost entirely abandoned in practice'); Ryngaert (2015), p. 29 ('[i]n practice, a consensus opinion has crystallized. This opinion seems mainly informed by the restrictive approach, in that it requires States to justify their jurisdictional assertion in terms of a permissive international law rule').

[22]See Qureshi and Ziegler (2011), pp. 85 f., with further references.

jurisdiction can be extraterritorial, as long as it respects the limitations placed by international law. In her view, the adoption of an extraterritorial rule is contrary to international law when it does not have a reasonable link with the state enacting such a rule.[23]

The main jurisdictional bases are territoriality and nationality. It is uncontested that states have jurisdiction over persons or things located on their territory or activities occurring within their borders. Neither is it contested that states have jurisdiction to adopt laws applicable to their nationals, wherever they are located.[24] Other jurisdictional claims include protective jurisdiction (prescriptive jurisdiction exercised in relation to activities affecting national security), universal jurisdiction (in relation to universally recognised crime, such as piracy) and the effects doctrine.[25] Jurisdiction claims based on this latter criterion have considered that a state has jurisdiction to regulate an activity taking place abroad if its effects are felt within that state. The effects doctrine is thus an extensive interpretation of territorial jurisdiction, sometimes referred to as the 'objective territoriality' principle.[26] This doctrine, which has often been invoked by the United States, has not remained uncontested.[27] Certain European countries, in particular, have only recognised a more limited definition of this theory.[28] It is usually considered at least that the effects that may justify a jurisdictional assumption must be substantial, direct and foreseeable.[29]

When it comes to the focus of this study, the first concern is whether *trade measures* must be regarded in some cases as an exercise of extraterritorial jurisdiction. Many domestic regulations may indeed have some effects beyond the territory of the regulating state, but clearly not all will be considered as being applied extraterritorially.[30]

---

[23]See Stern (1986), pp. 19 ff.; Stern (1992), p. 251; Stern (1997), p. 11.

[24]See e.g. Stern (1986), pp. 24 f.

[25]See Restatement of the Law, Third, The Foreign Relations of the United States (1987), pp. 238 ff.; Stern (1986), pp. 23 ff.; Bartels (2002), pp. 368 f.; Qureshi and Ziegler (2011), pp. 86 f.; Cooreman (2017), pp. 90 ff.

[26]This principle was applied for instance in the *Lotus* case, in which the Court held that the authors of an offence who 'at the moment of commission are in the territory of another state, are nevertheless to be regarded as having been committed in the national territory, if one of the constituent elements of the offence, and more especially its effects, have taken place there'. See also Stern (1986), p. 24.

[27]See Restatement of the Law, Third, The Foreign Relations of the United States (1987), p. 239; Stern (1986), pp. 30 ff., with further references; Bartels (2002), p. 369.

[28]See Stern (1997), p. 13 ('[t]o European countries, the effects doctrine is only acceptable, if the effect on the territory of an activity outside the territory is one element of the wrong, without which there would be no wrong, and not if it is just an economic or consequential effect').

[29]See Restatement of the Law, Third, The Foreign Relations of the United States (1987), p. 239; Stern (1986), pp. 30 ff.; Horn and Mavroidis (2008), pp. 1126 ff.

[30]As the Panel in the *US – Shrimp* case has noted (para. 7.51). See also e.g. Bartels (2002), p. 379, who asserts that practically all domestic legislation, in particular in the economic field, will have some impact on activities, persons or things located abroad.

5.1.2 The Particular Case of Trade Measures: Sovereignty Over Import Policies vs. Sovereignty to Regulate Activities Occurring in a State's Jurisdiction

The rules on extraterritorial jurisdiction restrict the ability of states to adopt or enforce certain measures addressing situations occurring beyond the territory of the regulating state. As far as the focus of this study is concerned, one must determine if *trade measures* must be categorised as an exercise of extraterritorial jurisdiction.[31] If not, then there is no need for justification based on the rules on extraterritorial jurisdiction. Thus, it must be determined if an importing country, by enacting a trade measure, can 'make its law applicable' to the activities of persons abroad[32] or, in other words, if trade measures are 'meant to regulate' a situation occurring abroad.[33] This issue is particularly relevant in the case of non-product-related PPM measures since, in these cases, the importing state specifies production methods that are to be used in places located beyond its territory, which means that they influence activities occurring in a foreign country or in areas beyond any jurisdiction.

Commentators have expressed quite different views on the question whether trade measures require a justification based on the rules on extraterritorial jurisdiction.

Under a *first* approach, the rules on extraterritorial jurisdiction apply to all trade measures. It has been argued that a state wishing to request foreigners to respect its public order must demonstrate that it can legitimately legislate on the issue at stake.[34] In this view, when a state defines the production methods that must be used in the exporting country, and when it restricts the rights of the exporting country's producers to export products to that state, solely because these persons do not comply with the standards set by the importing country, it regulates an activity occurring abroad.[35] The claimants in the *US – Shrimp* case have, for instance, argued that the United States' measure requiring the adoption of a particular fishing method for harvesting shrimp prescribed a conduct occurring beyond the United States territory. It conflicted, in their view, with their own jurisdiction and with their 'sovereign right to regulate persons, animal or things within their jurisdiction'.[36] The view that trade measures require justification based on the rules on extraterritorial jurisdiction has some support in academic writings.[37]

---

[31]See Vranes (2009), pp. 157 f. and Bartels (2002), pp. 376 ff.

[32]Using the terminology of the Restatement of the Law, Third, The Foreign Relations of the United States (1987), p. 232.

[33]Using the terminology of Stern (1998), p. 199.

[34]See Bagwell et al. (2002), p. 76.

[35]See Nollkaemper (1998), p. 188 (who criticises this argument); Bartels (2002), p. 381 ff.; Bagwell et al. (2002), p. 76.

[36]*US – Shrimp*, Panel Report, para. 3.163 *et passim*.

[37]See Jansen and Lugard (1999), p. 533 and n. 6 p. 535; Schobenaum (1997), pp. 279 f.; Bagwell et al. (2002), p. 76; Horn and Mavroidis (2008), p. 1125 *et passim*; Cooreman (2017), pp. 89 ff. See

Since the adoption of a measure addressing a situation occurring abroad is qualified in this approach as an exercise of legislative jurisdiction, its enforcement at the point of importation by non-judicial measures (i.e., trade restrictions) can be seen as the exercise of indirect enforcement jurisdiction by the importing country, i.e. some form of sanction for non-compliance with an extraterritorial norm, subject to the rules on extraterritorial jurisdiction.[38]

A justification based on the rules on extraterritorial jurisdiction would have to show the existence of a nexus between the foreign situation concerned and their own jurisdiction. It could be based on the *territoriality* and *nationality* principles or possibly on the *effects doctrine*.[39] The territoriality principle could also be invoked in cases of transboundary physical externalities affecting the environment of the importing state.[40] In the absence of territorial nexus, it would mainly be the effects doctrine, which requires that the effects be substantial, direct and foreseeable,[41] which could be invoked.[42]

In the view of Horn and Mavroidis, if the applicability of the rules on extraterritorial jurisdiction were not recognised, it would lead to absurd results. They reason by analogy with the situation in which a state would be allowed to tax the income of another state nationals' made in that country, which would be clearly not acceptable.[43] This analogy is, however, somewhat misleading. In this example, the regulating state would apply its taxes *regardless* of any particular territorial or nationality-related link with the persons concerned, which can indeed be qualified

---

also *US – Tuna II*, para. 5.17. Note that these commentators do not always explain why they consider that trade measures should be categorised as extraterritorial.

[38] See e.g. the Restatement of the Law, Third, The Foreign Relations of the United States (1987), § 431 ('[a] state may employ judicial or nonjudicial measures to induce or compel compliance with its laws or regulations, provided it has jurisdiction to prescribe') and related comment, p. 322 ('enforcement measures comprise not only the orders of a court [. . .] but also measures such as the following, when used to induce compliance with or as sanctions for violation of laws or regulations of the enforcing state: denial of the right to engage in export of import transactions; [. . .]').

[39] See Horn and Mavroidis (2008), *passim*; Appleton (1997a), pp. 62 ff.; Jansen and Lugard (1999), pp. 533 ff. As to whether environmental harm could justify in certain circumstances universal jurisdiction, Jansen and Lugard leave the question open (p. 535) and Horn and Mavroidis answer negatively, because environmental harm is not recognised (yet, at least) as a violation of *jus cogens* (p. 1134). See also Appleton (1997a), p. 59 (rejecting the applicability of the principle of universal jurisdiction).

[40] See Horn and Mavroidis (2008), p. 1133 *et passim*.

[41] See Restatement of the Law, Third, The Foreign Relations of the United States (1987), § 403, which subjects jurisdiction based on the effects doctrine on a reasonableness test, which requires to examine if the regulated activity has substantial, direct, and foreseeable effect upon or in the territory of the regulating state.

[42] See Horn and Mavroidis (2008), p. 1133; Appleton (1997a), p. 74 (rejecting a broad applicability of the effects doctrine in this context).

[43] See Horn and Mavroidis (2008), p. 1132.

as an exercise of extraterritorial jurisdiction.[44] Yet most restrictive trade measures are usually not meant to apply to all products produced abroad, even those that are not exported to the regulating country.

There might be some instances in which an importing country would adopt a trade measure meant to apply to all foreign producers (or all producers of a particular country), regardless of whether these producers actually export their products to that state. For instance, in the Pacific Fur Seals Arbitration, the United States sought to restrict activities of ships beyond its territorial waters, even though the harvested furs were not exported to the United States but were sent to the United Kingdom.[45] The United States thus meant to regulate the activities of all foreign hunters abroad, without making a distinction between products sent in the United States and those sent elsewhere.

However, trade measures usually do not prescribe that *all* the producers of the exporting country adopt the particular PPM standard but only *those who choose to export* their product to the importing state's market. For instance, the *US – Shrimp* case concerned a measure that requested foreign producers that chose to export shrimp to the United States to adopt particular fishing methods.

Based on these considerations, other commentators suggest a *second* approach. This view is based on the assumption that a territorial link does exist with the behaviour that trade restrictions regulating the conditions on the entry into the regulating state *immediately* target, i.e., the crossing of the frontier or, more generally, the conditions on imports and sale of products in the internal market.[46] If proponents of the first view are likely to argue that the adoption of restrictive process-based measures by the importing country violate the sovereignty of the exporting country to regulate activities occurring in its territory, proponents of the second view contend that the sovereignty of the exporting country to regulate such activities does not authorise it to say where in the rest of the world its producers may export their products.[47] Thus, it has been maintained that as long as the importing country only defines the conditions of importation, it does not *directly regulate*, from a legal viewpoint, activities occurring abroad.[48] Such measures are not meant

---

[44] See e.g. the analysis made by Stern concerning the Helms-Burton Act, under which nobody in the world is authorised to traffic in properties which belonged to US citizens and which were expropriated in 1959–1960 by Cuba: Stern (1997), pp. 5 ff.

[45] See *Behring Sea Fur Seals Fisheries Arbitration* (Great Britain v. United States), Moore's International Arbitrations (1893) 755.

[46] See Wiers (2002), p. 286; Vranes (2009), p. 166.

[47] See Howse and Regan (2000), p. 275.

[48] See Howse and Regan (2000), pp. 274 ('[p]rocess-based restrictions do not directly regulate any behaviour occurring outside the border') and 278 ('[w]e have argued that as long as the importing country regulates directly only behaviour within [or at] its borders, then it is not regulating extra-territorially even if its goal is to avoid encouraging behaviour beyond its borders'); Nollkaemper (1998), p. 189 ('[a]lthough a measure like this one aims to influence the conduct of legal subjects abroad, it does not *legally regulate* such conduct and as such does not run counter to international law'; original emphasis); Vranes (2009), p. 166 ('a state measure that imposes *conditions on the entry* into the regulating country applies to a conduct [the crossing of the frontier] which occurs in

to apply to all foreign producers regardless of whether they export their products to the importing country. The concrete way a product has been produced abroad has legal consequences only at the time of importation, for foreign producers who want their products to access the importing country's market. But the measure does not directly apply to these foreign production activities preceding importation,[49] and foreign producers can choose to disregard the PPM regulation without suffering any consequence.[50] In that sense, PPM measures are not meant to be a general obligation applicable to the production of all goods of a particular type produced abroad and are therefore not 'made applicable' in a foreign jurisdiction for purposes of the rules on extraterritorial jurisdiction. In other words, PPM measures can give rise to extraterritorial *effects* since they may eventually influence and target behaviour abroad, but they do not amount to extraterritorial *application*.[51] For these reasons, most commentators share the view that trade measures are territorial, i.e. that they do not require a justification based on the rules on extraterritorial jurisdiction.[52]

A further question that is usually not explicitly addressed by commentators is whether this conclusion is valid only for trade measures defining the conditions of importation on the market of the importing country or rather for *all* trade measures, including those that are, for instance, meant to be applicable to foreign producers *whether or not* they export goods to the importing country. As it has been mentioned above, such measure would be arguably an extraterritorial norm under the rules on *prescriptive* jurisdiction. This concerns in particular the case of secondary embargoes, in which the importing country prohibits exporting states to have particular trade transactions with third countries and imposes trade sanctions in cases of non-compliance. It has been argued that such measures are adopted in the absence of any territorial jurisdiction or any other jurisdictional basis.[53] Some have pointed out that certain trade measures can be clearly designed to influence, and be capable of influencing, the concrete conduct occurring abroad in a way essentially

---

its territory. [. . .] Moreover, if such a measure makes *importation dependent* e.g. on the characteristics of products or on the way they have been produced or processed, it does *not directly apply* to conduct occurring abroad: the concrete conduct of producing products with given characteristics or by means of given production and processing methods is not regulated itself, as there are no norms directly applying to these foreign acts which precede importation [. . .]'; original emphasis).

[49] See Vranes (2009), p. 166.

[50] See Charnovitz (1994a), p. 38; Nollkaemper (1998), p. 189; Howse and Regan (2000), p. 274.

[51] See Wiers (2002), p. 286; Vranes (2009), pp. 165 ff. *Contra*: Bartels (2002), p. 381, arguing that the notion of the application of legislation to a matter should be extended, in a way that would basically include PPM measures. He has suggested that 'a measure *defined* by something located or occurring abroad should be considered just as extraterritorial as a measure specifically mandating or forbidding conduct abroad'. This view is further commented *infra*, 7.1.2.2.

[52] See Anderson (1993), pp. 754 f.; Chang (1995), p. 2194; Charnovitz (1998), p. 720, n. 179; Nollkaemper (1998), pp. 188 f.; Stern (1998), p. 206; Howse and Regan (2000), p. 274 ff.; Wiers (2002), pp. 275 f.; Luff (2004), p. 156; Nielsen (2007), p. 264; Vranes (2009), p. 166; Will (2016), p. 617.

[53] See Luff (2004), p. 156.

similar to a direct regulation of foreign conduct and that such measures may arguably have to be justified under the rules on extraterritorial jurisdiction.[54]

As far as the rules on extraterritorial jurisdiction are concerned, the *adoption* of an extraterritorial measure does not necessarily mean that its *application* within the territory of the regulating country violates international law. Prescriptive jurisdiction is one thing; enforcement jurisdiction is another. As Stern has shown, a distinction must be made in public international law between enforcement measures (sanctions) that could be adopted legally even without the extraterritorial regulation and those that are exclusively based on this extraterritorial regulation and not on any other jurisdictional basis, i.e. which could not have been adopted in the absence of the extraterritorial norm. Only the latter sanctions must be *qualified* as extraterritorial in a legal sense, not the former.[55]

When it comes to trade, in the absence of any treaty commitment, an importing country can apply an import restriction *even* in the absence of a regulation prescribing the adoption of a process standard by all producers in the exporting country. Despite the absence of such a measure, the importing country can indeed still deny market access by invoking its sovereignty over its import policies. It is in general uncontested in customary international law that a state has the sovereign right to choose the conditions to which goods produced abroad can be imported into its territory.[56] This means that exporting countries do not have any right to access foreign markets because trade is a *privilege*,[57] which is unilaterally granted, in the absence of a treaty. This has been reminded by the International Court of Justice in the Nicaragua case, in which the ICJ stated that a state 'is not bound to continue particular trade relations longer than it sees fit to do so, in the absence of a treaty commitment or other specific legal obligation'.[58] Thus, a state has the sovereign right to choose its trading partners and the conditions to which the privilege of market access will be granted. The exercise of this sovereign right allows the importing state to enact import prohibitions or to regulate the conditions to which exporters can access the regulating country's market. In terms of international

---

[54]See Vranes (2009), p. 166, n. 424. In the same vein, Bartels (2002), p. 381, argues that the practical effect of measures requesting the adoption of a conduct abroad on private persons abroad that renders it potentially excessive. He has suggested that 'a measure *defined* by something located or occurring abroad should be considered just as extraterritorial as a measure specifically mandating or forbidding conduct abroad' (original emphasis).

[55]See Stern (1998), pp. 203 f.

[56]See Anderson (1993), pp. 754 f.; Chang (1995), p. 2194; Appleton (1997a), p. 82; Nollkaemper (1998), pp. 188 f.; Zeitler (2000), p. 184; Bartels (2002), p. 382; Gaines (2002), p. 412; Wiers (2002), p. 276; Luff (2004), p. 156; Nielsen (2007), p. 264; Carreau and Juillard (2013), p. 197, n. 492.

[57]See Carreau and Juillard (2013), p. 197, n. 492.

[58]*Military and Paramilitary Activities in and against Nicaragua* (Nicaragua v. United States), Merits, Judgment, ICJ Reports (1986), para. 276.

principles on countermeasures, trade restrictions are at most retorsion but not reprisals since they deny no right to foreign countries.[59]

In other words, an importing state could apply an import restriction even in the absence of this allegedly extraterritorial measure. Hence, it is submitted by the present author that even if trade measures requiring the adoption of a conduct abroad were qualified, under the rules on *prescriptive* jurisdiction, as extraterritorial regulations (i.e., measure requiring a justification on the basis of the rule on extraterritorial jurisdiction), they could not be qualified as extraterritorial enforcement measures (exercise of indirect enforcement jurisdiction) under the rules on *enforcement* jurisdiction because the regulating state can apply import restrictions, whether or not it adopts the 'extraterritorial' norm.[60] On the basis of this reasoning as well, it can be concluded that under customary international law, trade measures do not require a justification on the basis of the rules on extraterritorial jurisdiction.

In brief, the two different approaches described above are based on two opposing views. Under the first one, trade measures that require the adoption of a particular conduct in the exporting country are viewed as *indirect enforcement measures* of an extraterritorial norm, and they require a justification on the basis of the rules on extraterritorial jurisdiction. The crux of the analysis is thus the *object* of the regulation itself. The legality of trade measures under the rules on extraterritorial jurisdiction consequently depends on it. In the second approach, import policies represent the exercise of the importing state's sovereignty over its *import policies*. Hence, they are as such territorial and lawful, regardless of the policy reason underlying the measure.[61]

These two opposing views also explain why diverging opinions exist on the applicability of other principles, such as *comity*. When two states can potentially claim jurisdiction over a matter, it may give rise to conflicting exercises of

---

[59]The difference between the two is that retorsion is a legal act, adopted by one state against activities of another state perceived as injurious. They may be unfriendly and harmful for the targeted state. On the other hand, reprisals are acts 'which are in themselves illegal and have been adopted by one state in retaliation for the commission of an earlier act by another state' (Shaw 2014, pp. 818 f.). See also in another context, Stern (1998) who analyses the d'Amato-Kennedy Act and asserts that few reproaches can be addressed to it since most of the unilateral economic measures provided as sanctions in that law can only be considered as retorsion measures, since they consist in the suppression of privileges rather than rights.

[60]Under the *Restatement*, a state needs jurisdiction to prescribe to have enforcement jurisdiction, which is necessary in particular to adopt 'denial of the right to engage in export or import transaction' (Restatement of the Law, Third, The Foreign Relations of the United States 1987, p. 322). No right to trade exists under customary international law, as the ICJ has confirmed in the *Nicaragua* case. But some have argued that such a right does exist under the GATT, which would make the rules on extraterritorial jurisdiction applicable. It will be argued below that this reasoning is not convincing (see *infra*, 7.1.2).

[61]See e.g. Nollkaemper (1998), p. 188 ('under international law, import policies and corresponding measures at the border or in the national market are a prerogative of sovereign states, and as such lawful. It does therefore not appear to be helpful to include such measures because of their underlying *policy reason* in a category of measures that are considered unlawful because they subject to jurisdiction non-nationals or nationals for activity undertaken abroad').

jurisdiction. In that case, the *Restatement* suggests that they should evaluate the respective interests of both countries in regulating a particular transaction, on the basis of a series of factors, such as the link of the activity to the territory of the importing state, the importance of the regulated activity for the exporting state, etc.[62] These criteria basically allow to assess the intensity of the nexus between the regulating country and the matter concerned. If a state has a greater interest to regulate, the other should refrain from exercising jurisdiction and yield to that other state.[63] This rule is commonly referred to as comity.[64] It is based on the principle that even if one basis for jurisdiction is present, a state may not exercise prescriptive jurisdiction when the exercise of such jurisdiction is 'unreasonable'.[65]

It has been asserted that trade measures requiring the adoption of process standards abroad give rise to a conflict of jurisdiction, which could be resolved by applying the comity principle, i.e. by examining which country has the greater interest in regulating a particular matter.[66] Hence, the view that the comity principle should apply is based on the assumption that the importing country *exercises jurisdiction* on activities occurring abroad, when it enacts trade measures subordinating market access to the adoption of process standards by foreign producers.

By contrast, under the view that trade measures are by definition territorial, there is no conflict of jurisdiction. The importing country merely exercises its territorial jurisdiction when it defines the conditions to which products can be imported in its internal market, and such exercise of prescriptive jurisdiction does not represent a form of extraterritorial regulation in a legal sense. In the absence of a conflict of jurisdiction, the comity principle is not applicable.

In the view of this author, the second view is legally correct. It is indeed uncontested in international law that states do not have the obligation to have trade relations with foreign countries. A state is thus in principle free to prohibit the importation of all goods originating from one particular country (with the sole limit of coercion, as it will be seen in the next section). If a state has the right to exclude all products, it has *a fortiori* the right to exclude only some of them. Admitting that process-based measures legally regulate a conduct occurring abroad and are thus subject to the rules on extraterritorial jurisdiction and the comity principle would not be compatible with this conclusion. It would indeed imply

---

[62]See Restatement of the Law, Third, The Foreign Relations of the United States (1987), § 403 (2); Zeitler (2000), pp. 184 f.; Horn and Mavroidis (2008) p. 1129.

[63]See Restatement of the Law, Third, The Foreign Relations of the United States (1987), § 403, p. 247; Horn and Mavroidis (2008), pp. 1128 ff.

[64]See e.g. Horn and Mavroidis (2008), p. 1128.

[65]The Restatement of the Law, Third, The Foreign Relations of the United States (1987), § 403 (1) reads *in extenso*: '[e]ven when one of the bases for jurisdiction under § 402 is present, a state may not exercise jurisdiction to prescribe law with respect to a person or activity having connections with another state when the exercise of such jurisdiction is unreasonable'.

[66]See Zeitler (2000), p. 184. See also Mavroidis (2008b), p. 277, who maintains that the 'destination principle is at odds with the classic bases for regulating jurisdictional issues under public international law, in that no balancing of interests (to regulate) will ever take place'.

that foreign countries have a *conditional* right to trade: exporting countries would have the right in certain circumstances to demand market access for PPM-non-complying products, if PPM-complying products are granted market access. There is no indication in customary international law as it stands at present that such a conditional right to trade exists.

In the same vein, stating that the rules on extraterritorial jurisdiction are a *lex specialis* compared to the sovereignty of a state over its import policies would result in endorsing some form of conditional right to trade, since a state would not be entitled to exclude certain products not complying with a process standard, if it had granted market access to similar products complying with this standard.

Based on the preceding analysis, it is argued by this author that public international law does not require that trade measures be justified on the basis of the rules on extraterritorial jurisdiction. On the one hand, trade measures that regulate the conditions of importation do not directly regulate an activity abroad. On the other hand, states do not have any obligation under international law to have trading relations with other countries (with the sole exception of the principle of non-interference in internal affairs examined in the next section), which means that the reason why a state decides to apply a trade restriction does not seem to be relevant for its legality. A state can always restrict its imports under international law, irrespectively of the adoption of a norm requiring the adoption of process standards by foreign exporters. In this sense, the adoption of trade measures cannot in principle be qualified as an exercise of extraterritorial jurisdiction.

It remains less clear if there might be some exceptions, in particular when the importing country enacts a secondary embargo. It has been suggested that secondary embargoes may be regarded as lacking any justification under the rules on extraterritorial jurisdiction and that trade measures applied as a sanction of such embargo should be regarded as its accessory and should not, as such, grant jurisdictional basis to the main measure.[67] However, it could be argued that even though these kinds of measures could represent an exercise of extraterritorial *prescriptive* jurisdiction, it does not necessarily mean that the trade restrictions applied must be qualified as extraterritorial since the importing state retains the right under international law to define the conditions on importation in its internal market.[68] Hence, some might still contend that even in such cases, trade measures would not amount to an exercise of extraterritorial jurisdiction under customary international law.

It must be pointed out that this does not mean that a trade measure requiring the adoption of a process standard in the producing country is necessarily lawful. Such

---

[67] See Luff (2004), p. 156, n. 613, stating that a trade measure applied as a sanction of a secondary embargo appears 'comme l'accessoire d'une mesure principale d'embargo secondaire prise en dehors de toute compétence nationale reconnue. Elle ne devrait pas conférer de titre de compétence à la mesure principale'.

[68] This difficulty has been mentioned by Luff (2004), p. 156, n. 613, who concedes that a trade measure taken as a sanction to a secondary embargo could be seen as having automatically a territorial nature.

measures might be illegal not under the rules on extraterritorial jurisdiction but under a material obligation of the regulating state, for instance if the sanction interferes with a right of the state concerned (a legally protected interest) and not only with privileges conferred by the regulating state (mere economical interests), i.e. if the measure amounts to reprisals and not only to retorsion.[69] The next chapters of this book will thus examine the relevant commitments made by WTO Members in the covered agreements.

Another limit to the ability of states to adopt trade measures is related to the effects that they can have on foreign producers.[70] International law prohibits coercion based on the principle of non-intervention. It is thus necessary to examine in the next section if trade measures may amount in certain circumstances to coercion in a legal sense.

5.2   The Principle of Non-interference in Internal Affairs

The preceding section has shown that trade measures are in principle justified on the basis of the territoriality principle. These measures are not applied extraterritorially; however, they may have extraterritorial effects on producers abroad, which are basically faced with the choice to comply with the standard set by the importing country or to accept losing opportunities to export goods to that particular market.

On the other hand, international law recognises the principle of permanent sovereignty over natural resources, which entitles states to exploit their resources pursuant to their own environmental and developmental policies, as it has been shown in Chap. 4 above.[71] Moreover, states have the exclusive jurisdiction to regulate matters in their respective territory, and in particular to choose domestic environmental policies, in the absence of any transboundary effects or treaty commitments. A corollary of these different rights is that states are prohibited in

---

[69]See Stern (1998), pp. 203 f. and 206 f.

[70]Bartels, on the basis of an argument of Mann, has contended that the effects of a trade measures on foreign producers caused by its sole existence, regardless of whether it is enforced, could make the rules on extraterritorial jurisdiction applicable (Bartels 2002, p. 381). These impermissible effects are in his view those caused by the suspension of a right to access the importing country's market, in particular those provided for in the WTO agreements. This view has been criticised by Vranes (2009), p. 165, in particular because it introduces an element of contingency—the existence of a right to trade—in the examination of whether a measure must be qualified as extraterritorial or not. Stern has maintained that measures that violate a substantive rule of international law may be illegal on the basis of this rule but it does not make it extraterritorial (Stern 1998, pp. 206 f.). It is also submitted here that this view would have the consequence that one would presume that a state which grants a right to trade to foreign countries also accepts to restrict its sovereignty through the application of the rules on extraterritorial jurisdiction. It seems very unlikely that such a restriction to states' sovereignty can be presumed.

[71]See Rio Declaration, Principle 2.

international law to intervene in the domestic affairs of other states.[72] Some could thus argue that the effects of trade measures on the exporting country, in matters upon which the latter has exclusive jurisdiction, violate the principle of non-intervention. In this view, PPM trade measures must be regarded as attempts to force the exporting country to adopt particular process standards, which affect internal matters of that state.

The relevant question is thus whether the use of trade measures, in particular to induce changes in the environmental policies of foreign states, can amount to a violation of the principle of non-intervention and thus impose a limitation on the ability of importing countries to adopt trade measures requiring the adoption of process standards in exporting countries.[73]

It is uncontested in customary international law that the use of force represents a violation of the principle of non-intervention. However, it is much more debated whether economic coercion amounts to a form of intervention in domestic affairs. The ICJ had the opportunity to shed light on this debate, in the *Nicaragua* case decision. Various measures adopted by the United States against Nicaragua were at stake. The United States sought to support the Contras in their rebellion against the Nicaraguan government. Among other measures, the United States had used economic instruments in order to put pressure on the government of Nicaragua, the most important of which was a trade embargo. The question arose whether this embargo was an illegal intervention in the domestic affairs of a foreign state. The Court first stated:

> The principle of non-intervention forbids all states or groups of states to intervene directly or indirectly in internal or external affairs of other states. A prohibited intervention must accordingly be one bearing on matters in which each state is permitted, by the principle of state sovereignty, to decide freely. One of these is the choice of a political, economic, social and cultural system, and the formulation of foreign policy. Intervention is wrongful when it uses methods of coercion in regard to such choices, which must remain free ones. The element of coercion, which defines, and indeed forms the very essence of, prohibited intervention is particularly obvious in the case of an intervention which uses force (. . .).[74]

Thus, the ICJ expressed clearly the view that the use of force would violate the principle of non-intervention. The Court stated moreover that intervention is unlawful if it used 'methods of coercion'.

When it comes to economic measures, many developing countries have sought since the 1960s to obtain international recognition that economic coercion amounts to a breach of the principle of non-intervention under Article 2(7) of the UN Charter.[75] Thus, several United Nations General Assembly resolutions

---

[72]See Nollkaemper (1998), p. 184.

[73]New Zealand expressed as third party in the *US – Tuna II* dispute that the United States' measure violated the principle of non-intervention and could not be justified under Article XX (*US – Tuna II*, Report of the Panel, para. 4.38).

[74]*Military and Paramilitary Activities in and against Nicaragua* (Nicaragua v. United States), Merits, Judgment, ICJ Reports (1986), para. 205.

[75]See Gathii (2000), pp. 2029 f.

acknowledge that economic coercion violates national economic sovereignty and the non-intervention norm.[76]

The UN General Assembly Resolution 2131 of 21 December 1965 states, for instance:

> No state may use or encourage the use of economic, political or any other type of measures to coerce another state in order to obtain from it the subordination of the exercise of its sovereign rights or to secure from it advantages of any kind.

It further indicates:

> Every state has an inalienable right to choose its political, economic, social and cultural systems, without interference in any form by another state.[77]

These resolutions are, however, not binding.[78] This point was apparent in particular in the findings of the ICJ in the *Nicaragua* case.

In this case, as already mentioned, the United States had adopted a series of economic measures, in particular a complete embargo both for imports from and exports to Nicaragua. The explicit objective of this embargo was to put pressure on the Sandinista government in order to achieve political changes in Nicaragua, i.e. to obtain that this government implemented its commitments to political pluralism, human rights, free elections, non-alignment and a mixed economy.[79] Despite this objective and the important extent of the United States' economic sanctions against Nicaragua, the Court held that 'it [was] unable to regard such action on the economic plane as is here complained a breach of the customary-law principle of non-intervention'.[80]

In brief, the ICJ took the view that customary international law recognises that each state has the sovereign right to choose its trading partners and to use economic instruments to put pressure on foreign governments to adopt political changes abroad. The widely shared view among commentators is thus that international law does not treat economic pressure as a legal form of coercion.[81]

---

[76]See in particular UNGA Declaration on the Inadmissibility of Intervention in the Domestic Affairs of States and the Protection of the Independence and Sovereignty, UNGA Resolution 2131 (XX) of 21 December 1965; UNGA Declaration on Principles of International Law Concerning Friendly Relations and Co-operation among States in accordance with the Charter of the United Nations, UNGA Resolution 2625 (XXV) of 24 October 1970; Charter of Economic Rights and Duties of States, UNGA Resolution 3281 (XXIX), 12 December 1974 (Art. 1: '[e]very state has the sovereign and inalienable right to choose its economic system as well as its political, social and cultural systems in accordance with the will of its people, without outside interference, coercion or threat in any form whatsoever').

[77]UNGA Resolution 2131 (XX) of 21 December 1965, paragraphs 2 and 5.

[78]See e.g. Stern (1998), p. 189.

[79]See *Military and Paramilitary Activities in and against Nicaragua* (Nicaragua v. United States), Merits, Judgment, ICJ Reports (1986), para. 169.

[80]*Military and Paramilitary Activities in and against Nicaragua* (Nicaragua v. United States), Merits, Judgment, ICJ Reports (1986), para. 245.

[81]See Stern (1998), p. 195; Nollkaemper (1998), pp. 185 f.; Gathii (2000), p. 2030 (criticising the view that international legal opinion, especially in the West, does not regard economic coercion as intervention); Condon (2006), p. 253; Luff (2004), pp. 158 f.

Some commentators have expressed the view that there might be exceptional circumstances in which trade measures might amount to coercion, depending on the particular circumstances of the case, such as the importance of the products concerned for the exporting country, its level of economic development, its dependence to exportations, more specifically the importance of the particular export market concerned, etc.[82] It has been contended that these concerns are likely to be confined to instances in which the state to which a trade measure is applied is largely dependent on the export of the products concerned and, as a result of the adoption of the measure, has thus little economic choice but to modify its environmental practices.[83] In any event, it seems highly unlikely, in particular in the light of the *Nicaragua* case reasoning, in which a broad embargo was not qualified as unlawful coercion, that a PPM measure could amount to coercion in a legal sense. The extent of the pressure put on foreign government by PPM measures is often limited, and exporting states retain in principle the choice not to comply with the PPM standard and to sell their products to other states than those having adopted the measures at issue.[84]

As a result, even if PPM measures may have very real effects on foreign producers—namely to make them change their production practices or make them accept losing export opportunities—the effects of PPM measures on foreign producers and on foreign countries are not 'coercive' in a legal sense, which means that PPM measures do not amount to a violation of the principle of non-interference.[85] Moreover, because PPM measures deny no right to foreign countries, they cannot be seen as potentially illegal reprisals but at most as legal forms of retorsion.[86]

---

[82]See Luff (2004), pp. 158 f.

[83]See Appleton (1997a), p. 83.

[84]See Luff (2004), p. 159.

[85]See Condon (2006), p. 253 ('[i]nternational law is ambiguous regarding the consistency of economic coercion with the principle of non-intervention. Given the absence of international consensus and the decision of the ICJ in the Nicaragua case, the inconsistency of economic coercion with the principle of non-intervention cannot be established as a customary rule of international law. [...] Under the current state of international law, economic coercion does not violate non-intervention, and thus does not violate sovereign equality').

[86]See Condon (2006), p. 250; Gathii (2000), p. 2028. This does not mean that PPM measures may not be taken in certain cases in response to the violation by the exporting state of its international obligations concerning conservation of natural resources under its jurisdiction. In such circumstances, states may be authorised to take reprisals, for instance by adopting trade restrictions as countermeasures. The legality of such measures is however subject to certain conditions under international law, because not all international obligation violations justify the adoption of countermeasures.

5.3   Conclusion

Although it is frequently repeated that PPM measures are 'extraterritorial', they do not require a justification on the basis of the rules on extraterritorial jurisdiction since trade measures are by definition territorial. The sole recognised limit of the exercise of the importing country's sovereignty over its import policies is coercion, but it is highly unlikely that a PPM measure may amount to coercion in the legal sense.

In other words, the rules on extraterritorial jurisdiction or the principle of non-intervention is not, as such, useful to distinguish between permissible and impermissible PPM measures.

Nevertheless, states often conclude trade agreements and restrict their sovereignty over their import policies. A PPM measure addressing a situation occurring abroad can be unlawful on the basis of treaty commitments. It is thus necessary to examine the commitments made by WTO Members in the GATT to determine if a trade measure addressing a situation occurring abroad might be viewed as illegal under the GATT obligations.

The next chapters analyse in detail GATT Articles III and XX. The 'extraterritoriality' issue is specifically examined below in Chap. 7.[87]

---

[87]See *infra*, 7.1.2.

Chapter 6
National Treatment

The GATT is based on two main pillars: the prohibition of quantitative restrictions (which must be replaced by tariffs), enshrined in Article XI, and the principle of non-discrimination, which has been described as perhaps *the* fundamental pillar in the law of the World Trade Organization.[1] The non-discrimination principle contains two different elements: the most-favoured-nation principle (Art. I) and national treatment (Art. III).

The most-favoured-nation principle provides that any advantage granted by any Member to any product originating in or destined for any other Member shall be accorded immediately and unconditionally to the like products originating in or destined for the territories of all other contracting parties. This prohibition of favouritism in the concessions granted to foreign countries guarantees non-discrimination between the different trading partners of each WTO Member.

On the other hand, national treatment guarantees non-discrimination within the internal market of each particular state. WTO Members have the obligation to accord imported products no less favourable treatment than that granted to like domestic products, both for fiscal (Art. III:2) and regulatory measures (Art. III:4). The objective of national treatment is that internal regulations are not applied so as to afford protection to domestic production. This prohibition of protectionism must ensure that imported products are not discriminated against like domestic products in the internal market once they have passed customs.

The PPM issue has arisen in particular in the context of the application of national treatment. The debates concerning PPMs have mainly focused on the notion of like products and the question of whether differences in production methods could render two products 'unlike'. Since the most-favoured-nation clause refers as well to the concept of like products, certain developments made in the context of Article III could probably also be applied *mutatis mutandis* to Article I.

---

[1]Ortino (2004), p. 217.

© Springer International Publishing AG 2018
D. Sifonios, *Environmental Process and Production Methods (PPMs) in WTO Law*,
European Yearbook of International Economic Law 3,
DOI 10.1007/978-3-319-65726-4_6

This study does not, however, examine in further detail the most-favoured-nation principle and focuses on national treatment.

This chapter assesses whether PPM measures are covered by Article III (Sect. 6.1). After a few comments on the issue of the scope of Article III (Sect. 6.2), it analyses the two main conditions of national treatment, i.e. like products (Sect. 6.3) and discriminatory treatment (Sect. 6.4). It makes then some critical comments on the evolution of national treatment jurisprudence (Sect. 6.5) before some concluding remarks on the legality of PPM measures under Article III (Sect. 6.6).

6.1 The Issue of Coverage

6.1.1 Internal Measures vs. Border Measures in the GATT

It has been debated whether Article III 'covers' PPM measures or whether such measures do not fall within the scope of national treatment. The central aspect of this issue is that the GATT contains much more stringent rules for measures applying only to imports but not to domestic products.

As regards *financial contributions* imposed on imported products, they can be regarded either as border tariffs (Art. II) or as domestic taxes (Art. III:2). In the former case, Article II prohibits tariffs above the level specified in the concessions made by WTO Members. In the latter case, in which Article III applies, WTO Members have in principle retained their regulatory autonomy, provided that their internal fiscal measures do not discriminate against imported products.

Similarly, with respect to *regulatory measures*, quantitative restrictions are prohibited (Art. XI), while regulatory measures applying both to imports and domestic products are in principle GATT consistent, as long as they do not discriminate between imported and domestic products (Art. III) or between imported products originating from different exporting countries (Art. I).

The limits between these two categories of measures—i.e. the strict rules of Articles II and XI and the more lenient ones of Articles III:2 and III:4—may be subject to debate, in particular when it comes to PPM measures. It may be contended that such measures must be considered as internal regulations 'affecting the internal sale' of products in the sense of Article III:1, which means that the coverage of Article III must be interpreted broadly. On the other hand, one might also focus on the reference to 'products' in Article III and emphasise that process standards do not directly regulate or tax the products themselves but only their production processes, which justifies a restrictive coverage of the national treatment clause.

The two *US – Tuna* Panels applied this latter approach, referring extensively to the use of the word 'product' in the text of Article III and its Ad Note. In the view of the *US – Tuna I* Panel, this textual argument implied that Article III covered only 'measures affecting products as such'.[2] It held that the United States' measure at issue could not be regarded as being applied to tuna products 'as such' because it did not regulate the sale of tuna and 'could not possibly affect tuna as a product'. Therefore, the Panel concluded that these measures did not constitute internal regulations covered by the national treatment provision.[3] The *US – Tuna II* Panel similarly relied on the use of the word 'product' in the text of Article III, to conclude that Article III was not applicable to the contested measure, since the required PPMs could not have 'any impact on the inherent character of tuna as a product'.[4] As a consequence, the United States' measures concerned in these cases were examined under the more stringent quantitative restrictions provision of Article XI.

This use of the concept of 'product as such' was confirmed neither by subsequent Panels nor by the Appellate Body. The evolution of case law suggests that a broad interpretation of Article III's coverage now prevails, both for Article III:2 (*infra*, Sect. 6.1.2) and Article III:4 (*infra*, Sect. 6.1.3).

6.1.2 Article III:2

As far as fiscal measures are concerned, Article II does not prevent the adoption of a charge imposed on imported products *equivalent to an internal tax*. Internal taxes are defined in Article III:2, which refers to internal charges *directly or indirectly applied* to domestic and imported products. The limit between tariffs and internal taxes and the question whether PPM fiscal measures are subject to the strict rule of Article II or to the less restrictive regime of Article III are thus dependent on the broad or restrictive interpretation of what amounts to a 'charge directly or indirectly imposed on products'.

A GATT Working Party examined this issue in 1970. The *Border Tax Adjustment* report made some distinctions between different kinds of taxes. It considered, for instance, that specific excise duties, sales taxes, cascade taxes and the tax on value added were taxes *directly levied on products*, which were eligible for tax adjustment. On the other hand, it mentioned social security charges and payroll taxes as examples of taxes that were *not* directly levied on products and that were *not* eligible for tax adjustment.[5] In other words, the importing state's *product* taxes can be imposed on imported products but not its *producer* taxes.[6]

The *Border Tax Adjustment* report also mentioned certain categories of tax for which there were divergent views with regard to the eligibility for adjustment,

---

[2]*US – Tuna I*, Panel Report, para. 5.11.

[3]*Ibid.*, para. 5.14.

[4]*US – Tuna II*, Panel Report, para. 5.9.

[5]See GATT, *Border Tax Adjustments Report*, para. 14.

[6]See Pauwelyn (2007), pp. 17 f.

which were notably the 'taxes occultes'. They were defined as 'consumption taxes on capital equipment, auxiliary materials and services used in the transportation and production of other taxable goods. Taxes on advertising, energy, machinery and transport were among the more important taxes which might be involved.'[7] These taxes apply on inputs that are not physically incorporated in the final product, i.e. to npr-PPMs. Taxes on pollution emitted during the production process of a product, such as a carbon tax, might thus fall into this category of 'taxes occultes'. No consensus was reached on the question of whether such taxes could be adjusted at the border. The *Border Tax Adjustments* report thus offers limited guidance for the treatment of such cases.

Three reports suggest, however, that a broad interpretation of Article III:2's coverage should prevail.

The first case is the *US – Superfund* report, rendered by a GATT 1947 Panel in 1987, which addressed the issue of the definition of 'measures directly levied on products'. In this case, the Panel had to examine a complaint against a United States' domestic tax on certain chemicals, which was also applied on imported products that had used these chemicals during their manufacturing process.[8] The United States argued that this tax was consistent with GATT Articles II:2(a) and III:2.

The complainants EEC and Canada had argued that 'the pollution created in the production of the imported substances did not occur in the United States. It was therefore inappropriate to tax these substances upon entry in the United States.'[9] The United States replied that 'the Superfund Act's primary function was to raise revenue, not to alter consumer or producer behaviour to take into account the cost of environmental resources'.[10] The Panel accepted that argument and considered that what was important was the distinction between taxes *directly or indirectly levied on products* and not the distinction between taxes with different policy purposes.[11] It held that 'the tax on certain chemicals, being a tax directly imposed on products, was eligible for border tax adjustment independent of the purpose it served'.[12]

Thus, the Panel permitted the United States to apply border tax adjustments for the imported products concerned, even though they were taxed on the basis of chemicals *used during their production process*, which caused pollution *in the exporting countries*. This was insufficient to exclude the application of GATT Article III:2. Interestingly, the Panel did not say that the chemicals used to produce

---

[7]Using a definition of the OECD. See the GATT *Border Tax Adjustments* report, para. 15.

[8]See *US – Superfund*, Panel Report, para. 3.2.5: '[t]he principle to be applied in implementing the legislation was that the amount of tax to be imposed on the imported substances would equal the amount of tax that would have been imposed *on the chemicals used in producing the imported substances* if the chemicals had been sold in the United States for an equivalent use' (emphasis added).

[9]*US – Superfund*, GATT 1947 Panel Report, para. 3.2.7.

[10]*US – Superfund*, Panel Report, para. 3.2.9.

[11]*Ibid.*, para. 5.2.4.

[12]*Ibid.*

the taxed substances had to be still present in them in order to qualify as a tax applied to 'products'.[13]

A parallel can easily be made between this case and the possible taxation of CO_2 emissions that occurred in a foreign country during the production process of imported goods. Under the *US – Superfund* approach, it seems that such a measure could amount to a domestic measure under Article III:2 and not as a border tariff subject to Article II.

The second case is the 2001 *Argentina – Bovine Hides and Leather* report. In this case, the respondent referred to the concept of 'product as such', but its line of argumentation was not followed by the Panel, which applied instead a broad interpretation of the scope of Article III.[14] It held that three elements must exist for Article III:2 to apply: the measures at issue must (i) constitute taxes or other charges of any kind, (ii) constitute internal measures, (iii) apply directly or indirectly to imported and domestic products.[15]

The first condition should be interpreted in a large way, especially because of the words 'charges of any kind'. The Panel considered that the term 'charge' denoted, *inter alia*, a 'pecuniary burden' and a 'liability to pay money laid on a person'.[16] Thus, two measures qualified by the Panel as mechanisms for the collection of taxes, and not as taxes in their own right, were considered as 'tax measures' because there were no doubts that they imposed a pecuniary burden and created a liability to pay money.[17]

The second condition implies that the tax imposed on imported products must be the equivalent of a tax imposed on domestic products. This ensues from the wording of Article II:2(a). It does not matter if the tax is collected at the point of importation, pursuant to the Note *Ad* Article III.[18]

The third element is whether the measure is directly or indirectly applied to imported and domestic products. This issue has been central in the determination of the coverage of Article III. As indicated above, the logic of the *Border Tax Adjustments* report was that taxes applied on *products* were covered by Article III, whereas taxes on *producers* were not.

---

[13]See Pauwelyn (2007), p. 20. The Panel simply explained that the Superfund Act provided that '[a] substance shall be added to the list if the Secretary of the Treasury (. . .) determined that chemicals subject to the tax on certain chemicals constitute more than 50 per cent of the weight of the materials used to produce such substance (determined on the basis of the predominant method of production). He may also, to the extent necessary to carry out the purposes of the legislation, add any substance to the list if the value of the taxable chemicals constitutes more than 50 per cent of the total value of the materials used to produce the substance' (para. 2.4).

[14]See *Argentina – Bovine Hides and Leather*, Panel Report, para. 11.157.

[15]*Ibid.*, para. 11.139 ff.

[16]*Ibid.*, para. 11.143.

[17]*Ibid.*

[18]The Note *Ad* Article III provides that '[a]ny internal tax or other internal charge (. . .) which applies to an imported product and to the like domestic product and is collected or enforced in the case of the imported product at the time or point of importation, is nevertheless to be regarded as an internal tax or other internal charge (. . .) and is accordingly subject to the provisions of Article III'.

In this case, the Panel had to examine a tax applied to imported and domestic products, which was basically a mechanism providing for the prepayment of an income tax on natural and juridical persons. The amount of tax paid on all internal sales, or on the definitive importation of goods in Argentina, was then credited at the time of settlement of the definitive tax liability arising from the income tax law. Neither the parties to this case nor the Panel contested that the basic tax was an income tax, which is not in principle levied on products and thus not subject to Article III:2. Argentina thus argued that since the contested measure was a mechanism providing for the prepayment of this income tax, its collection mechanism could not be covered by Article III:2.

The Panel rejected this argument because, in its view, the provisions of the measure clearly stated that they applied to goods.[19] Another reason that the Panel mentioned was the fact that the amount to be collected was determined by applying the tax rate to the normal price defined for the application of import duties.[20] In consequence, this tax was regarded as *applying to products* and was subject to the conditions of Article III:2, regardless of the purpose it served, i.e. assuring the prepayment of an income tax.

Finally, a third relevant case is the 1997 *Canada – Periodicals* report, rendered a few years before the *Argentina – Bovine Hides and Leather* case. In this case, the United States brought a complainant to the Dispute Settlement Body after Canada had imposed an excise tax on advertisements in split-run periodicals, applied to the value of advertising of each issue of a split-run magazine.[21] Canada argued that its measure concerned advertising services, regulated by the GATS. The Appellate Body held that the GATT was applicable because the tax at issue was an excise tax that was applied on a physical good, a split-run edition of a periodical, on a 'per issue' basis, even though this product contained components having service attributes, namely editorial content and advertising content.[22] The Appellate Body concluded that by its very structure and design, the measure at hand was a tax levied on a product (a periodical), which was covered by Article III:2.[23]

All three cases referred to above seem to emphasise that the predominant issue is *whether the tax is applied to individual imported goods*, regardless of the motivation for the perception of this financial contribution, which can, for instance, be raising revenue (*US – Superfund*), assuring the prepayment of an income tax (*Argentina – Bovine Hides and Leather*) or taxing advertisement in split-run periodicals (*Canada – Periodicals*). In each of these cases, the reports determined the value to be taxed in relation to this individual product (amount of taxed chemicals used in the production process, value of the advertisement contained in a periodical or product prices). Hence, these reports have applied a broad definition

---

[19]See *Argentina – Bovine Hides and Leather,* Panel Report, para. 11.158.

[20]*Ibid.*

[21]See *Canada – Periodicals*, Appellate Body Report, p. 5.

[22]*Ibid.*, p. 17.

[23]*Ibid.*, p. 18.

of taxes directly or indirectly levied on products in the sense of Article III:2, which is very different from the restrictive approach applied by the *US – Tuna* Panels.

In the light of this broad definition, it thus seems that a measure imposing a tax on inputs used during the production process of imported products could be considered as an 'internal tax applied indirectly to products' in the sense of Article III:2, as long as this tax is levied on particular products. In other words, the broad interpretation adopted by the Appellate Body, which focuses on whether a tax is levied on products, probably means that the 'taxes occultes' referred to above are covered by Article III:2 and are eligible for adjustment at the border.

It should be pointed out, however, that this broad interpretation does certainly not mean that producer taxes, such as social security charges, can be considered as taxes 'levied on products' and adjustable at the border.[24] As Pauwelyn has suggested, a possibility to differentiate between producer taxes and 'taxes occultes' is to focus on the *nexus* between the tax and the products concerned, which should be tight enough.[25] As far as environmental taxes are concerned, measures taxing externalities produced during the manufacturing process of a particular product can potentially have some environmental effect even in the absence of any changes in the policies of the producing country. Indeed, the internalisation of externalities through the tax at issue would, all other things being equal, reduce the demand for this good and thus reduce the environmental harm concerned. By contrast, border tax adjustments aimed at producer taxes such as social security charges would not improve social protection in the exporting country without any change enacted in that state's legislation. There is thus arguably a closer nexus between the product itself and the tax for such environmental charges than for typical producer taxes. It is submitted that a sufficient nexus should be recognised at least when the tax aims at internalising the external costs of particular environmental practices, such as the social cost of carbon, in the ultimate price of the product, in order to correct a market failure.

6.1.3 Article III:4

When it comes to Article III:4, a similar evolution can be seen in case law. WTO adjudicating bodies have not confirmed the restrictive interpretation of the *US – Tuna* Panels, which based their interpretation almost exclusively on the word 'products' to exclude any regulation that could not affect a particular good 'as a product'. They have rather focused on whether a regulation 'affects' the sale of products in the internal market of the importing country.

---

[24]The Report of the Working Party on Border Tax Adjustments denied this possibility (see para. 14).

[25]See Pauwelyn (2007), pp. 20 f.

Article III:4 applies to *laws, regulations or requirements* (1), which *affect the internal sale*, offering for sale, purchase, transportation, distribution or use of imported products (2).

One Panel was of the view that the words 'laws, regulations and requirements' in Article III:4 'should be interpreted as encompassing a [...] broad range of government action and action by private parties that may be assimilated to government action'.[26] 'Regulations' are equivalent to 'mandatory rules applying across-the-board'.[27] 'Requirements' encompass 'commitments entered into on a voluntary basis by individual firms as a condition to obtaining an advantage'.[28] This could apply both to obligations that an enterprise is legally bound to carry out and to those that an enterprise voluntarily accepts in order to obtain an advantage from the government.[29]

Once a WTO Member's measure has been characterised as a law, regulation or requirement, the next step is to examine if it *affects the internal sale* of imported products.[30] The word 'affecting' serves to define the type of measures that must conform to the obligation not to accord 'less favourable treatment' to like imported products but does not, in itself, impose any obligation.[31] The word 'affecting' has consistently been defined broadly in GATT and WTO case law.[32] It has been interpreted as meaning that a measure has 'an effect on' the internal sale of imported products, which indicates a broader scope than such terms as 'regulating' or 'governing'.[33] Thus, this term 'goes beyond laws and regulations which directly govern the conditions of sale or purchase to cover also any laws or regulations which might *adversely modify the conditions of competition* between domestic and imported products'.[34] In the view of one Panel, Article III:4 also covers laws,

---

[26] *Japan – Films*, Panel Report, para. 10.376. In that respect, the Panel considered that the scope of the words 'laws, regulations and requirements' in Article III:4 should be as broad as the word 'measure' in Article XXIII:1(b) on nullification or impairment, which was interpreted broadly in the same report (para. 10.47–10.50).

[27] See *Canada – FIRA*, Panel Report (1947), para. 5.5; *India – Autos*, Panel Report, para. 8.181; *China – Auto Parts*, Panel Report, para. 7.239.

[28] See *Canada – FIRA*, Panel Report (1947), para. 5.4; *India – Autos*, Panel Report, para. 8.184; *China – Auto Parts*, Panel Report, para. 7.240.

[29] See *India – Autos*, Panel Report, para. 7.184; *China – Auto Parts*, Panel Report, para. 7.240; *Canada – Autos*, Panel Report, para. 10.73.

[30] See e.g. *China – Auto Parts*, Panel Report, para. 7.251.

[31] See *US – FSC (21.5)*, Appellate Body Report, para. 208 f.

[32] See *India – Autos*, Panel Report, para. 7.196; *US – FSC (21.5)*, Appellate Body Report, para. 210: '[i]n view of the similar function of the identical word, "affecting", in Article III:4 of the GATT 1994 [compared to Article I:1 GATS], we also interpret this word, in this provision, as having a "broad scope of application"'.

[33] See *China – Auto Parts*, Panel Report, para. 7.251; *EC – Bananas III*, Appellate Body Report, para. 220; *India – Autos*, Panel Report, para. 7.196; *Canada – Autos*, Panel Report, para. 10.80; *Dominican Republic – Cigarettes*, Panel Report, para. 7.278.

[34] *India – Autos*, Panel Report, para. 7.196 (emphasis added). See also *Canada – Autos*, Panel Report, para. 10.80; *Italian Agricultural Machinery*, GATT Panel Report, para. 12; *China – Auto Parts*, Panel Report, para. 7.251.

regulations or requirements that apply only to imported products, for instance a requirement imposed as a condition on importation.[35] The applicable criterion is whether these laws, regulations or requirements have an effect on specific trans-actions, activities and uses relating to products in the marketplace.[36]

In the *US – Tuna II (Mexico) 21.5* Panel report, the Panel mentioned the issue of coverage in a single paragraph only. It noted that 'previous panels and the Appellate Body have interpreted broadly what falls within the ambit of "laws and regulations" in the context of Article III:4'.[37]

In conclusion, it seems clear for the present author, in the view of these different reports, that the logic of the unadopted *US – Tuna* cases, according to which PPM measures are not covered by Article III, is not relevant in current case law since process-based measures are indeed capable of 'affecting' the sale of imported products.[38]

6.1.4   Comments

It is submitted here that the restrictive interpretation of the *US – Tuna* Panels was not consistent with the customary rules on treaty interpretation. It was based on a restrictive reading of the word 'products', which was basically the only word that mattered in the eyes of the *US – Tuna I* Panel.[39] This strict, and arguably too narrow, textual reading of Article III was not supplemented by an examination of the object and purpose of that provision, in application of the customary rules on interpretation, which would not have confirmed that interpretation. A word must be given its ordinary interpretation in the light of the object and purpose of the provision and the treaty.[40] As it will be shown below, the Appellate Body considers that Article III is about avoiding protectionism and protecting the competitive relationship between products in the importing country's market. In order to guarantee the equality of competitive conditions of products, it is necessary to subject all internal regulations affecting that competitive relation to the strictures of Article III. If Article III does not cover PPM measures, internally enforced process

---

[35]See *India – Autos*, Panel Report, para. 306.

[36]See *China – Auto Parts*, Panel Report, para. 7.253; *US – FSC (21.5)*, Appellate Body Report, para. 208.

[37]*US – Tuna II (Mexico) 21.5*, Panel Report, para. 7.474.

[38]Supporting the view that the words 'affecting' the sale includes PPM measures, see Howse and Regan (2000), p. 254; Hudec (2000), p. 198; Vranes (2009), pp. 322 f.; Conrad (2011), p. 155.

[39]See *US – Tuna I*, Panel Report, para. 5.11.

[40]See Article 31(1) of the Vienna Convention on the Law of Treaties ('[a] treaty shall be interpreted in good faith in accordance with the ordinary meaning to be given to the terms of the treaty in their context and in the light of its object and purpose').

measures would not be subject to any GATT scrutiny since they would not amount to a quantitative restriction in the sense of Article XI either.[41]

Moreover, the restrictive approach of the *US – Tuna* Panels was based on an 'objective' analysis of like products, where *the* determinative criterion was physical characteristics. In current case law, as it will be shown below, the most important criteria is the competitive relationship between products and not physical characteristics. On the basis of this approach, it is in principle possible that two physically identical products could be considered unlike because they would not be in a competitive relationship in the marketplace. Therefore, there is no reason to exclude PPM regulations, insofar as differences in production methods could possibly render two products unlike in the eyes of the consumers.

It is generally rightly argued in academic writings that PPM measures are in principle covered by Article III.[42] This view seems to have been at least implicitly endorsed by the Appellate Body, through the broad coverage given to the terms of Article III:2 (taxes applied 'directly or indirectly' to products) and III:4 ('affecting' the internal sale of products). In the light of the object and purpose of Article III, it is submitted that this broad interpretation must be endorsed.

With respect to internal taxes subject to Article III:2, there might be, however, certain limits, as mentioned above, due to the fact that 'producer taxes' should not be eligible for border tax adjustments. When there is no close nexus between the tax and the product at issue, such as in the case of social security taxes, adjustment at the border would not be possible.

6.2 The Scope of National Treatment

Article III covers both fiscal (Art. III:2) and regulatory (Art. III:4) measures. National treatment requires a two-step analysis. First, it is necessary to determine if two products are 'like' (Art. III:2, first sentence, and Art. III:4) or 'directly competitive or substitutable' (Art. III:2, second sentence). Second, one must determine if the treatment accorded to these products discriminates imported products compared to domestic products. The standards used to analyse discrimination differ in each case. As regards fiscal measures, imported *like* products must not be subject to taxes 'in excess of' those applied to domestic products (Art. III:2, first sentence). When it comes to *directly competitive or substitutable* products, an internal tax measure is inconsistent with Article III if such products are 'not similarly taxed' and if this dissimilar taxation is applied 'so as to afford protection to domestic production' (Art. III:2, second sentence). As for internal regulatory measures, the national

---

[41]See Howse and Regan (2000), p. 256; Hudec (2000), p. 194; Vranes (2009), p. 323.

[42]See Howse and Regan (2000), p. 254; Hudec (2000), pp. 194 ff., in particular p. 198; Vranes (2009), p. 322; Conrad (2011), p. 155; Holzer (2014), p. 130.

treatment clause requires that imported products be granted treatment 'no less favourable' than that accorded to *like* domestic products.[43]

The prohibition of protectionism enshrined in Article III guarantees that imported products are not discriminated against domestic like (or directly competitive or substitutable) products in the internal market of the importing Member. It represents one of the essential aspects of trade liberalisation.

The perceived importance of national treatment within the General Agreement has, however, evolved since the inception of the GATT in 1947. The main objective at that time was to lower tariff barriers. One of the great successes of the GATT is the important reduction in tariffs in industrialised countries since the middle of the twentieth century. Since tariffs do not represent a major obstacle to trade in developed states any more, the attention has gradually shifted on non-tariff barriers, which can also be used for protectionist purposes.

On the other hand, regulations in non-economic areas that may have an impact on trade, such as prescriptions related to health, safety, labour or consumer and environmental protection, have been increasingly used these last four decades, possibly because they can be viewed as part of the elaboration of a 'modern welfare state'.[44] However, trade liberals tend to see these kinds of regulatory measures as the most costly form of non-tariff barriers to trade, and they argue that these instruments require new disciplines under international trade rules.[45]

Article III has thus been gradually seen as one of the major tools necessary to discipline non-tariff barriers, along with the new instruments of the TBT and SPS agreements. Adopting a broad interpretation of national treatment is an efficient

---

[43] Article III:2, first sentence, provides:

> The products of the territory of any contracting party imported into the territory of any other contracting party shall not be subject, directly or indirectly, to internal taxes or other internal charges of any kind in excess of those applied, directly or indirectly, to like domestic products.

Article III:2, second sentence, is supplemented by the note *Ad* Article III. They respectively state:

> No contracting party shall otherwise apply internal taxes or other internal charges to imported or domestic products in a manner contrary to the principles set forth in paragraph 1.

> A tax conforming to the requirements of the first sentence of paragraph 2 would be considered to be inconsistent with the provisions of the second sentence only in cases where competition was involved between, on the one hand, the taxed product and, on the other hand, a directly competitive or substitutable product which was not similarly taxed.

Finally, Article III:4 provides, with respect to regulatory measures, as follows:

> The products of the territory of any contracting party imported into the territory of any other contracting party shall be accorded treatment no less favourable than that accorded to like products of national origin in respect of all laws, regulations and requirements affecting their internal sale, offering for sale, purchase, transportation, distribution or use.

[44] Trebilcock and Howse (1998), p. 6.
[45] *Ibid.*

way to prevent the risks of protectionist abuses through the use of internal regulations. However, endorsing such a broad interpretation can also have a disproportionate impact on WTO Members' regulatory autonomy in non-economic fields. As
a consequence, the scope one gives to national treatment is directly related to the
balance that must be found within the WTO system between trade liberalisation and
its Members' regulatory autonomy. In the light of this challenge, it is not surprising
that the interpretation of Article III is one of the most controversial issues of the
GATT.[46]

The debate on the appropriate scope of the conditions of Article III forms part of
the more general issue of defining adequate rules for cases of *de facto* discrimination. Panels have focused in the first decades of the GATT 1947 on cases of *de jure*
discrimination, for which they adopted a restrictive interpretation of the conditions
of Article III. However, modern disputes often concern cases of indirect discrimination, which require a more flexible definition of the conditions of Article III, in
order to determine if a measure that does not expressly discriminate imported and
domestic products must nonetheless be regarded as protectionist.

Technically, this controversy has focused mainly on the definition of *like
products*. The idea is that a Member is free to grant less favourable treatment to
products that are not deemed to be like. Thus, the broader is the definition of like
products, the larger is the scope of national treatment. The next sections show that
the definition of like products has fluctuated in practice, between quite broad
approaches and rather restrictive ones. Commentators likewise have quite divergent
views on the appropriate definition of like products.

It should be pointed out that the scope of national treatment also depends on the
interpretation of the second condition of Article III, *discriminatory treatment*. The
attention of jurisprudence and scholars has more recently tended to shift towards
this condition.

Both for like products and for discriminatory treatment, as it will be shown
below, three main theories exist, with very different consequences on the restrictiveness of these conditions.[47] Their combination thus allows for quite different
scopes for Article III as a whole.

One should also keep in mind that the extent to which GATT restricts WTO
Members' regulatory autonomy also depends on the interpretations of the *conditions of Article XX*, which are also debated.[48] Hence, a broad interpretation of the
disciplines of Article III, combined with an extensive interpretation of the possibilities to justify a measure under the general exceptions provision, may lead to a
similar practical result than a restrictive interpretation of Article III's disciplines.
There are thus many different variables that are relevant to determine the extent to
which GATT as a whole restricts WTO Members' regulatory autonomy.

---

[46]See, e.g., concerning 'like products': Choi (2003), p. xi.

[47]See *infra*, 6.3 and 6.4.

[48]See *infra*, Chap. 7.

The objective of this section is to present the different theories of the definition of like products and discriminatory treatment and to examine the extent to which they allow a WTO Member to take into account differences in protection methods in the context of Article III.

One should keep in mind in this context that a recurrent question related to the debates on the interpretation of the conditions of Articles III and XX is to determine the appropriate place in which the regulatory purpose of the measure, which may explain a distinction between domestic and imported products, should be taken into account: in the concept of like products, in the discriminatory treatment conditions of Article III or in the general exceptions provision of Article XX.

When it comes to the issue of the relevance of PPM distinctions in the context of Article III, it has not been addressed thoroughly by case law to date. However, the scope and the interpretation of the conditions of Article III have an influence on the extent to which trade measures based on differences in production processes may be compatible with the national treatment obligation. Hence, this chapter examines in particular the general debates on the conditions of Article III, which have direct consequences as far as the justifiability of PPM measures is concerned.

6.3 Like Products

As it has been mentioned above, the concept of like products has received most of the attention in academic debates relating to Article III, in particular because it can be seen as assuming a pivotal role in national treatment, which applies only between like products (or directly competitive or substitutable products in the case of Art. III:2, second sentence). Conversely, WTO Members remain free to grant less favourable treatment to 'unlike' products. In that view, the concept of like products has a fundamental importance on the scope of national treatment and consequently on the extent to which Article III restricts WTO Members regulatory autonomy.[49] The definition of 'like products' is in fact one of the most controversial issues of the WTO law,[50] both in case law and in academic writings.

---

[49] See e.g. Choi (2003), p. ix. This view is most clearly explained by proponents of the aim-and-effects theory: *US – Malt Beverages*, Panel Report, para. 5.72 ('once products are designated as like products, a regulatory product differentiation, e.g. for standardization or environmental purposes, becomes inconsistent with Article III even if the regulation is not "applied ... so as to afford protection"'); Roessler (2003), p. 772 ('a determination that [...] two products are "like products" within the meaning of Article III:4 [...] has the consequence that any regulatory distinction between those products is inconsistent with that provision'); Regan (2002), pp. 448 ff. This view overlooks that a violation of Article III also requires that like products would be granted less favourable but it illustrates at least clearly the importance attached to like products in certain debates relating to National Treatment.

[50] See e.g. Choi (2003), p. xi.

For the sake of clarity, and because of the diversity of the different approaches to the definition of like products and the fluctuations in the scope given to this concept, this section examines separately the different theories successively applied in case law (Sect. 6.3.1) and the different approaches advocated by commentators in academic writings (Sect. 6.3.2).

6.3.1 The Concept of Like Products in Case Law

6.3.1.1 The 'Accordion' of Like Products

One of the difficulties relating to the interpretation of 'like products' is that neither Article III nor the GATT defines this concept, which is used in many other provisions of the GATT and other WTO agreements (such as GATT Articles II:2, VI:1, IX:1, XI:2(c), XIII:1, XVI:4 and XIX:1; specific provisions of the TBT and SPS agreements; the Agreement on Safeguards; or the Anti-Dumping Agreement[51]).

Many reports rendered in GATT or WTO dispute settlement proceedings had to interpret the concept of like products.[52] However, case law has not established a particular test that has to be strictly followed in order to define likeness.[53] The Appellate Body stated that there 'can be no one precise and absolute definition of what is "like"'[54] because '[n]o one approach (. . .) will be appropriate for all cases'.[55]

This can be explained mainly by two reasons. First, in the view of the Appellate Body, the scope of 'like products' may be different in *each particular provision* referring to it. The Appellate Body explained it in the following way:

> The concept of 'likeness' is a relative one that evokes the image of an accordion. The accordion of 'likeness' stretches and squeezes in different places as different provisions of the WTO Agreement are applied. The width of the accordion in any one of those places must be determined by the particular provision in which the term 'like' is encountered (. . .).[56]

For instance, in the particular case of national treatment, the Appellate Body has construed the concept of like products narrowly in Article III:2, first sentence, since

---

[51]The Anti-Dumping Agreement is the only one containing a definition of like products, which is however only applicable to this particular field. Article 2.6 of the Anti-Dumping Agreement states that '[t]hroughout this agreement the term "like product" ("produit similaire") shall be interpreted to mean a product which is identical, i.e. alike in all respects to the product under consideration, or in the absence of such product, another product which, although not alike in all respects, has characteristics closely resembling those of the product under consideration'.

[52]See e.g. the list of cases cited by the Appellate Body in the *EC – Asbestos* report, p. 33, note 58.

[53]See *Japan – Alcohol II*, Panel Report, para. 6.21.

[54]*Japan – Alcohol II*, Appellate Body Report, p. 21.

[55]*Ibid.*

[56]*Ibid.*

its second sentence refers to the concept of directly competitive or substitutable products, whereas Article III:4 only uses the notion of like products. At the same time, the Appellate Body implied that the scope of Articles III:2 and III:4 must be construed in a similar manner to avoid that a WTO Member could freely make regulatory distinctions but not fiscal distinctions or vice versa.

Second, GATT case law and practice have usually considered that likeness must be determined on a *case-by-case basis*.[57] In other words, 'the context and the circumstances that prevail in any given case' have also a significant influence on the width of the 'accordion' of likeness.[58] This case-by-case approach implies that the likeness analysis always involves 'an unavoidable element of individual, discretionary judgement'.[59] This discretionary decision must be made in considering the various characteristics of products in each individual case.[60] In the view of the Appellate Body, Panels must evaluate *all* of the relevant evidence.[61]

Traditionally, GATT and WTO adjudicating bodies have examined likeness through the criteria mentioned by the 1970 Report of the Working Party on *Border Tax Adjustments*, namely (1) the properties, nature and quality of the products (the physical properties of the product[62]); (2) the end uses of the products (the extent to which the products are capable of serving the same or similar end uses[63]); (3) consumers' tastes and habits (the extent to which consumers perceive and treat the products as alternative means of performing a particular function in order to satisfy a particular want or demand[64]); and (4) tariff classification of the products.[65]

---

[57]The need to examine likeness on a case-by-case basis was already mentioned in the 1970 *Border Tax Adjustments* report.

[58]*Japan – Alcohol II*, Appellate Body Report, p. 21.

[59]*Japan – Alcohol II*, Appellate Body Report, p. 21; *EC – Asbestos*, Appellate Body Report, para. 101.

[60]*Japan – Alcohol II*, Appellate Body Report, pp. 20 f.; *Thailand – Cigarettes (Philippines)*, Panel Report, para. 7.437.

[61]*EC – Asbestos*, Appellate Body Report, para. 113.

[62]*Ibid.*, para. 101.

[63]*Ibid.*

[64]*Ibid.*

[65]*Japan – Alcohol II*, Panel Report, para 6.21; *Border Tax Adjustment*, Report of the Working Party, p. 3, para. 18 (criteria developed in order to define permissible internal tax adjustments applicable to like imported products): 'With regard to the interpretation of the term "... like or similar products ...", which occurs some sixteen times throughout the General Agreement, it was recalled that considerable discussion had taken place in the past, both in GATT and in other bodies, but that no further improvement of the term had been achieved. The Working Party concluded that problems arising from the interpretation of the term should be examined on a case-by-case basis. This would allow a fair assessment in each case of the different elements that constitute a "similar" product. Some criteria were suggested for determining, on a case-by-case basis, whether a product is "similar": the product's end-uses in a given market; consumers' tastes and habits, which change from country to country; the product's properties, nature and quality. It was observed, however, that the term "... like or similar products ..." caused some uncertainty and that it would be desirable to improve on it; however, no improved term was arrived at'.

If most of the reports that interpreted the notion of like products referred to these four criteria, the relative weight they were given in each case evolved, and the debates on the definition of like products is far from being over, as this chapter explains below.

There have been many debates on the definition of likeness, which have quite different consequences on the scope of like products and thus potentially on the scope of national treatment itself (even though this last issue depends also on the definition of the discriminatory treatment conditions). National treatment tests applied by panels and the Appellate Body have cycled through varying degrees of strictness or laxity over time,[66] in search of the right balance between disciplining non-tariff barriers and safeguarding WTO Members' regulatory autonomy.

These debates all relate basically to three main theories: the objective, economic and subjective approaches of like products. The two former are based to a certain extent on the criteria of the *Border Tax Adjustments* Report, while the latter is mainly based on the further criterion of the regulatory purpose of the measure. It will also be shown that the objective approach resulted in a large scope of like products and that the economic and subjective approaches may be seen as attempts to restrict it.[67]

6.3.1.2   The Objective Approach

6.3.1.2.1   A Focus on Physical Characteristics

A first possible approach for the definition of likeness is what could be referred to as the objective approach, which consists in concentrating on the products' most objective features, in particular physical characteristics and tariff classifications.

Early GATT 1947 panels' practice applied a fairly restrictive objective approach and considered that products could be considered as unlike based on small differences in their physical characteristics. For instance, in the 1949 *Brazilian Internal Taxes* report, local Brazilian *conhaque* and French cognac were not considered as like products due to differences in additives and aromas. Brazil had simply explained that local beverages containing aromatic or medicinal substances and known as tar, honey or ginger *conhaque* were 'quite different from French cognac'.[68] Brazil also assured that the authorities responsible for administering the taxes were able to distinguish between those products and cognac from abroad.[69]

---

[66]See DiMaschio and Pauwelyn (2008), p. 62.

[67]See, e.g., Pauwelyn (2004), pp. 585 f., who argues that the notion of like products has been 'restricted considerably' since it longer suffices with the economic approach that two products are physically the same for there to be an obligation to treat them the same way; rather, it is the marketplace that decides whether products are like.

[68]*Brazilian Internal Taxes*, Working Party Report (First Report), para. 7.

[69]*Ibid.*

Other reports mainly focused on differences in tariff classifications. In the 1950 *Australia – Ammonium Sulphate* report, the Panel concluded purely on the basis of differences in tariff classifications that ammonium sulphate fertiliser was not 'like' nitrate fertiliser within the meaning of Article III:4.[70] In the 1978 *EEC – Animal Feed Proteins* report, the Panel had to decide whether vegetable proteins and denatured skimmed milk powder were like, within the meaning of Articles I and III. It denied that qualification on the basis of differences in tariff classifications, contents of protein and origin of the protein products.[71]

In the 1980s, GATT panels started to apply a more extended objective approach, in which physical differences between products were not necessarily deemed to be sufficient to consider products as unlike. For instance, in the 1981 *Spain – Unroasted Coffee* report, the Panel considered two products to be like, despite organoleptic differences resulting from geographical factors, cultivation methods, processing of beans, genetic factors, taste and aromas.[72] In the 1987 *Japan – Alcohol* report, the Panel took the view that vodka, whisky, grape brandy, other fruit brandy, 'classic liqueurs', still wine and sparkling wine were all like products and that 'minor differences in taste, colour and other properties did not prevent products qualifying as "like products"'.[73]

6.3.1.2.2 The Product-Process Distinction

One of the main and most controversial evolutions of this 'extended' objective approach has been the product-process distinction applied in the two 1991 and 1994 *US – Tuna* reports. Basically, this approach consisted in considering that two physically identical or similar products would be considered like regardless of differences in their production processes. In the view of the *US – Tuna I* Panel, Article III covered only taxes and regulation applied to 'product as such' and not process-based measures since differences in production methods could not affect tuna 'as a product'.[74] In an *obiter dictum*, the Panel held that even if the PPM measure at issue had been regarded as regulating the sale of tuna 'as a product', Article III called for a comparison between imported tuna 'as a product' and domestic tuna 'as a product'. Since regulations governing the taking of dolphins incidental to the taking of tuna 'could not possibly affect tuna as a product', the Panel concluded that the United States could not grant a less favourable treatment to Mexican tuna compared to US tuna based on differences in production methods.[75]

---

[70] See *Australia – Ammonium Sulphate*, Working Party Report, para. 9.

[71] See *EEC – Measures on Animal Feed Proteins*, Panel Report, para. 4.1 ff.

[72] See *Spain –Unroasted Coffee,* Panel Report, para. 4.5 ff.

[73] *Japan – Alcohol I*, Panel Report, para. 5.6.

[74] See *US – Tuna I*, Panel Report, para. 5.8 ff.

[75] *Ibid.*, para. 5.15.

The Panel did not elaborate on the applicable criteria to define likeness. It exclusively emphasised the use of the word 'product' in Article III to conclude that production methods could not affect tuna as a product or, in other words, that PPMs could not be taken into account in a likeness analysis. The only criterion that mattered in the view of the Panel was hence physical characteristics. This conclusion was based exclusively on a textual interpretation, without any analysis of the context or objective of national treatment, and led to broad criticism.[76]

Similarly, the second *US – Tuna* report held that none of the practices, policies and methods concerning the harvesting of tuna 'could have any impact on the inherent character of tuna as a product'.[77] If this finding was made in relation to the Article III's 'coverage' issue, it indicates rather clearly that the Panel also meant that in the absence of any changes in the physical characteristics of products, a PPM could not render two products unlike.

The *US – Tuna* reports concerned the way tuna was harvested, or in other words a 'how-produced' standard.[78] Other cases concerned measures that distinguished products on the basis of the characteristics of the producers (producer characteristics standard).[79] Such measures are not PPM measures in a strict sense,[80] but they have been treated in GATT 1947 jurisprudence in a way that is quite similar to 'how-produced' standards. They have seemingly been perceived as part of the corpus of decisions upon which the product-process distinction was based.[81]

First, in the 1992 *US – Malt Beverages* case, Canada complained about an excise tax credit in Minnesota for small (domestic or foreign) beer breweries. The complainant had argued that this measure resulted in discrimination against its large breweries. The Panel considered that beer produced by large breweries was 'not unlike' beer produced by small breweries.[82]

Second, the unadopted 1994 *US – Taxes on Automobiles* report concerned, in particular, the US Corporate Average Fuel Economy (CAFE) regulation, which required manufacturers and importers of automobiles to reach certain fuel efficiency values. They were calculated on the basis of a fleet averaging method treating domestic and imported cars separately. The Panel expressed the view that 'Article III:4 does not permit treatment of an imported product less favourable than that accorded to a like domestic product, based on factors not directly relating to the product as such'.[83] It concluded that the contested measure violated national

---

[76]See Howse and Regan (2000), pp. 249 ff.; Hudec (2000), pp. 187 ff., in particular p. 194; Vranes (2009), pp. 322 f.

[77]*US – Tuna II*, Panel Report, para. 5.9.

[78]See Charnovitz (2002), p. 67.

[79]*Ibid.*

[80]See Charnovitz (2002), p. 67; Conrad (2011), p. 183.

[81]See in particular Hudec (2000), p. 189.

[82]See *US – Malt Beverages*, Panel Report, para. 5.19.

[83]*US – Taxes on Automobiles*, Panel Report, para. 5.54.

treatment because its method was 'based on the ownership or control relationship of the car manufacturer' and 'did not relate to cars as products'.[84]

Finally, the early WTO *US – Gasoline* case concerned a complaint brought in 1996 against a United States' measure that required pollution reduction from a specific baseline. Pollution reduction obligations were calculated, in principle, according to an individual baseline based on the characteristics of the gasoline sold in 1990 by that refiner or importer. However, if the refiner or importer could not provide reliable data to establish an individual baseline, a statutory baseline was applied.[85] Since data from foreign producers were most often not verifiable, they were usually assigned, in practice, a (less favourable) statutory baseline. The Panel held that Article III:4 'deals with the treatment to be accorded to like products; its wording does not allow less favourable treatment dependent on the characteristics of the producer and the nature of the data held by it'.[86]

The *US – Tuna* reports and the different cases concerning producer's characteristics standards that have been described above have in common a focus on the objective features of the product itself, i.e. on its physical characteristics, to the exclusion of other factors that do not leave any trace on the product, such as unincorporated PPMs or the characteristics of the producer. If only 'how-produced' standards are PPM measures in a strict sense, this corpus of (mainly unadopted) decisions, including those concerning producer's characteristics standard, seems to have been perceived as part of the 'product-process doctrine', which authorised only regulatory distinctions that have some impact on the product itself.[87]

The GATT contracting parties never adopted the two *US – Tuna* reports, and the Appellate Body never confirmed either the product-process doctrine. Unadopted reports have no legal status as such in the GATT or WTO system.[88] Hence, the *US – Tuna* reports do not formally have any legal significance.[89] Yet the Appellate Body has also expressed the view that a panel could nevertheless find 'useful guidance' in the reasoning of an unadopted panel report that it considered to be relevant.[90] In practice, despite the fact that the *US – Tuna* reports were never adopted, many commentators have referred to the product-process distinction in the early years following these reports, sometimes even considering that it was 'settled case law'.[91]

Some pointed out that the merit of the product-process distinction was that it represents a 'bright-line rule', which might serve as a simple tool to distinguish

---

[84]*Ibid.*, para. 5.55.

[85]See *US – Gasoline*, Panel Report, para. 2.4.

[86]*Ibid.*, para. 6.11.

[87]See Hudec (2000), pp.187 ff.

[88]See *Japan – Alcohol II*, Appellate Body Report, p. 15.

[89]See, e.g., Pauwelyn (2004), p. 585 (stating that the value of the *US – Tuna* reports is 'almost nil').

[90]See *Japan – Alcohol II*, Appellate Body Report, p. 16.

[91]See Schoenbaum (1997), pp. 288 and 290; Okubo (1999), pp. 618 ff.; Hudec (2000), p. 189, with further references; Charnovitz (2002), pp. 76 f., with further references; Marceau (2002), p. 807; Joshi (2004), p. 79; Pauwelyn (2004), p. 585.

between products at the border.[92] However, overall, this approach has been widely criticised as overly literalist and context independent and as basically lacking justification under the rules of interpretation.[93] Its result also led to broad criticism from environmental groups since the product-process distinction was perceived as resulting in unwarranted legal constraints on trade measures designed to discourage environmentally harmful activities occurring in other countries.[94]

More generally, the economic approach to likeness that will be discussed below also means implicitly that the objective approach, focusing essentially on physical characteristics and tariff classifications, is no longer applicable.[95] Yet the Appellate Body has not stated either that differences in production processes could be an independent criterion to define likeness (even though the Appellate Body considers that all circumstances must be taken into account, which theoretically does not exclude this possibility).

---

[92]See Jackson (2000), p. 303.

[93]See Hudec (2000), pp. 187 ff.; Howse and Regan (2000), pp. 249 ff.; Trebilcock and Giri (2004), p. 55 (they do not object to the exclusion of PPM-related criteria but apparently to the exclusive focus on physical characteristics rather than on economic factors); Vranes (2009), p. 322; Cooreman (2017), pp. 29 and 52.

[94]See Jackson (1997), p. 238; Hudec (2000), p. 188; Charnovitz (2002), p. 60.

[95]See e.g. Pauwelyn (2004), p. 586 ('[i]t no longer suffices to show that two products are *physically* the same [. . .] for there to be an obligation to treat them in the same way'). *Contra*: Conrad (2011), pp. 231 f. (p. 239: '[w]hile some decisions show that the WTO adjudicatory bodies were inspired by ideas and contemplations considered crucial in the alternative approaches, the objective approach in the determination of likeness clearly prevails'). She contends that the constant practice of the GATT and WTO dispute settlement bodies has been to focus on the products' physical characteristics and to a lesser extent on tariff classifications. In her opinion, even in the *EC – Asbestos* case, the Appellate Body has primarily focused on physical characteristics to conclude that asbestos and substitutes fibres were unlike. She maintains that even though the Appellate Body seems to make concessions to the aim-and-effects doctrine, which considers the genuineness of the underlying policies such as health policies as crucial in the determination of likeness, a merely objective approach focusing on the physical characteristics would have reached the same conclusion, which 'waters down' the relevance of consumer preferences (p. 239). In her view, the *EC – Asbestos* report confirms the paramount importance of the criterion of physical characteristics, in particular because the Appellate Body stated that a higher burden would be placed on complainants to establish the existence of a competitive relationship between physically very different products. The criterion of consumer preferences would only be useful to correct findings based on physical properties in 'unusual circumstances' (p. 231). In the view of the present author, this opinion seems difficult to reconcile with the recent reports of the Appellate Body, in which it has confirmed its economic approach, for instance in the *Philippines – Distilled Spirits* under Article III:2, first sentence. For further discussion, see *infra*, 6.3.3.

6.3.1.3 The Aim-and-Effects Theory

6.3.1.3.1 The *US – Malt Beverages* and *US – Taxes on Automobiles* Cases

At the beginning of the 1990s, two GATT 1947 panels did not apply the traditional criteria of the *Border Tax Adjustment* report but developed a quite different alternative approach commonly referred to as the 'aim-and-effects' test. This approach resulted in a much more restricted definition of like products, possibly in reaction to the broad definition applied by the *Japan – Alcohol I* and the *US – Tuna* reports a few years earlier.

Basically, under the aim-and-effects approach, two products are like if the regulatory measure distinguishing between them pursues protectionist intent and results in protectionist effects. The main basis of this approach was to interpret the concept of like products in line with the basic purpose of Article III, enshrined in Article III:1, that internal measures should not be applied so as to afford protection to domestic production. In the view of the *US – Malt Beverages* Panel, the following was clear from the text of this provision:

> The purpose of Article III is thus not to prevent contracting parties from using their fiscal and regulatory powers for purposes other than to afford protection to domestic production. Specifically, the purpose of Article III is not to prevent contracting parties from differentiating between different products categories for policy purposes unrelated to the protection of domestic production. The Panel considered that the limited purpose of Article III has to be taken into account in interpreting the term 'like products' in this Article. Consequently, in determining whether two products subject to different treatment are like products, it is necessary to consider whether such product differentiation is being made 'so as to afford protection to domestic production'.[96]

In the view of the *US – Malt Beverages* Panel, this 'limited purpose' of national treatment justified a restrictive interpretation of like products.

The unadopted 1994 *US – Taxes on Automobiles* report developed this approach. It held the view that '[n]on-protectionist government policies might (...) require regulatory distinctions that were not based on the product's end use, its physical characteristics, or the other factors mentioned'.[97] It added that 'a primary purpose of the General Agreement was to lower barriers to trade between markets, and not to harmonize the regulatory treatment of products within them'.[98]

More specifically, the Panel examined more closely the meaning of the phrase 'so as to afford protection' and stated:

> The Panel noted that the term 'so as to' suggested both aim and effect. Thus the phrase 'so as to afford protection' called for an analysis of elements including the aim of the measure and the resulting effects. A measure could be said to have the aim of affording protection if an analysis of the circumstances in which it was adopted, in particular an analysis of the instruments available to the contracting party to achieve the declared domestic policy goal,

---

[96]*US – Malt Beverages*, Panel Report, para. 5.25.
[97]*US – Taxes on Automobiles*, Panel Report, para. 5.8.
[98]*Ibid.*

demonstrated that a change in competitive opportunities in favour of domestic products was a desired outcome and not merely an incidental consequence of the pursuit of a legitimate policy goal. A measure could be said to have the effect of affording protection to domestic production if it accorded greater competitive opportunities to domestic products than to imported products. The effect of a measure in terms of trade flows was not relevant for the purposes of Article III, since a change in the volume or proportion of imports could be due to many factors other than government measures.[99]

In this case, the Panel examined a luxury tax enacted by the United States that was applied to vehicles sold in the United States above USD 30,000. The Panel considered that the aim of the measure was to raise revenue from sales of perceived luxury products and that the principal aim of the measure was not to target imported cars.[100] As to the effect of the legislation, the Panel did not find that the sales data provided conclusive evidence of a change in the conditions of competition favouring US cars.[101] Therefore, it concluded that the threshold of USD 30,000 did not create conditions of competition that divided products inherently into two classes, one of foreign origin and the other of domestic origin.[102] This meant that the US legislation was not applied so as to afford protection to the domestic production of automobiles and that, therefore, cars below and above the USD 30,000 threshold were not 'like products'.[103] Consequently, in the view of the Panel, different treatment could be accorded to cars above and below this threshold.[104]

In brief, after the extension of the scope of like products implied by the evolution from a restrictive to a broad objective definition of like products, the *aim-and-effect* theory resulted again in a more restrictive like products definition. The next evolution in the definition of likeness came from one of the very first reports of the new WTO dispute settlement system, the *Japan – Alcohol* case, which is examined next.

6.3.1.3.2   The *Japan – Alcohol II* Case

In the 1996 *Japan – Alcohol II* case, the relevance of the *aim-and-effects* theory arose. Both the Panel and the Appellate Body rejected it. The Appellate Body also moved away from a strict objective test, adopting an economic framework to define likeness, which focused on the competitive relationship between products on the market.[105] The Panel noted that the *US – Taxes on Automobiles* report had remained unadopted and did not therefore constitute subsequent practice. Moreover, the

---

[99] *US – Taxes on Automobiles*, Panel Report, para. 5.10.

[100] See *US – Taxes on Automobiles*, Panel Report, para. 5.12.

[101] *Ibid.*, para. 5.13.

[102] *Ibid.*, para. 5.14.

[103] *Ibid.*, para. 5.15.

[104] *Ibid.*

[105] See *infra*, 6.3.1.4.

Panel was of the view that the *aim-and-effects* test was inconsistent with the wording of Article III:2, first sentence, insofar as there was no explicit reference to the words 'so as to afford protection' in the text of that provision.[106] Another reason was the difficulty to assess the subjective intentions of the regulator because of the lack of access to the complete legislative history or the difficulty to determine which statements would be relevant.[107]

If the Appellate Body confirmed the reasoning of the Panel and thus the rejection of the *aim-and-effects* test, it did not directly elaborate on that issue. However, it explained its interpretation of the purpose of Article III, which is indirectly relevant since it was one of the main bases of the *aim-and-effects* test. The Appellate Body held:

> The broad and fundamental purpose of Article III is to avoid protectionism in the application of internal tax and regulatory measures. More specifically, the purpose of Article III 'is to ensure that internal measures "not be applied to imported or domestic products so as to afford protection to domestic production."' Towards this end, Article III obliges Members of the WTO to provide equality of competitive conditions for imported products in relation to domestic products. (. . .) [I]t is irrelevant that the 'trade effects' of the tax differential between imported and domestic products, as reflected in the volumes of imports, are insignificant or even non-existent; Article III protects expectations not of any particular trade volume but rather of the equal competitive relationship between imported and domestic products.[108]

If the Appellate Body did not make a direct correlation between these findings and its confirmation of the rejection of the *aim-and-effects* test, they were certainly relevant. While the *US – Malt Beverages* and *US – Taxes on Automobiles* Panels insisted on the 'limited purpose' of Article III[109] to justify an interpretation of likeness that would not prevent states from differentiating between different product categories for legitimate non-protectionist purposes, the Appellate Body in the *Japan – Alcohol II* report insisted on the 'broad purpose' of Article III, i.e. avoiding protectionism. First, in its view, Article III does not only guarantee that WTO Members will not undermine their tariff concessions through internal measures. The national treatment obligation also extends to products that are not subject to tariff concessions.[110] Second, whereas the *US – Taxes on Automobiles* Panel held that Article III did not prevent contracting parties to differentiate between different product categories 'for policy purposes unrelated to the protection of domestic production', the Appellate Body applied a much broader view that Article III protects expectations of the 'equal competitive relationship between imported and domestic products'.[111]

---

[106]*Japan – Alcohol*, Panel Report, para. 6.18.

[107]*Japan – Alcohol*, Panel Report, para. 6.16.

[108]*Japan – Alcohol II*, Appellate Body Report, p. 16.

[109]See *US – Malt Beverages*, Panel Report, para. 5.25; *US – Auto taxes*, Panel Report, para. 5.7.

[110]See *Japan – Alcohol II*, Appellate Body Report, p. 17.

[111]*Ibid.*, p. 16.

The formal rejection of the *aim-and-effects* test and the definition of the objective of Article III, which does not refer to the regulatory purpose of the measure but rather to the expectations of equal competitive relationship between products, seem to indicate that the Appellate Body has denied the relevance of the regulatory purpose of the measure in the likeness analysis. However, it will be illustrated below that scholarly debates on the influence of regulatory purpose in the likeness analysis are not over. Certain commentators interpret in fact case law as implying that the regulatory purpose does still implicitly play a role in the overall likeness assessment.

6.3.1.4 The Economic Approach

Since the very first reports of the new WTO dispute settlement system, the Appellate Body rejected the *aim-and-effects* theory.[112] It also moved away from a strict objective test,[113] adopting an economic framework to define likeness, which focuses on the competitive relationship between products on the market.

This economic framework applies to the three different cases covered by national treatment, namely Article III:2, first and second sentences, and Article III:4, even though the precise scope of each of these provisions differs to a certain extent.

The main principle on which the Appellate Body has relied to endorse an economic framework to the interpretation of Article III is the fundamental purpose of national treatment, namely to avoid protectionism in the application of internal fiscal and regulatory measures. This principle is embodied in Article III:1, which states that measures should not be applied so as to afford protection to domestic production.

Towards this end, Article III implies an obligation for WTO Members to provide 'equality of competitive conditions for imported products in relation to domestic products'.[114] The idea is that in the absence of any competitive relation between two products, a Member could not intervene through internal taxation or regulation to protect domestic production.[115] Thus, the Appellate Body considers that internal taxes and regulations should not be applied in a manner that affects the competitive relationship, in the marketplace, between domestic and imported products so as to afford protection to domestic production.[116]

Moreover, the Appellate Body stated that Article III protects *expectations* of the equal competitive conditions between imported and domestic products and not of

---

[112]See *supra*, 6.3.1.3.

[113]See *supra*, 6.3.1.2.

[114]*Japan – Alcohol II*, Appellate Body Report, p. 16; *EC – Asbestos*, Appellate Body Report, para. 98.

[115]See *EC – Asbestos*, Appellate Body Report, para. 117.

[116]*Ibid.*, para. 98 *in fine*.

any particular trade volume.[117] This view has important consequences since it implies that a measure may be regarded as protectionist and in violation of national treatment, even though there are no protectionist effects visible in actual trade flows.

This general principle should guide the interpretation of the other paragraphs of Article III. However, two textual differences give rise to difficulties in the interpretation of the conditions of this provision. First, only Article III:2, first sentence, contains an explicit reference to the general principle of Article III:1. Article III:2, second sentence, and Article III:4 do not. The Appellate Body has, however, stated that the general principle of the first paragraph 'informed' the rest of this provision, including Articles III:2, first sentence, and III:4.[118]

Second, the two sentences of Article III:2 use the different concepts of 'like' and 'directly competitive or substitutable' products, whereas Article III:4 refers only to the notion of 'like' product. It results in rather difficult distinctions on the definition and the scope of these different terms. It will, however, be shown that these different concepts are all interpreted by the Appellate Body within an economic framework and that the combined scope of the two sentences of Article III:2 is similar to the scope of Article III:4.

6.3.1.4.1 Article III:2, First Sentence

Fiscal measures of Article III:2 are subject either to the strict standard of the first sentence, which is applicable to 'like products' and prohibits any taxation of imported products 'in excess' of that applied to domestic like products, or to the less restrictive standard of the second sentence, which is applicable to 'directly competitive or substitutable' products and which forbids 'dissimilar' taxation, applied 'so as to afford protection to domestic production'. The Appellate Body stated that 'like' products, in the sense of Article III:2 first sentence, is a subset of 'directly competitive or substitutable' products, in the sense of Article III:2, second sentence.[119]

The concept of 'like products' has been interpreted *narrowly* in the context of Article III:2, first sentence.[120] The rationale is to protect 'like' products more strongly than 'directly competitive or substitutable' products. Under the first sentence, no additional taxation of imported products compared to 'like' domestic products is authorised, even very small one. By contrast, an infringement of Article

---

[117]See *Japan – Alcohol II*, Appellate Body Report, p. 16.

[118]*Ibid.*, p. 18. See also *EC – Asbestos*, Appellate Body Report, para. 98.

[119]See *Korea – Alcohol*, Appellate Body Report, para. 118.

[120]See *Japan – Alcohol II*, Panel Report, para. 6.22; *Korea – Alcohol*, Appellate Body Report, para. 118. The Panel in the *Thailand – Cigarettes (Philippines)* report, para. 7.438, even stated that 'the scope of likeness between imported and domestic products is to be construed *very* narrowly' (emphasis added).

III:2, second sentence, requires that the amount of differential taxation between 'directly competitive or substitutable' products be greater than *de minimis*.[121] Taxation must, in addition, be applied 'so as to afford protection to domestic production', unlike the first sentence, in which this condition is not examined independently.[122]

Therefore, the strict terms of the first sentence of Article III:2, which imply the 'inescapability of violation in case of taxation of foreign products in excess of like domestic products',[123] is counterbalanced by a narrow interpretation of 'like' products in order not to condemn measures that these strict terms 'are not meant to condemn'.[124]

Initially, jurisprudence considered that this narrow interpretation of likeness in the context of Article III:2 implied that the criterion of physical characteristics was particularly important and that likeness determination under this provision turned to a greater extent, although not exclusively, on the physical characteristics of products.[125] The *Korea – Alcohol* Panel stated that for two products to be considered 'like', they had to share 'essentially the same physical characteristics'.[126] Thus, relatively small differences in physical characteristics can be sufficient to consider products as unlike. For instance, with respect to alcohols, the use of different additives, ingredients or different appearances was deemed sufficient to render products unlike.[127] On the other hand, beet sugar and cane sugar were considered to be like because of an identical molecular structure, same end uses and consumers' perceptions that both products were almost identical and under the same tariff classification.[128]

More recently, the Appellate Body has endorsed an economic definition of likeness in Article III:2, reducing the importance of physical similarities or differences. It held in the *Philippines – Distilled Spirits* report that while a panel could start by examining the physical characteristics of the products, none of the criteria that a panel considers necessarily have an 'overarching role' under Article III:2. These criteria have to be examined 'in order to make a determination about the nature and extent of a competitive relationship between and among products'.[129] The Appellate Body added that products with very similar physical characteristics might not be like within the meaning of Article III:2 if their competitiveness or substitutability is low. Conversely, products that have certain physical differences

---

[121]See *Japan – Alcohol II*, Appellate Body Report, p. 27.

[122]*Ibid.*, p. 24.

[123]*Japan – Alcohol II*, Panel Report, para. 6.22.

[124]*Japan – Alcohol II*, Appellate Body Report, pp. 19 f. See also, Diebold (2010), p. 107.

[125]See *Korea – Alcohol*, Panel Report, para. 10.66.

[126]*Ibid.*

[127]See the *Japan – Alcohol II* reports. These products were however considered as directly competitive or substitutable and fell within Article III:2, second sentence.

[128]See *Mexico – Soft Drinks*, Panel Report, para. 8.27–8.36.

[129]*Philippines – Distilled Spirits*, Appellate Body Report, para. 119.

may still be considered like if such physical differences have a limited impact on the competitive relationship between and among products.[130]

Physical characteristics are thus not crucial in the likeness analysis under Article III:2, first sentence. They are only useful to assess, along with other criteria, the intensity of the competitive relationship between products. Certain reports stated that like products, within the meaning of the first sentence of Article III:2 encompassed 'perfectly' substitutable products, whereas directly competitive or substitutable products comprised 'imperfectly' substitutable products.[131] If the Appellate Body did not define 'perfect' substitutability, this finding shows that both 'like' and 'directly competitive or substitutable' products must be in a competitive relationship, which must be more intense in the former case than in the latter.

In brief, the Appellate Body has endorsed an economic definition of the notion of like products, in the sense of Article III:2, first sentence, which requires a particularly close competitive relationship between products.

6.3.1.4.2   Article III:2, Second Sentence

When it comes to defining 'directly competitive or substitutable' products in the sense of Article III:2, second sentence, WTO adjudicating bodies have mentioned products' physical characteristics, their tariff classifications and their common end uses as possible criteria.[132] However, the two first criteria are not decisive. The *Japan – Alcohol II* Panel stated that the wording of the terms 'directly competitive or substitutable' 'does not suggest at all that physical resemblance is required in order to establish whether two products fall under this category'.[133] The crucial criterion to determine if two products are directly competitive or substitutable is

---

[130]See *Philippines – Distilled Spirits*, Appellate Body Report, para. 120.

[131]See *Canada – Periodicals*, Appellate Body Report, p. 28; *Korea – Alcohol*, Appellate Body Report, para. 118. See however the Panel Report in the *Thailand – Cigarettes (Philippines)* case, para. 7.436, in which the Panel expressed the view that perfect substitutability could not be a necessary condition to establish 'likeness' under Article III:2 ('[a]lthough we agree that perfectly substitutable products will clearly be 'like products' within the meaning of Article III:2, first sentence, we do not consider that the Appellate Body meant to restrict the scope of like products to identical products. While this interpretation may be consistent with the economic definition of 'perfectly substitutable', it would render a finding of likeness under Article III:2, first sentence, almost impossible').

See also *Thailand – Cigarettes (Philippines)*, Panel Report, para. 7.447: 'the econometric studies put forward by the Philippines purport to prove the substitutability between all imported and all domestic cigarettes. The more convincing the evidence shows the substitutability between the cigarette brands concerned, the more likely the imported and domestic cigarettes are like within the meaning of Article III:2, because they show consumer habits and preferences that treat them alike.'

[132]See e.g. *Japan – Alcohol II*, Appellate Body Report, p. 25.

[133]*Japan – Alcohol II*, Panel Report, para. 6.22.

their end uses, which can be shown by their elasticity of substitution.[134] The word 'directly' suggests a degree of proximity in the competitive relationship between the domestic and the imported products.[135] More specifically, products are competitive or substitutable when they are interchangeable or if they offer alternative ways of satisfying a particular need or taste.[136]

The Appellate Body also emphasised the need to take into account not only extant demand but also latent demand. In other words, the Appellate Body refused to limit the analysis to situations in which consumers already regard products as alternatives. Otherwise, consumer behaviour could be influenced by protectionist internal taxation. Examining only extant competition could lead to the result that a protectionist measure could create or freeze preferences for domestic products.[137] These preferences could then justify trade-restrictive measures and thus defeat national treatment purpose. Consequently, particularly in a market where regulatory barriers to trade exist, the Appellate Body found that there may well be latent demand,[138] and in some cases, it might be 'highly relevant' to examine it.[139]

As a result, the Appellate Body refused to consider cross-price elasticity as *the* decisive criterion in determining whether two products are directly competitive or substitutable.[140] WTO adjudicating bodies have been therefore reluctant to rely extensively on quantitative analyses of the competitive relationship between products and have rather focused on the 'quality' or 'nature' of the competition (which means examining both existing and potential demand).[141]

In brief, the Appellate Body has endorsed a view in which both 'like' products and 'directly competitive or substitutable' products are economic concepts.[142] Both require an examination of the competitive relationship between products. Like products are a subset of directly competitive or substitutable products, which means that they require a particularly close competitive relationship and possibly that they should share most physical characteristics. The Appellate Body has, however, not drawn a precise line between these two categories or products, which thus remains to a large extent to the discretion of panels in each individual case. In addition, the Appellate Body has not endorsed a purely economic approach

---

[134]See *Japan – Alcohol II,* Panel Report, para. 6.22; *Japan – Alcohol II*, Appellate Body Report, p. 26; *Korea – Alcohol*, Panel Report, para. 10.4.

[135]See *Korea – Alcohol*, Appellate Body Report, para. 116.

[136]See *Korea – Alcohol*, Panel Report, para. 10.40; *Korea – Alcohol*, Appellate Body Report, para. 115. Thus, the Panel stated that because of their limited financial resources, consumers may have to arbitrate between different needs, such as giving up going on a vacation to buy a car or abstaining from eating in restaurants to buy new shoes or a television set. This would not be regarded as a 'direct' competitive relationship.

[137]See *Japan – Alcohol II*, Panel Report, para. 6.28.

[138]See *Korea – Alcohol*, Appellate Body Report, para. 115, 116 and 120.

[139]See *Korea – Alcohol*, Appellate Body Report, para. 120 *in fine*.

[140]See *Japan – Alcohol II*, Appellate Body Report, p. 25; *Korea – Alcohol*, Appellate Body Report, para. 134.

[141]See *Korea – Alcohol*, Appellate Body Report, para. 132 ff.

[142]See Diebold (2010), p. 108; Vranes (2009), pp. 197 ff.

based on econometric instruments, which means that the analysis of whether two products are like or directly competitive or substitutable is largely left to the discretion of panels and to their overall assessment of the relevant factors.

6.3.1.4.3 Article III:4

When it comes to regulatory measures, Article III:4 only refers to 'like' products and not to 'directly competitive or substitutable' products. However, there are no sharp differences between fiscal and non-fiscal regulation because both forms of regulation can achieve the same ends.[143] Hence, the Appellate Body stated that the notion of like products is broader in Article III:4 than in Article III:2. It held, moreover, that the scope of like products in Article III:4 is *not broader* than the combined scope of the 'like' and 'directly competitive or substitutable' products in Article III:2.[144] This arguably means that the scope of like products in Article III:4 is *essentially the same* as the scope of the combined scope of like products and directly competitive or substitutable products in Article III:2.[145] The Appellate Body intends to avoid that differences in the scope of these two provisions would mean that Members were prevented from using one form of regulation (fiscal, for instance) to protect domestic production but were allowed to use another form of regulation (non-fiscal, for instance) to achieve the same objectives.[146]

The approach applied by the Appellate Body for the definition of like products in Article III:4 is thus an economic approach. The Appellate Body held that 'a determination of "likeness" under Article III:4 is, fundamentally, a determination about the nature and extent of a competitive relationship between and among products'.[147] Thus, it is important 'to take account of evidence which indicate[s] whether and to what extent, the products involved are—or could be—in a competitive relationship in the marketplace'.[148] The Appellate Body did not indicate which degree of competitiveness or substitutability is required in the abstract for a finding of likeness under Article III:4.[149]

---

[143]See *EC – Asbestos*, Appellate Body Report, para. 99.

[144]*Ibid.*

[145]See Quick and Lau (2003), pp. 428 f. (arguing that case law suggests 'that notwithstanding their different wording, the product scope of both provisions is identical'); Mavroidis (2000), pp. 133 f.; Vranes (2009), pp. 199 f. ('the scopes of both provisions should essentially be identical'); Diebold (2010), p. 115, stating that 'the Appellate Body implicitly confirmed that [the breadth of "like products"] should be essentially identical to the breadth of "directly competitive or substitutable products"'.

[146]See *EC – Asbestos*, Appellate Body Report, para. 99.

[147]*EC – Asbestos*, Appellate Body Report, para. 99.

[148]*Ibid.*, para. 103.

[149]The Appellate Body stated that it was 'mindful that there is a spectrum of degrees of "competitiveness" or "substitutability" of products in the marketplace, and that it is difficult, if not impossible, in the abstract, to indicate precisely where on this spectrum the word "like" in Article III:4 of the GATT 1994 falls' (*EC – Asbestos*, Appellate Body Report, para. 99).

The Appellate Body recalled that it is necessary to examine *all* relevant evidence in the determination of likeness and not only one or some of the criteria mentioned in the *Border Tax Adjustment* report.[150] Other factors, not included in this list, may also be taken into account, although the Appellate Body did not provide any example. Indeed, the Appellate Body noted that neither the text of Article III:4 nor the practice of panels and the Appellate Body suggested that any evidence should be excluded *a priori* from a panel's examination of 'likeness'.[151] Then a panel should make an *overall* determination of whether the products at issue must be characterised as 'like'.[152]

Two criteria seem, however, to be particularly relevant in the view of the Appellate Body in this assessment of the competitive relationship between goods: products' end uses and consumers' tastes and habits, which involve certain of the 'key elements' relating to the competitive relationship between products in the marketplace.[153] These criteria may show the extent to which products can serve the same end uses and the extent to which consumers are willing to choose one product instead of another to perform those end uses.[154]

With respect to the criterion of consumers' tastes and habits, the Appellate Body has seemingly considered that it played an important part in the *EC – Asbestos* report. However, it did not rely on any empirical econometric studies but simply depended on its own assumptions of how consumers would react. The Appellate Body thus held that it was persuaded that evidence relating to consumers' tastes and habits *would* establish that the health risks involved influence consumers' behaviour. It was of the view that consumers' tastes and habits were 'very likely (. . .) to be shaped by health risks associated with a product which is known to be highly carcinogenic'.[155] Thus, in this case, the Appellate Body did not rely or require any

---

[150]See *EC – Asbestos*, Appellate Body Report, para. 109. The Panel had examined only physical properties and end-uses of products but dismissed the relevance of the two other criteria.

[151]See *EC – Asbestos*, Appellate Body Report, para. 113.

[152]*Ibid.*, para. 109.

[153]*Ibid.*, para. 117.

[154]*Ibid.*

[155]*Ibid.*, para. 122: 'In this case especially, we are also persuaded that evidence relating to consumers' tastes and habits *would* establish that the health risks associated with chrysotile asbestos fibres influence consumers' behaviour with respect to the different fibres at issue. We observe that, as regards chrysotile asbestos and PCG fibres, the consumer of the fibres is a manufacturer who incorporates the fibres into another product, such as cement-based products or brake linings. We do not wish to speculate on what the evidence regarding these consumers would have indicated; rather, we wish to highlight that consumers' tastes and habits regarding fibres, even in the case of commercial parties, such as manufacturers, are *very likely* to be shaped by the health risks associated with a product which is known to be highly carcinogenic. A manufacturer cannot, for instance, ignore the preferences of the ultimate consumer of its products. If the risks posed by a particular product are sufficiently great, the ultimate consumer *may simply cease to buy* that product. This *would*, undoubtedly, affect a manufacturer's decisions in the marketplace. Moreover, in the case of products posing risks to human health, we think it *likely* that manufacturers' decisions will be influenced by other factors, such as the potential civil liability that might flow from marketing products posing a health risk to the ultimate consumer, or the

empirical evidence of the consumers' tastes and habits. This shows that recourse to econometric indicators establishing the products' substitutability is not necessarily required. In that sense, the Appellate Body has *not* endorsed a purely economic approach, in which likeness would be defined by the competitive relationship between products, determined by econometric instruments.

6.3.1.4.4 Likeness and Differences in PPMs

As it will be explained in the next chapter, the *US – Shrimp* case, which was factually quite comparable to the *US – Tuna* cases as far as the PPM debate is concerned, showed that PPM measures were not, as such, GATT illegal and could be justified in certain circumstances under Article XX. In the *US – Shrimp* case, the United States did not argue that its measure complied with national treatment, and Article III was thus not examined. No clarifications were thus brought in this case concerning the definition of like products and the relevance of PPM differences.

The endorsement of an economic approach has, however, had important implicit consequences on the relevance of differences in production methods in the likeness analysis. Indeed, the focus on the consumers' perspective logically means that products with different PPMs could be regarded as unlike if consumers treat them as unlike, which, in the view of this author, implicitly rejects the relevance of the product-process distinction. Physical identity between two products, in other words, does not necessarily entail an obligation to treat them the same way. This viewpoint is widely shared in academic writings,[156] even though it is also often pointed out that there would probably be few situations in which enough consumers would indeed distinguish physically identical products on the basis of their PPM to make them 'unlike'.[157]

The findings of the Appellate Body in the *US – Tuna II (Mexico)* case also tend to confirm this conclusion. This case was examined not under GATT Article III but under the TBT Agreement, in particular TBT Article 2.1, the equivalent of GATT Article III.[158] The Appellate Body noted that the tuna products at issue shared common physical characteristics and properties, end uses and tariff classifications, which was not surprising since they were 'in essence the same products, processed in a different country'.[159] Yet the Appellate Body also recognised that the

---

additional costs associated with safety procedures required to use such products in the manufacturing process' (emphasis added).

[156]See Bronckers and McNelis (2000), p. 376; Marceau and Trachtman (2002), p. 859 and note 181, p. 858; Quick and Lau (2003), p. 431; Pauwelyn (2004), p. 586; Green (2005), p. 160; Vranes (2009), p. 324; Conrad (2011), p. 227; Marceau and Trachtman (2014), p. 412.

[157]See Marceau and Trachtman (2002), p. 859; Quick and Lau (2003), p. 432; Vranes (2009), p. 324; Marceau and Trachtman (2014), p. 412.

[158]See *infra*, 8.2.

[159]*US – Tuna II (Mexico)*, Appellate Body Report, para. 7.249.

information brought to the Panel suggested that US consumers had certain preferences with respect to tuna products based on their dolphin-safe status. It then held:

> We do not exclude that such preferences may be relevant to an assessment of likeness. To the extent that consumer preferences, including preferences relating to the manner in which the product has been obtained, may have an impact on the competitive relationship between these products, we consider it a priori relevant to take them into consideration in an assessment of the likeness.[160]

The Appellate Body did not conclude, however, that, in the circumstances of the case, consumer preferences to the dolphin-safe status of tuna products did lead to a finding that these products were not like.

It seems likely that the Appellate Body would apply a similar approach in the context of GATT Article III, which means that consumer preferences could *in theory* render two products unlike. The requirements for consumer preferences to outweigh the other criteria might, however, be difficult to meet. This seems true in particular for 'producers characteristics standard' (measure requiring that the producers have certain characteristics) and 'government policy standard' (measure prescribing the adoption of certain environmental policies by the exporting country),[161] which seems unlikely to be reflected in consumers' preferences, in practice.

6.3.1.5 Conclusion

In conclusion, the Appellate Body has rejected both the objective approach and the *aim-and-effects* theory and has endorsed an economic definition of 'like' and 'directly competitive or substitutable' products both under Article III:2, first and second sentences, and under Article III:4. Likeness is determined by assessing the intensity of the competitive relationship between products, through the examination of all relevant circumstances. In practice, panels and the Appellate Body have focused on the four traditional criteria for determining likeness, without formally giving a preeminent weight to one of them.

The focus on the consumers' perspective means that products with different PPMs could be regarded as unlike if consumers treat them as unlike, which results implicitly in a rejection of the product-process distinction, as argued above.[162]

The Appellate Body has not adopted a 'purely' economic approach since it has refused to give a predominant importance to econometric instruments to define likeness, which means that likeness determination remains a qualitative assessment of all the relevant evidence rather than a pure quantitative test of substitutability.

GATT and WTO case law on like products has evolved, fluctuated and may not always be entirely clear. As the next section shows, it has thus given rise to many scholarly debates on the definition of like products.

---

[160]*Ibid.*

[161]This taxonomy of PPM measures has been suggested by Charnovitz (2002), p. 67.

[162]See *supra*, 6.3.1.4.4.

6.3.2 Scholarly Debates on 'Like Products'

The definition of likeness has been a very controversial issue in academic writings. Certain commentators argue that case law contains some indication that WTO adjudicating bodies take the regulatory purpose into account in the likeness examination and that it should in any case do so (Sect. 6.3.2.1). Others contend that a coherent economic approach to like products requires a systematic use of econometric instruments, which should play a decisive role in the likeness analysis (Sect. 6.3.2.2).

6.3.2.1 The Regulatory Purpose Approach

6.3.2.1.1 Proponents

The Appellate Body clearly rejected the *aim-and-effects* test in the *EC – Asbestos* report.[163] However, some commentators argue that the Appellate Body has continued to a certain extent—or at least should continue—to take the regulatory purpose into account in the examination of likeness.[164] Even if the regulatory purpose approach has several forms, which slightly vary, the central elements of this theory seem to be shared. The main fear of proponents of the regulatory purpose approach is that the interpretation of Article III results in a too large national treatment scope, restricting excessively WTO Members' regulatory autonomy, in particular, in cases of *de facto* discrimination.[165]

It has also been argued that this theory is a solution to the issue of the closed list of public interests that may justify an otherwise inconsistent measure under Article XX[166] since any legitimate non-protectionist policy could potentially lead to a conclusion that two products are not 'like' under Article III. Moreover, the proponents of this approach maintain that examining the regulatory purpose in Article III would not render Article XX *inutile* since this provision could still be used to justify cases of *de jure* discrimination or to defend violations of a number of other GATT provisions.[167]

---

[163] See *supra*, 6.3.1.4.

[164] See Howse and Regan (2000), p. 266 ('in its discussion of "affording protection", the Appellate Body in *Japanese Alcohol* may or may not have rejected the "aims and effects test", but it clearly did not reject consideration of aims and effects'). See also in particular Regan (2002), p. 443; Hudec (1998), pp. 619 ff.; Horn and Weiler (2003), pp. 25 ff.; Roessler (2003), pp. 771 ff.

[165] See Hudec (1998), p. 623; Diebold (2010), pp. 79 f.; Conrad (2011), p. 220. More generally, on the issue of the evolution of case law and its consequences on the intrusiveness of National Treatment, see e.g. DiMascio and Pauwelyn (2008), pp. 62 ff.

[166] See Roessler (2003), pp. 777 ff.; Hudec (1998), pp. 626 ff.; Howse and Regan (2000), pp. 260 f.; Regan (2002), p. 454.

[167] See Pauwelyn (2008), p. 368; Howse and Regan (2000), p. 266; Regan (2002), pp. 454 f.; Conrad (2011), p. 221. The Appellate Body held in *Asbestos* that the health risks were relevant in Article III in assessing the competitive relationship in the marketplace between allegedly like

Some share the view of the two GATT 1947 panels that have developed the *aim-and-effects* test, according to which Article III does not prevent WTO Members to use internal regulations for other purposes than the protection of domestic production, even if it implies distinguishing between several categories of products.[168] The main basis of this theory is that Article III should prohibit only measures that are discriminatory and have a protectionist purpose[169] but not measures that distinguish between products for legitimate non-protectionist reasons, which could, for instance, be the environmental impact of the product concerned, including the impact caused by their production processes. Proponents of the regulatory purpose approach contend that the legitimacy of the measure should be examined in the likeness analysis. Two products that could be physically identical but that would have notable differences from the viewpoint of a non-protectionist policy, for instance because one of them is produced in a much more polluting way, could thus be qualified as unlike. Howse and Regan have thus suggested that likeness should be defined as meaning that two products are 'not differing in any respect relevant to an actual non-protectionist policy'.[170]

This would not necessarily mean that panels could not examine in a first stage whether the products at issue are in a competitive relationship on the market.[171] Regan has, however, suggested that the existence of a competitive relationship should not be a sufficient condition for a finding of likeness. It is necessary in his opinion to additionally show that products are 'not distinguished by any non-protectionist policy which actually underlies the challenged regulation'.[172] Such non-protectionist policy could demonstrate that products are distinguished in order not to protect domestic products but rather, for instance, to favour environmental-friendly products. In the view of Regan, this examination intends not to determine the individual motivation of the legislator but to show which political forces are responsible for the final result, be it environmental or consumers' protection groups or industrial groups seeking a competitive advantage.[173]

A slightly different alternative to this approach is the one presented, in particular, by Horn and Weiler. They point out that any case of non-discrimination embodies explicitly or implicitly a comparator[174] (*tertium comparationis*), which

---

products and that they served in Article XX(b) the purpose of assessing whether a Member has a sufficient basis for adopting and enforcing a WTO inconsistent measure on the grounds of human health (*EC – Asbestos*, Appellate Body, para. 115).

[168]See Roessler (2003), pp. 773 f. (the purpose of Article III 'is to prevent internal measures imposed "so as to afford protection". It is not intended to curtail the exercise of the regulatory freedom of WTO Members for any other purpose'); Regan (2002), pp. 450 f. See also *US – Malt Beverages*, Panel Report, para. 5.25.

[169]See Howse and Regan (2000), p. 253; Sykes (1999), pp. 1 ff.; Regan (2002), p. 451.

[170]Howse and Regan (2000), p. 260.

[171]See Regan (2003), p. 752; Trebilcock et al. (2013), p. 169.

[172]Regan (2003), p. 752. See also Horn and Weiler (2003), p. 23; Trebilcock et al. (2013), p. 169.

[173]See Regan (2002), pp. 458 ff.

[174]See Horn and Weiler (2003), p. 25.

can be defined as the quality or element that two situations or objects should have in common for the conclusion that they are 'alike' for the purpose of the comparison.[175] Generally, non-discrimination prohibitions exclude certain factors as illegitimate comparators, such as gender, race, religion or nationality,[176] without, however, defining all the comparators upon which distinctions may be freely made (such as education, skill or experience in cases of gender discrimination). In the context of Article III, the Appellate Body seems to have defined implicitly the comparator that is relevant, in its view, in the likeness analysis, namely the competitive relationship between products.[177] Some point out that the competitive relationship may not always be the adequate comparator and that, in certain circumstances, this very comparator should be put in question by examining if other criteria should not be used for the basis of the comparison.[178] After all, national treatment is concerned with discrimination—both *de jure* and *de facto*—based on origin.[179] Thus, the only comparator prohibited by Article III is national origin.[180]

Thus, Horn and Weiler suggest that a possible approach would be to require first a complaint establishing a *prima facie* violation of Article III, in the form of an alleged discriminatory treatment of products in competition. In a second phase, the regulating state could have the opportunity to challenge the very market comparator and show that an alternative comparator, such as ecological efficiency, is the implicit comparator of the contested measure, not market functionality. Therefore, products should not be considered like in such circumstances.[181] It will also be shown below that some commentators share the view that the real issue concerns the comparator underlying the measure (the only prohibited one being national origin) but consider that the examination of this comparator should intervene in the less favourable treatment analysis and not in the like product context.[182] It has been noted that consideration of the regulatory purpose could even come in theory as a separate third step of the non-discrimination analysis but that Article III lacks a textual basis for such an approach.[183]

Some of the proponents of the regulatory purpose approach do not only support the view that the policy objective underlying the measure *should* be examined in the

---

[175]See Diebold (2010), p. 69.

[176]See Horn and Weiler (2003), p. 25; Pauwelyn (2008), p. 361.

[177]See Horn and Weiler (2003), p. 25; Diebold (2010), p. 70.

[178]See Horn and Weiler (2003), p. 26; Diebold (2010), p. 78; Mavroidis (2012), p. 302.

[179]See Pauwelyn (2008), p. 363.

[180]*Ibid.*, p. 361.

[181]See Horn and Weiler (2003), p. 26. See also Mavroidis (2012), p. 302, submitting that two products should be regarded as like 'if they are both market and policy like'.

[182]See Pauwelyn (2008), pp. 358 ff. He also argues that one should not attempt to define all the criteria that could be relied on legitimately to distinguish two products but that one should rather focus on the real issue of whether the only forbidden comparator of national origin has been used. See *infra*, 6.4.3.3.

[183]See Diebold (2010), p. 83.

likeness analysis but also argue that the Appellate Body *does* take the regulatory purpose into account in its jurisprudence. There are two main aspects of case law on which they rely.

The *first* concerns the definition of like products itself. The Appellate Body clearly stated that it analyses likeness by examining the competition relationship between products. Yet it seems that certain elements pertaining to the regulatory purpose influence this analysis. With respect to Article III:2, the Appellate Body has been reluctant to use econometric instruments to analyse the competitive relationship and has refused to make cross-price elasticity *the* decisive criterion in determining whether two products are 'directly competitive or substitutable'.[184] It has also held that potential competition and data from other markets could be relevant in this analysis.[185] In the view of certain commentators, this shift from an economic notion of substitutability to a juridical conception of competitive equality looks, in some respects, like the *aim-and-effects* test 'or at least views the issue of competition as a normative question about whether consumers ought to look at two products as substitutable given their preferences and needs, rather than as an empirical economic question about revealed consumer behaviour'.[186]

This may be a bold conclusion insofar as the Appellate Body does not to refer—explicitly at least—to the regulatory purpose in this case. But a similar tendency is more clearly formulated in the context of Article III:4. In the *Asbestos* report, the Appellate Body relied not on econometric studies either but simply on its own assumptions of how consumers would react in relation to the health risks associated with asbestos. The Appellate Body thus stated that it was 'persuaded that evidence relating to consumers' tastes and habits would establish that the health risks associated with chrysotile asbestos fibres influence consumers' behaviour with respect to the different fibres at issue'.[187] It further noted that consumers' tastes and habits were 'very likely' to be shaped by the health risks associated with a product that is known to be highly carcinogenic and that 'in case of products posing risks to human health, we think it likely that manufacturers' decisions will be influenced by other factors, such as potential civil liability that might flow from marketing products posing a health risk to the ultimate consumer'.[188]

Certain commentators consider that, in these findings, the Appellate Body examined the perspective of consumers in an *idealised* marketplace, in which consumers have full information and where negative externalities have been internalised through tort law. In doing so, it has been argued that the Appellate Body has taken into account the kind of regulatory interests that were considered through the *aim-and-effects* test, the difference being that those interests are taken into consideration by adopting not the perspective of the regulator as such but the

---

[184]See *Korea – Alcohol*, Appellate Body, para. 134.

[185]*Ibid.*, para. 115 f. and 135 ff.

[186]Trebilcock et al. (2013), p. 149.

[187]*EC – Asbestos*, Appellate Body, para. 122.

[188]*Ibid.* (emphasis added).

perspective of consumer preferences in an idealised marketplace.[189] Through this concept, the Appellate Body would have 'through the back door' brought into the picture regulatory interests.[190]

It could also be noted that, in the same *EC – Asbestos* report, even though the Appellate Body relied on the four traditional criteria to define likeness, it also held as follows:

> [I]n examining the 'likeness' of products, Panels must evaluate all of the relevant evidence. We are very much of the view that evidence relating to the health risks associated with a product may be pertinent in an examination of 'likeness' under Article III:4 of the GATT 1994.[191]

This statement seems to imply that the underlying policy—in this case, health concerns related to a known carcinogenic substance—may to a certain extent be taken into account in the likeness examination.[192] It may be conceded that the Appellate Body also held that the evidence relating to health risks associated with chrysotile asbestos fibres did not need to be examined under a *separate* criterion but that it could be evaluated under the criteria of physical properties and of consumers' tastes and habits.[193] Yet, in this case, it was indeed the *underlying policy* of health protection that made certain physical differences between products (implying the carcinogenicity of asbestos) 'highly significant' in the determination of likeness.[194]

A *second* argument of commentators who claim that the Appellate Body does take the regulatory purpose into account in the likeness analysis concerns the interpretation of the phrase 'so as to afford protection' of Article III:1. The Appellate Body has held that the objective purpose of the measure (and not the subjective intent of the legislator) was relevant in the assessment of whether a measure is applied 'so as to afford protection to domestic production' under Article III:1.[195] On the other hand, the Appellate Body stated that Article III:1 'informs' the

---

[189]See Trebilcock et al. (2013), p. 161; Howse and Tuerk (2001), p. 301.

[190]See Trebilcock et al. (2013), p. 161.

[191]*EC – Asbestos*, Appellate Body, para. 113.

[192]See Howse and Tuerk (2001), p. 300; Conrad (2011), p. 239 (pointing out that 'it seems that the Appellate Body at this point makes concessions to the aim and effects doctrine, which considers the genuineness of the underlying policies, such as health policies, as crucial in the determination of likeness'. She argues however that differences in physical characteristics would have been sufficient to consider the products at issue as unlike in this case).

[193]See *EC – Asbestos*, Appellate Body, para. 113.

[194]*Ibid.*, para. 114.

[195]See *Japan – Alcohol II*, Appellate Body Report, p. 29. In this case, the Appellate Body held that '[a]lthough it is true that the aim of a measure may not be easily ascertained, nevertheless its protective application can most often be discerned from the design, the architecture, and the revealing structure of a measure'.
In the view of Hudec, 'protective application' was 'a concept that for all the world looked like an objective analysis of regulatory purpose' (Hudec 1998, p. 631). Sharing Hudec's view, see also Howse and Regan (2000), p. 265 ('"[p]rotective application" seems very much a matter of the best understanding of the apparent purpose, gleaned from objective evidence') and Regan (2002), p. 477 (who adds that 'what may be "revealed" by contemplation of the measure's design,

different sub-paragraphs of this provision.[196] The Appellate Body held in the *EC – Asbestos* report that, therefore, 'the term "like product" in Article III:4 must be interpreted to give proper scope and meaning to this principle'.[197] Some have thus concluded on this basis that the regulatory purpose is relevant in the examination of likeness under Article III:4.[198]

However, the meaning of the Appellate Body's reference to the objective purpose of the measure is debated. Some argue that the Appellate Body has focused, in practice, on whether measures were *objectively capable* of producing competitive effects on imported products rather than on protectionist intent.[199] In any case, it is doubtful that the Appellate Body meant that its developments on the principle of Article III:1 could be applied directly to the definition of likeness itself since the Appellate Body has not examined explicitly the regulatory purpose in the likeness analysis in the *EC – Asbestos* report[200] and since it has clearly rejected the *aim-and-effects* test. It should indeed be pointed out that this theory was precisely based on the same argument, i.e. that Article III:1 required that likeness be assessed in the light of the aim of the measure. But in any event, if the objective purpose of the measure may have an influence on the national treatment analysis, it does not necessarily mean that it should be examined in the likeness condition. It may seem more coherent to take the regulatory purpose into account in the discriminatory treatment conditions.

---

architecture, and "revealing" structure is protectionist purpose'). See also *Chile – Alcohol*, Appellate Body, para. 62: '[w]e emphasized in that Report that, in examining the issue of "so as to afford protection", "it is not necessary for a Panel to sort through the many reasons legislators and regulators often have for what they do and weigh the relative significance of those reasons to establish legislative or regulatory intent." The subjective intentions inhabiting the minds of individual legislators or regulators do not bear upon the inquiry, if only because they are not accessible to treaty interpreters. It does not follow, however, that the statutory purposes or objectives—that is, the purpose or objectives of a Member's legislature and government as a whole—to the extent that they are given objective expression in the statute itself, are not pertinent.'

[196]See *Japan – Alcohol II*, Appellate Body Report, p. 18.

[197]*EC – Asbestos*, Appellate Body Report, para. 98.

[198]In the view of Regan, since the Appellate Body held that in interpreting Article III:4, it is necessary to take into account the policy laid down in Article III:1, under which measures should not be applied so as to afford protection, and since the Appellate Body interpreted Article III:1 as implying the examination of 'the purposes or objectives of a Member's legislature and government as a whole' (*Chile-Alcohol*, Appellate Body Report para. 62), panels must consider the regulatory purpose of the measure under review in their examination of Article III:4; see Regan (2002), p. 443.

[199]See Vranes (2009), pp. 244 and 247. In the view of the present author, if the Appellate Body's findings concerned may not be entirely clear, it would however seem rather odd that the Appellate Body would exclude explicitly the subjective intent of the legislator, while indicating that the objective purpose is 'intensely' pertinent (*Chile – Alcohol*, Appellate Body Report, para. 71), if the Appellate Body simply meant that the phrase 'so as to afford protection' is only concerned with competitive effects. Moreover, it seems artificial to examine a non-discrimination provision without ever examining the regulatory purpose.

[200]See Vranes (2009), pp. 212 f. He also opposes this interpretation because in his view the Appellate Body simply referred to Article III:1 to make it clear that competitive relations between domestic and imported products are particularly important in the determination of likeness.

With respect to Article III:2, first sentence, the Appellate Body held that 'the presence of a protective application need not be established separately from the specific requirements that are included in the first sentence in order to show that a tax measure is inconsistent with the general principle set out in the first sentence'.[201] It seems therefore more difficult to contend that the regulatory purpose should be taken into account in this case, even though certain commentators do maintain such view.[202]

In brief, the regulatory purpose approach has been seen as a way to relax the restrictiveness of trade rules, in particular, in cases of *de facto* discrimination.[203] Certain commentators interpret current case law as requiring implicitly the examination of the regulatory purpose in the likeness analysis. However, this interpretation has not been clearly endorsed by the Appellate Body and is quite controversial, as it will be shown in the next section.

The regulatory purpose approach does not focus directly on the legality of PPM measures. Clearly, however, the endorsement of this theory would give WTO Members more leeway to distinguish products sold on their internal market on the basis of legitimate reasons, including the cases in which the PPMs used by a set of similar products have a different environmental impact.

6.3.2.1.2 Opponents

Many scholars and trade practitioners have rejected the regulatory purpose approach, for different reasons. One of the most controversial issues related to national treatment is the scope that this principle should have. While proponents of the regulatory purpose approach argue that the economic approach restricts too much WTO Members' regulatory autonomy, its opponents assert that this theory unduly restricts the scope of Article III, in a way that prevents national treatment to fulfil properly its function to prevent covert protectionism. Some argue that in order to guarantee the expectations of equal competitive conditions between imported and domestic products, Article III must focus on discriminatory effects and not on the regulatory purpose.[204] With a similar concern in mind, it has been often argued that examining the aim of the measure in Article III would render the exhaustive list of the general exceptions of Article XX *inutile*.[205] At the same time, it is often contended that it would allow the achievement of other public interests to the detriment of free trade, which would contradict the intentions of GATT negotiators

---

[201] *Japan – Alcohol II*, Appellate Body Report, p. 18.

[202] See e.g. Regan (2002), pp. 471 ff.

[203] See e.g. Hudec (1998), p. 631.

[204] See e.g. Vranes (2009), pp. 203 f. *et passim*.

[205] See *Japan – Alcohol II*, Panel Report, para. 6.17. See also Bronckers and McNelis (2000), p. 371.

through judicial activism.[206] A fear exists among free traders that taking the regulatory purpose into account could jeopardise the fundamental objective of the GATT to counter protectionist measures unrelated to any environmental concerns.[207]

More precisely, opponents of the regulatory purpose approach point out that entrusting panels with the task of deciding subjectively which criteria are relevant for distinguishing products in the light of the regulatory purpose would give rise to important concerns relating to a lack of security and predictability.[208] It is true that in the constitutional structure of the WTO, the checks and balances between the 'judicial' and the 'legislative' branches do not work the same way as they do in a traditional internal state system, in which the parliament can correct tribunals' interpretations by changing the applicable laws. Achieving a consensus among WTO Members, in order to modify the covered agreements or to adopt a formal interpretation, has proved to be very challenging. This can explain in part the reluctance of WTO Members to approaches mostly based on teleological rather than textual interpretations since they may be politically perceived as undue judicial activism, even though this may not be correct from a strictly legal viewpoint.

Problems related to the practical difficulty to determine the regulatory purpose are also pointed out. It has been maintained that the regulating state often pursues simultaneously multiple aims, which makes the identification of the genuine regulatory purpose difficult.[209] The burden of proving the aim, like all other relevant facts, would be on the complainant, who does not necessarily have access to the relevant legislative history.[210] It might also lead to the undesirable outcome that a particular measure would be allowed in a WTO Member because its aims were considered authentic, while it would be prohibited in another WTO member because of considerable doubts about the real motivation.[211] Some also fear that assessing which purposes are legitimate, in the absence of any list of policy objectives comparable to that of Article XX, would be problematic and would imply entrusting panels and the Appellate Body with the task of determining which criteria for distinguishing between products are acceptable and thus which purposes are legitimate, in the process or making a decision on likeness.[212]

---

[206]See Diebold (2010), pp. 78 f.; Mavroidis (2000), p. 130. See also Matsushita et al. (2015), stating that the 'major problem' with the regulatory purpose approach 'is that it opens the door too wide. Every kind of PPM, no matter how irrational or silly, may be permitted'.

[207]See Bronckers and McNelis (2000), p. 371.

[208]See Gaines (2002), p. 426; Conrad (2011), p. 221.

[209]See *Japan – Alcohol II*, Panel Report, para. 6.16. See also Cottier and Oesch (2005), p. 407; Vranes (2009), p. 205; Diebold (2010), p. 78.

[210]See *Japan – Alcohol II*, Panel Report, para. 6.16. See also Trebilcock et al. (2013), p. 146.

[211]Conrad (2011), p. 221. However, the focus on the objective purpose of the measure and the exclusion of the subjective intent would arguably reduce such a risk.

[212]See Davey and Pauwelyn (2000), p. 38; Diebold (2010), p. 78; Conrad (2011), pp. 221 f.

It is also sometimes argued that Article III lacks the textual basis for the consideration of regulatory purpose.[213] This argument is, however, not convincing since the words 'so as to' may be interpreted as referring both to intent and effects,[214] or at least are ambiguous.[215] Moreover, there is in any case no clear guidance from the text of Article III, which means that a teleological interpretation must prevail.[216] All the controversies on the scope of Article III and on the definition of like products are precisely based on differing views on the purpose of national treatment, i.e. on a teleological interpretation. Such interpretation does not necessarily exclude the examination of regulatory purpose.

Finally, some point out that the objective of the *aim-and-effects* theory is to adopt less stringent standards in cases of *de facto* discrimination but that other, more adequate, approaches exist, such as to interpret the conditions of Article XX more broadly[217] or to examine the regulatory purpose in the less favourable treatment condition of Article III.[218]

6.3.2.2 The Pure Economic Approach

6.3.2.2.1 Proponents

As it has been shown above, the Appellate Body has seemingly adopted an economic approach to define like products, in which a determination of likeness is 'fundamentally a determination about the nature and extent of a competitive relationship between and among products'.[219] At the same time, the Appellate Body refused both in the context of the 'directly competitive and substitutable products' of Article III:2, second sentence, and in that of 'like products' of Article III:4, to rely predominantly or exclusively on quantitative analyses of the competitive relationship among products and thus to make cross-price elasticity the decisive criterion in this analysis.[220]

Some have submitted that relying solely on the criterion of consumers' tastes and habits in such a way poses risks of protectionist abuses.[221] Many commentators

---

[213]See *Japan – Alcohol II*, Panel Report, para. 6.16. See also Bronckers and McNelis (2000), p. 371; Hudec (1998), p. 628.

[214]*US – Taxes on Automobiles*, Panel Report, para. 5.10 ('[t]he Panel noted that the term "so as to" suggested both aim and effect').

[215]See Vranes (2009), p. 243.

[216]See Conrad (2011), p. 221.

[217]See Vranes (2009), p. 214 *et passim*.

[218]See Pauwelyn (2008), pp. 358 ff.

[219]*EC – Asbestos*, Appellate Body Report, para. 99.

[220]See *Korea – Alcohol*, Appellate Body Report, para. 134; *EC – Asbestos*, Appellate Body Report, para. 122.

[221]See Quick and Lau (2003), p. 432.

who agree that the competitive relation between products is the decisive criterion, or at least one of the relevant elements, in determining likeness have argued that the economic approach of the Appellate Body in defining competition should be more tightly structured in order to be as objective as possible, in particular by using econometric instruments.[222] It is often suggested that WTO adjudicating authorities could rely whenever possible on instruments developed to address similar problems in the field of competition law, which use substitutability of demand and supply.[223] Some suggest that the use of econometric instruments could increase consistency and predictability of the decisions of WTO adjudicating authorities and set limits to their possible undue discretion.[224]

As it has been seen above, if likeness were determined through an examination of consumer preferences, established by econometric instruments, it would mean that, theoretically, two products with similar or identical physical characteristics could be considered as unlike if the market instruments showed that consumers treat them as unlike.[225] However, most commentators also point out that such circumstances may be rather exceptional.[226] This would be especially true in the pure economic approach, in which likeness would be determined by econometric tools: many environmental regulations respond to a market failure, such as externalities. In such cases, the market may only confirm that consumers treat products as 'like', and no consideration of how a reasonable and informed consumer *would* react in an idealised marketplace[227] could contradict such result.

6.3.2.2.2   Opponents

The view that the use of econometric instruments would necessarily guarantee greater predictability has not remained uncontested. Some have argued that even though such tools would provide absolute numbers, they would show only the actual competitive relationship and not the potential one, which is also relevant.[228]

---

[222]See Trebilcock and Giri (2004), p. 60; Quick and Lau (2003), p. 433; Choi (2003), pp. 7 f. *et passim;* Horn and Mavroidis (2004), p. 62. Even Regan (2003), note 52, p. 751—who is one of the main proponents of the regulatory purpose approach—does not oppose to the use of econometric tools in a first step. He argues however that the regulatory purpose must be taken into account in a second step, if a competitive relation exists.

[223]See Quick and Lau (2003), p. 433; Trebilcock and Giri (2004), p. 60; Horn and Mavroidis (2004), p. 62.

[224]See Choi (2003), pp. 43 and 62 ff. See also Quick and Lau (2003), pp. 432 f.

[225]See Marceau and Trachtman (2002), p. 859 and note 181, p. 858; Quick and Lau (2003), p. 431; Pauwelyn (2004), p. 586; Green (2005), p. 160; Vranes (2009), p. 324; Conrad (2011), p. 227; Marceau and Trachtman (2014), p. 412.

[226]See Marceau and Trachtman (2002), p. 859; Quick and Lau (2003), p. 432; Vranes (2009), p. 324; Marceau and Trachtman (2014), p. 412.

[227]See the approach of the Appellate Body in the *EC – Asbestos* report, para. 122 and *supra*, 6.3.2.1.1.

[228]See Conrad (2011), pp. 232 f.

Potential competition would arguably be determined mainly on the basis of end uses and physical characteristics.[229] It has also been contested that economic instruments necessarily allow more objective determination of likeness since different studies may result in different numbers, which may thus be contested by the parties to the dispute.[230] Moreover, since the purpose of state interventions is often to correct a market result in order to achieve policy goals that cannot be achieved by the market, an economic approach to likeness would merely reinforce market outcomes, insofar as only national measures distinguishing between products that would anyway be considered 'unlike' by consumers would be permissible.[231] Finally, it has been argued that consumers may also distinguish products for 'unacceptable' reasons, which could render products 'unlike' in a market-based approach.[232]

More generally, it can be pointed out that the pure economic approach is based on the view that the broad purpose of Article III is to protect conditions of competition, which requires a large scope of national treatment to prevent all kinds of covert protectionism. However, as it has been shown above, this view has been contested by some, who argue that the purpose of Article III is narrower, i.e. that it must be interpreted as preventing WTO Members to distinguish *de jure* or *de facto* between products on the basis of their national origin. In such a view, it is not justified to give a predominant importance to econometric instruments, at least without inquiring at all about the reasons justifying the product distinction, which are in principle not reflected in these instruments. This issue is further discussed below.[233]

6.3.3 Consequences for PPM Measures of the Debates on the Definition of 'Like Products'

The preceding sections have shown that the debate on the justifiability of PPM measures under Article III has mainly focused on the interpretation of the notion of like products. The product-process distinction itself was based on an objective definition of like products, under which tax or regulatory measures could not comply with Article III if they did not have any impact on the physical characteristics of the product. At the end of the GATT 1947 era and at the beginning of the WTO, the product-process distinction has often been considered in literature as

---

[229]See Conrad (2011), p. 233.

[230]*Ibid.*

[231]See Conrad (2011), p. 235.

[232]See Conrad (2011), p. 236. She gives the example of distinctions between products produced by ethnic minorities following a popular campaign that would have led consumers in the regulating country to boycott those products, thus rendering them 'unlike'.

[233]See *infra*, 6.5.1.

settled case law,[234] even though the main reports that actually applied this theory, in particular the *US – Tuna* cases, have not been adopted by the GATT contracting parties. This issue has, on the other hand, not yet been addressed *explicitly* by WTO adjudicating bodies.

Several scholars have argued at the beginning of the 2000s that the notion of like products should be defined in a much broader way, taking into account the regulatory purpose of the measure. These theories were probably in part a reaction to the product-process distinction applied in the *US – Tuna* cases and an attempt, more generally, to interpret Article III in a more deferent way for cases of *de facto* discrimination. The subjective definition of likeness would have indeed allowed more leeway to regulating Members in the adoption of environmental trade measures, including those applying to differences in production methods. This theory has, however, not been endorsed as such by the Appellate Body, which has rejected the *aim-and-effects* test applied by two GATT 1947 panels.

The Appellate Body did not confirm either the strict objective approach on which the product-process doctrine was based. Rather, it has developed an economic definition of like products, which consists in examining if products are in a competitive relationship on the market. It is possible in theory that two physically identical products may be considered as unlike by consumers because of differences in their production processes. Consumers, for instance, may consider that dolphin-friendly tuna is not 'like' tuna caught in a way that harms dolphin or that a product produced in a carbon-intensive manner is not like a physically similar product produced by clean technologies. In the view of this author, these developments of case law have thus implicitly repudiated the relevance of the product-process distinction since both product and process characteristics may influence consumer preferences. [235]

The economic definition of like product endorsed by the Appellate Body is, however, not an exclusively economic approach. Indeed, even though the Appellate Body considers that likeness must be examined on the market, it does not consider that it should necessarily be assessed by an examination of the elasticity of demand, established on the basis of econometric instruments. It has considered that consumers' preferences could in certain circumstances be established through reasonable assumptions about how an informed consumer would behave. It thus seems that social concerns about, for instance, health or environmental protection could indirectly be taken into account through such 'reasonable consumer test'. Proponents of the subjective approach tend to interpret these findings as a sign that the regulatory purpose of the measure may thus indeed influence the likeness

---

[234]See Schoenbaum (1997), pp. 288 and 290; Okubo (1999), pp. 618 ff.; Hudec (2000), p. 189, with further references; Charnovitz (2002), pp. 76 f., with further references; Marceau (2002), p. 807; Joshi (2004), p. 79; Pauwelyn (2004), p. 585.

[235]Of the same view, see Bronckers and McNelis (2000), p. 376; Marceau and Trachtman (2002), p. 859 and note 181, p. 858; Quick and Lau (2003), p. 431; Pauwelyn (2004), p. 586; Green (2005), p. 160; Vranes (2009), p. 324; Conrad (2011), p. 227; Marceau and Trachtman (2014), p. 412.

analysis. Other scholars have argued in favour of the adoption of a pure economic definition of likeness, based on the use of econometric instruments.

In any event, both the current approach of the Appellate Body and a pure economic approach could theoretically allow regulatory distinctions based on differences in PPMs if consumers treat two products with different PPMs as unlike. But if consumers do differentiate between two products based on their PPMs, the regulator is likely to consider that state intervention by taxation or regulation is not necessary.[236] It is rather when the market does not differentiate between two products that should be distinguished from an environmental viewpoint, i.e. when a market failure exists, that state intervention is required.

A definition of likeness mainly based on the examination of the market would not allow a conclusion that products are unlike in cases of market failures. By contrast, the 'reasonable consumer test' that the Appellate Body has applied in the *EC – Asbestos* case could possibly allow consideration of broader social concerns, which would be irrelevant if the elasticity of demand established by econometric instruments were the decisive criterion.

More recently, as the next section shows, the attention has tended to turn to the discriminatory treatment conditions of national treatment. It has been argued that the regulatory purpose of the measure could be relevant in the analysis of whether a measure is discriminatory in the sense of Article III.

6.4 Discriminatory Treatment

Once two products are regarded as 'like', or 'directly competitive or substitutable' in the case of Article III:2, second sentence, the treatment granted to these products must be compared in order to determine if the measure discriminates directly or indirectly imported products compared to domestic products. Article III:2, first sentence, provides that imported products must not be subject to internal taxes 'in excess' of those applied to like domestic products. A measure would be inconsistent with Article III:2, second sentence, if imported products and directly competitive or substitutable products were 'not similarly taxed' and if the measure were applied 'so as to afford protection to domestic production'. As for Article III:4, it provides that imported products shall be accorded 'treatment no less favourable' than that accorded to like domestic products in respect of all internal regulations. These different standards can be viewed as constituting the 'essence' of discrimination, insofar as they contain the basic discriminatory component.[237]

---

[236]See Marceau and Trachtman (2002), note 181, p. 858 and Marceau and Trachtman (2014), note 219, p. 412, noting that if consumer preferences are strong enough to make products unlike, there is little need for regulation.

[237]Diebold (2010), p. 33. See also Pauwelyn (2008), *passim.*

If the wording differs between the different cases covered by Article III, it is necessary in all cases to compare the treatment granted to imported and domestic products. Several different tests could be applied, the restrictiveness of which varies considerably.

This section presents these different possible theories on the definition of discriminatory treatment (Sect. 6.4.1) and analyses the applicable jurisprudence to cases of *de jure* discrimination (Sect. 6.4.2) and *de facto* discrimination (Sect. 6.4.3).

6.4.1 Different Theories on the Definition of Discriminatory Treatment

There are basically four possible ways to define discriminatory treatment, which could potentially be applicable to Article III. They have very different consequences on the restrictiveness of the national treatment obligation and the extent to which it limits WTO Members' regulatory autonomy.

Treatment granted to the products at issue is usually compared by dividing them into four categories, depending on whether they are imported or domestic and on whether they are subject to favourable or less favourable treatment.

A first possible comparison between these different categories of products is to compare the least favourably treated imported good and the most favourably treated domestic good. In such a view, the measure at issue would be discriminatory if *any* imported product were treated less favourably than any like domestic products, even if imported products overwhelmingly received the better treatment and if most domestic goods were treated less favourably.[238] This has been referred to as the 'diagonal test'[239] or the 'most-favoured domestic product' rule,[240] which constitutes a particularly restrictive approach.

Second, one could compare the respective ratios of favoured and disfavoured products within the group of imported products on the one hand and within that of domestic products on the other. A measure would be discriminatory only should the ratio of *imported* products falling into the less favourable category be greater than the ratio of *domestic* products within this same category. For instance, 60% of imported products and only 20% of domestic products would fall within the least favoured category, while 40% of imports and 80% of domestic products would be subject to the more favourable regime. This test has been referred to as the 'asymmetric impact test',[241] the 'disparate impact' theory[242] or the 'discriminatory

---

[238]See Ehring (2002), p. 924.

[239]See Ehring (2002), p. 924. See also Ortino (2004), p. 258; Vranes (2009), p. 231; Diebold (2010), p. 40; Conrad (2011), p. 241.

[240]*US – Malt Beverages*, Panel Report, para. 5.17.

[241]See Ehring (2002), p. 924.

[242]See Regan (2003), p. 756; Vranes (2009), p. 235.

effects test'.[243] In this model, some imported products may be accorded less favourable treatment than some domestic products, as long as the less favourable treatment is not heavier for the category of imported products than for the category of domestic products. The asymmetric impact view gives thus considerably more regulatory autonomy to WTO Members than the diagonal test.

A third theoretical possibility is to examine separately the situations of imported and domestic products, respectively, in each regulatory or fiscal category. This has been referred to as the 'horizontal test'.[244] There are two main possibilities to understand this test. Under a first one, it consists in comparing the treatment granted to domestic and imported products within a particular fiscal or regulatory category.[245] In such case, it can never result in a violation of Article III since products would be compared within a particular regulatory category and would thus be treated by definition equally, which means that, in that view, the horizontal test cannot be useful to discipline *de facto* discrimination.[246] A second possibility to interpret a 'horizontal test' is to consider that it consists in comparing the relative ratios of domestic and imported products within the different fiscal or regulatory categories, i.e. within the *favoured* or *disfavoured* category, in order to determine if a majority of domestic or imported products fall within the less favoured category and in the more favoured one.[247] There would be an indication of discrimination if the more favoured category were mainly composed of domestic products, whereas imported products comprised the majority of the less favoured category.

Finally, a fourth possible way to examine discrimination under Article III is to focus not only on the discriminatory effects of the measure but also on the objective underlying state intervention. This has been referred to as a 'subjective theory' of less favourable treatment.[248] The basis of this approach is that Article III prohibits only discrimination based directly or indirectly on origin and that therefore WTO adjudicating bodies must examine whether the measure discriminates imported

---

[243] See Davey and Pauwelyn (2000), pp. 38 ff.

[244] See Ehring (2002), p. 927; Vranes (2009), p. 233; Conrad (2011), pp. 240 f.

[245] See the argument made by Chile in para. 51 of the Appellate Body Report in the *Chile – Alcohol* case that all domestic and imported products entering into a particular fiscal category (determined by the alcohol content) were subject to identical *ad valorem* tax rates and that the Panel should 'focus exclusively on a comparison of the relative tax burden on domestic and imported products *within each fiscal category* and to disregard the differences of tax burden on distilled alcoholic beverages which have different alcohol contents and which are, therefore, in *different fiscal categories*' (original emphasis).

[246] See Ehring (2002), p. 927; Vranes (2009), p. 233; Conrad (2011), pp. 240 f.

[247] See e.g. Mavroidis (2008b), p. 228, commenting the argument made by Chile in para. 67 of the Appellate Body Report that domestic products comprised in that case the major part of the volume of sale in the least favoured fiscal category. See also Ortino, who implicitly argues that such comparison is relevant. He contends that WTO adjudicating bodies should take into account in the less favourable treatment analysis *inter alia* 'past, current and potential *ratio* of domestic and imported *favoured* products, as well as the ratio of domestic and imported *disfavoured* products' (Ortino 2004, p. 261; original emphasis).

[248] See Diebold (2010), p. 45.

products because of their foreign origin or because of a legitimate reason, such as environmental impact.[249] This analysis requires consideration of the regulatory purpose of the measure.

The different theories described above have been examined more or less explicitly by GATT and WTO jurisprudence. The main difference on this applicability concerns cases of *de jure* and *de facto* discrimination.

6.4.2   De Jure *Discrimination*

A measure amounts to *de jure* discrimination if it differentiates the treatment accorded to imported and domestic products on the basis of their origin. In that sense, discrimination based directly on nationality is rather easy to identify, insofar as the measure itself differentiates between products on the basis of their origin.[250]

GATT and WTO jurisprudence has traditionally applied a *diagonal test* in cases of *de jure* discrimination. It is thus irrelevant that only few imported products are accorded less favourable treatment. No imported products can be granted a treatment less favourable than domestic products because of their foreign origin.[251]

Typical examples are those of the *US – Superfund*[252] and *US – Malt Beverages* cases. In the latter, the United States had applied a measure that provided that a lower rate of the federal excise tax was applicable on domestic beer. This measure was challenged before a GATT Panel because the tax at issue was applicable to small US producers, while that lower rate was not available to imported beer. In other words, the US legislation differentiated products on the basis of their foreign or national origin. The lower rate concerned around 1.5% of the total US production. The United States argued that its exception for small brewers could not 'protect' its domestic production because it was applicable to such a small proportion of its producers that it could not have any protectionist effect. The Panel held that this measure was nonetheless inconsistent with Article III because Article III protected not the expectations on export volumes but the expectations on the competitive relationship between imported and domestic products.[253] Hence, Article III required 'treatment of imported products no less favourable than that accorded to the most-favoured domestic products'.[254]

---

[249]See in particular Pauwelyn (2008), pp. 358 ff.

[250]See Ortino (2004), p. 219.

[251]See e.g. Ehring (2014), p. 54.

[252]In that case, the United States had argued that the tax differential between these two categories of product was so small that its trade effects were minimal or nil. The Panel rejected this argument because the purpose of Article III was in its view to 'establish certain competitive conditions for imported products in relation to domestic products' (*US – Superfund*, Panel Report, para. 5.1.9).

[253]See *US – Malt Beverages*, Panel Report, para. 5.4 ff.

[254]*Ibid.*, para. 5.17.

In brief, Article III protects WTO Members against discrimination; if a measure explicitly discriminates on the basis of the origin of the products, it violates the principle of non-discrimination. Thus, when it comes to *de jure* discrimination, there is no tolerance for distinctions based explicitly on the foreign origin of products, regardless of how few imported products are granted less favourable treatment.[255]

6.4.3 De Facto *Discrimination*

De facto discrimination can be defined as cases in which a measure does not overtly differentiate on the basis of origin but discriminates indirectly or implicitly imported products.[256] The way discriminatory treatment has to be examined in cases of *de facto* discrimination has given rise to debates.

6.4.3.1 Types of Comparison

Case law may not be entirely consistent on whether a diagonal test or disparate impact test is applicable to Article III.[257] These uncertainties concern mostly Article III:2. While most reports that applied this provision concerned cases in which a disparate impact existed, some commentators interpret certain findings of the Appellate Body as the application of a diagonal test, which would prevent WTO Members to distinguish between two products that are in a competitive relationship in the eyes in the consumer.[258] It has, however, been pointed out that even though WTO adjudicating bodies have not explicitly endorsed the relevance of the disparate impact test in the context of Article III:2, this test has been underlying more or less openly most dispute settlement reports that have applied this provision.[259]

In any event, many commentators point out that applying a diagonal test to Article III would be inconsistent with the objective pursued by the national treatment obligation. It has been argued that it would transform the nature of Article III from an obligation of non-discrimination to an obligation of non-restriction[260] or

---

[255]See Ortino (2004), p. 260; Vranes (2009), p. 227.

[256]Ehring (2002), p. 922, note 3.

[257]For a detailed examination of case law, see in particular Ehring (2002), pp. 931 ff. See also Vranes (2009), pp. 236 ff.

[258]See the interpretation of Mavroidis (2008b), p. 228, who interprets the *Chile – Alcohol* Appellate Body Report as endorsing a diagonal test (in his view, this report 'essentially means that states cannot intervene and distinguish between two products that are in a DCS relationship in the eyes of the consumer').

[259]See Ehring (2002), p. 948; Ortino (2004), pp. 241 ff.; Vranes (2009), pp. 236. *Contra*: Conrad (2011), p. 241.

[260]See Diebold (2010), p. 41.

equal treatment[261] since no single imported product could ever be taxed more than any domestic products without being inconsistent with Article III. This interpretation would go much further in trade liberalisation than the principle of non-discrimination.[262] Moreover, non-restriction requires a certain level of confidence in one another's form of government and regulatory system, as well as an institutional framework based on constitutional principles, which are lacking in the WTO context.[263] It would contradict the nature of the GATT, which is a negative integration system, in which WTO Members have made no commitments to deregulate or harmonise their standards across markets.[264]

On the other hand, the applicability of a disparate impact test has been clearly endorsed by the Appellate Body in the context of Article III:4. In the *EC – Asbestos* case, the Panel had applied a diagonal test. The Appellate Body overturned these findings by holding as follows:

> [E]ven if two products are 'like', that does not mean that a measure is inconsistent with Article III:4. A complaining Member must still establish that the measure accords to the group of 'like' *imported* products 'less favourable treatment' than it accords to the group of 'like' *domestic* products. The term 'less favourable treatment' expresses the general principle, in Article III:1, that internal regulations 'should not be applied . . . so as to afford protection to domestic production'. If there is 'less favourable treatment' of the group of 'like' imported products, there is, conversely, 'protection' of the group of 'like' domestic products. However, a Member may draw distinctions between products which have been found to be 'like', without, for this reason alone, according to the group of 'like' *imported* products 'less favourable treatment' than that accorded to the group of 'like' *domestic* products.[265]

These findings were confirmed in subsequent Appellate Body reports.[266]

If a more deferent disparate impact test is applicable for Article III:4 regulatory measures, it seems unjustified that a more restrictive diagonal test should be relevant for Article III:2 fiscal measures. Otherwise, it would mean that a WTO

---

[261]See Ehring (2002), p. 954; Ortino (2004), p. 259.

[262]See Diebold (2010), p. 41.

[263]See Diebold (2010), p. 43.

[264]See Mavroidis (2008b), p. 228; Cottier and Mavroidis (2000), p. 4 ('[t]he WTO contract is not [and should not be interpreted as] an instrument for deregulation'); Mavroidis (2000), pp. 125 f. ('[t]he WTO is, at the present stage of integration, an instrument for trade liberalization. It does not aim at establishing a unified market where all factors of production circulate without any restriction. [. . .] the WTO contract imposes on its parties negative integration-type ["thou shall not"]. The inference from the mandate is that the WTO is an instrument prescribing non-discrimination and not an instrument for deregulation since [. . .] no common policies are established. In fact, this point is reflected black and white in Article III'); Diebold (2010), p. 43 ('it is very questionable whether an interpretation of WTO non-discrimination rules in accordance with the diagonal test and the principle of non-restriction is in line with the objective and purpose of the WTO framework'). See also Vogel (1995), pp. 14 f.; Trebilcock and Howse (1998), p.7; Afilalo and Foster (2003), p. 638.

[265]*EC – Asbestos*, Appellate Body Report, para. 100 (original emphasis).

[266]See *Dominican Republic – Cigarettes*, Appellate Body Report, para. 92; *US – Clove Cigarettes*, Appellate Body Report, para. 179; *EC – Seal Products*, Appellate Body Report, para. 5.117.

Member could more easily take a regulatory measure than a fiscal one, which is precisely a result that the Appellate Body wishes to avoid.[267]

Most commentators thus agree that despite certain inconsistencies in case law, the Appellate body has endorsed the view that a *disparate impact test* is applicable in cases of *de facto* discrimination.[268] Discrimination based on a diagonal test is thus not sufficient for a finding of 'less favourable treatment' (or taxation 'in excess' or 'dissimilar' taxation) in such cases.

It has been debated whether the existence of an asymmetric impact is the only criterion that should be taken into account by WTO adjudicating bodies in the examination of differential treatment. One could also require that some form of protectionist effects would be caused by the contested measure (Sect. 6.4.3.2) and even, additionally, that possible discriminatory effects would not be explained by the regulatory purpose of the measure (Sect. 6.4.3.3).

6.4.3.2 Protectionist Effects?

In the examination of the discriminatory treatment conditions, the Appellate Body focuses on the *expectations of the equality of the competitive conditions* between imported products and like domestic products and not on the practical impact of the measure at issue.[269] The examination of the impact of a measure on the conditions of competition requires a 'careful scrutiny of the measure, including consideration of the design, structure, and expected operation of the measure at issue'.[270] The Appellate Body held that, in any event, 'there must be in every case a *genuine relationship* between the measure at issue and its adverse impact on competitive opportunities for imported versus like domestic products to support a finding that imported products are treated less favourably'.[271] The analysis of the existence of a genuine relationship between the measure at issue and its adverse impact on competitive opportunities for imported products requires an examination of whether it is the *measure at issue* that 'affects the conditions under which like goods, domestic and imported, compete in the market within a Member's territory'.[272]

---

[267]See *EC – Asbestos*, Appellate Body Report, para. 99.

[268]See Ehring (2002), pp. 942 ff.; Porges and Trachtman (2003), p. 796; Ortino (2004), pp. 258 ff.; Pauwelyn (2008), p. 364; Vranes (2009), pp. 236 ff.; Diebold (2010) p. 44. *Contra*: Regan (2003), pp. 756 f.

[269]See *Japan – Alcohol II*, Appellate Body Report, p. 16; *Thailand – Cigarettes (Philippines)*, Appellate Body Report, para. 135; *EC – Seal Products*, Appellate Body Report, para. 5.108 ff.

[270]*Thailand – Cigarettes (Philippines)*, Appellate Body Report, para. 134.

[271]*Ibid.* (emphasis added). This statement has been confirmed in several subsequent reports: *US – Clove Cigarettes*, Appellate Body Report, fn 373 to para. 179; *US – COOL*, Appellate Body Report, para. 270; *EC – Seal Products*, Appellate Body Report, para. 5.105.

[272]*EC – Seal Products*, Appellate Body Report, para. 5.105 (quoting its reports in the *US – COOL* and *Korea – Beef* cases).

When it comes to *trade effects* as such, the Appellate Body held that the analysis of whether a measure has a detrimental impact on the competitive opportunities between imported and domestic products 'involves, but does not require' an examination of the actual trade effects of the measure on the market.[273] In other words, a measure may have *no effects* at all on the actual trade flows and still be considered as distorting the competitive conditions between imported and domestic like products. These findings are relevant both for fiscal and regulatory measures since the Appellate Body held the view that Article III itself protects expectations not of any particular trade volume but rather of the equal competitive conditions between imported and domestic products.[274]

It remains uncertain whether other types of comparison than the disparate impact test[275] are also relevant in the view of the Appellate Body. In particular, the horizontal comparison[276] could provide in certain circumstances additional elements on which discriminatory treatment could be examined. For instance, in the *Chile – Alcohol* case, 95% of imported products were subject to the higher tax, while 75% of domestic products were subject to the lower tax. Yet it was uncontested that domestic products comprised the major part of the volume of sales in the high tax category. In this case, the Appellate Body stated that this fact, 'by itself', did not outweigh the other relevant factors that tended to reveal protective application of the measure. Some have concluded that such horizontal comparison is irrelevant in the view of the Appellate Body.[277] But these findings could also be interpreted as a sign that the horizontal comparison is not necessarily excluded in the examination of the discriminatory conditions of Article III.[278] A comparison within the different regulatory categories may provide information on the actual or potential impact of the measure on competitive conditions, which may be viewed as an inquiry on whether the measure results in trade effects. It must be conceded that since no trade effects are required, it is unlikely that such comparison could lead to a conclusion that there is no 'protective application', at least when a clear disparate impact exists at the same time.

The absence of any trade effects test has been criticised in academic writings, in particular because the examination of whether a measure *protects* domestic

---

[273]See *Thailand – Cigarettes (Philippines)*, Appellate Body Report, para. 134 (see also para. 129). See also, in the context of Article III:4, *US – FSC 21.5*, Appellate Body Report, para. 215; *EC – Seal Products*, Appellate Body Report, para. 5.82. When it comes to Article III:2, see *Japan – Alcohol II*, Appellate Body Report, p. 23; *Thailand – Cigarettes (Philippines)*, Appellate Body Report, para. 112.

[274]See *Japan – Alcohol II*, Appellate Body Report, p. 16.

[275]The disparate impact test compares the ratios of favoured and disfavoured products within the respective categories of imported and domestic products.

[276]The horizontal comparison test compares the ratios of imported and domestic products within the respective categories of favoured and disfavoured products.

[277]See Mavroidis (2008b), pp. 226 ff.

[278]At least when it comes to Article III:2, second sentence ('so as to afford protection') and III:4 ('less favourable treatment').

producers logically requires an examination of the actual or potential effects of the measure and of the regulatory intent of the regulating Member.[279] The absence of any trade effects test may thus considerably stretch the scope of Article III, at least when national treatment is viewed only as a means to prevent WTO Members from protecting their producers through other means than import tariffs.[280]

6.4.3.3 Protectionist Objective?

A further question that has been debated is whether the existence of discriminatory treatment is a sufficient condition or if the regulating Member may still show that discriminatory treatment stems from a legitimate regulatory distinction.[281] Indeed, under the subjective approach to less favourable treatment, a finding of national treatment violation requires an examination of the regulatory purpose of the measure, which may justify discriminatory treatment, when it can be shown that imported products are more heavily affected by the contested measure not because of their foreign origin but because of another characteristic relevant to a legitimate regulatory objective, such as their environmental impact. Several reports had seemed to leave the door open to this possibility.

First, some commentators relied on a finding of the Appellate Body in the 2001 *EC – Asbestos* report that a Member could draw distinctions between products that have been found to be like, without, for this reason alone, according to the group of like *imported* products less favourable treatment than that accorded to the group of like *domestic* products.[282] On the other hand, the Appellate Body clearly expressed that it considered the objective aim of the measure manifested in the design and structure of a measure—to the exclusion of the subjective intent of the legislator— to be relevant in the examination of whether the measure is applied 'so as to afford protection to domestic production', in the sense of Article III:1. This approach was first mentioned in the 1996 *Japan – Alcohol* report[283] and then confirmed in the 2001 *Chile – Alcohol* report.[284] Therefore, certain commentators interpreted case

---

[279]See in particular Mavroidis (2008b), pp. 227 f. and 242 ff.

[280]See Mavroidis (2008b), p. 227. See further developments *infra*, 6.5.1.

[281]See Horn and Mavroidis (2004), pp. 60 ff.; Pauwelyn (2008), pp. 358 ff.

[282]*EC – Asbestos*, Appellate Body Report, para. 100.

[283]See *Japan – Alcohol II*, Appellate Body Report, p. 29: '[a]s in that case, we believe that an examination in any case of whether dissimilar taxation has been applied so as to afford protection requires a comprehensive and objective analysis of the structure and application of the measure in question on domestic as compared to imported products. We believe it is possible to examine objectively the underlying criteria used in a particular tax measure, its structure, and its overall application to ascertain whether it is applied in a way that affords protection to domestic products. Although it is true that the aim of a measure may not be easily ascertained, nevertheless its protective application can most often be discerned from the design, the architecture, and the revealing structure of a measure.'

[284]See *Chile – Alcohol*, Appellate Body Report, para. 71.

law as meaning that the analysis of the regulatory purpose had been reintroduced in the discriminatory treatment conditions of Article III since 'less favourable treatment' was equated with 'protection' and since establishing protection of domestic production may imply 'intent-based' evidence.[285] Some have thus concluded that the *aim-and-effects* test had been brought back in Article III.[286] Others have opposed this conclusion, arguing that the Appellate Body had simply endorsed a disparate impact test, thereby rejecting the applicability of the diagonal test.[287]

Second, several subsequent reports seemed to signal an evolution towards the examination of the regulatory purpose in the discriminatory treatment provisions of Article III. In the *Chile – Alcohol* case, the Appellate Body stated that the objective purpose of a measure manifested in the design, architecture and structure of the measure was 'intensely pertinent' in the evaluation of whether the measure was applied so as to afford protection to domestic production. The Appellate Body also considered that the conclusion of protective application was very difficult to resist in the light of 'anomalies' in the progression of the tax rates applied (two levels of taxation of 27% and 47% *ad valorem* separated by four degrees of alcohol content) and in the absence of 'countervailing explanations' by Chile.[288] Some have interpreted these findings as meaning that Chile could still have shown that the design of its measure was explained not by the foreign origin of the product but by another objective purpose manifested in the architecture of the measure itself.[289]

This trend that seemed to allow a defending Member to justify some discriminatory effects by relying on the regulatory purpose of the measure was also visible in the 2004 *Dominican Republic – Cigarettes* case. Case law has established that a formal difference in treatment between imported and like domestic products was not sufficient for a violation of Article III:4. A finding of less favourable implies, in the view of the Appellate Body, that a measure 'modifies the conditions of competition in the relevant market to the detriment of imported products',[290] i.e. that it

---

[285]See Hudec (1998), p. 631; Howse and Regan (2000), p. 265; Howse and Tuerk (2001), p. 299 and note 56; Regan (2002), p. 477; Trebilcock et al. (2013), p. 159 and note 53.

[286]See Howse and Tuerk (2001), p. 299; Howse (2002), p. 515; Porges and Trachtman (2003), p. 796; Green (2005), p. 161; Trebilcock et al. (2013), p. 159.

[287]See Ehring (2002), pp. 945 f.; Vranes (2009), p. 239; Diebold (2010), p. 82. See also Trebilcock and Giri (2004), p. 62 (stating that the Appellate Body merely had in mind the examination of the impact of the measure on effective equality of competitive opportunities of imports and domestic products).

[288]See *Chile – Alcohol*, Appellate Body Report, para. 71 (emphasis added).

[289]See Ortino (2004), pp. 182 f., who interprets this finding as meaning that the existence of a detrimental effect against imported products functions as a threshold for a presumption of 'less favourable treatment'. In his view, the Appellate Body seemed to allow consideration of a measure's purpose to rebut a finding of 'protective application'). *Contra*: Vranes (2009), pp. 247 f. (arguing that the Appellate Body focused exclusively on the objective design of the measure and its suitability to produce negative competitive effects and did not refer to the regulatory intent).

[290]*Korea – Beef*, Appellate Body Report, para. 137; *Dominican Republic – Cigarettes*, Appellate Body Report, para. 93.

'gives domestic like products a competitive advantage in the market to the detriment of imported products'.[291] The Appellate Body held in the *Dominican Republic – Cigarettes* report:

> [T]he existence of a detrimental effect on a given imported product resulting from a measure does not necessarily imply that this measure accords less favourable treatment to imports if the detrimental effect is explained by factors or circumstances unrelated to the foreign origin of the product, such as the market share of the importer in this case.[292]

Some have interpreted this report as meaning that a detrimental effect on imports as opposed to like domestic products may not be sufficient proof of less favourable treatment. A non-protectionist explanation, such as a non-protectionist alternative purpose, could in this view demonstrate that the regulation is not based *de facto* on origin.[293]

Finally, in the 2006 *EC – Biotech* report, the Panel took the view that the EC treated all biotech and non-biotech products alike irrespective of their origin. It stated:

> Argentina is not alleging that the treatment of products has differed depending on their origin. In these circumstances, it is not self-evident that the alleged less favourable treatment of imported biotech products is explained by the foreign origin of these products rather than, for instance, a perceived difference between biotech products and non-biotech products in terms of their safety, etc. In our view, Argentina has not adduced argument and evidence sufficient to raise a presumption that the alleged less favourable treatment is explained by the foreign origin of the relevant biotech products.[294]

It has been contended that the Panel required in this case that the complainant submitted evidence showing that the discriminatory treatment of imports was explained by their origin and not by a permitted criterion such as safety.[295] Some have, however, interpreted these findings simply as indications that the complainant had not established that the measure predominantly disadvantaged imported products, in line with previous jurisprudence on the disparate impact test.[296]

---

[291]*Dominican Republic – Cigarettes*, Appellate Body Report, para. 93.

[292]*Ibid.*, para. 96.

[293]See Leroux (2007), p. 782; Pauwelyn (2008), p. 365; Regan (2009), p. 122. *Contra*: Ortino (2004), p. 184 ('[c]ontrary to what may appear at first sight, the Appellate Body's statements in *Dominican Republic – Cigarettes* are in line with the previous jurisprudence on the relevance of 'detrimental effect' or 'adverse impact' for purposes of establishing the existence of less favourable treatment vis-à-vis imported products'); Diebold (2010), p. 82; Ehring (2014), pp. 48 ff.

[294]*EC – Biotech,* Panel Report, para. 7.2514.

[295]See Diebold (2010), p. 83. Not as conclusive: Ortino (2008), p. 185. See also Pauwelyn (2008), p. 366.

[296]See Ortino (2008), p. 185, who argues that '[i]n the Panel's view, (...) it was not clear that the EC measure was predominately disadvantaging products of non-EC origin. This at least was not enough to raise a presumption that the EC measure was *de facto* discriminating on the basis of the origin of the product.' Ortino, however, concedes that 'the Panel's reference to other possible explanations for the discrimination leaves open the door for the respondent to rebut a preliminary finding of de facto discrimination by putting forward possible justification for the adverse effect

However, the Appellate Body had the occasion to explain its findings of the *EC – Asbestos* and *Dominican Republic – Cigarettes* cases, in a way that clearly rejected the possibility that the regulatory purpose of the measure may prevent a conclusion of discriminatory treatment under Article III, despite the existence of a detrimental effect on the competitive opportunities for imported products.

In the 2012 *US – Clove Cigarettes*, the Appellate Body recognised that the statement of the *Dominican Republic – Cigarettes* quoted above 'could be viewed as suggesting that further inquiry into the rationale for the detrimental impact is necessary'.[297] In its view, this interpretation was not correct, however; it stated that, in that case, the Appellate Body 'merely held' that the higher *per unit* costs of the bond requirement for imported cigarettes (detrimental impact) was attributable to the sales volume of the importer and not to the measure at issue.[298] The Appellate Body thus rejected the interpretation of the *Dominican Republic – Cigarettes* report, under which the regulatory purpose could 'explain' a detrimental effect on competitive opportunities for imported products.

In the subsequent 2014 *EC – Seal Products* case, the European Union argued on appeal that the legal standard under Article III:4 entailed an inquiry into whether the detrimental impact of the measure on competitive opportunities for like imported products stemmed 'exclusively from a legitimate regulatory distinction'.[299] In such a case, it could have been concluded that the measure was not 'protectionist' in a relevant sense and could not be deemed to have violated Article III. The Appellate Body rejected this argument and held, on the basis of prior reports, that Article III:4 only required an analysis of whether the detrimental impact on competitive opportunities for like imported products was attributable to the specific measure at issue, which did not involve an assessment of whether such detrimental impact stemmed exclusively from a legitimate regulatory distinction.[300]

The European Communities had also supported its argument that an examination of the regulatory distinction made by the measure at issue was necessary by relying on the statement of the Appellate Body in the *EC – Asbestos* case referred to above.[301] Under these findings, a WTO Member can draw distinction between like products, without, for this reason alone, according to the group of like imported

---

predominantly on imported products'. He does not stipulate if in his view arguments based on the regulatory purpose of the measure could be advanced in such as case.

[297] *US – Clove Cigarettes*, Appellate Body Report, note 372 to para. 179. See also Crowley and Howse, p. 332, who still argued after the *US – Clove Cigarettes* report (but before the *EC – Seal Products* report was released) that the regulatory purpose may be relevant in the examination of the discriminatory treatment conditions of Article III (they based their argument on the fact that the interpretation of TBT Article 2.1 made by the Appellate Body in the *US – Tuna II (Mexico)* report, in which the regulatory purpose was examined under the 'less favourable treatment' condition, could influence the interpretation of Article III).

[298] *Ibid.*

[299] See *EC – Seal Products*, Appellate Body Report, para. 5.97.

[300] *Ibid.*, para. 5.103 ff.

[301] See *EC – Asbestos*, Appellate Body Report, para. 100.

products less favourable treatment than that accorded to the group of like domestic products.[302] The Appellate Body rejected this argument as well, stating that these findings merely meant that Article III required not identical treatment but rather the equality of competitive conditions between like products. It held:

> [T]he mere fact that a Member draws regulatory distinctions between imported and like domestic products is, in itself, not determinative of whether imported products are treated less favourably within the meaning of Article III:4. Rather, what is relevant is whether such regulatory differences distort the conditions of competition to the detriment of imported products. If so, then the differential treatment will amount to treatment that is 'less favourable' within the meaning of Article III:4.[303]

The Appellate Body concluded:

> We do not consider (...) that for the purposes of an analysis under Article III:4, a panel is required to examine whether the detrimental impact of a measure on competitive opportunities for like imported products stems exclusively from a legitimate regulatory distinction.[304]

In this report, the Appellate Body has thus rejected the different arguments that the regulatory purpose of the measure had a role to play in the discriminatory treatment conditions of Article III, both those based on the *EC – Asbestos* and *Dominican Republic – Cigarettes* report. In the view of the Appellate Body, the existence of a detrimental impact of the measure on the conditions of competition for imported like products compared to domestic like products is a *necessary* and *sufficient* condition to conclude that the measure at issue amounts to less favourable treatment.[305]

6.4.4   Conclusion

Under WTO case law on Article III, there is discriminatory treatment if the specific measure at issue results in a detrimental impact on the competitive opportunities of imported products compared to domestic like (or directly competitive or

---

[302]See *EC – Seal Products*, Appellate Body Report, para. 5.106.

[303]*Thailand – Cigarettes*, Appellate Body, para. 128, quoted by the Appellate Body in its *EC – Seal Products* report, para. 5.109.

[304]*EC – Seal Products*, Appellate Body Report, para. 5.117. This paragraph has been referred to by the *US – Tuna II (Mexico) 21.5*, Panel report, para. 7.479.

[305]See also *US – Tuna II (Mexico) 21.5*, Panel Report, para. 7.481, comparing the regime applicable to TBT Article 2.1 and GATT Article III:4, in the light of the *EC – Seal Products* Appellate Body report: '[a]s the Panel understands it, the key difference between the two provisions is that while a showing of detrimental impact is in itself sufficient to establish a violation of Article III:4 of the GATT 1994, a further analysis of whether detrimental treatment stems exclusively from a legitimate regulatory distinction may be required under Article 2.1 of the TBT Agreement, at least where the detrimental treatment identified is de facto'. See also *US – Tuna II (Mexico) 21.5*, Appellate Body Report, para. 7.277.

substitutable) products. The fundamental question is whether the measure at issue, including any relevant regulatory distinctions, distorts the conditions of competition to the detriment of imported products. In the examination of the conditions of competition, potential competition is also relevant, and the complaining party does not have to establish that the contested measure does affect in practice the actual trade flows. The relevant effects, which may be viewed as the effects that are considered as 'protectionist effects' for the purpose of national treatment, are thus defined in a very broad manner by this jurisprudence.

In cases of *de facto* discrimination, the analysis of whether such detrimental impact exists seems to consist mainly in a disparate impact test, which consists in examining whether the treatment accorded to certain products is more burdensome than that accorded to other like products and whether the group of imported products is affected more heavily by this less favourable treatment than the group of like domestic products. The Appellate Body clearly endorsed the disparate impact test in the context of Article III:4. It did not clearly state that this test is also applicable to Article III:2, but it seems unjustified that the test applicable to fiscal measures should be more restrictive than that relevant for regulatory measures. The Appellate Body stated, moreover, that the objective of the national treatment provision as a whole was to achieve the equality of competitive conditions, which means that a similar approach should be adopted in the context of Articles III:2 and III:4.

The disparate impact test requires a comparison of the respective proportions of favoured and disfavoured products within the respective categories of imported and domestic products. It is necessary to show that it is the measure at issue, and not other factors, that result in a detrimental impact on the competitive conditions between imported and domestic products. By contrast, it is irrelevant in the view of the Appellate Body if the contested measure does not have any effects on actual trade flows. This probably means that circumstances related to imports volumes, or the fact that domestic products comprise the vast majority of the disfavoured categories, cannot prevent a finding of discrimination when a disparate impact between imported and domestic products occurs.

At the same time, the Appellate Body held that the examination of 'less favourable treatment' did not involve any assessment of whether a detrimental impact on imported products stemmed from a legitimate regulatory distinction.[306] In this view, it does not matter if imported products are more heavily affected by a particular measure because they are, for instance, more environmentally harmful and not because they are produced in a foreign country. In other words, the regulatory intent of the Member adopting the contested measure is irrelevant for the examination of the 'less favourable treatment' condition and may thus not limit

---

[306]Cooreman (2017), p. 42 argues that in light of the previous turns that the Appellate Body has taken in this matter, further confirmation is to be awaited. But in the view of the present author the fact that case law has fluctuated much before the *EC – Seal Products* case could precisely be seen as a sign that case law has now settled and that the Appellate Body is thus unlikely to change its view on this point.

the aforementioned broad scope given to national treatment by the absence of any trade effects test.

In brief, the definitions given by the Appellate Body to the discriminatory treatment conditions have been described elsewhere as a 'no effects no intent test',[307] even though it has been argued by proponents of the subjective approaches to like products and discriminatory treatment that the objective of the prohibition of protectionism precisely requires the examination of both protectionist effects and intent.

6.5 Critique

6.5.1 The Fluctuations of Case Law on National Treatment

The previous sections of this chapter have shown that the interpretation of the notions of like products and discriminatory treatment has fluctuated in case law between restrictive and broad definitions.[308]

When it comes to the notion of 'like products', as explained above, GATT 1947 panels initially construed it narrowly, until the 1980s. Relatively small differences in physical characteristics were sufficient to consider products 'unlike'.[309] At that moment, the scope of like products was broadened a first time in particular with the 1987 *Japan – Alcohol I* report and in the *US – Tuna* reports, which applied a broad objective definition of like products.[310] A few years later, the two panels that applied the *aim-and-effects* test shifted back to a restrictive approach to like products. The Appellate Body then rejected the *aim-and-effects* theory in the 1996 *Japan – Alcohol II* report and thereby swung back towards a large scope of like products by endorsing an economic definition of like products focusing on competition in the marketplace. Finally, a last tendency of case law, evidenced by the 2001 *EC – Asbestos* report, seems to restrict somewhat this large definition of likeness, by taking into account non-economic concerns such as health, at least indirectly, in the likeness analysis, through assumptions on consumers' preferences in an idealised marketplace.[311]

---

[307]Mavroidis (2008b), p. 244. Professor Mavroidis has argued in details that both intent and effect should be relevant in the National Treatment analysis (Mavroidis 2012, pp. 302 ff., in particular p. 306). See also Mavroidis (2016a), p. 395, where he argues that '[i]t is high time for the senseless "no effects cum no intent" test to be abandoned'.

[308]See also DiMascio and Pauwelyn (2008); Du (2016), p. 139.

[309]See e.g. *Brazilian Internal Taxes*, Panel Report (GATT/CP.3/42 – II/181), adopted on 30 June 1949, para. 7. See also *supra*, 6.3.1.2.1.

[310]See *supra*, 6.3.1.2.2.

[311]For a description of these different phases, see DiMascio and Pauwelyn (2008), pp. 61 ff.

A somewhat similar trend has been followed with respect to discriminatory treatment.[312] GATT case law initially focused on the broad definition of discrimination implied by the diagonal test. The Appellate Body then endorsed the more restrictive disparate impact test for cases of *de facto* discrimination, which reduces the number of cases considered as discrimination. At the same time, by holding that the discriminatory treatment conditions of Article III do not contain any 'trade effects' test, in particular the 1996 *Japan – Alcohol II* report, the Appellate Body has considerably broadened again the possibilities of finding discriminatory treatment. In subsequent cases such as the 2000 *Chile – Alcohol* report or the 2004 *Dominican Republic – Cigarettes* report, there were signs that the Appellate Body could limit to a certain extent this broad test by examining explanations of the defendant showing that the detrimental effect on imported products was explained not by their foreign origin but by other factors. Finally, the Appellate Body clearly indicated in its 2014 *EC – Seal Products* report that the regulatory purpose of the measure was not among these other factors.

These important fluctuations of the conditions of Article III and, more generally, the many scholarly debates on this issue may be first explained by the fact that the text of Article III contains many undefined and rather vague terms and thus provides little guidance on the appropriate scope of national treatment.[313] Hence, this provision must be interpreted on the basis of a teleological approach, which requires defining the objective of Article III. Commentators usually agree that the principle that measures should not be applied 'so as to afford protection' contained in Article III:1 means that the objective of Article III is to avoid protectionism.

But protectionism is not defined, and the words 'so as to' are ambiguous and may be interpreted as referring both to the intent and effects of the measure at issue.[314] Consequently, the definition of protectionism and of the objective of national treatment is also debated, and by defining the objective of Article III, one defines indirectly the scope of national treatment. As a result, the debates on the interpretation of the conditions of Article III must also be understood as elements of the broader controversy on the appropriate scope that national treatment should have and the extent to which it should be construed as restricting WTO Members' regulatory autonomy.

This broader debate on the scope of Article III is influenced by the importance that national treatment has gradually gained in the GATT system since its inception in 1947. Initially, the main objective of the GATT was regarded as lowering tariff barriers, and it achieved that objective quite successfully. As tariffs did not represent significant barriers to trade, the attention gradually turned towards non-tariff

---

[312]See e.g. Mavroidis (2016a), pp. 389 ff., referring to the 'Sultans of Swing' to describe the different phases in the evolution of the notion of 'less favourable treatment' in WTO case law.

[313]See e.g. Broude and Levy (2014), who analyse what they call the 'indeterminacy' of the national treatment conditions.

[314]See *US – Taxes on Automobiles*, Panel Report, para. 5.10 ('[t]he Panel noted that the term 'so as to' suggested both aim and effect'). See also Vranes (2009), p. 243.

barriers, such as internal regulation pursuing non-economic objective like health, environmental protection or safety, and the way such regulation could influence competitive condition between products.

The evolution in the importance of national treatment in the GATT system has influenced in turn the interpretation of Article III and of its objectives. Initially, the main objective of Article III was regarded as ensuring that GATT contracting parties would not circumvent their tariff reduction commitments of Article II through discriminatory fiscal or regulatory internal measures.[315] Some contend that until the end of the 1980s, national treatment was considered to be 'relatively unimportant'[316] because of this merely secondary function it had to fulfil. But as tariff barriers diminished, the importance of disciplining non-tariff barriers grew. Panels have started to emphasise that the objective of national treatment was not only reinforcing tariff commitments but also avoiding protectionism and providing equality of competitive conditions for imported products in relation to domestic products,[317] which represents a much broader purpose.

This controversy concerning the objective of Article III explains in part the fundamental divide between proponents of the subjective and economic approaches to the definition of the conditions of Article III. The former tend to emphasise that the objective of Article III is to prevent the achievement of results that would otherwise be achieved by negotiated tariff concessions.[318] Since a tariff has a protectionist goal (insofar as simple revenue goals can be achieved by a neutral tax) and since national treatment must prevent states from doing indirectly through internal measures what tariff do directly, it might be concluded that the internal measures prohibited by Article III are those with protectionist purpose.[319] More generally, many commentators defend the view that the objective of Article III is to prevent protectionism, which means that the sole prohibited product distinctions are those based directly or indirectly on national origin[320] and that the examination of whether a measure is protectionist requires an inquiry into the regulatory purpose of

---

[315]See, e.g., *Italy – Agricultural Machinery*, Panel Report, para. 11; *Japan – Alcohol II*, Panel Report, para. 6.13 ('[t]he Panel concluded, as had previous Panels that dealt with the same issue, that one of the main purposes of Article III is to guarantee that WTO Members will not undermine through internal measures their commitments under Article II').

[316]See DiMascio and Pauwelyn (2008), p. 61.

[317]*Japan – Alcohol II*, Appellate Body, pp. 16–17.

[318]See Regan (2002), p. 450 ('[w]hy do we have Article III? We have it to prevent the use of internal restrictions to achieve goals that would otherwise be achieved by tariffs—both to preserve the value of negotiated tariff concessions, and, even where there are no concessions, as part of the project of channelling protectionism into the tariff mode so that it can be more easily negotiated down'); Mavroidis (2008b), p. 227 (stating that WTO Members 'did not, by virtue of Art. III of the GATT, promised to *de-regulate*; [they] simply promised not to *discriminate*, that is, not to protect [their] domestic producers through means other than import tariffs'; original emphasis).

[319]See Regan (2002), pp. 450 f. See also Roessler (2003), pp. 773 f. (the purpose of Article III "is to prevent internal measures imposed 'so as to afford protection'. It is not intended to curtail the exercise of the regulatory freedom of WTO Members for any other purpose).

[320]See e.g. Pauwelyn (2008), p. 361.

the measure and its trade impact.[321] In such view, the default principle is states' regulatory autonomy, which is only limited by the commitment not to discriminate directly or indirectly on the basis of national origin.

On the other hand, proponents of the economic approach base their reasoning on the view that the purpose of Article III is much broader, i.e. that it guarantees the expectations of equality of the competitive conditions between products. They argue that this objective implies that Article III is concerned only with competitive effects of a measure, not with its regulatory purpose.[322] In this view, the default basic principle is arguably market access, subject to certain defined and limited exceptions.[323] Therefore, regulatory interventions are viewed with suspicion, especially PPM measures, which are regarded as entailing important risks of covert protectionism. Some would thus simply prohibit PPM measures to avoid these risks and guarantee market access.

Schematically, the first view reflects in particular the concerns of the civil society, which focuses often its attention on the extent to which trade rules restrict states' autonomy in pursuing non-economic policy objectives through trade-related measures and tend to file *amicus curiae* briefs.[324] Taking these views into account can be crucial in what can be referred to as the 'external' legitimacy of the WTO.[325] The second approach is arguably that of many trade officials.[326] Taking their concerns into account is necessary for the Appellate Body to guarantee the 'internal' legitimacy of the dispute settlement system.[327]

The Appellate Body's jurisprudence with respect to the conditions of Article III can be considered as navigating between these two opposing views. It may have tried to take into account their respective interests, in an attempt to find a compromise guaranteeing both the external and internal legitimacy of the jurisprudence.[328] Another objective, however, is to guarantee legal predictability. These objectives

---

[321]See Howse and Regan (2000), p. 268 *et passim*; Horn and Mavroidis (2004), p. 60; Mavroidis (2008b), p. 228; Grossman et al. (2013) and Mavroidis (2016a), pp. 396 f. (who suggest various proxies that can be helpful in assessing whether a measure distinguishes between two products based on their origin, such as origin neutrality, the use of first-best instruments in terms of efficiency, scientific evidence justifying the contested measure, necessity of the measure, who bears the adjustment costs, consistency in the application of similar policies in other industries, international standards).

[322]See e.g. Vranes (2009), p. 204 *et passim*.

[323]See Howse and Tuerk (2001), p. 304 (who do not share this view); Horn and Weiler (2003), p. 144 (who do not share this view); Du (2016), pp. 153 ff.

[324]*Ibid*. See also DiMascio and Pauwelyn (2008), p. 65, who state that if the reasons for which case law seems recently to have reintroduced 'some form of aim-and-effects test' are difficult to ascertain, they 'may lie in the fear that WTO disciplines are becoming too intrusive and in the resulting pressure on WTO adjudicators'.

[325]Using the terminology of Weiler (2001), pp. 191 ff.

[326]See Howse and Tuerk (2001), p. 304.

[327]Using the terminology of Weiler (2001), pp. 191 ff.

[328]See Howse and Tuerk (2001), pp. 304 f.

are partly competing and may require some indispensable trade-offs, as it will be argued below and in the last chapter of this book.

6.5.2 Comments on the Appellate Body's Approach to National Treatment

The debates on the definition of the conditions of Article III are all part of a larger debate on the appropriate scope of national treatment and the extent to which the GATT as a whole restricts WTO Members' regulatory autonomy. This regulatory autonomy depends in a large part on the manner and the context in which the regulatory purpose underlying a particular measure is examined. More precisely, the regulatory purpose can, in theory, be examined in the like products analysis, in the review of the discriminatory treatment conditions or in the context of Article XX general exceptions.

It has been shown that in the Appellate Body's practice, the regulatory purpose seems to be able to indirectly play some role in the likeness analysis and is completely absent from the discriminatory treatment examination, which means that it will be relevant mainly in the context of Article XX. Before analysing in detail the conditions of the general exceptions provision in the next chapter, this section makes some comments on the Appellate Body's definition of like products (Sect. 6.5.2.1) and discriminatory treatment (Sect. 6.5.2.2).

6.5.2.1 The Definition of Like Products

It has been seen that, on the one hand, the Appellate Body has given an economic framework to the definition of like products. A logical corollary to the view that the likeness analysis consists in an examination of the competitive relation between products on the marketplace is that likeness is determined through the eyes of the consumer, not of the regulator.[329]

On the other hand, the Appellate Body has not endorsed a purely economic approach. It seems that it considers that, within this economic framework, broader human interests and values such as health may be taken into account.[330] There might be some flexibility in the way WTO adjudicating bodies will use the different

---

[329]See Bronckers and McNelis (2000), p. 376 ('[w]hen assessing market conditions under Article III, government regulation cannot be deemed to anticipate or guide consumer perceptions'); Vranes (2009), pp. 194 f. ('[t]his focus on competition not only has the consequence of making the perspective of consumers central to the determination of likeness. [...] it is a further corollary of this view that the relevance of the perspective that a regulator may have on the similarity of products finds no obvious confirmation in Article III:2 and III:4').

[330]See Howse and Tuerk (2001), p. 305.

criteria to determine likeness.[331] Econometric instruments are not necessary to determine the competitive relation between products. In certain circumstances, assumptions on the preferences of a 'reasonable consumer' in an idealised market-place in which externalities are internalised may be sufficient. In the *EC – Asbestos* report, the Appellate Body has examined how consumers *should* behave rather than how they *did* behave on the market. It allowed the Appellate Body to introduce some of the regulator's concerns, especially those related to market failures, into the consumers' preference criterion. Thus, the Appellate Body obviously showed *deference* in this case to the defending Member, in its analysis of consumers' tastes and habits.

As mentioned above, the fact that the Appellate Body did not endorse a purely economic approach can be viewed as a way to reconcile both the trade community and civil society constituencies, in an effort to safeguard both the internal and external legitimacy of the WTO.[332] The result is, however, not transparent and is thus questionable. The 'ideal consumer test' was a way to introduce some of the regulator's concerns in the likeness analysis. Yet the economic definition of like-ness (assessment of the competitive relationship on the marketplace) means that likeness should be examined in the eyes of the consumer. In this case, asbestos and its substitutes were certainly in a competitive relationship since otherwise state intervention may not have been necessary.[333] If the Appellate Body considered that the importance of the health concerns were such that they had to be taken into account in the likeness analysis, it would have been more transparent to examine these risks as an independent criterion, rather than doing so rather artificially through assumptions about the behaviour of fully informed consumers. Consider-ation of this factor would appear as an exception to the principle that likeness is about competitiveness on the market. Such exception could be viewed as justified when the non-economic interests underlying the measure are particularly important.

In other words, case law would seem more transparent and coherent if, in such circumstances, WTO adjudicating bodies applied an approach similar to that suggested *inter alia* by Horn and Weiler, i.e. examine the competitive relationship between products in a first phase and leave the opportunity to the regulating state to show that, in the circumstances of the case, the relevant comparator underlying the measure is not market functionality but, for instance, ecological efficiency.[334] The likeness analysis would remain in principle an economic analysis, with a possible exception when the magnitude of the risks addressed by the measure shows that, in the light of all the relevant circumstances of the case, the competitive relationship should not be the decisive criterion.

---

[331]See, e.g., Du (2016), pp. 160 f. (who argues that a more 'flexible and imaginative use of "like products" analysis is surely a promising path to open up more regulatory space for a regulating WTO Member').

[332]See Howse and Tuerk (2001), pp. 304 f.

[333]See Trebilcock and Giri (2004), p. 61; Mavroidis (2012), p. 283; Mavroidis (2016a), p. 384.

[334]Horn and Weiler (2003), p. 26 and *supra*, 6.3.2.1.1.

In the view of this author, another possible way to grant additional leeway to WTO Members to adopt internal measures addressing important non-economic concerns, without calling into question the economic nature of the likeness analysis, would be to hold that the intensity of the competitive relationship between products, i.e. the degree of likeness, that is required in a particular case for two products to be considered as like should vary according to the importance of the non-economic interests at stake.[335] At least, a higher substitutability could be required when the non-economic interests underlying the measure are particularly important, which was arguably the case in *EC – Asbestos*, which concerned protection against life-threatening risks of a known carcinogenic substance. This approach would be in line with the Appellate Body's findings that the term 'like' can encompass a spectrum of differing degrees of 'likeness'[336] and that the width of the 'accordion' of like products depends in particular on the context and the circumstances that prevail in any given case.[337]

Nevertheless, requiring a higher degree of likeness in certain circumstances may not necessarily grant additional leeway to WTO Members when two products are substitutable because of a market failure (which was arguably the case in *EC – Asbestos*). It is precisely in these cases that exclusive reliance on the market may seem questionable, in particular in the light of the Appellate Body's definition of discriminatory treatment conditions and the related implications on the scope of national treatment and the relation between Articles III and XX.

In any event, the definition of like products cannot be examined in isolation of the discriminatory conditions of Article III since both steps are important in determining the scope of the national treatment obligation. A large definition of like products combined with a narrow definition of discrimination may lead to the same result as the other way round. Eventually, the interpretation given to the conditions of Article XX matters as well since it determines the extent to which the GATT restricts WTO Members' regulatory autonomy. This issue will be further examined in Chap. 9 below.

6.5.2.2 Discriminatory Treatment and the Relation Between Articles III and XX

It seems now clear that the Appellate Body has rejected the subjective approach to differential treatment, denying that the regulatory purpose of the measure could have any relevance in the examination of whether a measure accords less favourable treatment to imported products.[338] The Appellate Body has thus endorsed a very formal economic definition to the discriminatory treatment

---

[335]For further details, see also *infra*, 9.4.1.

[336]See *EC – Asbestos*, Appellate Body Report, para. 92.

[337]See *Japan – Alcohol II*, Appellate Body Report, p. 21.

[338]See *supra*, 6.4.3.3.

conditions of Article III, which focuses exclusively on whether the measure at issue has a detrimental impact on the conditions of competition of the group of imported products, without requiring any actual trade effects. It thus seems that the only relevant analysis in the view of the Appellate Body is whether imported products are affected more heavily than domestic products, as shown by a disparate impact test and whether it is the measure at issue, and not other factors, that caused these effects.

Discrimination has thus been defined in a particularly broad fashion, which means that a very broad spectrum of internal regulations are likely to be found in violation of GATT Article III, a result that has been viewed as 'extreme' and hard to reconcile with the intent of the GATT.[339] Indeed, neither protectionist trade effects nor protectionist intent is considered as necessary factors. A disparate impact on imports is sufficient, even if this impact does not result in any protection of domestic producers. Yet this approach is precisely based on the view that the objective of national treatment is to prevent protectionism. As explained above, there are, however, two very different ways to interpret the consequences of this objective. Under a first one, Article III is considered as only prohibiting regulatory distinctions based directly or indirectly on national origin, i.e. non-tariff barriers that would protect domestic producers. In this case, the default principle is regulatory autonomy: states are free to make any regulatory distinctions, as long as they are not directly or indirectly based on national origin of the products. Under a second view, Article III guarantees the expectations of equality of the competitive conditions between imported and domestic products. The default principle is thus arguably market access, which should be granted unless a measure is justified under specific exceptions. As explained below, such approach may be appropriate for highly integrated regimes but arguably not for negative integration system such as the WTO, which does not seek to harmonise standards across its Members.

Under current case law, it could be argued that not all internal measures, in particular PPM measures, would necessarily violate Article III and be subject to Article XX: indeed, physically similar or identical products with different PPMs may be considered as unlike if consumers treat them as unlike. However, if market regulation is needed in the first place, it means most often that the market itself does not differentiate the products concerned and thus that a market failures exists. In such a case, examination of the preferences of consumers will simply confirm this market failure. In addition, the market may be influenced by collective action problems. Consumers may not accept to differentiate between two products with different environmental PPMs, and pay a premium for environmental friendly products, as long as they know that other consumers will be able to free ride on these efforts, which could limit or even prevent any effective results from an environmental viewpoint.[340] In such typical prisoner's dilemma situation, consumers' dominant strategy is to defect and to refuse to cooperate by differentiating

---

[339]See Howse et al. (2014); Du (2016), p. 155.
[340]See Trebilcock and Giri (2004), p. 57.

the products concerned.[341] Focusing exclusively on the market would simply illustrate this non-cooperative outcome. The adoption of a broader perspective, based *inter alia* on assumptions on how reasonable and informed consumers are likely to act, if, for instance, they had the assurance that other consumers would cooperate, could reduce this problem but probably not solve it completely. In brief, in cases of state intervention to correct a market failure, it is likely that the products concerned would be viewed as like.

They would thus be subject to the discriminatory conditions of Article III. Compliance is theoretically possible if there is no disparate impact on imported products compared to domestic products. But since no protectionist trade effects are required, and since it does not matter if a disparate impact on imported products is explained not by their foreign origin but by another factor such as their environmental impact, most internal measures are likely to be found to be discriminatory and would have to be justified under Article XX. Thus, the Appellate Body's approach to the discriminatory treatment conditions seems to correspond to the second approach described above, in which market access is the basic principle, which means that any exception has to be justified by the regulating Member.

Such definition of protectionism seems to go beyond a non-discrimination obligation such as national treatment. It is submitted here that the 'so as to afford protection' (Art. III:2, second sentence) and 'less favourable treatment' (Art. III:4) conditions should examine various factors showing that the measure has actual or potential effects. The existence of a disparate impact may be viewed with suspicion but should not mean in all cases that the measure is protectionist in a relevant sense. Other circumstances, showing if the measure may actually or potentially result in protectionist effects should be examined as well. This should include in particular, as it has also been suggested elsewhere,[342] the comparison of the actual and potential proportion of domestic and imported goods within, respectively, the disfavoured and the favoured categories (horizontal comparison), actual and potential respective size of the groups of domestic and imported products, actual and potential imports from other third-party Member.

If the examination of all the relevant evidence leads to the conclusion that the measure has actual or potential protectionist effects, then the regulatory purpose may be invoked to justify these effects and to show that they are not intended but the consequences of a legitimate objective. The Appellate Body has made it clear, by rejecting the subjective approach to less favourable treatment, that it is not in Article III that the regulatory purpose is relevant but that it must instead be examined in the context of Article XX. In the resolution of disputes concerning the application of the TBT Agreement, which will be examined in Chap. 8 below, the Appellate Body explained that the exclusion of the regulatory intent from Article III's discriminatory treatment conditions was justified on the basis that the GATT contained a general exceptions provision, Article XX. The regulatory

---

[341] See *supra*, 3.4.3.

[342] See Ortino (2004), pp. 261 ff.

purpose is thus examined under Article XX in the context of the GATT, while it has to be considered directly in the non-discrimination analysis in the context of TBT Article 2.1 because the TBT Agreement does not contain any equivalent to GATT Article XX.

However, subjecting all measures having a disparate impact on imported products to the conditions of Article XX would mean that the regulating Member would systematically have to comply, in particular, with the necessity test and the conditions of the chapeau of Article XX. This may not be coherent with the negative integration system of the GATT. WTO Members have created in the GATT a system in which each Member can regulate its internal market according to its own political choices, provided that it does not discriminate between imported and domestic products.[343] This choice means, in particular, that there are no obligations of WTO Members to harmonise standards across markets or to deregulate.[344] In other words, non-discriminatory measures cannot be challenged, unlike the regime that prevails in more integrated system such as the European Union, in which even non-discriminatory obstacles to trade are prohibited unless they are justified under a non-protectionist objective.[345] In 1995, WTO Members decided to adopt a different regime in the TBT and SPS agreements, which discipline non-discriminatory barriers as well, but they did not change the GATT non-discrimination regime.

The principle that WTO Members are free to adopt non-discriminatory measures, which was thus confirmed in 1995, can be considerably restricted by a pure economic definition of national treatment. By limiting the cases in which a measure is found to be non-discriminatory, one increases the cases in which justification under the conditions of Article XX is required. Thereby, the GATT system could evolve towards a regime in which justification is required most of the time (or at least every time that a measure is capable of having a detrimental impact on the conditions of competition of imported products). In other words, one would risk making the GATT evolve, through the interpretation of the conditions of Article III, towards a more integrated system, similar to those in which even non-discriminatory measures must be justified (although this final result would also depend on the interpretation of the conditions of Article XX and the difficulty to comply with them).

It is also questionable whether such interpretation, which would require that most state interventions to correct a market failure be justified under the conditions of Article XX, would be compatible with the objective of sustainable development of the WTO agreement. Many principles related to sustainable development require the correction of market failures, such as the elimination of unsustainable production and consumption practices, the internalisation of externalities, the polluter-

---

[343]See e.g. Mavroidis (2016a), p. 335.

[344]See Cottier and Mavroidis (2000), p. 4; Mavroidis (2000), pp. 125 f.; Mavroidis (2008b), p. 228; Diebold (2010), p. 43; Mavroidis (2016a), p. 336. See also Vogel (1995), pp. 14 f.; Trebilcock and Howse (1998), p. 7; Afilalo and Foster (2003), p. 638.

[345]See e.g. Pauwelyn (2004), p. 580.

pays principle, etc.[346] By adopting an exclusively economic definition of like products, combined with a discriminatory treatment test that ignores both trade effects and the reasons for which a regulatory distinctions has been enacted, one would exclude any possibility in Article III to examine whether the market fails and whether the regulating state has made legitimate distinctions between products in order to correct it and not in order to discriminate goods on the basis of their national origin. Justification under Article XX could make it more difficult for WTO Members to adopt policies aiming at the implementation of these different environmental principles.

The Appellate Body's exclusion of the subjective approach to less favourable treatment must probably be explained by a systematic interpretation of the GATT (relation between Articles III and XX) and the relevant WTO agreements (the GATT and the TBT Agreement), as it will be further explained in Chap. 9. However, since justification under Article XX requires compliance with conditions that are not present in Article III, this approach can potentially represent an important restriction of WTO Members' regulatory autonomy and could potentially lead to an excessively broad interpretation of national treatment.

However, the extent to which this result does occur in practice depends on the way the conditions of Article XX are interpreted and on the extent to which they represent important hurdles for a regulating Member.[347] Indeed, as indicated at the beginning of this chapter, the debate on whether PPM measures, and more generally measures pursuing non-economic goals, can comply with the conditions of Article III cannot be examined in a total independence from Article XX. Even if one adopts a very broad definition of national treatment, which would increase the number of measures subject to justification under Article XX, WTO Members' regulatory autonomy will eventually depend on whether the conditions of Article XX are interpreted broadly or restrictively. Article XX has been traditionally interpreted restrictively by GATT 1947 panels, but the Appellate Body has endorsed a much more flexible approach, as the next chapter will show.

This issue will thus be explored further below (Chap. 9), after having examined in detail the conditions of Article XX (Chap. 7) and of the relevant provisions of the TBT Agreement (Chap. 8).

---

[346]See *supra*, 4.1.

[347]See e.g. Du (2016), p. 154, who argues that there is not much difference with regard to the outcome of the dispute to examine the regulatory purpose in Article III or in Article XX.

6.6 Conclusion: The Legality of PPM Measures Under Article III

This chapter has shown first that the two unadopted *US – Tuna* reports considered that internal PPM regulatory measures were not covered by Article III but represented quantitative restrictions subject to Article XI. This reasoning could have meant similarly that taxes on particular PPMs used during the manufacturing process could have been considered as being subject to the restrictive Article II on border tariffs rather than to Article III:2. The Appellate Body has not endorsed this view but has instead applied a reasoning that implies that PPM measures, both fiscal and regulatory measures, are indeed covered by Article III.

Concerning the conditions of Article III, the intense debates that have arisen have often not focused specifically on the issue of PPM measures but have centred rather on the different approaches to like products and discriminatory treatment described in the previous sections. However, even though case law has not addressed specifically the question of whether PPM measures could comply with the conditions of Article III, it has had important implicit consequences for this debate.

In particular, the endorsement of the subjective approach to the definition of likeness and less favourable treatment would have given WTO Members a significant margin for manoeuvre to enact regulations distinguishing between products on the basis of a legitimate purpose, including (but not limited to) cases of differences in production methods. As it has been shown above, the Appellate Body has rejected both the *aim-and-effects* test and the subjective approach to less favourable treatment, which means that these theories, as such, cannot be used to justify PPM measures.

However, the interpretation of the conditions of Article III made by the Appellate Body implicitly means that certain PPM measures could comply with Article III. First, the adoption of an economic definition of 'like products' means that if consumers do not consider two products to be like, including because of differences in their production processes, they will not be regarded as 'like products'.[348] Therefore, this approach has implicitly repudiated the product-process distinction.[349]

On the other hand, even if products that have different process and production methods are considered to be like, regulatory distinctions may be made between them provided that the group of imported products is not affected more heavily than the group of domestic like products. This confirms as well the inapplicability of the product-process distinction[350] since a measure that accords differential treatment to

---

[348]See Bronckers and McNelis (2000), p. 376; Marceau and Trachtman (2002), p. 859 and note 181, p. 858; Quick and Lau (2003), p. 431; Pauwelyn (2004), p. 586; Green (2005), p. 160; Vranes (2009), p. 324; Conrad (2011), p. 227; Marceau and Trachtman (2014), p. 412.

[349]See e.g. Pauwelyn (2004), p. 586.

[350]See Howse and Tuerk (2001), p. 289; Trebilcock and Howse (2013), p. 159.

'like products' because of differences in their production processes may comply in theory with Article III, as long as the measure does not have a detrimental impact on the competitive conditions of the group of imported products.

In sum, in WTO adjudicating bodies' practice, there seems, in the view of the present author, to be no fundamental divide left in Article III between legal product standards and illegal process standards, which means that not much remains, in Article III, of the product-process distinction as such. The extent to which WTO Members may adopt PPM measures depends much more on the general interpretation given to the conditions of Articles III and XX. Yet, since the Appellate Body has endorsed a very broad definition of national treatment, it is likely that few PPM measures would in practice comply with Article III, even though it remains theoretically possible. As a result, the extent to which WTO Members can adopt PPM measures depends largely on the interpretation of the conditions of Article XX, which are examined in the next chapter.

Chapter 7
The General Exceptions Provision

If a trade measure adopted by a WTO Member conflicts with GATT commitments, such as the non-discrimination provisions or the quantitative restrictions prohibition, the regulating Member still has the possibility to invoke the general exceptions of Article XX to justify its measure. Under Article XX, the defending Member bears the burden of proof and must in particular show that the contested measure falls within one of the policy goals listed in the sub-paragraphs and complies with the means-ends relationship specified therein. Two of them are particularly relevant as far as environmental policies are concerned: Article XX(b), which applies to measures necessary to protect human, animal or plant life or health, and Article XX(g), which concerns measures relating to the conservation of exhaustible natural resources.

If a measure is provisionally justified under the sub-paragraphs, the defending Member must still show that the conditions of the chapeau are met, i.e. that the application of the measure does not result in unjustifiable or arbitrary discrimination or disguised restriction to international trade.

This chapter critically examines in turn the scope of the relevant policy goals listed in the sub-paragraphs (Sect. 7.1), the means-ends relationship (Sect. 7.2) and the conditions of the chapeau (Sect. 7.3).

7.1 The Policy Goals Listed in the Sub-paragraphs

This section analyses first jurisprudence relating to the policy goals listed in Article XX sub-paragraphs (Sect. 7.1.1) before focusing more particularly on the issue of extraterritoriality (Sect. 7.1.2), which is particularly important in the context of PPM measures.

© Springer International Publishing AG 2018
D. Sifonios, *Environmental Process and Production Methods (PPMs) in WTO Law*,
European Yearbook of International Economic Law 3,
DOI 10.1007/978-3-319-65726-4_7

7.1.1   The Coverage of Environmental Concerns by the Policy Goals Listed in Article XX

Within the policy goals listed in Article XX, which may justify a measure that violates otherwise GATT commitments, environmental policies are not explicitly mentioned. Environmental concerns are, however, at least partly covered in practice by Article XX(b), which protects human, animal or plant life or health (Sect. 7.1.1.1), and Article XX(g), which deals with conservation of exhaustible natural resources (Sect. 7.1.1.2). Article XX(a), which protects public morals, could be invoked to justify measures taken to protect, for instance, animal welfare. Such measures could be regarded as environmental measures in a very large sense but are not examined in detail in this study.

7.1.1.1   Article XX(b): Protection of Human, Animal or Plant Life or Health

Article XX(b) allows a WTO Member to enact trade measures that otherwise violate GATT commitments, provided that they are 'necessary to protect human, animal or plant life or health'.

For this provision to apply, a WTO Member must first establish that the trade measure at issue falls within the range of policies designed to protect human, animal or plant life or health.[1] This requirement has not provoked significant controversy within the WTO dispute resolution system, except when it comes to the possible jurisdiction limitations of that provision,[2] which are examined below.

WTO adjudicating bodies have applied a two-step test. The defending Member must first show the *existence of a risk* to human, animal or plant life or health.[3] Under established case law, the defending state must make a *prima facie* case for the existence of such risk, which the complainant may attempt to rebut.[4] The role of a panel is not to become an 'arbiter of the opinions expressed by the scientific community'.[5] The *EC – Asbestos* case illustrates this view. The Panel held that it felt 'bound to point out that it is not its function to settle a scientific debate, not being composed of experts in the field of the possible human health risks posed by asbestos'.[6] The Appellate Body added that since a WTO Member has no obligation to automatically follow a possible majority scientific opinion but may rely on scientific sources that may represent a divergent but qualified and respected

---

[1]See *US – Gasoline*, Panel Report, para. 6.20; *EC – Asbestos*, Panel Report, para. 8.171 and 8.184.

[2]See Guzman and Pauwelyn (2016), p. 401.

[3]See *EC – Asbestos*, Panel Report, para. 8.184; *Brazil – Tyres*, Panel Report, para. 7.42.

[4]See e.g. *EC – Asbestos*, Panel Report, para. 8.194.

[5]*EC – Asbestos*, Panel Report, para. 8.181.

[6]*Ibid.*

opinion,[7] a Panel 'need not, necessarily, reach a decision under Article XX(b) of the GATT 1994 on the basis of the "preponderant" weight of the evidence'.[8] Thus, a Panel may assess the nature and character of a risk on the basis of all scientific means available, including qualitative and quantitative assessment.[9]

In past reports, examples of restrictions applied to certain products to reduce health risks include regulations of tobacco,[10] gasoline,[11] asbestos[12] and the accumulation of waste tyres.[13] They were all considered to be policies aimed at reducing risks to human health or life.

A question that arose in the *Brazil – Tyres* case was whether risks to 'the environment' were covered by Article XX(b).[14] The complainant had argued that they were excluded because Article XX(b) did not cover measures designed to protect environmental concerns not related to human, animal or plant life or health.[15] The Panel did not have to explicitly address this issue. It held that although Brazil had often argued in its submissions that its import ban was necessary to protect 'human life and health and the environment', Brazil had used the term 'environment' as shorthand for 'animal or plant life or health'.[16] In its view, the complainant had to establish under Article XX(b) the existence not only of risks to the environment generally but specifically of risks 'to animal or plant life or health' as well.[17] It added that preservation of animal and plant life and health constituted an essential part of the protection of the environment and was an important value, recognised in the WTO Agreement.[18] It considered that the reference to the objective of achieving sustainable development mentioned in the Preamble of the Marrakesh Agreement showed that WTO Members were fully aware of the importance and legitimacy of environmental protection as a goal of national and international policy.[19] The *Brazil –Tyres* Panel seems thus to have adopted the view that

---

[7]*EC – Asbestos*, Appellate Body Report, para. 178; *EC – Hormones*, Appellate Body Report, para. 194.

[8]*EC – Asbestos*, Appellate Body Report, para. 178.

[9]See *EC – Asbestos*, Appellate Body Report, para. 167. The Appellate Body held in that paragraph that 'there is no requirement under Article XX(b) of the GATT 1994 to quantify, as such, the risk to human life or health'. See also *Brazil – Tyres*, Appellate Body Report, para. 146.

[10]See *Thailand – Cigarettes*, Panel Report, para. 73.

[11]See *US – Gasoline*, Panel Report, para. 6.21.

[12]See *EC – Asbestos*, Panel Report, para. 8.184 ff.

[13]See *Brazil – Tyres*, Panel Report, para. 7.53 ff.

[14]*Ibid.*, para. 7.44 ff.

[15]*Ibid.*, para. 7.45.

[16]*Ibid.*, para. 7.46.

[17]*Ibid.*

[18]*Ibid.*, para. 7.112.

[19]*Ibid.*, para. 7.112 and note 1193. The Appellate Body concurred. It stated that '[t]he Panel noted that the objective of the Import Ban also relates to the protection of the environment, a value that it considered – correctly, in our view – important' (*Brazil – Tyres*, Appellate Body Report, para. 179).

a large interpretation of the terms of Article XX(b) is justified,[20] which could lead to the acceptance that wider concerns relating to environmental protection are covered by this provision.

This could include, for instance, the use of certain substances in the production processes of a particular product, which threaten human, animal or plant health, or restrictions of PPMs causing destruction of natural habitats or the incidental killings of animals. More generally, pollution of natural resources such as air, water or soil—which could be viewed as more general risks to the 'environment'—may often entail certain risks for human, animal or plant life or health and could thus possibly come within the ambit of Article XX(b). In any event, such risks would certainly fall under Article XX(g), which applies to 'exhaustible natural resources' and contains a less stringent 'relating to' test, instead of the necessity test of Article XX(b). A defending Member may thus prefer for this reason to invoke Article XX(g) than Article XX(b) in such circumstances.

Once a risk for human, animal or plant life or health has been established, a panel should determine in a *second* stage if the objective of the measure is to *reduce such risk* and if it thus falls within the range of policies covered by Article XX(b).[21] The trade measure at issue must be designed to prevent the relevant risks and be limited to the products that entail such risk.[22]

In this respect, the Appellate Body reminded on numerous occasions that a WTO Member might choose its level of protection.[23] WTO adjudicating bodies examine neither the desirability of the declared policy goal as such, i.e. the policy choice to protect human, animal or plant life or health against certain risks,[24] nor the level of protection that the regulating Member wishes to achieve.

It can also be pointed out that in a trade-related environmental dispute, a complaining Member may often suggest that the real objective of the defending Member's measure is to protect the domestic industry and not life or health. However, this kind of argument should not be examined at this stage of the analysis, which focuses only on whether the declared policy objective of the measure falls within the range of policies covered under Article XX(b). What is relevant at this stage is the existence of a risk and whether the policy objective to reduce such a risk falls within the scope of policies to protect human, animal or plant life or health.[25]

A debated issue concerns the geographical location of the health or environmental risks at stake, i.e. whether only the risks affecting the territory of the

---

[20]The Appellate Body has applied an evolutionary interpretation of the terms 'exhaustible natural resources' in Article XX(g), which has also led to a large scope given to these terms. See *infra*, 7.1.1.2.

[21]See *Brazil – Tyres*, Panel Report, para. 7.42; *EC – Asbestos*, Panel Report, para. 8. 186.

[22]See Luff (2004), p. 165.

[23]See *EC – Asbestos*, Appellate Body Report, para. 168; *EC – Asbestos*, Panel Report, para. 8.210; *Brazil – Tyres*, Appellate Body Report, para. 7.97.

[24]See *Brazil – Tyres*, Panel Report, para. 7.97.

[25]*Ibid.*, para. 7.101.

importing state are relevant or if those affecting shared resources or global ecosystems can also be taken into account. This issue is addressed below (Sect. 7.1.2).

7.1.1.2 Article XX(g): Conservation of Exhaustible Natural Resources

Article XX(g) covers measures relating to the conservation of exhaustible natural resources. Many environmental disputes brought before GATT 1947 panels or the WTO Dispute Settlement Body were examined under sub-paragraph (g), which has thus a fundamental importance for the legal principles applicable to environmental trade measures.[26]

In the *US – Shrimp* case, the complainants had argued that the term 'exhaustible' should be interpreted as referring to finite resources such as minerals, rather than biological or renewable resources, or in other words non-living exhaustible natural resources.[27] This interpretation would have excluded *living resources* from Article XX(g) and would have consequently drastically limited the possibilities of WTO Members to justify environmental trade measures under this sub-paragraph. The Appellate Body was aware of this fact and did not endorse the view of the complainants. It confirmed that measures to conserve exhaustible natural resources, whether *living* or *non-living*, might fall within Article XX(g).[28]

That conclusion gave rise to controversial issues since it was in part based on an 'evolutionary' interpretation of the terms 'exhaustible natural resources'. Complainants had mainly referred to the drafting history of Article XX, which, they argued, supported their interpretation.[29] The Appellate Body disagreed[30] and held that the term 'exhaustible natural resources', which was crafted more than 50 years before this case was brought to the Dispute Settlement Body, had to be read in the light of contemporary concerns of the community of nations about the protection and conservation of the environment.[31] It added that the generic term 'natural resources' in Article XX(g) is not 'static' in its content or reference but is rather 'by definition, evolutionary'.[32]

With these considerations in mind, the Appellate Body first analysed the WTO Preamble, which explicitly acknowledges the objective of sustainable development. Second, the Appellate Body examined several modern international conventions referring to natural resources, such as the United Nations Convention on the Law of

---

[26]See e.g. Chi (2014) (who analyses all the disputes in which Article XX(g) has been applied).

[27]See *US – Shrimp*, Appellate Body Report, para. 127.

[28]*Ibid.*, para. 131.

[29]*Ibid.*, para. 127.

[30]It held that 'the drafting history does not demonstrate an intent on the part of the framers of the GATT 1947 *to exclude* "living" natural resources from the scope of application of Article XX(g)' (*US – Shrimp*, Appellate Body Report, note 114, para. 131; original emphasis).

[31]See *US – Shrimp*, Appellate Body Report, para. 129.

[32]*US – Shrimp*, Appellate Body Report, para. 130.

the Sea (UNCLOS), the Convention on Biological Diversity (CBD), Agenda 21 or the Convention on the Conservation of Migratory Species of Wild Animals, which define natural resources as including living and non-living resources. The Appellate Body concluded that it was 'too late in the day' to suppose that Article XX(g) might be read as referring only to the conservation of exhaustible mineral or other non-living natural resources.[33]

The Appellate Body also noted that there was no textual limitation to the conservation of 'mineral' or 'non-living' natural resources in Article XX(g)[34] and cited two adopted GATT 1947 Panel reports that had followed the same interpretation,[35] i.e. the *US – Canadian Tuna*[36] and *Canada – Salmon and Herring*[37] reports. It is true that both panels had considered living resources (tuna, salmon, herring) to be exhaustible natural resources within the meaning of Article XX(g).[38]

This part of the *US – Shrimp* report can be seen by some as controversial, first because it applied an evolutionary interpretation and also because the Appellate Body based its conclusion that living resources were covered by Article XX(g) at least in part on non-WTO law, referring to several MEAs, which were not ratified by all parties, were not necessarily binding, and some of which were not in force. However, it should be reminded that the *travaux préparatoires* are only a supplementary means of interpretation. On the other hand, sustainable development is one of the objectives of the WTO mentioned in the Marrakesh Agreement, and Article XX may be one of the main provisions the interpretation of which may be influenced by this goal. The objective of sustainable development was introduced nearly 50 years after the *travaux préparatoires* of the GATT 1947 have taken place and environmental concerns have considerably grown during this period. Hence, the concerns that prevailed in 1947 have largely become old-fashioned.[39] On the other hand, it may be inevitable to examine MEAs in order to interpret the implications that the objective of sustainable development may have in a particular case.[40] In brief, the evolutionary interpretation of the terms 'exhaustible natural resources' seems in the view of this author to be a positive and necessary development of WTO law, insofar as a strict interpretation would limit the possibilities of WTO Members to enact environmental trade measures to a large extent.[41]

---

[33]*Ibid.*, para. 131.

[34]*Ibid.*, para. 128.

[35]*Ibid.*, para. 131.

[36]See *US – Canadian Tuna*, GATT Panel Report (1982).

[37]See *Canada – Herring and Salmon*, GATT Panel Report (1988).

[38]The definition and scope of exhaustible natural resources were however not analysed at length in these reports since the parties to the disputes agreed that the fish species concerned were covered by Article XX(g).

[39]See Prost (2005), p. 49.

[40]See *supra*, 4.1.

[41]*Idem.*

Nonetheless, some unresolved questions remain about the precise scope and definition of the terms 'natural resources' and 'exhaustible'. If one admits that exhaustible natural resources cover living resources, it raises certain issues on the definition of the term 'exhaustible'. The main issue is whether this term should be interpreted in this context as 'endangered'.

Case law suggests that it would not necessarily be the case, i.e. that species that are not recognised as 'endangered' may be deemed to be 'exhaustible'. Thus far, living resources that were regarded as exhaustible natural resources were tuna,[42] salmon and herring,[43] dolphins[44] and sea turtles.[45] Among them, only sea turtles were listed in an international agreement (i.e., CITES) as endangered species. In addition, the *US – Tuna II* Panel held the view that dolphin stocks could be 'potentially exhausted' and that a state could adopt a policy to conserve them whether or not their present stocks were depleted. It concluded that a policy to conserve dolphins was a policy to conserve exhaustible natural resources.[46]

In the *US – Shrimp* report, the Appellate Body indicated that one lesson 'that modern biological sciences teach us is that living species, though in principle, capable of reproduction and, in that sense, "renewable", are in certain circumstances indeed susceptible of depletion, exhaustion and extinction, frequently because of human activities'.[47]

These findings seem to suggest that, potentially, all living natural resources could thus be covered by the term 'exhaustible'. However, the Appellate Body stated that living species are susceptible of exhaustion *in certain circumstances*. It did not expand on the nature of such circumstances. But it could mean that the Appellate Body would examine if the environmental harm at issue involves some risks of depletion or extinction of the species concerned in the mid or long term. For instance, the United States had argued in the *US – Tuna II* case that prior to the adoption of the dolphin protection measures of the United States, mortality attributable to the eastern tropical Pacific tuna fishery was at levels that *threatened the sustainability* of several species of dolphins.[48]

As the complainants in the *US – Shrimp* case argued, considering that all natural resources would be defined as 'exhaustible' within the meaning of

---

[42] See *US – Canadian Tuna*, Panel Report. See para. 4.4: '[t]he Panel agreed with the parties that salmon and herring stocks are "exhaustible natural resources" [. . .] within the meaning of Article XX(g)'.

[43] See *Canada – Herring and Salmon*. Panel Report. See para. 4.9: '[t]he Panel furthermore noted that both parties considered tuna stocks, including albacore tuna, to be an exhaustible natural resource in need of conservation management and that both parties were participating in international conventions aimed, *inter alia*, at a better conservation of such stocks'.

[44] See *US – Tuna II*, Panel Report, para. 5.13.

[45] See *US – Shrimp*, Appellate Body Report, para. 127 ff.

[46] See *US – Tuna II*, Panel Report, para. 5.13.

[47] *US – Shrimp*, Appellate Body Report, para. 128.

[48] See *US – Tuna II*, Panel Report, para. 3.50.

Article XX(g) would risk rendering that term superfluous.[49] By requiring that 'certain circumstances' indicating the existence of a risk of mid- or long-term depletion of the natural resources concerned would avoid such a result. Future case law may have to specify what the nature and extent are of these circumstances.

A last noteworthy issue that was raised in dispute settlement proceedings is whether the natural resources concerned by Article XX(g) are only those that have an *economic value*. In the *US – Tuna II* case, the complainants had argued that dolphins were not exhaustible natural resources within the meaning of Article XX(g) because they were not a resource in any economic sense of the term, insofar as no trade in dolphin species was allowed under CITES.[50] The Panel did not explicitly answer to that argument, which may imply that it rejected it.[51] Accepting this argument would have implied that recognised endangered species for which no trade is allowed under international agreements would not necessarily be qualified as exhaustible natural resources under Article XX(g).

However, in the *US – Gasoline* Panel report, the Panel held that 'clean air was a resource (it had value)'.[52] If one interprets such reference to resources that have a *commercial* value, it could mean that resources that are not commercially exploited are not covered by Article XX(g), in the same line as the argument mentioned by the EEC in the *US – Tuna II* case. Such interpretation would limit the possibilities of WTO Members to enact trade-related environmental policies to a very important extent since even endangered species, for which no trade is allowed, could not be protected by measures justifiable under Article XX(g). State interventions to correct a market failure affecting natural resources that are not commercially exploited would not be allowed either under this view, even though market failures are particularly likely to occur precisely in cases in which certain costs are externalised on environmental resources that are not commercially exploited (conservation of natural habitats, of unexploited wild species, etc.). Hence, such a reference to a *commercial* value should not be endorsed.[53]

Moreover, the *US – Gasoline* Panel referred only to the 'value' of clean air. Stating that an environmental resource has a value does not necessarily mean that it has a *commercial* value. It is usually considered in economic theory that the total value of environmental goods is not limited to the 'use value' of that good but includes also 'non-use value'.[54] The former refers to goods that are directly 'consumed' and the value of which is established by the market or to goods that are used indirectly, such as the services rendered by ecosystems, like carbon sinks or waste assimilation. The latter (non-use value) captures cases in which people put monetary values on natural resources that are independent of any present or future

---

[49]See *US – Shrimp*, Appellate Body Report, para. 127.

[50]See *US – Tuna II*, Panel Report, para. 3.52.

[51]See Prost (2005), p. 45.

[52]See *US – Gasoline*, Panel Report, para. 6.37.

[53]See also Prost (2005), pp. 44 f.

[54]See e.g. the analysis of Freeman (2003), in particular pp. 137 ff. See also Chang (1995), pp. 18 ff.

use that these people may have of these resources.[55] These non-use values encompass, for instance, 'existence' value (willingness to pay to ensure the survival of certain species without any expectations to see them) or 'bequest' value (preserving resources for future generations).[56]

It has been suggested that the term 'resource' in Article XX(g) should be given not an economic definition but a 'biological' or 'ecological' definition, in order to avoid to restrict unduly the scope of this provision,[57] which would seem logical insofar as Article XX deals mainly with non-economic policies that may have a trade impact. In that respect, Article XX(g) should not be restricted to 'exhaustible natural resources' that have a 'commercial' value. However, it is submitted that even if WTO adjudicating bodies gave an economic definition to the term 'resources', they should in any case have to take into account not only its 'commercial' value (or use value) but potentially also its non-use value, the preservation of which may encompass many environmental concerns resulting in state intervention.

There might, however, be some limits to the consideration of non-use value related to the intensity of the nexus between the regulating country and the environmental resources concerned. The nature of this nexus can show that the preservation of non-use value of a particular resource amounts to a legitimate international concern because of the importance of the resource at stake, or it can alternatively show that it is rather a local issue, for which an importing country may have only moral concerns and which does not necessarily justify a restrictive trade measure. This raises the issue of 'extraterritoriality'.

7.1.2 'Extraterritoriality' and 'Coercion'

Chapter 5 has shown that public international law does not bring significant restrictions to the ability of states to take import restrictions in order to address environmental harm occurring abroad, the sole limit being coercion, which is unlikely to occur when only economic measures are concerned. Possible geographical limits are therefore those contained in the WTO agreements.[58]

A controversial issue when it comes to the definition of policies that would fall within the range of those covered by Article XX(b) and (g) is whether measures taken to protect environmental resources located outside the territorial jurisdiction of the importing country can be justified by Article XX or, in other words, whether this provision contains what the Appellate Body has called an 'implied jurisdictional limitation',[59] even though the text of Article XX does not contain any explicit

---

[55]See Freeman (2003), in particular pp. 137 ff. See also Chang (1995), pp. 18 ff.

[56]*Ibid.*

[57]See Prost (2005), p. 45.

[58]See *supra*, Chap. 5.

[59]*US – Shrimp*, Appellate Body Report, para. 133.

limit of that sort. This issue has a considerable importance when it comes to PPM measures because the environmental resources that such measures aim to protect are frequently located partly or wholly outside the territory of the regulating state, such as dolphins or sea turtles in the high seas, or protection of the global atmosphere. If one would accept that PPM measures could only protect resources located on the territory of the importing state, it would considerably limit the possibility for WTO Members to take PPM measures.

Case law provides little guidance on that issue in the context of Article XX(b). It has merely been examined in the two unadopted *Tuna* reports and has not been addressed directly since the inception of the WTO. Nevertheless, the *US – Shrimp* Appellate Body's report, which was examined exclusively under Article XX(g), contains findings that may be applicable to other sub-paragraphs, particularly Article XX(b). After having examined the relevant case law (Sect. 7.1.2.1), this section will critically analyse the extraterritorial issue, which represents one of the most controversial aspects of PPM measures (Sect. 7.1.2.2).

7.1.2.1   Case Law

7.1.2.1.1   The *US – Tuna* and *US – Shrimp* Panel Reports

The first two *US – Tuna* and the *US – Shrimp* panels all mentioned briefly the issue of extraterritoriality and applied a restrictive approach concerning this issue.

In the 1991 *US – Tuna I* case, the United States asserted that Articles XX(b) and (g) were applicable to justify a measure aiming at the protection of dolphins outside its jurisdiction. Mexico invoked an opposite argument.

The Panel expressed the view that Article XX(b) concerned the use of sanitary measures to safeguard life or health of humans, animals or plants *within* the jurisdiction of the importing country.[60] It further described the argument made by the United States as an 'extrajurisdictional interpretation' of Article XX.[61] The Panel finally held as follows:

> [I]f the broad interpretation of Article XX(b) suggested by the United States were accepted, each contracting party could unilaterally determine the life or health protection policies from which other contracting parties could not deviate without jeopardizing their rights under the General Agreement. The General Agreement would then no longer constitute a multilateral framework for trade among all contracting parties but would provide legal security only in respect of trade between a limited number of contracting parties with identical internal regulations.[62]

The Panel applied a similar reasoning with respect to Article XX(g).[63]

---

[60]See *US –Tuna I*, Panel Report, para. 5.26.

[61]*Ibid.*, para. 5.28 and 5.32.

[62]*US –Tuna I*, Panel Report, para. 5.28.

[63]*Ibid.*, Panel Report, para. 5.32.

Thus, in the view of the *US – Tuna I* Panel, Article XX could not justify measures taken to protect animal life or health outside the jurisdiction of the importing state, by which it probably meant its territory.[64] This conclusion was mainly based on the perceived risks for the multilateral trading system entailed by a widespread use of such measures, but the report lacks any detailed analysis of the principles governing prescriptive jurisdiction and of the influence that the commitments made in the GATT has upon them.[65]

The 1994 *US – Tuna II* report resulted in similar findings of the Panel. It stated that it could not be held that Article XX(g) applied only to policies related to the conservation of exhaustible natural resources *within the territory* of the regulating Member[66] because states were not in principle barred under international law from regulating the conduct of their *nationals* and their vessels having their nationality, or any persons on these vessels, with respect to persons, animals, plants and natural resources outside their territory.[67] It also seemed to consider that measures addressing situations occurring abroad fell in the range of policies covered by Article XX if they could 'by themselves' further the conservation policy pursued, i.e. if they did not force other countries to change their own policies in order to achieve its intended effects.[68]

In other words, the *US – Tuna II* Panel seemed to assume that restrictive *trade measures* adopted by importing GATT Members and addressing situations, persons or resources located abroad required a justification based on the principles of extraterritorial jurisdiction, such as the nationality or territoriality principles. It is, however, quite debatable that the WTO commitments would render the rules on extraterritoriality applicable, as it will be shown below.[69] It did not explain why it had considered that trade measures required such a justification, i.e. why, in its view, a trade measure would 'regulate the conduct' of persons abroad in a *legal* sense.

The second *Tuna* Panel, like the first one, was also concerned with the perceived 'coercive' effects of certain PPM measures. It expressed the view that if Article XX were interpreted to permit an importing state to take trade measures to 'force' other countries to change their conservation policies within their own jurisdiction, the GATT 'could no longer serve as a multilateral framework for trade among contracting parties'.[70]

---

[64]Since the Panel did not mention that the United States might have taken measures addressing situations outside its territory on the basis of the rules on extraterritorial jurisdiction, like the *US – Tuna II* Panel did.

[65]See *supra*, Chap. 5 and *infra*, 7.1.2.2.1.

[66]See *US – Tuna II*, Panel Report, para. 5.20.

[67]*Ibid.*, para. 5.17.

[68]*Ibid.*, para. 5.23 ff.

[69]See *infra*, 7.1.2.2.1.

[70]*US – Tuna II*, Panel Report, para. 5.26. '[i]f Article XX were interpreted to permit contracting parties to deviate from the obligations of the General Agreement by taking trade measures to implement policies, including conservation policies, within their own jurisdiction, the basic

The 1998 *US – Shrimp* Panel report does not contain any clear findings in relation to the issue of extraterritorial jurisdiction. The United States had argued that the complainants confused the 'difference between extrajurisdictional application of a country's law and the application by a country of its law, within its jurisdiction, in order to protect resources located outside its jurisdiction'. The Panel simply held that it was not basing its findings on an 'extrajurisdictional' application of US law, pointing out that many domestic governmental measures could have an effect outside the jurisdiction of the government that takes them.[71] Neither the argument of the United States[72] nor the relevant findings of the Panel[73] shed much light on the debate on extraterritorial jurisdiction.

Like the *US – Tuna* panels, the *US – Shrimp* Panel was concerned about the effects of measures requiring a change in a foreign government's policies, which could 'threaten' the security and predictability of trade relations. The main fear was apparently that of conflicting requirements between several importing countries, applying to the same subject for the same exporting countries, making it impossible for the states concerned to comply with both requirements.[74] The Panel even stated that allowing such measures could 'rapidly lead to the end of the WTO multilateral trading system'.[75]

A parallel can be made between these findings and the general international law context, in which developing countries have regularly attempted to define economic pressure by a state to induce political changes in a foreign country as a form of illegal coercion. Such form of coercion is not recognised under general international law.[76] However, the view of the *US – Tuna* and *US – Shrimp* panels can be seen as meaning that, in their view, certain form of economic 'coercion' is not allowed under the GATT, at least when it 'threatens' the multilateral trading system.

---

objectives of the General Agreement would be maintained. If however Article XX were interpreted to permit contracting parties to take trade measures so as to force other contracting parties to change their policies within their jurisdiction, including their conservation policies, the balance of rights and obligations among contracting parties, in particular the right of access to markets, would be seriously impaired. Under such an interpretation the General Agreement could no longer serve as a multilateral framework for trade among contracting parties.'

[71] See *US – Shrimp*, Panel Report, para. 7.51.

[72] Was the Panel referring to extraterritorial enforcement measures? Or to measures taken in the absence of any jurisdictional basis, i.e. 'extra'-jurisdictional? Or simply to the adoption of PPM measures requiring the adoption of process-standards abroad?

[73] It remains unknown if the Panel was of the view that the United States had to justify its measure on the basis of the rules on extraterritorial jurisdiction.

[74] See *US – Shrimp*, Panel Report, para. 7.45.

[75] *Ibid.*, para. 7.45 *in fine*.

[76] See *supra*, Chap. 5.

7.1.2.1.2   The Appellate Body *US – Shrimp* Report

This restrictive approach was not upheld by the Appellate Body, which overturned the arguments on which the *US – Shrimp* Panel had relied. In one of the most significant paragraphs of that report, the Appellate Body stated:

> It appears to us, however, that conditioning access to a Member's domestic market on whether exporting Members comply with, or adopt, a policy or policies unilaterally prescribed by the importing Member may, to some degree, be a common aspect of measures falling within the scope of one or another of the exceptions (a) to (j) of Article XX. Paragraphs (a) to (j) comprise measures that are recognized as exceptions to substantive obligations established in the GATT 1994, because the domestic policies embodied in such measures have been recognized as important and legitimate in character. It is not necessary to assume that requiring from exporting countries compliance with, or adoption of, certain policies (although covered in principle by one or another of the exceptions) prescribed by the importing country, renders a measure a priori incapable of justification under Article XX. Such an interpretation renders most, if not all, of the specific exceptions of Article XX inutile, a result abhorrent to the principles of interpretation we are bound to apply.[77]

The Appellate Body entirely overturned the logic of the *Shrimp* and *Tuna* Panel reports and did not accept that a perceived 'threat' to the multilateral trading system was a relevant element for the interpretation of the GATT. This finding has far-reaching consequences for PPM measures since it implies that their possible 'unilateral' or 'coercive' character is not sufficient to render the measure incapable of justification. This is also shown by the fact that the United States was eventually able, in the *US – Shrimp 21.5* case, to successfully defend a unilateral PPM measure, which conditioned access to the United States market to the adoption by exporting WTO Members of certain conservation policies. Thus, the argument that PPM measures are 'coercive', insofar as they require the adoption of certain practices or policies in the exporting country, is not in itself sufficient to conclude that WTO law has been violated.[78]

As regards the applicability of the rules on *extraterritorial jurisdiction* to trade measures, more uncertainties remain. The Appellate Body was aware of the debate concerning the possible implied jurisdictional limitation of Article XX. However, it did not need to clarify this point in the *US – Shrimp* report because of the specific circumstances of the case: the protected sea turtles at issue were migratory animals, and some of them were present at some moment of their lives in the United States territorial waters. Thus, the Appellate Body stated:

---

[77] *US – Shrimp*, Appellate Body Report, para. 121.

[78] It does not mean that the 'coercive effect' of a measure is irrelevant. It may well play a role in the context of the chapeau, in the negotiations and flexibility requirements (see *infra*, 7.3.2. See also *US – Shrimp*, Appellate Body Report, para. 161: 'perhaps the most conspicuous flaw in [the] measure's application relates to its intended and actual coercive effect on the specific policy decisions made by foreign governments, Members of the WTO'). However, a WTO Member may in certain circumstances unilaterally impose a policy, such as avoiding incidental killing of sea turtles in the harvesting of shrimp.

We do not pass upon the question of whether there is an implied jurisdictional limitation in Article XX(g), and if so, the nature or extent of that limitation. We only note that in the specific circumstances of the case before us, there is a *sufficient nexus* between the migratory and endangered marine populations involved and the United States for purposes of Article XX(g).[79]

The Appellate Body did not elaborate on the meaning or the implications of the concept of 'sufficient nexus', which seemed to be critical to define the limits of the ability of WTO Members to take PPM measures to protect environmental goods located beyond their territory. It could be interpreted as a reference to the rules on extraterritorial jurisdiction. But it could equally be construed as merely being a concept of WTO law, indicating that the importing country has a sufficient interest in the natural resource concerned to take a restrictive trade measure aiming at its protection, despite the commitments made in the GATT.[80]

7.1.2.1.3 The *EC – Seal Products* and *US – Tuna II (Mexico)* Reports

The Appellate Body briefly mentioned the 'sufficient nexus' issue in the 2014 *EC – Seal Products* report. This case was examined under Article XX(a), which can be invoked for the protection of public morals. The measure at issue was designed to address seal hunting activities occurring within and outside the European Union and the seal welfare concerns of citizens and consumers in EU Member States. Because participants did not address this issue in their submissions on appeal, the Appellate Body did not examine it further. It stated nonetheless that it recognised the 'systemic importance of the question of whether there is an implied jurisdictional limitation in Article XX(a), and, if so, the nature or extent of that limitation'.[81]

It noted that in response to questioning at the oral hearing, the participants expressed their agreement that *there was a sufficient nexus* between the public moral concerns and activities addressed by the measure, on the one hand, and the European Union, on the other.[82]

Another noteworthy aspect of this report is that the Appellate Body recognised that the measure was not merely aimed at avoiding the 'moral taint' of consuming products made of seal that were killed by cruel manners. In the necessity analysis, the Panel accepted the assumption that the import ban made a contribution to reducing the demand for seal products *within* the European Union and, to a certain extent, to reducing global demand.[83] This reasoning could imply that the trade

---

[79]*US – Shrimp*, Appellate Body Report, para. 133 (emphasis added).

[80]For further analysis, see *infra*, 7.2.1.2.

[81]*EC – Seal Products*, Appellate Body Report, para. 5.173.

[82]*Ibid.*, para. 5.173, n. 1191.

[83]*Ibid.*, para. 7.459; *EC – Seal Products*, Appellate Body Report, para. 5.225.

measure is viewed as a *territorial* measure taken by the importing Member in order to achieve a moral (or environmental) result.

This tendency seems even clearer in the 2012 *US – Tuna II (Mexico)* reports and in the 2015 *US – Tuna II (Mexico) 21.5* Panel report. This case was examined under the TBT Agreement, and the issue of the possible GATT Article XX implied that jurisdictional limitation was not examined in the original report. The perceived extraterritorial character of PPM measures should, however, logically not be different in the GATT or the TBT Agreement, in particular because the Appellate Body seeks to interpret both agreements in a consistent and coherent manner.[84]

In this case, the United States explained that one of its objectives for the dolphin-safe label was contributing to the protection of dolphins, by ensuring that the US market was 'not used to encourage fishing fleets to catch tuna in a manner that adversely affects dolphins'.[85] The Panel and the Appellate Body recognised that the objective of the US dolphin-safe provisions was 'legitimate' within the meaning of Article 2.2 of the TBT Agreement.[86] The United States' measure at issue concerned fishing methods that had to be used to protect dolphins that did not live, even at some moment of their lives, in the United States' territorial waters. Certain WTO Members would thus certainly argue that such measures were 'extraterritorial'. Yet, by focusing on whether the importing Member sought to ensure that its *internal market* was not used to encourage environmentally harmful PPM abroad, the measure at hand was arguably viewed as *territorial* in nature.

The 2015 *US – Tuna II (Mexico) 21.5* Panel report examined under GATT Article XX the measures taken by the United States to comply with the *US – Tuna II (Mexico)* Appellate Body's report, even though the GATT had not been analysed in the original reports. The Panel applied a similar reasoning as that adopted by the Appellate Body in the context of Article 2.2 of the TBT Agreement and accepted that the US measure fell within the scope of Article XX(g).[87] Interestingly, the complainant had argued that the contested measure as a whole did not have a '*sufficient nexus* with the goal of conserving dolphins'.[88] Thus, Mexico did not argue that the fact that the dolphins concerned by the measure were located outside US territorial waters rendered the measure incapable of justification. It rather maintained that there was no sufficient nexus between the goal of conservation and the effective impact of the amended US measure on that objective, i.e. dolphins' conservation.[89] Neither the complainant nor the Panel discussed or even mentioned the issue of the existence of a sufficient 'jurisdictional' nexus. Instead, the parties to the dispute and the Panel agreed, as in the original reports,

---

[84]See *US – Clove Cigarettes*, Appellate Body Report, para. 91.

[85]*US – Tuna II (Mexico)*, Panel Report, para. 7.401 and 7.425.

[86]*Ibid.*, para. 7.444; Appellate Body Report, para. 338.

[87]See *US – Tuna II (Mexico) 21.5*, Panel Report, para. 7.525. This finding was not challenged before the Appellate Body (see Appellate Body Report, para. 7.284).

[88]*Ibid.*, para. 7.522.

[89]*Ibid.*, para. 7.526 ff.

that one of the goals of the challenged measure was ensuring that the US market was not used to encourage fishing fleets to catch tuna in a manner that adversely affected dolphins.[90]

Therefore, it seems that the 'extraterritoriality' issue has clearly lost importance in recent WTO case law.[91]

7.1.2.2 Critique

7.1.2.2.1 Comments on Case Law

It has been shown that the two unadopted *US – Tuna* Panel reports referred to the rules on extraterritorial jurisdiction in their examination of the contested PPM measures at issue. They did not explain, however, why these rules were relevant in their view. Yet, in public international law, the ability of states to adopt trade measures is only limited by coercion, which means that the first two *Tuna* Panel findings concerning the inadmissibility of so-called extraterritorial measures under GATT Article XX are much more restrictive than the applicable default rules of international law, despite opposite statements or assumptions of these panels.[92]

In the *US – Shrimp* case, the Appellate Body did not refer to the rules on extraterritorial jurisdiction but mentioned the issue of whether Article XX contained an 'implied jurisdictional limitation'. It did not elaborate on this issue, having exercised judicial economy, and merely stated that a 'sufficient nexus' existed in the circumstances of the case between the regulating country and the protected situation for purposes of Article XX(g)[93] because the protected turtles were present at some moment of their lives in the territory of the importing state. This statement might be interpreted either as meaning that a territorial link was required under Article XX or as meaning that a sufficiently close relationship existed to justify the exercise of extraterritorial jurisdiction by the United States.[94] As it will be further elaborated below, it could also simply be seen as the sign that the existence of a legitimate interest in the environmental resources at stake is sufficient, irrespective of the rules on extraterritorial jurisdiction. This largely depends on the interpretation of the commitments that WTO Members made in the GATT and on the extent to which it implies restrictions to states' sovereignty over import policies.[95]

---

[90]*Ibid.*, para. 7.523.

[91]See also Young (2014), p. 317, who argues that if the scope of the 'sufficient nexus' is still uncertain, it is likely to be easily satisfied, in particular in the light of the impact environmental problems may have on public morals or citizens of the importing country.

[92]See Luff (2004), p. 161.

[93]See *US – Shrimp*, Appellate Body Report, para. 133.

[94]See e.g. Vranes (2009), p. 161, with further references.

[95]Howse has argued that the reference to a 'sufficient nexus' simply echoes the requirement of Article XX(g) that the measure be applied in conjunction with restriction on domestic production or consumption and that the question of whether an implied jurisdictional limitation exists is

Before examining this matter, it must be noted that the issue of the existence of an 'implied jurisdictional limitation' has not even been mentioned in the context of the TBT Agreement, in the *US – Tuna II (Mexico)* reports. Yet this case concerned npr-PPM labelling requirements that aimed at the protection of dolphins abroad. There was no territorial nexus between the importing Member and the animals concerned, which means that this measure was as 'extraterritorial' as those of the first two *Tuna* cases. The Appellate Body accepted nevertheless that this measure contributed to the protection of dolphins, by ensuring that the US market was not used to encourage fishing fleets to catch tuna in a manner that adversely affected dolphins. This reasoning arguably implies that a PPM measure is by nature territorial because it concerns the influence that the internal market of the importing Member has on domestic or foreign environmentally harmful practices. As such, it enables WTO Members to apply principles of international environmental law that encourage states, and in particular developed nations, to eliminate unsustainable production and consumption practices.[96] Moreover, there are no obvious reasons why this reasoning would be relevant in the context of the TBT Agreement but not in that of the GATT, taking into consideration that by adopting the TBT, WTO Members expressed their desire to 'further the objectives of the GATT'[97] and since the Appellate Body purports to interpret both agreements in a coherent and consistent manner.[98]

On the basis of this evolution of case law, it seems likely that the Appellate Body would apply in the context of GATT Article XX a similar approach as that applied for the TBT Agreement and that the notion of 'sufficient nexus' refers not to the rules on extraterritorial jurisdiction but merely to the existence of a sufficient interest.

The next question is whether this interpretation is justified or whether the commitments by WTO Members in the GATT could make the rules on extraterritorial jurisdiction applicable.

States can restrict their sovereignty over their import policies in a treaty and commit to grant access to their internal market to their trading partners.[99] It has

---

largely moot (Howse 2002, p. 504 and Trebilcock et al. 2013, p. 676). However, the Appellate Body discussed in the *US – Shrimp* report the nexus that existed between the regulating country and the protected resources. If no similar restriction on domestic production can be introduced but only restrictions on domestic consumption, a risk of protectionist abuse exists, if there is no examination of the interest that the importing country may have in the foreign resource. In particular, as it will be shown, an importing country cannot impose trade restrictions to achieve competitiveness objectives (level the playing field). To differentiate these motivations from environmental justification, it seems necessary to examine the interests at stake.

[96]See Rio Principle 8 and Agenda 21, Chapter 4, para. 4.8, (which states that 'developed countries should take the lead in achieving sustainable consumption patterns'). See also *supra*, Chap. 4.

[97]See TBT Agreement Preamble, second recital.

[98]See *US – Clove Cigarettes*, Appellate Body Report, para. 91.

[99]See Appleton (1997a), p. 82; Wiers (2002), p. 276; Nielsen (2007), p. 265. See also *supra*, Chap. 5.

been contended that granting a right to market access to foreign producers entitles them to complain about the effects of trade-restrictive measures. These effects would not be 'mere' extraterritorial effects any longer but would become 'coercive' effects.[100] In this view, foreign producers would be forced to adopt the prescribed behaviour or to accept the 'sanction' of being denied market access. It has been therefore argued that, in such a case, the rules on extraterritorial jurisdiction might be applicable, at least when it comes to measures prescribing the adoption of a conduct abroad.[101]

For instance, Bartels has contended that enacting an import prohibition amounts to a denial of the right to market access granted under the GATT, i.e. a right 'normally available'[102] and would constitute a form of indirect enforcement measure of an extraterritorial regulation.[103] According to him, such measures require a justification based on the rules on extraterritorial jurisdiction, such as territoriality, nationality or the effects doctrine (under which a state may have prescriptive jurisdiction over activities occurring abroad when they have substantial and foreseeable effects on its territory).

It is, however, doubtful that the GATT grants WTO Members a 'right' to market access. Bartels argues that such right stems from the non-violation complaint provision (GATT Article XXIII), which protects the benefits accruing to WTO Members whether or not the contested measures at stake conflict with the GATT.[104] However, Article XXIII:1(b) does not require the withdrawal of such measures resulting in nullification or impairment of benefits. It simply provides that compensation can be sought under certain circumstances, which must be 'serious enough'.[105] Case law has thus considered that 'the remedy in Article XXIII:1(b) should be approached with caution and should remain an exceptional remedy'.[106] The rationale is that 'Members negotiate the rules that they agree and only *exceptionally* would expect to be challenged for actions not in contravention of those

---

[100]See e.g. Howse and Regan (2000), p. 277, stating that '[d]enying someone something they have a right to (such as market access, on the first view of the GATT) is a way of coercing them; whereas merely choosing not to deal with them, when that violates no right (as on the second view of GATT), (...) is not'.

[101]See Bartels (2002), pp. 381 ff.

[102]See the terminology of the Restatement of the Law, Third, The Foreign Relations of the United States (1987).

[103]See Bartels (2002), p. 378 (arguing that trade measures are non-judicial enforcement measures in the form of the 'denial of the right to engage in export or import transactions [...] and comparable denial of opportunities normally open to the person against whom enforcement is directed', in the sense of the Third Restatement of the Foreign Relations Law of the United States).

[104]See Bartels (2002), p. 383.

[105]GATT Article XXIII provides that the contracting parties may authorise the complainant to take action against the regulating country if they consider that the circumstances are 'serious enough'. Article 26:1b of the DSU provides that 'where a measure has been found to nullify or impair benefits under, or impede the attainment of objectives, of the relevant covered agreement without violation thereof, there is no obligation to withdraw the measure'.

[106]*EC – Asbestos*, Appellate Body Report, para. 186.

rules'.[107] Therefore, the argument that such an exceptional provision could justify that a *general* right to market access exists in the GATT seems untenable.

Moreover, as the Appellate Body has pointed out, Article XX does not contain any *explicit* jurisdictional limitation.[108] The Appellate Body's emphasis on the importance of the ordinary meaning of the text makes it unlikely that it would find that a general right to market access exists under the GATT.[109] On the other hand, the Appellate Body might also apply the principle of interpretation *in dubio mitius*—i.e., that a restriction to sovereignty cannot be presumed[110]—in order to deny the existence of a general right to market access, which could imply that the sovereignty of WTO Members would be restricted by rules on extraterritorial jurisdiction in addition to their obligations under the GATT.[111] When it comes to the object and purpose of the GATT, it can also be underlined that the GATT is not a free trade system but a trade liberalisation system. The objective is thus 'expanding trade' and not 'free trade'.[112] WTO Members have committed to substantially reduce obstacles to trade, but there is no commitment to eliminate them. Thus, it has been contended that the GATT introduces not a general right to trade but only a negative system prohibiting certain forms of discriminatory treatment.[113] The existence of numerous exceptions to WTO Members 'rights',

---

[107]Excerpt from the Panel Report in *Japan – Films*, para. 10.36, quoted by the Appellate Body in *EC – Asbestos*, para. 186 (emphasis added).

[108]See *US – Shrimp*, Appellate Body Report, para. 133. If the issue of the existence of an *implied* jurisdictional limitation arises, then it logically means that there is no *explicit* jurisdictional limitation.

[109]See Chang (2005), pp. 28 f. and p. 36.

[110]The Appellate Body applied this principle in the *EC – Hormone* case (p. 64). The Appellate Body referred to R. Jennings and A. Watts (eds.), *Oppenheim's International Law*, 9th ed., Vol. I (Longman 1992), p. 1278 and cited the following statement: '[t]he principle of *in dubio mitius* applies in interpreting treaties, in deference to the sovereignty of states. If the meaning of a term is ambiguous, that meaning is to be preferred which is less onerous to the party assuming an obligation, or which interferes less with the territorial and personal supremacy of a party, or involves less general restrictions upon the parties.'

[111]See Howse and Regan (2000), p. 276 ('[t]he doctrine *in dubio mitius* counsels against finding such a derogation without much clearer textual support'); Wiers (2002), p. 292 ('[i]n cases of doubt, the *in dubio mitius* principle would point towards a limited interpretation of those rights in favour of the remaining state sovereignty reflected in Article XX'). Note, however, that some have argued that this doctrine is controversial because to 'interpret obligations of one state restrictively could amount to not giving the intended effect to the rights of another state' (Pauwelyn 2003a, p. 186); Charnovitz (2007), p. 701 ('[p]erhaps, the principle *in dubio mitius* would be helpful to the adjudicator on the grounds that governments drafting Article XX did not impose on themselves more onerous requirements than those specifically mentioned in Article XX').

[112]See Wiers (2002), p. 290.

[113]See Howse and Regan (2000), p. 257 ('GATT creates no such general right of access [...]; it creates only a negative right that access shall not be restricted by discriminatory measures of various sorts'); Gaines (2002), p. 412 ('GATT creates no general right of market access'); Charnovitz (2007), p. 703 ('[a] puzzling, and I believe unfortunate, feature of the Appellate Body's holdings on the chapeau is the notion that WTO Members have a legal "right" in WTO law to have their exports accepted by other WTO Members. [...] surely, no practical right to trade exists under WTO law'). See also Howse and Regan (2000), pp. 276 ff.

even apart from the Article XX exceptions, could also be a factor showing that there is precisely no 'right' to market access.[114]

On the basis of these different arguments, it does not seem possible, in the view of the present author, to conclude that the GATT introduces a general right to market access. In the GATT, WTO Members committed, *inter alia*, to apply the principle of non-discrimination and to avoid quantitative restrictions. They have thereby limited their original sovereignty. At the same time, WTO Members have introduced general exceptions to these commitments in Article XX. The chapeau of this provision states that subject to certain requirements, 'nothing in this Agreement shall be construed to prevent the adoption or enforcement by any contracting party of measures' listed in sub-paragraphs (a) to (j). It is submitted that the words 'nothing in this agreement' in the chapeau of Article XX refer to this *original sovereignty*: the commitments made by WTO Members do not apply to policy goals listed in Article XX, subject to certain conditions specified in that provision.[115] In other words, the term 'nothing in this agreement' could be interpreted as a hierarchy in favour of non-economic goals, with a number of specific disciplines to prevent abuses and control the legitimacy of the non-economic goals pursued.[116]

Since WTO Members exercise their original sovereignty over their import policies when they take measures pursuing one of the policy goals mentioned in Article XX, they are not subject to any significant jurisdictional limitations resulting from customary international law. Any possible 'implied jurisdictional limitations' in Article XX are therefore those resulting from the GATT itself.

The tendency of the Appellate Body, in the light of the TBT Agreement case law, seems to be an evolution towards the application of the destination principle, which would enable an importing Member to choose the conditions upon which market access is granted.[117] Such approach would potentially render the 'extraterritoriality' debate largely irrelevant.

---

[114]See Charnovitz (2007), p. 703 ('[g]iven the myriad of trade barriers tolerated by WTO law, I would have thought that it is too late in the day for the Appellate Body to suppose that US trading partners have a legal right to export shrimp to the US economy').

[115]See also Wiers (2002), p. 292 ('Article XX reflects the sovereign right to protect life and health, natural resources and other things, a right which is not conferred by the trade treaty but which already existed'). See also Mavroidis (2016a), p. 416 ('there should thus be no doubt that the framers' intent was that all the grounds mentioned in this provision [Article XX] trump any trade-liberalizing obligation reflected in the rest of the GATT').

[116]It must be pointed out that diverging views exist in case law. Some GATT 1947 Panels held that the exception of Article XX had to be interpreted narrowly. Such approach has not been endorsed by the Appellate Body, which has rather emphasised that the function of the chapeau was to find a 'line of equilibrium' between the GATT obligations and the general exceptions. See discussion *infra*, 7.3.1.

[117]See on this score Mavroidis (2008b), pp. 277 ff., discussing whether an 'unconditional destination principle, whereby the country granting market access has the right to impose conditions, upon the satisfaction of which, market will be granted' should be applicable. In the context of tax measures, discussions have been made in the 1970 GATT report on *Border Tax Adjustment*, to examine the extent to which the destination principle applies in the GATT context. This principle

However, the WTO system would not allow either that a Member imposed all its internal rules to exporting countries, i.e. a full destination principle. The multilateral trading system is based on certain differences in internal regulations of states, without any will to harmonise the applicable standards. It represents, in other words, a negative rather than a positive integration system.[118] It has thus been argued that a WTO Member could not request other WTO Members to apply all its domestic environmental law within their jurisdiction in order to obtain access to the importing country's market. WTO Members have indeed, in principle, accepted to conduct trade on the basis of differences in internal regulations.[119] But the importing Member can also be particularly affected by an environmental harm caused by the production practices in the exporting country, and the GATT contains no commitment to refrain from enacting regulation to address such measures, in particular in the light of Article XX(b) and (g).

When an importing WTO Member purports to request compliance with environmental process standards by foreign producers for the products imported in its territory, it may theoretically seek, broadly speaking, either to foster environmental protection or to compensate the cost advantages that foreign producers that do not have to comply with these standards may have compared to domestic producers, which are subject to these requirements. It has therefore been contended in academic writings that a distinction should be made between these two general kinds of motivations, i.e. *environmental* and *competitiveness-based* motivations.[120] While the former seeks to address some form of environmental harm, the latter is mainly concerned with the negative competitive effects of lax environmental regulations of foreign exporting countries on the importing country's producers,[121] which may be seen as resulting in 'social dumping' from 'pollution havens'.[122]

Another way to describe this distinction is to refer to *comparative advantages*, compared to mere *competitive advantages*.[123] Comparative advantages include costs advantages, which do not result in externalities affecting other countries and

---

enables exported products to be relieved of some or all of the tax charged in the exporting country in respect of similar domestic products sold to consumers on the home market. Conversely, imported products sold to consumers may be charged with some or all of the tax charged in the importing country in respect of similar domestic products.

[118]See, e.g., Afilalo and Foster (2003), pp. 633 ff.; Horn and Mavroidis (2008), p. 1111. See also Wiers (2002), pp. 345–366 with comparison with EC law.

[119]Horn and Mavroidis (2008), p. 1132.

[120]For a distinction between environmentally based and competitiveness-based trade measures, see e.g. Trebilcock et al. (2013), pp. 658 ff. See also Chambers and Kohn (2001), p. 130 (concluding that '[t]here is little justification for such restraints of trade when the environmental standard is used solely to enhance the welfare of the regulated industry, but growing support exists when the primary intent of the import restriction is to increase environmental standards for foreign and domestic producers alike'); Stern (2006), pp. 150 f.

[121]See Trebilcock et al. (2013), p. 661.

[122]See Bhagwati (2004), pp. 146 ff.

[123]See Howse and Regan (2000), p. 281; Trebilcock et al. (2013), p. 661.

which might be attributable to diverging policies, characteristics of local factors of production or differences in geographical or demographic conditions. It has been argued that proposals to apply 'countervailing duties' to imported products to compensate comparative advantages would be primarily motivated not by an effort to improve environmental protection abroad but instead on competitiveness concerns because it would negatively affect producers of the importing country through 'unfair' competition, which requires measures to 'level the playing field'.[124] Competitive advantages, on the other hand, are those derived from the situation in which both the importing and the exporting countries cause the same externality but in which only the importing country enacts a measure to internalise these environmental costs. As a result, the producers of the exporting country profit from a cost advantage compared to those of the importing state. It has been maintained that such advantages are not relevant for the achievement of efficiency and should consequently not be regarded as a relevant comparative advantage.[125] The importing country's justification for imposing the same standards to imported products can be regarded in principle, in such a case, as an environmental justification.

Others refer to *'commercial' externalities* (negative effects on domestic producers) as opposed to *'transboundary' externalities* (negative effects on the importing country's environment or on shared resources) to distinguish these two broad categories of cases in which an importing country may wish to impose environmental trade measures.[126] While the GATT regulates trade (commercial externalities), it is not meant to regulate certain environmental externalities,[127] which may affect importing states' environment or shared resources. In that case, negative integration implies that there are no obligations to deregulate and restrictive trade measures are imaginable.[128]

Finally, one can also describe this distinction by opposing internal environmental matters of the exporting state to international environmental concerns.[129]

---

[124]Trebilcock et al. (2013), p. 661. It implies that it is not the same externality that is produced abroad, i.e. that domestic and foreign activities do not harm a shared environmental resource.

[125]See Howse and Regan (2000), p. 281. As it will be further explained below, they argue that these costs advantages would be derived to mere legal facts, while foreign producers would produce the same externality on a shared resource as domestic producers. See also Chang (2000), p. 36 and the detailed analysis in Chang (1995), pp. 2131 ff.

[126]See Horn and Mavroidis (2008), p. 1132; Cooreman (2017), p. 126.

[127]*Ibid.*

[128]See also Mavroidis (2016a), p. 423 (referring to the risk that a strict interpretation of the closed list of policy goals justifying an Article XX exception could lead to interpreting the GATT as an instrument for deregulation, as opposed to an instrument condoning negative integration).

[129]See e.g. the distinctions made in OECD (1997b), pp. 15 ff. See also Bhagwati (1993), pp. 164 f. (distinguishing between 'environmental problems that are intrinsically *domestic* in nature' and 'those that are intrinsically *international* in nature because they inherently involve spillovers across national borders').

In general terms, environmental motivations can justify a restrictive trade measure, but not competitiveness concerns,[130] because WTO Members have accepted in principle to conduct trade on the basis of differences in internal regulations since there are no commitments in the GATT to achieve positive integration.[131] The challenge is, of course, to draw the limit between internal matters of the exporting state and international environmental concerns. The crux of this debate consists in finding criteria that may be applied to verify that an environmental justification exists,[132] showing that the measure is not simply a pretext to pursue protectionist purposes.[133] In other words, the importing Member has to show that it can rely on a *sufficient legitimate interest.*[134]

7.1.2.2.2   Externalities and Proximity of Interests

A possible way to assess whether a sufficient legitimate interest exists would be to focus on the externalities that the measure at issue aims to address. The nature and the geographical scope of such externalities influence what will be referred to in this study as the 'proximity of interests' between the importing Member and the

---

[130]See Chang (1995), p. 2190 (discussing proposals to apply countervailing duties to offset 'ecodumping'); Bhagwati (2004), pp. 146 ff.; Horn and Mavroidis (2008), p. 1132; Trebilcock et al. (2013), p. 661.

[131]See Horn and Mavroidis (2008), p. 1132.

[132]See Charnovitz (2002), p. 104.

[133]See Stern (2006), p. 150 ('[e]ach State must be free to exercise its own sovereignty, each must be able to work towards common goals, but none should use the pretext of common goals to protect its commercial interests').

[134]See Esty (1994), pp. 117 f. ('[t]he use of trade restrictions to reinforce environmental standards should generally be seen as appropriate if they are used in response to an environmental injury in which the country using the measures has a legitimate interest'); Farber (1996), p. 1276 ('the ultimate test is whether some legitimate regulatory interest sufficiently justifies the measure'); Sands (2000), p. 299 ('[t]here was [. . .] no international instrument that entitles one state to take measures to protect turtles located in another jurisdiction. The Appellate Body nevertheless concluded that the United States had a legitimate interest in the conservation of turtles located outside its jurisdiction'); Bartels (2002) (he argues that the relevant question is whether a 'legitimate state interest' exists); Marceau (2002), p. 810 ('[r]eference to "shared values" in the interpretation of Article XX(g) in *US – Shrimp* may be seen as an attempt to formulate a coherent jurisdictional test to assess when a country has a sufficient interest in a policy such that Article XX will excuse unilateral action against a producer who violates that policy'); Puth (2004), p. 316 ('[d]ie Rechtfertigung nichtproduktbezogener Handelsmassnahmen des Importstaates nach Art. XX(g) darf danach nur soweit reichen, als ein legitimes Nutzungsinteresse des handelnden Staates an den betreffen Naturschätzen anzuerkennen ist'); Nielsen (2007), p. 307 ('the argument in Article XX must be that the wrong-doing is of "sufficient" "interest" to the country enacting the NPR-PPM to warrant a trade measure'). Outside the context of the WTO, Perrez (2000), p. 167, has argued that in international law, 'inhabitants and states at the other side of the globe may have a legitimate interest in the survival of a specific species, in the protection of the biodiversity, in the reduction of greenhouse gas emissions or the preservation of the rain forests at distant places'.

environmental situation at stake and thus the extent to which they might be viewed as a controversial basis for a restrictive trade measure.[135]

(i) Physical transboundary externalities affecting the environment of the importing Member: when the exporting Member causes externalities that have negative physical effects on the importing country's own domestic environment, there are no doubts that WTO Members have a legitimate interest in the way the activities concerned are conducted abroad. Nothing in the GATT indicates that WTO Members committed to refrain from taking trade measures to protect their own environment from negative physical transboundary externalities generated by production activities abroad.[136] Moreover, international law recognises that states have the duty not to cause damage to the environment of other states and thus to prevent transboundary harm.[137] Thus, an importing state negatively affected by a transboundary externality obviously has an interest in the environmental harm caused. Even the very restrictive *US – Tuna* Panel's view would allow such basis for enacting a restrictive trade measure.

(ii) Physical externalities affecting shared resources partly located on the territory of the importing Member: in cases of shared resources (such as migratory animals or shared watercourses or fish stocks), domestic and foreign producers may cause the same externality, and such externality can harm the same natural resource stock. If the importing country were concerned about externalities caused by its domestic producers, it would have equal concerns about the same externality caused by foreign producers and affecting the same resources. In other words, it

---

[135]The 'proximity test' suggested here should be distinguished both from the 'sufficient nexus' test mentioned by the Appellate Body in the *US – Shrimp* case and from any jurisdictional test based for instance on the effects doctrine. The proximity test is different from that latter, insofar as its goal is not to distinguish between two categories of measures, one for which the importing state has a jurisdictional basis allowing the adoption of legislation, the other for which it does not. The purpose of the proximity test is rather to determine one element of the importance of the goal pursued by the importing state, which should influence in turn the degree to which the conditions of Article XX are interpreted restrictively (see *infra*, 9.4.1). On the other hand, the proximity test is more precise than the Appellate Body's 'sufficient nexus' test (see *supra*, 7.1.2.2.2). It remains unclear if this 'sufficient nexus' implies in the view of the Appellate Body some form of territorial nexus or if it only requires the existence of a sufficient interest of the importing country. In that case, the level at which a particular interest is 'sufficient' is also unknown. Logically, under this 'sufficient nexus' test, some measures could in theory be rejected directly at the very first stage of Article XX analysis, namely the examination of whether the purpose pursued by the measure falls within the goals listed in the sub-paragraphs. It would thus also result in two categories of measures, one which cannot be justified under Article XX and the other which may, provided that they comply with the other conditions of the general exceptions provision. The proximity test indicates more clearly that no territorial nexus is required. With this test, most measures would not be rejected at the very first stage of Article XX analysis but the intensity of the interests at stake would influence the restrictiveness of the other conditions of Article XX, which allows a more subtle analysis of all the circumstances of the case.

[136]See Horn and Mavroidis (2008), p. 1132.

[137]See *supra*, Chap. 4.

would have an interest in the internalisation of all externalities affecting the natural resources concerned, irrespective of the location of these externalities' source.

Moreover, various principles of international law indicate that such environmental interest of the importing country is in principle legitimate, such as the principles of prevention of transboundary harm, sustainable use and equitable use.[138] The latter specifically applies to cases of shared resources. These principles may not necessarily imply that the exporting country has international binding obligations, the violation of which could justify countermeasures. However, they indicate that other states have a recognised *legitimate interest* in the sustainable management of shared natural resources. The recognition of this legitimate interest should be taken into account in the analysis of Article XX.

Besides, the Appellate Body confirmed in the *US – Shrimp* reports that PPM import measures aimed at the protection of resources at least partly under the territorial jurisdiction of the importing state could be consistent with Article XX.[139]

(iii) Physical externalities affecting common pool resources shared by all states: PPMs used abroad may physically affect common pool resources shared by all states (the 'global commons'), which encompass resources located beyond any jurisdiction, such as fish stocks of the high seas, and global ecosystems, such as the atmosphere or the ozone layer, which may be partially within the jurisdiction of specific states and partially in areas beyond any jurisdiction.

The contested measure in the *US – Tuna II (Mexico)* case concerned such a situation, i.e. the protection of dolphins located in the high seas. This characteristic was not deemed to be problematic by the Panel and the Appellate Body. Even though this measure was only examined under the relevant provisions of the TBT Agreement and not under Article XX, it seems likely that both agreements would be interpreted in a similar fashion.[140] On the other hand, in the *US – Shrimp* case, the protected sea turtles were migratory animals present at some moment of their lives in US territorial waters. But if the facts had been different and if these animals had not been migrating at some moment in US waters, it seems quite unlikely that the Appellate Body would have concluded that the United States had no legitimate interest in the protection of sea turtles. The contested measure would probably not have been rejected merely because of the absence of any territorial nexus.

Moreover, various arguments show that an importing Member may have a legitimate interest in externalities affecting the global commons. First, resources located beyond any jurisdiction are subject to a common property regime, which means that all states can exploit them and all have thus an interest in their sustainable management.[141] Likewise, a serious pollution of the atmosphere can affect several states or even all of them, regardless of the location of the source of

---

[138]*Idem.*

[139]See *supra*, 7.1.2.1.2.

[140]See *US – Tuna II (Mexico) 21.5*, Panel Report, para. 7.525, in which the compliance Panel did apply this reasoning to Article XX.

[141]See *supra*, Chap. 3.

the pollution. It is thus generally accepted that trade restrictions based on the amount of greenhouse gases emitted in the production of imported products would comply with the 'sufficient nexus' requirement because CO_2 emitted abroad affects the global atmosphere and has the same effects on global climate than CO_2 emitted domestically.[142] More generally, each state exploiting common pool resources cause similar externalities, in particular through appropriation of exploited resources, pollution or damaging practices. For efficiency reasons, when a state decides to internalise these externalities with respect to its own producers, it must do the same with externalities produced by foreign producers. If WTO Members were not allowed to apply the same standards to domestic and foreign producers, they would have an incentive not to regulate at all, which would then lead to a prisoner's dilemma situation. The ensuing non-cooperative outcome conversely risks leading to a tragedy of the commons.[143] Thus, in such cases, it cannot be said that the primary motivation for applying the same standards to imported products is generally based on competitiveness concerns.

Second, international law recognises that states should not harm areas beyond any jurisdiction. The principle of sustainable use has been specifically acknowledged in various fields, in particular in the United Nations Convention on the Law of the Sea, with respect to fish populations. Likewise, the Biodiversity Convention refers to the objective of conservation and sustainable use of biological diversity. On the other hand, climate change has been recognised as an issue of 'common

---

[142]See e.g. Bierman (2001), p. 431; Pauwelyn (2007), p. 35; Condon (2009), p. 912; Hufbauer et al. (2009), p. 83.

[143]Internalising an externality only with respect to domestic producers but not foreign producers would create a cost advantage for foreign producers, even though the physical externality caused is exactly the same. If the importing country does not impose the same regulation to imported products, then price differences between domestic and imported products will make the demand for the environmental-unfriendly product rise, all other things being equal. As a result, a PPM measure applicable only to domestic producers could fail to achieve any environmental outcome, but could threaten at the same time domestic producers. Therefore, the exclusion *per se* of all PPM measures addressing environmental harm caused to the 'global commons' would lead to inefficient results, since governments would have incentives not to regulate the activities of their own producers. In other words, their dominant strategy in the absence of an enforceable international agreement would be not to regulate, even if the adoption of such behaviour by all countries would result in a Pareto-suboptimal outcome, which is a form of prisoner's dilemma situation (see *supra*, 3.4.3). This could then lead to overexploitation and the 'tragedy of the commons' (see *supra*, 3.4.4). The same result could ensue if countries could not enact trade measures as a response to free riding or continuing practices harming resources located in areas beyond any jurisdiction or global ecosystems. For instance, more than any other common pool resources, the high seas are truly non-excludable, which means that enforcement of any resources management standard in the high seas is extremely difficult and costly. Similarly, it is impossible to prevent countries not participating in efforts to mitigate climate change to enjoy the benefits of a stable climate. Such situations increase the incentives to free ride on international efforts for sustainable management of these common resources, which risks leading to cooperation failures. In such context, trade measures are one of the main—and one of the only—concrete instruments to effectively protect such goods, if cooperation cannot be achieved (see *supra*, Chap. 3).

concern of humankind'.[144] These different concepts and principles show that an importing country has a legitimate interest in the production practices of foreign exporters, which could harm global ecosystems or resources located beyond any jurisdiction. On the other hand, the internalisation of externalities and the elimination of unsustainable production and consumption practices have been acknowledged as principles of international environmental law.[145] It must also be reminded that developed countries have a particular role in achieving these objectives: the size of their markets implies greater responsibilities in the elimination of unsustainable production and consumption patterns.[146] Such responsibilities should not be overlooked in the GATT context, and in particular in the interpretation of Article XX, in the light of the objective of the WTO of achieving sustainable development.

It must be pointed out that these principles of international environmental law may not entail precise rules as to the practices or level of exploitation that should be allowed. They can be viewed, however, as *shared goals* of the international community. In the presence of shared goals or values, it has been suggested that legitimacy should depend mainly on *scientific evidence*,[147] which could establish in particular the intensity of environmental harm in a particular case and the consequence it could have on other resources or on whole ecosystems or show patterns of unsustainable exploitation. The existence of shared goals does not mean that all states may have the same view on the priorities and the appropriate balance between economic, environmental and development objectives. In addition, states may have different responsibilities and capabilities in relation to the environmental harm concerned. These elements should be taken into account under the chapeau of Article XX and may influence the eventual compliance with Article XX as a whole. They should not, however, be examined in the context of whether a 'sufficient nexus' exists since they constitute a different issue. The interests pursued may be legitimate, but the allocation of the burden of environmental protection may be inappropriate.

(iv) Physical externalities affecting exclusively the environment of the exporting state but which also result in loss of global positive externalities: even in the absence of physical externalities affecting the environment of the importing state or shared resources, environmental practices in the exporting country may affect global positive externalities, such as biodiversity, and thus also affect the importing state. Such cases have not yet been submitted to WTO adjudicating bodies. However, if the Appellate Body applied a reasoning similar to that of the *US – Tuna II*

---

[144]See *supra*, 4.2.2.3.

[145]See *supra*, 4.1.1.

[146]*Idem.*

[147]See Bodansky (2007), p. 721 (he states that although 'science cannot answer questions of value, expertise can provide a legitimate basis of decision-making when there is no significant disagreement over values—when people have shared goals and the principal issue is how to achieve those goals').

(Mexico) case, it could consider that avoiding that the importing state's internal market could be used to encourage PPMs that reduce a global public good represents a legitimate interest. Besides, the Appellate Body could also consider, like it did in the *EC – Seal Products*, that such measures aim at reducing the global demand for a product produced through environmentally harmful PPMs, which could in turn reduce the production of that product.

International environmental law may show that the importance of certain global public goods has been acknowledged. For instance, biodiversity has been recognised as a 'common concern' of mankind.[148] It must be noted that relevant MEAs may show that a particular global public good represents a form of 'shared value'.[149] But since the adopted trade measures are based on the importing Member's original sovereignty, it is irrelevant if these MEAs are binding or if they authorise trade measures.

There is no doubt that the question of whether losses of global positive externalities justify a reaction by the importing state in the form of a *trade measure* is likely to be controversial. Besides the traditional arguments against the use of PPM measures, such as the alleged 'eco-imperialist' nature of such measures or the differing priorities that states might have, the exporting country may also argue that it would not be legitimate for an importing country to impose restrictive trade measures in reaction to the reduction in the supply of global public goods without *sharing* part of the conservation *costs* of these global benefits. If the loss of global positive externalities as a result of the environmental policies of the exporting country may be a legitimate concern for the importing country, it may not be legitimate in the light of the chapeau of Article XX to *require* foreign states to supply global positive benefits without participating in the costs of conservation.[150] These different objections are legitimate and should be taken into account not in Article XX but rather in the examination of the necessity test and of the conditions of the chapeau. At this stage, the focus should remain exclusively on whether the importing state can legitimately be concerned with the environmental harm occurring abroad, which indirectly affects it through a loss of global positive externalities.

(v) Physical externalities affecting exclusively the environment of the exporting state: it is questionable whether, even in this case, recent case law may imply that measures addressing externalities that affect exclusively the environment of the exporting state are justifiable. It could be contended that the importing Member may not want that products sold in its internal market favour environmentally

---

[148]See *supra*, 4.2.2.3.

[149]See Jansen (2000), p. 313 (discussing whether the extinction of an endangered species might be a ground of 'universal jurisdiction', becoming a matter of international concern. This author interprets this discussion as a reference to 'clearly shared values'); Sands (2000), pp. 299 f. (distinguishing between community values [the resource is shared], conservation value [conservation is desirable] and cooperation value [consensual approach is desirable]); Marceau (2002), p. 810.

[150]See *infra*, 7.3.4.2.2.

harmful production methods abroad, even if these PPMs do not result in transboundary physical externalities, in damage to common pool resources or in loss of global public goods.

Such reasoning would, however, result in the application of a pure destination principle, which seems incompatible with the multilateral trading system, as explained above. One of the problems with such justification is that it would be difficult to distinguish it from protectionist pretexts. There might be, however, certain circumstances in which a legitimate interest might be recognised by the Appellate Body.

First, international environmental law may show that the objective pursued is legitimate.[151] In that case, the fact that the resources concerned are located wholly within the territory of the exporting state may not seem relevant.

Second, the nature and intensity of the environmental harm at issue might possibly hurt the importing Member's public morals and be justifiable under Article XX(a).

These different types of externalities represent bases for the adoption of trade measures, which have a gradual degree of controversy. While it is clear in WTO law that the first three categories can represent a valid basis for enacting a restrictive trade measure, the fourth is likely to be more controversial and the fifth even more. Case law suggests nonetheless that even these last two categories might justify the adoption of PPM trade measures, in certain circumstances. However, in order to recognise the existence of a sufficient legitimate interest in these last two cases, it would probably be necessary to show at least that the environmental harm at issue is particularly intense.

7.1.2.3 Conclusion

It has been shown above that the tendency in WTO adjudicating bodies' practice seems to be a gradual reduction of the importance of the role of the 'extraterritoriality' issue. It seems likely that the issue of the 'implied jurisdictional limitation' in Article XX will not, in many cases, play a significant role.

This means that the attention of the Appellate Body is likely to focus rather on the specific conditions of Article XX, in particular the necessity test and the conditions of the chapeau.

The types of externalities that may be invoked to justify a restrictive trade measure do not all have the same proximity of interests. In order to find the balance between trade and environmental concerns, this proximity of interests could be taken into account. This means, for instance, that the environmental harm may have to be particularly intense to justify a measure targeting production methods in the exporting country that do not result in transboundary physical externalities. Conversely, it may appear justified to give WTO Members more leeway to adopt

---

[151] See *supra*, Chap. 4.

restrictive trade measures addressing externalities with which they have a particular close proximity of interests.

Moreover, the legitimacy of the goal pursued, as far as international trade law is concerned, may also depend on whether the goal pursued by the importing state has already been recognised by the international community, for instance in a multilateral environmental agreement. When it is the case, it may be argued that the trade measure aims at convincing the exporting state to adopt policies that further this goal. If, on the other hand, no such shared goal has already been recognised by the international community, trade measures rather aim at supporting the emergence of international standards or objectives. These two categories of measures have been described elsewhere as 'law-supporting' and 'law-creating' trade regulations.[152] It may be suggested that the multilateral trading system could take into account the international recognition of the legitimacy of a particular objective and give more leeway to WTO Members in the adoption of measures pursuing objectives that have been already recognised at an international level.

More precisely, the proximity of interests and the international recognition of the legitimacy of the goal pursued could influence the *importance of the goal* pursued by a particular measure.

As it will be shown in the next section, the importance of the goal is one of the criteria applied by the Appellate Body in the necessity test, which consists in its view in a 'weighing and balancing' analysis. It has been shown that WTO adjudicating bodies tend to be less strict than certain GATT 1947 panel reports on the extraterritoriality issue. At the same time, the absence of a close proximity of interests between the importing Member and the environmental situation at stake might result in a less deferent application of the necessity test, in the light of the criterion of the 'importance of the goal' pursued.

Likewise, it will be argued below that conditions of the chapeau should also be examined with a varying degree of deference depending on the importance of the goal,[153] which should be assessed, among other criteria, on the basis of the importance of the goal pursued.

In sum, it is submitted here that case law could continue its evolution towards a more subtle system, in which so-called 'extraterritorial' measures are not prohibited per se but are subject to a more or less strict scrutiny in the application of the conditions of Article XX depending on the importance of the goal pursued and the proximity of interests that prevail in any given case.

---

[152]See Nadakavukaren Schefer (2010), pp. 3 f.

[153]See *infra*, 9.4.1.

7.2 The Means-Ends Relationship in Article XX(b) and (g)

The two 'environmental' exceptions of Article XX do not contain the same standard concerning the nexus between the measure and the goal pursued. While sub-paragraph (b) refers to a necessity test, sub-paragraph (g) contains a 'relating to' test. These two standards are successively analysed below.

7.2.1 Article XX(b): The Necessity Test

7.2.1.1 Case Law

7.2.1.1.1 The New Necessity Test and the Right to Choose the Level
of Protection

Under GATT 1947 case law, the necessity test has been traditionally interpreted as a GATT inconsistency test. Panels examined if no alternative measure consistent, or less inconsistent, *with the GATT* was reasonably available to the regulating country, to further its objective of protecting human, animal or plant life or health.[154] Certain Panels focused rather on whether the adopted scheme was the *least trade restrictive* measure available.[155]

At the same time, GATT 1947 panel reports have repeatedly held that GATT Members had the right to choose their *level of protection*, which means that the only relevant alternatives in the necessity test were those that provided the same level of protection.[156]

The 'traditional' necessity test and the way it was actually applied in practice have been criticised as too restrictive.[157] Some have argued that the terms of the traditional necessity test were 'extraordinarily difficult to satisfy'.[158] Several commentators have thus argued that the necessity test had to be interpreted with a greater deference to the choices of an importing country in health matters.[159]

---

[154]See e.g. *US – Section 337*, Panel Report, para. 5.26: *Thailand – Cigarettes*, Panel Report, para. 75; *US – Gasoline*, Panel Report, para. 6.25.

[155]See e.g. *US – Malt Beverages*, Panel Report, para. 5.52.

[156]See e.g. *US – Section 337*, Panel Report, para. 5.26.

[157]See Esty (1994), pp. 48, 222 *et passim;* Appleton (1997b), p. 136; Schoenbaum (1997), pp. 276 f.; Neumann and Tuerk (2003), pp. 207 ff.

[158]Appleton (1997b), p. 136.

[159]See Esty (1994), p. 222 (stating that the traditional necessity test 'fails to give sufficient deference to the judgements of national politicians and officials concerning environmental goals and the means to pursuing them'); Schoenbaum (1997), p. 277 (stating that the traditional necessity test 'constitutes too great infringement on the sovereign powers of states to take decisions [one hopes] by democratic means [...]. An international organization such as the WTO should employ a deferential standard of review with respect to certain national decisions and policy choices').

In the *Korea – Beef* case, which concerned Article XX(d), the Appellate Body adopted what has been referred to as a 'new test' regarding the interpretation of necessity,[160] which did bring more flexibility to this test. It held that a panel had to apply a 'weighing and balancing' test in the determination of whether a WTO-consistent alternative measure that the Member concerned could 'reasonably be expected to employ' was available or whether a less WTO-inconsistent measure was 'reasonably available'.[161]

For the Appellate Body, the weighing and balancing test involves the examination of mainly three factors, which all influence the difficulty to comply with the necessity test. The Appellate Body held that a treaty interpreter had to

> (...) take into account the relative *importance of the common interests or values* that the law or regulation to be enforced is intended to protect. The more vital or important those common interests or values are, the easier it would be to accept as 'necessary' a measure designed as an enforcement instrument.

> There are other aspects of the enforcement measure to be considered in evaluating that measure as 'necessary'. One is the extent to which the measure *contributes to the realization of the end pursued*, the securing of compliance with the law or regulation at issue. The greater the contribution, the more easily a measure might be considered to be 'necessary'. Another aspect is the extent to which the compliance measure produces *restrictive effects on international commerce*, that is, in respect of a measure inconsistent with Article III:4, restrictive effects on imported goods. A measure with a relatively slight impact upon imported products might more easily be considered as 'necessary' than a measure with intense or broader restrictive effects.[162]

This approach was confirmed by several subsequent reports and transferred to the other provisions containing a necessity test, such as Article XX(b), in the *Brazil – Tyres* case; Article XX(a), in the *EC – Seal Products* case; and GATS Article XIV.

The Appellate Body has confirmed that WTO Members have the right to choose their level of (health or moral) protection, which means that they have the right to adopt the least trade-restrictive measure to achieve this level.[163] This right was also confirmed by the Appellate Body in the context of Article XX(a), in the *EC – Seal Products* case. Canada had argued that the European Union had to recognise the same level of animal welfare risk in seal hunts as it did in slaughterhouses and terrestrial wildlife hunts. The Appellate Body held that WTO Members had the right to determine the level of protection they consider appropriate, which meant that Members could set 'different levels of protection even when responding to similar interests of moral concern'.[164]

---

[160]See Neumann and Tuerk (2003), p. 210; Vranes (2009), p. 271.

[161]*Korea – Beef*, Appellate Body Report, para. 166.

[162]*Korea – Beef*, Appellate Body Report, para. 162 f. (emphasis added).

[163]Concerning Article XX(b), see in particular *EC – Asbestos*, Appellate Body Report, para. 168; *Brazil – Tyres*, Appellate Body Report, para. 156. Regarding Article XX(a), see *EC – Seal Products*, Appellate Body Report, para. 5.200. On the notion of trade-restrictiveness, see Voon (2015).

[164]*EC – Seal Products*, Appellate Body Report, para. 5.200.

But case law also appears ambiguous because in parallel to the confirmation of the right to choose the level of protection, the Appellate Body also applied a form of necessity test that could potentially be interpreted as an evolution towards a *proportionality* test. This would mean that, in certain circumstances, even the least trade-restrictive measure to achieve the level of protection sought by the importing country could be regarded as disproportional and thus not be deemed to comply with the necessity test. Such a result is incompatible with WTO Members' right to choose the level of protection.

First, the Appellate Body held in the *Brazil – Tyres* case that the contribution of the measure to the achievement of the goal must be 'material' and not simply 'marginal' or 'insignificant', especially when the measure at issue is as trade restrictive as an import ban.[165] The Appellate Body added that the contribution of the measure to the achievement of the goal was a 'key element' of the necessity analysis.[166] The Appellate Body thus explicitly rejected the defendant's argument that '[i]f the Panel finds that there are no reasonable alternatives to the measure, the measure is necessary—no matter how small its contribution—because the WTO does not second-guess the Member's chosen level of protection'.[167] Finally, the Appellate Body confirmed that 'in the light of the importance of the interests protected by the objective of the Import Ban, the contribution of the Import Ban to the achievement of its objective outweighs its trade restrictiveness'.[168]

Holding that the health benefits of the measure must outweigh its trade costs is a way of introducing a proportionality test *stricto sensu* in the necessity analysis. In this view, since even the least trade-restrictive measure might not comply with the necessity test should its efficiency not be 'material' enough, the right of WTO Members to choose their level of protection would be restricted.

However, in the *EC – Seal Products* report, the Appellate Body has seemed to distance itself from this conclusion. In this report, it interpreted its relevant findings of the *Brazil – Tyres* report. It denied that the contribution of the measure to its objective should have a decisive role in the necessity test. The *EC – Seal Products* Panel had stated, referring to the *Brazil – Tyres* Appellate Body's report, that the contribution made by the import ban to the identified objective had to be shown to be at least material, given the extent of its trade restrictiveness.[169] It added that in order to be considered necessary, the contribution of the measure to its objective

---

[165] See *Brazil – Tyres*, Appellate Body Report, para. 210. See also para 150, in which the Appellate Body held that it 'disagree[d] with Brazil's suggestion that, because it aims to reduce risk exposure to the maximum extent possible, an import ban that brings a marginal or insignificant contribution can nevertheless be considered necessary'.

[166] *Brazil – Tyres*, Appellate Body Report, para. 210.

[167] *Ibid.*, note 242.

[168] *Ibid.*, para. 179 (emphasis added). In a similar vein, the Appellate Body concludes its analysis of the necessity test in para. 210 by stating that '[t]hus, the contribution of the measure has to be weighed against its trade restrictiveness, taking into account the importance of the interests or the values underlying the objective pursued by it'.

[169] *EC – Seal Products*, Panel Report, para. 7.636.

had to reach a certain minimum threshold such as *material* or *significant* contribution.[170] The Appellate Body did not share the Panel's view. It held that it did not 'see that the Appellate Body's approach in *Brazil – Retreated Tyres* sets out a generally applicable standard requiring the use of pre-determined threshold of contribution in analysing the necessity of a measure under Article XX'.[171] It added that 'a measure contribution is thus only one component of the necessity calculus under Article XX. This means that whether a measure is "necessary" cannot be determined by the level of contribution alone, but will depend on the manner in which the other factors of the necessity analysis, including a consideration of potential alternative measures, inform the analysis'.[172] The Appellate Body thus emphasised the need to examine the different relevant factors as a part of a 'holistic' weighing and balancing exercise, the 'flexibility' of which did not allow for the setting of predetermined thresholds in respect of any particular factor.[173]

With these findings, the Appellate Body probably reduced the practical importance of the 'material' contribution issue, negating its self-standing relevance in a necessity test. It certainly did not mean that a measure may make no contribution at all to the objective but rather meant that the level of this contribution is not predetermined and depends on the other relevant factors, such as the importance of the goal pursued and the trade restrictiveness of the measure.

The 'material' contribution should thus probably be interpreted not as the introduction of a proportionality test but rather as a *suitability* test: in order to be necessary, a measure has to be suitable to achieve the objective pursued. It remains that the higher the efficiency threshold is set in practice, the closer one gets to a proportionality test *stricto sensu*.

A second element in the *Brazil – Tyres* case could be interpreted as an evolution towards a proportionality test. In its report, the Appellate Body stated that the necessity test consisted in a two-step approach. In the first phase of this analysis, a panel must consider in particular the importance of the interests and values at stake, the extent of the contribution of the measure to the achievement of the objective and its trade restrictiveness. This may yield a *preliminary* conclusion that the measure is necessary,[174] if the contribution of the measure to the achievement of the health or environmental objective outweighs its trade restrictiveness.[175] It is only in that case that this result must be confirmed by comparing the measure with possible alternatives.[176] This seems to imply that a WTO adjudicating body could potentially hold that a measure failed the necessity test on the basis of this first stage of the analysis. Certain findings of the *EC – Seal Products* Appellate Body's report seem to confirm

---

[170]*Ibid.*, fn. 977 to para. 7.635.

[171]*EC – Seal Products*, Appellate Body Report, para. 5.213.

[172]*Ibid.*, para. 5.215.

[173]*Ibid.*

[174]See *Brazil – Tyres*, Appellate Body Report, para. 178.

[175]*Ibid.*, para. 179.

[176]*Ibid.*, para. 178.

this two-step analysis. In this report, the Appellate Body stated that after having weighed and balanced the relevant factors (i.e., the importance of the objective, the contribution of the measure to that objective and the trade restrictiveness of the measure), 'in most cases', a comparison between the challenged measure and possible alternatives should 'then' be undertaken.[177]

Hence, the Appellate Body seemingly left the door open to the possibility that a measure might be considered as not 'necessary' under the first step of the necessity test, if the costs of the measure at issue (trade restrictiveness) are deemed to outweigh its benefits (contribution to the objective), in the light of the importance of the goal. In such a case, the necessity test would amount to a fully fledged proportionality test. It would represent an important limitation of WTO Members' right to choose their level of protection, which has been repeatedly recognised by the Appellate Body, since it could be concluded in certain circumstances that no measure to achieve that level is 'necessary' under Article XX(b). Moreover, it is possible that the requirement that the contribution of the measure be 'material' simply means that a measure should be suitable to achieve the objective of the measure. It could, however, also potentially imply some form of cost-benefit balancing, depending on the height at which the contribution threshold is set.

The main question here is thus whether the right to choose the level of protection should prevail, which means that the weighing and balancing test is not a proportionality test, or whether there might be restrictions to this right when the costs of the measure (trade-restrictive effects) outweigh its benefits (contribution to the achievement of the goal).

A close examination of case law provides certain interesting elements on this issue. In practice, it seems that the Appellate Body has applied a more or less restrictive approach of the necessity test depending on the circumstances of the case and, in particular, on the *importance of the goal* pursued, as the following analysis shows.

7.2.1.1.2 The *Brazil – Tyres* case

As explained above, in the 2007 *Brazil – Tyres* report, the Appellate Body introduced different new elements in the necessity test, which could have implied in theory a more restrictive test that could limit WTO Members' right to choose their level of protection: it held that the 'weighing and balancing' test comprises two phases, and it took the view that the measure must make a 'material' contribution to the achievement of the goal in order to be necessary.

However, when the Appellate Body applied its reasoning to the facts of the case, it took a deferent approach towards the regulating WTO Member. First, the *material contribution* threshold did not play an important role in practice. The Appellate Body merely stated that the Brazilian import ban was 'likely' to bring a

---

[177]*EC – Seal Products*, Appellate Body Report, para. 5.169 and 5.214.

material contribution to the achievement of its objective.[178] Hence, the Appellate Body showed much deference to the importing country in its examination of this condition. The efficiency threshold was set rather low, and the principle that a Member may choose its level of protection thus clearly prevailed in this case.[179] The Appellate Body also made clear that there was no need to quantify the efficiency of the measure and that, in certain cases, efficiency had to be examined on the long term, as in the case of global warming, since the results could only be evaluated with the benefits of time.[180]

Some have criticised this aspects of the Appellate Body's report, concluding that given the 'possibly minimal contribution' implied by the 'material contribution' threshold, it could be assumed in the future that any measure that contributes to health, no matter how minimally, would satisfy the necessity test under Article XX(b).[181] As mentioned above, the material contribution threshold probably rather means that the measure must be *suitable* to achieve the goal pursued. Besides, the fact that the Appellate Body applied a deferent approach in the *Brazil – Tyres* case does not mean that it would necessarily do so in all cases. In the view of this author, this deferent approach must rather be explained by the importance of the health interests at stake, i.e. the fight against a life-threatening disease.

Then, after having weighed and balanced the relevant factors, the *Brazil – Tyres* Panel examined the *alternative measures* available. A first issue was to determine what the relevant alternatives were that could achieve the same level of protection, which required a definition of the level of protection pursued.

The Panel considered as follows:

---

[178]See *Brazil – Tyres*, Appellate Body Report, para. 155.

[179]A parallel can be made here with the findings of the Appellate Body in the context of Article XX(g), in which it stated that a measure may fail to meet the requirement of this provision 'should it become clear that realistically, a specific measure cannot in any possible situation have any positive effect on conservation goals' (*US – Gasoline*, Appellate Body Report, pp. 21 f.). It seems that in both contexts of Article XX(b) and (g), the concern of the Appellate Body is to prevent abusive invocation of these exceptions for measures which are not even capable of meeting these low requirements, i.e. which constitute an unsuitable means to reach the purported goal.

[180]See *Brazil – Tyres*, Appellate Body Report, para. 151 ('certain complex public health or environmental problems may be tackled only with a comprehensive policy comprising a multiplicity of interacting measures. In the short-term, it may prove difficult to isolate the contribution to public health or environmental objectives of one specific measure from those attributable to the other measures that are part of the same comprehensive policy. Moreover, the results obtained from certain actions—for instance, measures adopted in order to attenuate global warming and climate change, or certain preventive actions to reduce the incidence of diseases that may manifest themselves only after a certain period of time—can only be evaluated with the benefit of time'). See also *US – Gasoline*, Appellate Body Report, p. 21, in which the Appellate Body similarly stated in the context of Article XX(g) that 'in the field of conservation of exhaustible natural resources, a substantial period of time, perhaps years, may have to elapse before the effects attributable to implementation of a given measure may be observable'.

[181]See Bown and Trachtman (2009), p. 126.

> Brazil's chosen level of protection is the reduction of the risks associated with waste tyres accumulation to the maximum extent possible and (. . .) Brazil purports to achieve this goal by reducing the 'generation' of tyre waste as much as possible. Thus, insofar as the level of protection pursued by Brazil involves the 'non-generation' of waste tyres in the first place, the Resolution would not seem able to achieve the same level of protection as the import ban.[182]

Thus, the Panel examined alternative measures that could decrease the generation of waste tyres in order to reduce the relevant health risks to the maximum extent possible.

In this case, Brazil sought to *reduce the health risks* associated with the accumulation of waste tyres. This could be referred to as the final goal of the measure or the objective *stricto sensu* (first level). To achieve that objective, Brazil had to choose one or several concrete measures of health or environmental policy. In that case, Brazil chose to reduce the *generation* of new waste tyres[183] rather than measures dealing with these wastes once they had accumulated. This choice of environmental or health policy can be seen either as an *objective lato sensu* (second level)—i.e., as a concrete goal of environmental or health policy to achieve the final objective of protecting health—or as a *means* to achieve the objective of protecting health. Finally, to achieve that goal *lato sensu*, Brazil adopted an import ban on retreated tyres, which have a shorter lifespan, as a means to achieve the 'non-generation' objective (third level).

The Panel hence considered in the *Brazil – Tyres* case that the right to choose the level of protection covered both the choice of the goal *stricto sensu* (reduction of health risks to the maximum extent possible) and the goal *lato sensu* (non-generation of waste tyres). The consequence of these findings is that measures reducing the risks associated with waste tyres by other means than the reduction of waste tyres generation, such as improved disposal methods of waste tyres, were not qualified as relevant alternatives.

These findings undoubtedly represented a deferent approach since Brazil's choice of environmental policy (the waste non-generation objective) was not questioned by the Panel. They have been criticised by the European Communities in their appeal, precisely because they would have preferred that the 'non-generation' goal be qualified as a *means* to achieve health protection, which could have been reviewed under the necessity test.[184] Some commentators similarly criticised this interpretation, considering that a reduced number of waste tyres is not a degree to which health is fulfilled. They have pointed out that there might have been other less restrictive ways to achieve the same health effects without reducing the number of waste tyres.[185]

---

[182]*Brazil – Tyres*, Panel Report, para. 7.177.

[183]Along with other complementary measures.

[184]See *Brazil – Tyres*, Appellate Body Report, para. 17. The EC argued that the approach of the Panel 'wrongly link[ed] the notion of alternative measures to the *means* (avoidance or non-generation of waste tyres) employed by the measure at issue to achieve its objective, rather than to the objective itself'.

[185]See Bown and Trachtman (2009), p. 124.

The Appellate Body did not overturn the Panel findings and made a similar reasoning, although its view is rather imprecise. It held that non-generation measures were 'more apt' to achieve the objective pursued because they prevented the accumulation of waste tyres, while waste management measures disposed of waste tyres once they had accumulated.[186] By maintaining that non-generation measures are 'more apt' to achieve the reduction of health risks arising from the accumulation of waste tyres, the Appellate Body may have recognised that the alternative measures of environmental policy (i.e., the other possible goals *lato sensu*) could not achieve the same reduction of health risks and could thus not be categorised as alternatives. But it could also mean that the Appellate Body did not want to review the choice of *lato sensu* goals, examining only alternative *trade* measures that could achieve the desired waste tyre 'non-generation' objective.

In any event, the Appellate Body did not rely on any quantitative data to conclude that non-generation measures were 'more apt' to prevent the accumulation of waste tyres than waste management measures, which denotes the application of a low standard of review as to the choice of the *lato sensu* goal.

When it comes to whether the less trade-restrictive *alternatives achieved the same level of protection*, the Appellate Body also applied a deferent approach. First, it did not require quantification of the reduction of the risks, accepting that a qualitative evaluation was enough.[187] Without any form of quantification, no reference exists to evaluate if the suggested alternatives make an 'equivalent contribution' to the achievement of the goal,[188] especially since the Appellate Body accepted that Brazil's level of protection was the reduction of health risks 'to the maximum extent possible'.[189]

In addition, the Panel qualified certain alternatives suggested by the complainant as 'cumulative rather than substitute',[190] which was criticised by the European Communities because, in their view, such measures were capable of achieving the same objective as the import ban and had therefore to be taken into account.[191] But the Appellate Body upheld this Panel's findings by recognising that Brazil had designed a comprehensive strategy to deal with waste tyres and that substituting 'one element of this comprehensive policy for another would weaken the policy by reducing the synergies between its components, as well as its total effect'.[192] These complementary measures were deemed to be 'mutually supportive elements of a comprehensive policy to deal with waste tyres'.[193]

---

[186]See *Brazil – Tyres*, Appellate Body Report, para. 174; see also para. 161.

[187]See *Brazil – Tyres*, Appellate Body Report, para. 146, in which the Appellate Body refers to its report in *EC – Asbestos*, para. 167.

[188]This was criticised *inter alia* by Bown and Trachtman (2009), pp. 126 f.

[189]See *Brazil – Tyres*, Appellate Body Report, para. 144; Panel Report, para. 7.108.

[190]*Brazil – Tyres*, Panel Report, para. 7.169.

[191]See *Brazil – Tyres*, Appellate Body Report, para. 18.

[192]*Ibid.*, para. 172.

[193]*Ibid.*, para. 211.

These findings may be surprising insofar as they exclude the view that in the least trade-restrictive alternative test, there is one and only one measure that achieves the chosen level of protection and causes the smallest trade costs. On the other hand, the enhanced regulatory autonomy that it gives WTO Members may be useful to address complex issues such as the fight against climate change, which also requires the adoption of comprehensive policies, which may be composed of a series of 'complementary' or 'cumulative' measures.

All the different aspects of the *Brazil – Tyres* case described above show that the Appellate Body applied a deferent standard of review when it actually applied the necessity test to the facts of this case. As it will be argued below, this deferent standard of review might be explained by the importance of the interests and values at stake in this dispute.

7.2.1.1.3   The *EC – Seal Products* Case

The Appellate Body also applied a deferent approach towards the regulating state in certain aspects of the 2014 *EC – Seal Products* report. Concerning the question whether a measure makes a 'material' contribution to the objective pursued, the Appellate Body stated, as mentioned above, that there was no predetermined threshold of 'materiality'.[194]

Moreover, the Panel held that the import ban made a contribution to reducing the demand for seal products within the European Union and, to a certain extent, to reducing global demand.[195] The complainants had argued on appeal that the Panel should have assessed whether a reduction in demand for seal products would have actually contributed to a reduction in inhumanely killed seals. They contended that it had not been established that the EU seal regime led to a reduction in demand for seal products and that the Panel had not demonstrated that reducing demand led to fewer inhumanely killed seals. Basically, their argument was that the import ban could not contribute to the achievement of the objective pursued since it would not reduce the number of inhumanely killed seals. This argument was rejected by the Appellate Body, which stated that 'it was not unreasonable for the Panel to assume that a decrease in demand, and hence a contraction of the seal products market, would have the effect of reducing the number of seals killed, and thus the number of inhumanely killed seals'.[196]

These findings have a great significance for PPM measures, arguably in the context of Article XX(b) as well. It has been contended that potential influence of PPM measures on the adoption of particular policies in the exporting country is very limited and depends in particular in private and public response in that country.[197] Some have thus claimed that PPM measures 'are inherently ineffective

---

[194]See *EC – Seal Products*, Appellate Body Report, para. 5.216.

[195]See *EC – Seal Products,* Panel Report, para. 7.459; Appellate Body Report, para. 5.225.

[196]*EC – Seal Products*, Appellate Body Report, para. 5.247.

[197]See Conrad (2011), p. 291.

or even unsuitable to further the policy goals they seek to achieve, since they do not have any actual effects on the circumstances or behaviour targeted'.[198] Such arguments would restrict to a large extent the admissibility of all PPM measures that seek to influence the adoption of particular policies abroad. However, the Appellate Body rejected this reasoning in the *EC – Seal Products* and thus applied a deferent approach towards the regulating state in the examination of the contribution of the measure to the objective pursued.

Finally, regarding the level of protection sought by the import ban, the complainants had highlighted that terrestrial wildlife hunts and slaughterhouse practices in the EU raised similar moral concerns as seal hunts. In their view, the EU had to apply the same level of protection of animal welfare risks in all these cases. The Appellate Body disagreed and held that 'Members have the right to determine the level of protection that they consider appropriate, which suggests that Members may set different levels of protection even when responding to similar interests of moral concern'.[199] It was thus recognised that the EU could have different, and higher, moral standards for seal hunts and for terrestrial wildlife hunts and slaughterhouses, which represented obviously a deferent approach towards the regulating state.

7.2.1.1.4   The *Korea – Beef* Case

If the Appellate Body has shown deference to the defending Member in many aspects of the necessity test in the *Brazil – Tyres* report and in some aspects of the *EC – Seal Products* report, the Appellate Body has been much less deferent when it has examined the necessity of a measure under Article XX(d).

The *Korea – Beef* case illustrates these differences. It should be pointed out that the Appellate Body's report in this case was rendered in 2001, before the *Brazil – Tyres* (2007) and *EC – Seal Products* (2014) reports commented above. But it seems unlikely that the Appellate Body's reasoning would be significantly different if a similar case had been brought to the dispute settlement body after these two cases.

In the *Korea – Beef* case, the Appellate Body did not accept the defendant's stated level of protection and thus corrected it. Korea had argued that its chosen level of enforcement was the *elimination* of fraud in beef retail market.[200] But the Appellate Body considered it unlikely that Korea intended to establish a level of protection that *totally eliminated* fraud. It rather assumed that, in effect, Korea intended to *reduce considerably* the number of cases of fraud.[201]

---

[198] *Ibid.*

[199] *EC – Seal Products*, Appellate Body Report, para. 5.200.

[200] See *Korea – Beef*, Appellate Body Report, para. 175.

[201] *Ibid.*, para. 178.

Moreover, it did not allow Korea to choose its *lato sensu* goal, which was in that case the introduction of a dual retail system for beef sale. This system was expressly categorised by the Appellate Body as an *instrument* to achieve the final objective, i.e. reduction of fraud with respect to the origin of beef sold by retailers.[202] This dual retain system was not regarded by the Appellate Body as the least trade-restrictive means to achieve Korea's objective.

Hence, the Appellate Body applied a high standard of review in the Article XX(d) necessity analysis, in the *Korea – Beef* case. There is therefore a striking contrast between the approach applied by the Appellate Body in the *Korea – Beef* case and that applied in the *Brazil – Tyres* case.

7.2.1.2   Critique

7.2.1.2.1   Necessity, Proportionality and the Right to Choose the Level of Protection

When it comes to whether the 'weighing and balancing' approach of the Appellate Body should be interpreted as a traditional necessity test or rather as some form of proportionality test, which could encroach on WTO Members' right to choose their level of protection, it must be emphasised that, so far, no panel or Appellate Body report has applied a genuine proportionality test *stricto sensu*. In other words, it has never been held that the least trade-restrictive measure to achieve the chosen level of protection did not pass the necessity test. On the other hand, the Appellate Body has always confirmed that WTO Members have the right to choose their level of protection, which implicitly rejects the applicability of the proportionality test. In addition, restriction of this right would imply very controversial limitations of WTO Members' regulatory autonomy to pursue non-economic objectives, which may contradict the negative integration system of the WTO by requiring some form of international standard harmonisation. It seems thus that case law on the necessity test should not be interpreted as having transformed it as a proportionality test *stricto sensu*.

If WTO Members can choose their level of protection, the measure at issue must in the first place be capable of achieving some protection. The 'material contribution' threshold could thus be seen as a suitability test, which would represent a limit to the right to choose the level of protection, when the contribution to the achievement of the goal is minimal and the underlying interests not particularly important.

However, it must be pointed out that the more efficient the measure is required to be, the closer one gets to a proportionality test, i.e. a situation in which it would be

---

[202]See *Korea – Beef*, Appellate Body Report, para. 178 ('it must be noted that the dual retail system is only an instrument to achieve a significant reduction of violations of the Unfair Competition Act. Therefore, the question remains whether other, conventional and WTO-consistent instruments can not reasonably be expected to be employed to achieve the same result').

held that the trade-restrictive effects of the measure outweigh the contribution of the measure to the achievement of the goal. In order to preserve WTO Members' right to choose their level of protection, the 'material contribution' threshold should not, in the view of the present author, be set at a level that would amount to a genuine cost-benefit balancing. It should remain a suitability test only.

7.2.1.2.2   A Varying Standard of Review According to the Importance of the Goal Pursued

It has been explained above that in the *Brazil – Tyres* case, the Appellate Body introduced some *potentially* restrictive elements in the necessity test, in particular through the two-phase analysis of the 'weighing and balancing' approach and the 'material contribution' test. At the same time, it applied a low degree of scrutiny when it *actually* applied the elements of the necessity test to the facts of the case. In other cases, such as the *Korea – Beef* report, the Appellate Body was much more restrictive. In that case, it corrected in particular Korea's stated level of protection.

A first possible explanation for these differences in the Appellate Body's approach is simply the fact that *Brazil – Tyres* was examined under Article XX(b) and *Korea – Beef* under Article XX(d). It is, however, submitted that a more fundamental element explains the differences in the degree of scrutiny applied, i.e. the importance of the goal pursued by the measure at issue. In *Brazil – Tyres*, the defendant's measure addressed particularly severe health risks, i.e. risks of life-threatening diseases implied by the accumulation of waste tyres. The non-economic interests underlying the measure were thus particularly important. In *Korea – Beef*, the objective pursued by the contested measure was the fight against fraud in the beef market, which does not have the same importance. Current case law on the necessity test may appear somewhat unclear, but it becomes easier to understand if one interprets the reference to the importance of the interests and values at stake, in the applicable criteria of the 'weighing and balancing test', as a reference to the *applicable standard of review*. [203]

---

[203]Of a similar opinion, see Sykes (2003), p. 416 (stating in particular that 'if the regulatory objective relates to some highly valued interest such as the protection of human life, then the challenged regulation will be upheld if there is any doubt as to the ability of the proposed alternative to achieve the same level of efficacy. This practice may be understood as a recognition of the fact that the costs of an erroneous decision—loss of life—would be extremely high, and that even a small probability of an erroneous decision counsels against condemning the measure under scrutiny'); Vranes (2009), p. 275 (arguing that the criteria of the weighing and balancing test 'have been referred to by the Appellate Body as well to demarcate the degree of scrutiny that was deemed applicable under the *necessity* test'); Mavroidis et al. (2010), p. 694 (suggesting that the degree of deference by the WTO adjudicating bodies might vary depending on the objective sought). See also Howse and Tuerk (2001), p. 325 (in the view of whom the Appellate Body has introduced the weighing and balancing test so as to provide WTO Members with an additional 'margin of appreciation' in making regulatory choices to achieve the purpose stated in those provisions of Article XX that entail a necessity test).

In the view of this author, the degree of scrutiny applied by a WTO adjudicating body in a particular case should indeed depend on the importance of the goal pursued. This argument is further developed in Chap. 9 below. As far as the necessity test is concerned, it should be noted that this approach would be coherent with current case law. The process by which the Appellate Body balances all relevant factors should be regarded as efforts to adapt the restrictiveness of the necessity test to the importance of the interests pursued by the importing country in order to guarantee a 'flexible' system.[204] More particularly, depending on the degree of deference applied in a particular case, the Appellate Body could examine more or less closely whether a measure makes a 'material' contribution to the achievement of the goal pursued, what the actual level of protection sought by the regulating country is, whether possible alternative measures were reasonably available, whether they could achieve the same level of protection, etc. If the Appellate Body showed an important deference to the defending Member in the *Brazil – Tyres* case, which involved particularly severe health risks, it may apply a more stringent standard of review in other cases in which the relevant risks may not be as high.[205]

In that respect, the Appellate Body has not introduced a generally applicable *in dubio mitius* rule in favour of respondents, as some have argued.[206] Rather, it results in a flexible system granting greater deference to the regulating state when the non-economic interests pursued are particularly important. The necessity test may be examined narrowly when the interests at stake are not particularly important but could be applied in a much more deferent fashion when the regulating Member pursues objectives of primary importance or urgency.

It might be objected by some that the Appellate Body lacks the legitimacy to review the importance of the goal pursued.[207] It is correct that the Appellate Body could, for instance, clearly not hold that the goal of protecting human, animal or plant life or health is 'unimportant'. The policy goals listed in Article XX have been recognised by WTO Members as legitimate objectives that could justify exceptions to GATT commitments if certain conditions are met. In practice, WTO adjudicating bodies have exercised self-restraint when it comes to evaluating the importance of the values at stake by stating, for instance, that they were not required to examine the 'desirability of the declared policy goal as such'.[208]

---

[204]In para. 5.215 of the *EC – Seal Products* Report, the Appellate Body referred to the 'flexibility' resulting from the application of the weighing and balancing test.

[205]*Contra*: Bown and Trachtman (2009), p. 126 ('we must assume in the future that any measure that contributes to health, no matter how minimally, will satisfy the necessity test under Article XX(b)').

[206]See Bown and Trachtman (2009), p. 133 (arguing that the necessity test as applied by the Appellate Body in the *Brazil – Tyres* case results in a rule of *in dubio mitius* in favour of the responding state.

[207]See Howse and Tuerk (2001), pp. 326 f.; Neumann and Tuerk (2003), p. 214; Regan (2007), p. 349.

[208]*Brazil – Tyres*, Panel Report, para. 7.97. The Panel referred to the following paragraphs of the *US – Gasoline* Panel Report: '[i]n concluding, the Panel wished to underline that it was not its task

It is submitted here that the examination of the importance of the goal by WTO adjudicating bodies must focus not on the importance of the *value* of protecting life or health as such but rather on the intensity of the *existing risks* for these values in a particular case, such as the nature and intensity of the health risks of asbestos or of the accumulation of waste tyres, or of the risks for the environment caused by climate change. When the Appellate Body has examined in past cases the importance of the interests and values at stake, it has relied clearly on the concrete risks for the values protected by Article XX(b) present under the circumstances of the case. For instance, the Appellate Body stated in the *EC – Asbestos* case that the objective pursued by the measure was the preservation of human life and health through the elimination of the 'well-known, and life-threatening, health risks posed by asbestos fibres', which was a value both 'vital and important to the highest degree'.[209]

In the context of the SPS Agreement, the Appellate Body similarly established a link between the existence of a reasonable relationship between the measure and risk assessment. It held in the *EC – Hormones* report that with respect to the requirement that a risk assessment be conducted, governments could act in good faith on the basis of divergent opinion coming from qualified and respected sources. It stated further that such conduct by itself did not necessarily signal the absence of a reasonable relationship between the SPS measure and the risk assessment, especially where the risk involved was 'life-threatening in character' and was perceived to constitute a 'clear and imminent threat' to public health and safety.[210] In other words, the Appellate Body explicitly linked the degree of deference that it would show to the defending Member regarding the relation between the risk assessment and the SPS measure to the intensity of the health risks involved and to the urgency of the intervention. In the view of this author, a similar approach should be applied in the context of Article XX(b).

In order to limit the legitimacy issues related to the assessment of the importance of the objective pursued, WTO adjudicating bodies should focus in a similar fashion on the factual aspects of the case establishing the nature of the risks (extent of environmental damage, intensity of the threat, importance of the ecosystem or species at issue, rate at which degradation occurs, urgency of intervention, etc.), the

---

to examine generally the desirability or necessity of the environmental objectives of the Clean Air Act or the Gasoline Rule' (para 7.1). See also para. 6.22: '[t]he Panel noted that it was not the necessity of the policy goal that was to be examined, but whether or not it was necessary that imported gasoline be effectively prevented from benefitting from as favourable sales conditions as were afforded by an individual baseline tied to the producer of a product. It was the task of the Panel to address whether these inconsistent measures were necessary to achieve the policy goal under Article XX(b). It was therefore not the task of the Panel to examine the necessity of the environmental objectives of the Gasoline Rule, or of parts of the Rule that the Panel did not specifically find to be inconsistent with the General Agreement.'

[209]See *EC –Asbestos*, Appellate Body Report, para. 172. See also *Brazil – Tyres*, Panel Report, para. 7.111 ('the objective of protecting human health and life against life-threatening diseases, such as dengue fever and malaria, is both vital and important to the highest degree').

[210]See *EC – Hormones*, Appellate Body Report, para. 194.

importance of the resources or ecosystems at stake for the conservation of a global public good, the need for urgent intervention, etc. The intensity of these interests determines the extent to which the underlying values are put at risk because of life-threatening diseases, possible irreversible environmental damages, etc. It is also clear that it is not the task of WTO adjudicating bodies 'to settle a scientific debate, not being composed of experts in the field of possible human health risks' and that therefore panels are not an 'arbiter of opinions expressed by the scientific community'.[211] They should thus be able to rely on 'divergent but qualified and respected opinion'.

7.2.1.2.3 PPM Measures and the Necessity Test

It has been suggested above that WTO adjudicating bodies should apply a varying standard of review under the necessity test, depending on the importance of the goal pursued. It has also been argued that assessing the importance of the goal in a particular case requires the examination of the specific facts of the case showing the nature and intensity of the environmental threat at issue and the urgency of intervention.

In the context of PPM measures, this analysis could also take into consideration the proximity of interests between the environmental harm addressed by the measure and the regulating country. The analysis of whether the regulating WTO Member can invoke a sufficient legitimate interest in environmental harm occurring abroad, which should be carried out in the examination of whether the measure falls within the scope of Article XX(b), could thus provide useful factual elements to determine the importance of the goal in the necessity test.[212]

Moreover, the intensity of the nexus between the regulating country and the environmental situation may influence the possibilities to comply with the test of the 'material contribution' to the achievement of the goal. A trade measure completing an internal measure addressing the same environmental externalities produced domestically and abroad may contribute to the achievement of internalising that externality. On the other hand, the efficiency of a trade measure addressing an environmental externality only produced in the exporting country would probably be less important. Depending on the applicable standard of review, the 'material contribution' test could thus be more difficult to meet in such a case.

Certain findings of the *EC – Seal Products* reports may be relevant for this issue. The European Union had chosen to address public moral concerns relating to the number of inhumanely killed seals by enacting a ban on the importation of certain seal products. In the examination of the necessity test under Article XX(a), the Panel concluded that this ban made 'a contribution to reducing the demand for seal

---

[211] See *EC – Asbestos*, Panel Report, para. 8.181.

[212] See *supra*, 7.1.2.2.2.

products within the European Union and, to a certain extent, to reducing global demand'.[213]

In the context of Article XX(b), a similar reasoning could be applied, according to which a restrictive trade measure targeting externalities caused only in the exporting country may contribute to the achievement of an environmental objective by *reducing the demand* for the goods the production processes of which cause that externality. Even though trade measures are not first-best solutions, they may represent the only available instrument to address an externality caused abroad, in the absence of international cooperation. They may thus be 'necessary' within the meaning of Article XX(b) in certain circumstances.[214] Similarly, a measure examined under Article XX(g) could be viewed as a suitable measure to achieve the objective, through a reduction of the demand for the products concerned, and thus comply with the 'relating to' test.

With respect to the choice of the level of protection, the previous sections have shown that in the *Brazil – Tyres* case, the Appellate Body applied a deferent standard of review as regards the determination of the level of health protection sought by Brazil. It concluded that the chosen level of protection implied a waste tyre *non-generation objective* and that only the alternative measures that could achieve this non-generation objective were relevant in the least trade-restrictive alternative test. In other words, the Appellate Body considered that Brazil had the right to choose its *lato sensu* goal (non-generation objective) and not only the degree to which it sought to protect life and health.

In the context of PPM measures, it is doubtful that a similar reasoning could apply. In the *US – Shrimp* case, the United States initially decided to require the adoption by shrimp exporting countries of essentially the same regulatory scheme for the protection of sea turtles from shrimp trawling. Thus, it required the adoption of the same instruments (or *lato sensu* goal) as the United States scheme. The Appellate Body held that United States could only ask for the adoption of a measure 'comparable in effectiveness'. In other words, a WTO Member can require the

---

[213]*EC – Seal Products,* Panel Report, para. 7.459; Appellate Body Report, para. 5.225.

[214]*Contra:* Conrad (2011), pp. 291 ff. She has argued that in the case of PPM measures, the importing country lacks legislative jurisdiction for the behaviour it seeks to influence and that therefore PPM measures are 'inherently ineffective or unsuitable to further the policy goals they seek to achieve, since they do not have any actual effects on the circumstances or behaviour targeted'. This implies, in her view, that such measures could not be justified under the necessity test, and possibly under the relating to test of Article XX(b) and (g) (Conrad 2011, pp. 291 ff). This reasoning seems difficult to reconcile with the fact that a reduction of the demand for a particular product may consequently reduce its supply and thus the damages caused by production. The *EC – Seal Products* reports acknowledge that such potential reduction of demand is relevant in the examination of the contribution of the measure to the achievement of the goal. The Appellate Body upheld the findings of the Panel under which it had assumed that a decrease in demand of seal products would result in a contraction of the seal products market and have the effect of reducing the numbers of seal killed, and thus the number of inhumanely killed seals (*EC – Seal Products,* Appellate Body Report, para. 5.247). The reasoning of Conrad appears untenable in the light of these recent developments of case law.

achievement of a goal *stricto sensu* (reduction of turtle mortality to a particular extent) but cannot impose the instruments to achieve this goal (reduction of turtle mortality by the adoption of essentially the same regulatory scheme).

To conclude, it is submitted that the developments of the necessity test made by the Appellate Body result in a more flexible system, which can be less restrictive than the traditional one when the objective pursued is of the highest importance and potentially more restrictive when the health risks or the environmental harm addressed are low.[215] The flexibility that would result may be a useful tool, in particular, to distinguish legitimate and illegitimate PPM measures. It could allow, for instance, applying differing standards on the basis of the intensity of the environmental threat at stake and on the intensity of the nexus between the importing country and the environmental harm at stake. This could allow WTO Members to take measures targeting PPMs causing the greatest damages to the global environment or shared resources, while at the same time providing useful disciplines, with a higher standard of review and efficiency requirement when the intensity of the nexus and the nature of the environmental harm are not as important.

7.2.2 Article XX(g): The 'Relating to' Test

7.2.2.1 Case Law

Article XX(g) concerns measures 'relating to' the conservation of exhaustible natural resources. The 'relating to' test is generally interpreted as requiring a less intense means-ends relationship than the necessity test applicable to Article XX(a) and (b).

It has been interpreted rather restrictively by different GATT 1947 panels, which held that it meant that measures had to be 'primarily aimed at' the conservation of exhaustible natural resources.[216] But the Appellate Body has not endorsed this rather restrictive interpretation.

In the *US – Gasoline* case, the Panel started its analysis by stating that the words 'related to' did not in isolation provide precise guidance as to the required link between the measures and the conservation objective.[217] Then it applied the 'primarily aimed at' approach suggested by the *Herring and Salmon* Panel report.

---

[215]Indeed, the conditions introduced by the Appellate Body in the necessity test, in particular the two-phases of the necessity test and the requirement that the measure makes a 'material contribution' to the achievement of the objective, *could* imply that a Panel found that no 'necessary' measure can actually achieve the chosen level of protection.

[216]See *Canada – Herring and Salmon*, Panel Report, para. 4.6; *US – Tuna I*, Panel Report, para. 5.30 ff.; *US – Tuna II*, Panel Report, para. 5.22; *US – Taxes on Automobiles*, Panel Report, para. 5.59.

[217]See *US – Gasoline*, Panel Report, para. 6.39.

In the report, the Panel never used the terms 'related to' from there on but used five times the words 'primarily aimed at'. In other words, it simply examined if the baseline establishment methods could be said to be 'primarily aimed at' achieving the conservation objectives of the Gasoline Rule and not if it 'related to' these objectives.[218]

The Appellate Body's *US – Gasoline* report contains several signs that the Appellate Body was not favourable to the interpretation of the words 'relating to' as meaning 'primarily aimed at'. However, the Appellate Body did not explicitly reverse this interpretation because all the participants in that appeal accepted it.[219] But it noted that the phrase 'primarily aimed at' was not itself treaty language and was not designed as simple litmus test for the inclusion or exclusion from Article XX(g).[220] In addition, it did not conclude that the environmental measure at stake was 'primarily aimed at' the conservation of clean air, but rather it held that it could not be regarded as 'merely incidentally or inadvertently aimed at'[221] this purpose, which was already a less strict definition.

In the *US – Shrimp* case, the Appellate Body distanced itself even further from the 'primarily aimed at' interpretation. Referring to the *US – Gasoline* case, the Appellate Body noted that it had found in that case a 'substantial relationship' between the US measure and the conservation of clean air, which was 'a close and genuine relationship of means and ends', even though it had never explicitly made such statement in its original report.[222]

The new approach of the Appellate Body pays probably more attention to the text of Article XX(g). The Appellate Body uses different terms to reach its conclusion, perhaps to avoid superseding the 'primarily aimed at' approach by another inflexible approach.

It held that it is necessary to make an examination of the relationship between the general structure and design of the measure at stake and the legitimate policy of conserving exhaustible natural resources.[223] The Appellate Body stated that in the circumstances of that case, the means-ends relationship was 'a close and real one'.[224] It held also that the means were 'directly connected to the policy of conservation of sea turtles' and 'reasonably related to the ends'.[225] It added that the measure was 'not disproportionately wide in its scope and reach' in relation to the policy objective of protection and conservation of the sea turtle species.[226]

---

[218]*Ibid.*, para. 6.40.

[219]See *US – Gasoline*, Appellate Body Report, p. 18.

[220]*Ibid.*, p. 19.

[221]*Ibid.*

[222]See *US – Shrimp*, Appellate Body Report, para. 136.

[223]*Ibid.*, para. 135 and 137.

[224]*Ibid.*, para. 141.

[225]*Ibid.*

[226]*Ibid.*

This approach, which has been described as a 'rational connection-standard', is more deferential towards regulating WTO Members than the 'primarily aimed at' standard.[227] Thus, even measures that do not *primarily aim* at the conservation of exhaustible natural resources can be justified under Article XX(g), as long as they have a rational connection to the objective pursued by the measure.[228]

In order to comply with Article XX(g), a measure relating to the conservation of exhaustible natural resources must also be made 'in conjunction with' restrictions on domestic consumption or production. In GATT 1947 panel practice, the term 'in conjunction with' was interpreted as meaning 'primarily aimed at', rendering effective restrictions on domestic production or consumption.[229]

This interpretation does not seem to have been endorsed in subsequent cases examined by WTO adjudicating bodies, which are apparently less restrictive in their interpretation of the 'in conjunction with' requirement.

In the *US – Gasoline* case, the Appellate Body started its analysis by stating that the ordinary meaning of these conditions imply that measures that are 'made effective' should be seen as a reference to measures that have 'come into effect'[230] and that the term 'in conjunction with' should be read plainly as 'together with'.[231] On that basis, the Appellate Body held that this meant that WTO Members could impose restrictions not only in respect of *imported* products but also with respect to *domestic* products. It concluded as follows:

> The clause is a requirement of even-handedness in the imposition of restrictions, in the name of conservation, upon the production or consumption of exhaustible natural resources.[232]

This requirement of *even-handedness* was justified by the Appellate Body in the *Gasoline* case on the assumption that if a restriction were imposed on imported products alone, then it was likely that the measure would 'simply be naked discrimination for protecting locally-produced goods'[233] and that it could not be justified as a measure designed for implementing conservationist goals.[234]

The interpretation of this obligation as a requirement of *even-handedness* was confirmed in the *US – Shrimp* case.[235] In the *US – Gasoline* case, the Appellate Body had held that the defendant complied with the requirement since 'restrictions on the consumption or depletion of clean air by regulating the domestic production

[227]See Mavroidis et al. (2010), p. 704.

[228]*Ibid.*

[229]See *Canada – Herring and Salmon*, Panel Report para. 4.6; *US – Tuna II*, Panel Report, para. 5.22 ff.; *US – Taxes on Automobiles*, para. 5.59 ff.

[230]The Appellate Body also held that it 'may be seen to refer to such measure being "operative" [or] as "in force"'. *US – Gasoline*, Appellate Body Report, p. 20.

[231]Or 'jointly with' (see *US – Gasoline*, Appellate Body Report, p. 20).

[232]*US – Gasoline*, Appellate Body Report, pp. 20 f.

[233]*US – Gasoline*, Appellate Body Report, p. 21.

[234]*Ibid.*

[235]See *US – Shrimp*, Appellate Body Report, para. 143 f.

of 'dirty' gasoline are established jointly with corresponding restriction with respect to imported gasoline'.[236] Similarly, in the *US – Shrimp* case, the Appellate Body held that the US measure was an 'even-handed' measure because the restrictions imposed to imported shrimp were also imposed to domestic shrimp.[237]

The Appellate Body specified that the 'in conjunction with' clause does not require *identical treatment* of domestic and imported products.[238] This result is quite logical since if identical treatment were granted to both categories of product, there would be no violation of the non-discrimination provision.

The Appellate Body finally noted that this criterion was not intended to establish an empirical 'effects test' for the availability of the Article XX(g) exception. One reason was that 'in the field of conservation of exhaustible natural resources, a substantial period of time, perhaps years, may have to elapse before the effects attributable to implementation of a given measure may be observable'.[239] It does not, however, imply that a measure may be clearly ineffective and still comply with this test. As the Appellate Body stated:

> [i]n a particular case, should it become clear that realistically, a specific measure cannot in any possible situation have any positive effect on conservation goals, it would probably be because that measure was not designed as a conservation regulation to begin with. In other words, it would not have been 'primarily aimed at' conservation of natural resources at all.[240]

7.2.2.2 Critique: The Differences in the Means-Ends Relationship in Article XX (b) and (g)

Even though Article XX does not provide that the commitments made by WTO Members in the GATT do not preclude measures taken to protect the 'environment', it is commonly assumed that Article XX(b) and (g) embraces the different situations in which protection of the 'environment' could be invoked, especially since the Appellate Body applied an evolutionary interpretation of the term 'exhaustible natural resources' so as to include living natural resources in the scope of this provision.[241]

Article XX(b) contains a necessity test, while Article XX(g) contains only a 'relating to' test. As a result, it might appear that it would be more difficult to justify a measure to protect life and health than to conserve exhaustible natural resources, which does not appear justified. It has, however, been contended that case law has evolved in a way that the means-ends relationship in these two provisions actually

---

[236]*US – Gasoline*, Appellate Body Report, p. 21.

[237]See *US – Shrimp*, Appellate Body Report, para. 144.

[238]See *US – Gasoline*, Appellate Body Report, p. 21.

[239]*Ibid.*

[240]*US – Gasoline*, Appellate Body Report, pp 21 f.

[241]See *supra*, 7.1.1.2.

converge. Some have indeed argued that the Appellate Body is in the process of harmonising the means-ends tests applicable in paragraphs (b) and (g), through the application of a proportionality test, in both cases.[242] It is, however, doubtful that the necessity test of Article XX(b) amounts to a proportionality test.[243] Applying a more restrictive test in sub-paragraph (g) than in sub-paragraph (b), by introducing in the former a proportionality test that the latter does not contain, would not seem coherent with the wording of Article XX. It seems therefore that the Appellate Body could not adopt an interpretation of the conditions of Article XX(b) and (g) that would imply a similarity of the applicable tests.

When a measure is provisionally justified under one of these sub-paragraphs, it must still comply with the conditions of the chapeau. Another possible convergence between Article XX(b) and Article XX(g) relates to the cumulative effects of the 'relating to' test and of the conditions of the chapeau. In other words, WTO adjudicating bodies may tend to be more restrictive in the examination of the conditions of the chapeau for measures falling under sub-paragraph (g) than for those examined under sub-paragraph (b). This issue is developed further below, after having examined the conditions of the chapeau.[244]

7.3 The Chapeau Requirements

This section critically examines the function of the chapeau in the view of WTO adjudicating bodies (Sect. 7.3.1) and the conditions of arbitrary or unjustifiable discrimination (Sect. 7.3.2) and disguised restriction on international trade (Sect. 7.3.3).

7.3.1 Function of the Chapeau

The introductory clause of Article XX (the 'chapeau') provides that measures must not be

> applied in a manner which would constitute a means of arbitrary or unjustifiable discrimination between countries where the same conditions prevail, or a disguised restriction on international trade.

When a measure is provisionally justified under one of the sub-paragraphs (a) to (j) of Article XX, WTO adjudicating bodies must then examine in a second step if its application complies with the requirements of the chapeau (two-tiered

---

[242] See Schoenbaum (1998), p. 37; Prost (2005), pp. 54 f.

[243] See *supra*, 7.2.1.2.1.

[244] See *infra*, 7.3.4.3.

analysis).[245] In that respect, the terms of the chapeau imply that Article XX is a 'limited and conditional exception' from the substantive obligations contained in other provisions of the GATT.[246]

In practice, the conditions of the introductory clause of Article XX have proved to be difficult to meet, and defendant Members have often lost on this basis, such as in the *US – Gasoline*, *US – Shrimp*, *Brazil – Tyres* or *EC – Seal Products* cases.

Hence, the interpretation of the conditions of the chapeau has considerable importance on the scope of Article XX and on the ability of WTO Members to take restrictive trade measures justified under the GATT. On the other hand, the terms used in the chapeau are rather vague and lack precise definition. The Appellate Body has recognised that the text of the chapeau is 'not without ambiguity', including when it comes to the field of application of its different standards.[247] Moreover, it has stated that the conditions of the chapeau could be read side by side and that they imparted meaning to one another.[248] The distinction between these three standards is sometimes regarded as artificial because they are all expressions of the same underlying concepts.[249]

The Appellate Body has adopted the view that the function of the chapeau is to prevent the 'abuse', 'illegitimate use' or 'misuse' of a Member's right to invoke an exception to the substantive rules of the GATT.[250] It has considered that the introductory clause of Article XX is an expression of the principle of good faith, which controls the exercise of rights by states.[251] One consequence of that principle is the doctrine of *abus de droit*, which prohibits the abusive exercise of a state's right.[252] The Appellate Body has stated that an abusive exercise by a Member of its own treaty right 'results in a breach of the treaty rights of the other Members and, as well, a violation of the treaty obligation of the Member so acting'.[253]

The Appellate Body has also expressed the view that the chapeau embodies the recognition on the part of WTO Members of the need to maintain a *balance of rights and obligations*,[254] between the right of the regulating Member to invoke an exception and the substantive rights of the other WTO Members under the GATT.

---

[245]See *US – Gasoline*, Appellate Body Report, p. 22; *US – Shrimp*, Appellate Body Report, para. 118.

[246]See *US – Shrimp*, Appellate Body Report, para. 157.

[247]See *US – Gasoline*, Appellate Body Report, p. 23.

[248]*Ibid.*, p. 25.

[249]See Desmedt (2001), p. 475; Vranes (2009), p. 278.

[250]See *US – Gasoline*, Appellate Body Report, p. 25; *EC – Seal Products*, Appellate Body Report, para. 5.297.

[251]See *US – Shrimp*, Appellate Body Report, para. 158.

[252]*Ibid.*

[253]*Ibid.*

[254]See *US – Shrimp*, Appellate Body Report, para. 156 (emphasis added).

Based on these considerations,[255] the Appellate Body used the metaphor of the 'line of equilibrium' to describe this objective:

> The task of interpreting and applying the chapeau is, hence, essentially the delicate one of locating and marking out a line of equilibrium between the right of a Member to invoke an exception under Article XX and the rights of the other Members under varying substantive provisions (e.g., Article XI) of the GATT 1994, so that neither of the competing rights will cancel out the other and thereby distort and nullify or impair the balance of rights and obligations constructed by the Members themselves in that Agreement. The location of the line of equilibrium, as expressed in the chapeau, is not fixed and unchanging; the line moves as the kind and the shape of the measures at stake vary and as the facts making up specific cases differ.[256]

The Appellate Body has further stated that the right to invoke an exception must be exercised *reasonably*.[257] Even if it did not explicitly elaborate on what should be construed as a reasonable exercise of an exception, it suggested that a 'reasonable and bona fide exercise of a right in such a case is one which is appropriate and necessary for the purpose of the right (. . .). It should at the same time be *fair and equitable as between the parties* and not one which is calculated to procure for one of them an unfair advantage in the light of the obligation assumed'.[258]

These different findings could thus seem to be an indication that some form of necessity test, or even of proportionality test, should be applied in the context of the chapeau. In particular, the reference to the 'line of equilibrium' might potentially be interpreted to imply some form of discretionary powers to strike a balance between the interests at stake according to the circumstances of the case, i.e. some form of balancing test or proportionality test.[259]

At the same time, other findings of the Appellate Body seem to underscore that only *clear or severe abuses* of the right to invoke Article XX would violate the chapeau of this provision. This is apparent in particular in the following findings:

> Exercise by an importing Member of its right to invoke an exception, if abused or misused, would erode or render naught the substantive treaty rights [. . .] of other Members. [. . .] If the abuse or misuse is *sufficiently grave or extensive*, the Member, in effect, reduces its treaty obligation to a merely facultative one and dissolves its juridical character, and, in so doing, negates altogether the treaty rights of other Members. The chapeau was installed at the head of the list of 'General Exceptions' in Article XX to prevent such far-reaching consequences.[260]

---

[255]After its paragraph on the principle of good faith and abuse of right, the Appellate Body stated that '[t]he task of interpreting and applying the chapeau is, *hence*, essentially . . .'. *US – Shrimp*, Appellate Body Report, para. 159 *in initio* (emphasis added).

[256]*US – Shrimp*, Appellate Body Report, para. 159.

[257]*Ibid.*, para. 158.

[258]*Ibid.*, para. 158, in footnote 156 (emphasis added by the Appellate Body) citing B. Cheng, *General Principles of Law as applied by International Courts and Tribunals*, Stevens and Sons, Ltd., 1953, p. 125.

[259]See Bown and Trachtman (2009), p. 132. See also Hilf (2001), p. 128. *Contra*: Desmedt (2001), p. 474.

[260]*US – Shrimp*, Appellate Body Report, para. 156 (emphasis added).

The Appellate Body expressly indicated that these 'far-reaching consequences' could occur if the abuses of the right to invoke Article XX were 'sufficiently grave or extensive' so as to reduce treaty obligations to a 'merely facultative one'. The use of the right to rely on the general exceptions provision should not, in its view, 'frustrate or defeat the legal obligations of the holder of that right' under the GATT.[261]

This interpretation seems more compatible with the terms used in the chapeau than that which consists in introducing in it a necessity or proportionality test. The drafters of the GATT used specific terms that refer to a common idea of *abuse* of the possibility to take restrictive trade measures for non-economic goals. The term 'unjustifiable' or 'arbitrary' discrimination implies not only the existence of discrimination but also some form of *qualified* one.

As regards the 'disguised' restriction on international trade standard, it has been held that a restriction that formally meets the requirements of Article XX(b) would constitute an *abuse* if such compliance were in fact only a disguise to *conceal* the pursuit of trade-restrictive objectives.[262]

In the view of the present author, these different terms imply that a violation of the chapeau requires a *clear disproportion* between the discrimination that has occurred and the goal pursued or between the trade effects of the measure and the purported non-economic goal. Examining if a clear disproportion exists is not the same task as balancing the rights and obligations of WTO Members in the circumstances of the case to see if trade or non-economic concerns must prevail. It is true that a claim that the invocation of Article XX in a specific case constitutes an abuse of right could rely on similar criteria as those applicable in a balancing test, with a different standard of review: invoking Article XX to justify a measure that is *clearly* unsuitable, unnecessary or disproportionate, or in other words that represents a *gross* imbalance, could be seen as an abuse of right.[263]

It is thus submitted that the concept of the 'line of equilibrium' is somewhat misleading, insofar as it might be seen as a mandate to WTO adjudicating bodies to tilt the balance in favour of free trade or non-economic concerns on the basis of the specific circumstances of the case, i.e. to apply a proportionality test in a strict sense. The author posits that the function of the chapeau should rather be described as a safeguard against 'clear disequilibrium' between the right to invoke an exception and the substantive rights under the GATT, which could occur as the result of abusive invocation of Article XX. In that respect, WTO adjudicating bodies may have a tendency to overestimate the role that can be given to the chapeau of Article XX, which has often had a crucial role in the analysis conducted

---

[261] *US – Gasoline*, Appellate Body Report, p. 22.

[262] See *EC – Asbestos*, Panel Report, para. 8.236 (emphasis added).

[263] See e.g. Neumann and Tuerk (2003), p. 231 ('the Appellate Body interpreted the chapeau to reflect the principle of good faith, including the prohibition of abuse of rights. While an abuse can occur when rights of other Members are unnecessarily curtailed, there is no common proportionality standard that would be included in the prohibition of abuse of rights').

under Article XX and which has often led in practice to a finding of Article XX violation.

This tendency may probably be explained to a certain extent by the outdated nature of the wording of Article XX, which does not mention explicitly environmental protection in the list of policy goals justifying an exception. To overcome this difficulty, the Appellate Body has applied an evolutionary interpretation of Article XX(g),[264] which allows many environmental trade measures to be covered by its scope. At the same time, Article XX(g) does not contain a necessity test but includes a less stringent 'relating to' test. As a result, WTO adjudicating bodies may have been tempted to be more stringent in the application of the chapeau for measures falling under sub-paragraph (g) and possibly to introduce in the chapeau some form of necessity test.

But the chapeau applies to all the sub-paragraphs, including (a) and (b), which do contain a necessity test. A restrictive interpretation of the conditions of the chapeau has consequences for all sub-paragraphs. This fact arguably results, at least when it comes to cases examined under Article XX(a) and (b), in an artificial interpretation of the chapeau and, consequently, to some overlaps between the chapeau and the necessity test contained in sub-paragraphs (a) and (b).

The evolutionary interpretation of Article XX(g) was probably the 'next best thing' insofar as it allowed the introduction of legitimate environmental concerns in Article XX, despite its outdated wording. However, the consequences that this evolution has had on the interpretation of the conditions of the chapeau, and consequently on the global coherence of Article XX interpretation, show that a better solution would be an amendment of Article XX so as to introduce a sub-paragraph applying to measures 'necessary for the protection of the environment'. The perspective of such a modification is unlikely in the current WTO negotiations context. It would, however, allow the Appellate Body to apply a more coherent approach, consisting in a generally more stringent interpretation of the necessity test and in a less strict examination of the chapeau.

In the meantime, it is submitted that the findings of the Appellate Body that the location of the 'line of equilibrium' moves according to the kind of measure at stake and the specific facts of the case should be understood as a reference to the degree of scrutiny applicable in each case (and not as a reference to the need to balance the different interests at stake). The degree of scrutiny in the examination of whether the invocation of Article XX constitutes an abuse of right could thus vary according to the importance of the interests and values concerned.[265] The more important the goal pursued is, the easier it should be for a defending Member to show that possible discrimination is not 'unjustifiable' or 'arbitrary' or that the application of the measure does not result in 'disguised' restriction on international trade. In any event, it should be recognised that only *clearly* abusive measures should be deemed to violate the chapeau.

---

[264]See *supra*, 7.1.1.2.

[265]For further details, see also *infra*, 9.4.1.

Another particularity regarding the chapeau is that it is supposed to be mainly concerned with the manner in which the measure is *applied*, while the sub-paragraphs focus on the design of the measure.[266] However, this distinction may often seem artificial or difficult to make and has been rightly criticised.[267] Indeed, the Appellate Body itself has stated that whether a measure is applied in a particular manner 'can most often be discerned from the design, the architecture and the revealing structure of a measure'.[268] Thus, what is relevant is not only the actual but also the *expected* application of a measure, determined by its design, architecture and revealing structure.[269] These findings seem to blur the distinction between the application of the measure and its design.

7.3.2   Arbitrary or Unjustifiable Discrimination

When a measure is provisionally justified under one of the sub-paragraphs, WTO adjudicating bodies examine if the application of the measure does not result in 'arbitrary' discrimination or in 'unjustifiable' discrimination. In the *US – Shrimp* report, the Appellate Body held that, under the terms of the chapeau, three elements must exist in order for a measure to be applied in a manner that would constitute arbitrary or unjustifiable discrimination between the countries where the same conditions prevail: the measure must result in *discrimination* (Sect. 7.3.2.1), which must be *arbitrary* or *unjustifiable* in character (Sect. 7.3.2.2) and which must occur *between countries where the same conditions prevail* (Sect. 7.3.2.3).[270]

7.3.2.1   'Discrimination'

The first element that must exist for a finding of 'unjustifiable or arbitrary discrimination' is, logically, that the application of the measure results in *discrimination*. An obvious question is therefore the relation that this condition may have with the non-discrimination provisions, when a regulating Member seeks precisely to justify a violation of the national treatment or most-favoured-nation clause.[271]

---

[266]See *US – Gasoline*, Appellate Body Report, p. 22; *US – Shrimp*, Appellate Body Report, para. 115; *Brazil – Tyres*, Appellate Body Report, para. 215; *EC – Seal Products*, Appellate Body Report, para. 5.302.

[267]See Desmedt (2001), p. 475; Vranes (2009), p. 278; Bartels (2015), pp. 98 ff.

[268]*Japan – Alcohol II*, Appellate Body Report, p. 29; *EC – Seal Products*, Appellate Body Report, para. 5.302.

[269]See *EC – Seal Products*, Appellate Body Report, para. 5.302.

[270]See *US – Shrimp*, Appellate Body Report, para. 150.

[271]On this issue, see e.g. Bartels (2015), pp. 109 ff.

WTO adjudicating bodies have considered that 'the nature and quality' of discrimination in the substantive provisions and in Article XX is 'different'.[272] The Appellate Body held:

> The provisions of the chapeau cannot logically refer to the same standard(s) by which a violation of a substantive rule has been determined to have occurred. To proceed down that path would be both to empty the chapeau of its contents and to deprive the exceptions in paragraphs (a) to (j) of meaning. Such recourse would also confuse the question of whether inconsistency with a substantive rule existed, with the further and separate question arising under the chapeau of Article XX as to whether that inconsistency was nevertheless justified.[273]

Thus, the 'same standards' of discrimination as those that led to a violation of Article III are insufficient. For instance, in the *EC – Asbestos* case, the Panel took the view that discrimination in the sense of the chapeau of Article XX did not exist on the basis of the less favourable treatment accorded to imports under Article III:4. Since the Panel did not find any other discriminatory provision in the contested measure, it concluded that there was therefore no 'unjustifiable discrimination' because there was no 'discrimination' in the first place.[274]

On the other hand, in the *US – Gasoline* report, the Appellate Body adopted the view that certain discriminatory elements[275] of the US measure went 'well beyond what was necessary for the Panel to determine that a violation of Article III:4 had occurred in the first place. The resulting discrimination must have been foreseen, and was not merely inadvertent or unavoidable.'[276] This suggests that there should be some additional discriminatory characteristics, compared to Article III, for a finding of 'discrimination' under the chapeau of Article XX, such as the presence of discriminatory *intent*.[277] For instance, while the *EC – Asbestos* Panel considered that the less favourable treatment accorded to imported products under Article III:4 could not be relied on by the complainant in the chapeau of Article XX,[278] the Appellate Body in the *US – Gasoline* case took the view that the nature and extent of the discriminatory character of the measure at issue were such that it had been intended and was not merely incidental.

Other forms of discrimination can also be relevant in the context of Article XX, such as discrimination in negotiations (e.g., the *US – Shrimp* case, in which the importing country had negotiated an international agreement on turtle protection

---

[272]See *US – Shrimp*, Appellate Body Report, para. 150.

[273]*US – Gasoline*, Appellate Body Report, p. 23.

[274]See *EC – Asbestos*, Panel Report, para. 8.227 ff.

[275]These discriminatory elements resulted from two omissions of the United States, namely to explore the possibility of cooperative arrangement and the omission to take into account the costs of foreign refiners.

[276]*US – Gasoline*, Appellate Body Report, p. 28.

[277]This is the reading of Lester (2012), p. 407 (who argues that the Appellate Body's findings in the *US – Gasoline* case could mean that discriminatory effects are enough for a violation of Article III, whereas a violation of the chapeau requires discriminatory intent as well).

[278]See *EC – Asbestos*, Panel Report, para. 8.227.

with certain exporting Members but not others) or discrimination in the imposition of an import ban (e.g., the *Brazil – Tyres* case, in which Brazil had exempted the MERCOSUR countries from the imposition of the import ban).

7.3.2.2 'Unjustifiable or Arbitrary' Discrimination

Once the application of a measure has been considered as resulting in 'discrimination' in the sense of the chapeau, the next step is to assess if this discrimination is 'unjustifiable or arbitrary'.

One of the basic principles in this analysis is the relationship between discrimination and the legitimate objective pursued. WTO adjudicating bodies have in particular examined if the policy goal of the measure, considered to be legitimate under the sub-paragraphs, could also be relied on under the chapeau of Article XX to justify some form of discrimination.

In the *Brazil – Tyres* report, the Appellate Body held that analysing whether discrimination is arbitrary or unjustifiable usually involves an analysis that relates 'primarily to the cause or the rationale of the discrimination'.[279] Recalling that the function of Article XX is to prevent abuses of the general exceptions, the Appellate Body stated:

> In our view, there is such an abuse, and therefore, there is arbitrary or unjustifiable discrimination when a measure provisionally justified under a paragraph of Article XX is applied in a discriminatory manner 'between countries where the same conditions prevail', and when the reasons given for this discrimination bear no rational connection to the objective falling within the purview of a paragraph of Article XX or would go against that objective.[280]

Determination of whether discrimination is 'unjustifiable' or 'arbitrary' thus requires the examination of the reasons given for the discrimination. For instance, in *Brazil – Tyres*, Brazil applied its import ban to all WTO Members except MERCOSUR countries, which constituted discrimination. Brazil had explained that the exemption of MERCOSUR countries had been introduced as a consequence of a ruling of a MERCOSUR tribunal. The Appellate Body then examined if a rational connection existed between the reasons invoked (i.e., the MERCOSUR tribunal ruling) and the objective of health and environmental protection of the import ban and noted that it did relate to the pursuit of this objective. In the absence of a rational relationship between this exemption and the legitimate health and environmental objective pursued by the import ban, the Appellate Body held that

---

[279]*Brazil – Tyres*, Appellate Body Report, para. 225. These findings contradicted the view adopted by the Appellate Body in the *US – Shrimp* case, in which it held that the policy goal of a measure at issue cannot provide its rationale or justification under the standards of the chapeau of Article XX, since it did not follow from the fact that a measure fell within the terms of Article XX(g) that it would necessarily comply with the requirements of the chapeau (*US – Shrimp*, Appellate Body Report, para. 149).

[280]*Brazil – Tyres*, Appellate Body Report, para. 227.

the measure was applied in a manner that constituted arbitrary or unjustifiable discrimination.[281]

Similarly, in the *EC – Seal Products* report, the Appellate Body held that whether discrimination could be reconciled with the policy objective pursued, or was rationally related to it, was 'one of the most important factors' in the assessment of arbitrary or unjustifiable discrimination.[282] It concluded that the manner in which the EU seal regime treated seal products derived from 'commercial' hunts (the products of which were prohibited based on animal welfare concerns) and seal products derived from Inuit communities' hunts (the importation of which was allowed in the EU even though it raised similar animal welfare concerns) could not be 'reconciled with the objective of addressing EU public moral concerns regarding seal welfare', at least on the basis of the European Union's explanations.[283]

In the *US – Tuna II (Mexico) 21.5* report, the Panel held that the different certification mechanisms within the Eastern Tropical Pacific Ocean (ETP, in which an independent observer had to be present on each ship to certify that no tuna was harmed during the sets in which tuna was caught) and outside the ETP (in which the ship's captain himself could certify that no dolphin was injured) were not justified by the objective of conserving dolphins by providing consumers with accurate information about dolphin-safe status of tuna products[284] since the Panel held that it had not been established that captains had the necessary expertise to certify compliance with the dolphin-safe label criteria.[285]

In the light of these cases, it thus seems that the Appellate Body has considered that it is only the objective invoked under the sub-paragraphs that can justify discrimination under the chapeau. Such general interpretation seems disputable in the view of the present author, insofar as a trade measure may pursue multiple goals, and in some cases discrimination under the chapeau may be explained by another legitimate objective than that invoked under the sub-paragraphs.[286] For instance, in the *EC – Seal Products* case, it appears questionable whether providing an exception to the import ban for Inuit communities' hunts, in order in particular to avoid depriving such communities of one of their main sources of income, really resulted in *unjustifiable* or *arbitrary* discrimination. When another goal than that invoked under the sub-paragraphs is advanced to show that discrimination under the chapeau is not unjustifiable or arbitrary, it should not be automatically rejected. WTO adjudicating bodies should rather examine if this objective is legitimate and if

---

[281] See *Brazil – Tyres*, Appellate Body Report, para. 228.

[282] See *EC – Seal Products*, Appellate Body Report, para. 5.306.

[283] *Ibid.*, para. 5.338.

[284] See *US – Tuna II (Mexico) 21.5*, Panel Report, para. 7.605.

[285] *Ibid.*, para. 7.603.

[286] The issue of 'multiple competing purposes' has been much commented in academic writings since the *EC – Seal Products* case. See e.g. Qin (2015); Levy and Regan (2015); pp. 361 ff.; Regan (2015); Marin Durán (2016); Herwig (2016); pp. 123 ff.; Conconi and Voon (2016), pp. 323 ff.

the possible discrimination that may result must be considered as an *abuse* of the right to invoke Article XX.

In the context of PPM measures, the Appellate Body considered in the *US – Shrimp* case that certain features of the challenged measure bore no relation with the environmental objective pursued. The United States had imposed a country-based restriction to enforce its PPM regulation, rather than only prohibiting the importation of products that did not comply with the PPM regulation. This measure prohibited the importation of all shrimp originating from countries that had not been certified, even shrimp caught using methods *identical* to those employed in the United States.[287] The Appellate Body considered that country-based restrictions would be 'difficult to reconcile' with the declared policy objective of protecting and conserving sea turtles.[288] It suggested that the United States was more concerned with effectively influencing WTO Members to adopt essentially the same comprehensive regulatory regime as that applied by the United States.[289] Following the first report of the Appellate Body in the *US – Shrimp* case, the United States modified its legislation so that shipments of shrimp that were harvested in non-certified countries could be imported in the United States, provided that a declaration that they were harvested under conditions that did not adversely affect sea turtles was issued (shipment-by-shipment restriction).[290] The Panel and the Appellate Body upheld this system in the *US – Shrimp 21.5* reports.

It may be conceded that country-based restrictions should be viewed with suspicion. Commentators usually call for the application of stricter scrutiny for this kind of measures.[291] In certain circumstances, it may, however, be legitimate to apply such restrictions, for instance when standards specifying the way that each products must be produced is impractical (for instance, when raw materials are co-mingled in production) or when shipment-by-shipment PPM restrictions do not prevent the environmental damage but only reallocate the product to different markets.[292] The nexus between the restrictive trade measure and the environmental objective is likely to be less intense in cases of country-based restrictions, and they may thus be harder to justify than product-based restrictions. However, there might be circumstances in which such a type of trade restrictions is justified from an environmental viewpoint, i.e. cases in which the choice to impose a restrictive

---

[287]See *US – Shrimp*, Appellate Body Report, para. 165.

[288]*Ibid.*

[289]*Ibid.*

[290]See *US – Shrimp 21.5*, Panel Report, para. 2.26.

[291]For instance, Howse and Regan argue that 'country-based' restrictions are *prima facie* illegal under Article III and require a justification under Article XX (Howse and Regan 2000, pp. 252 and 269 ff). Charnovitz (2002) considers that 'government standard PPM' (i.e. 'a government policy standard standards that specifies laws or regulations of a foreign government regarding production process, or its enforcement of them'; see p. 67) should in principle be disfavoured because they are coercive and abide origin-based discrimination, even though there might be exceptions depending on the relevant circumstances of the case. See also Chang (1995), pp. 278 ff.

[292]See Charnovitz (2002), pp. 106 f.

measure in this form does not appear to constitute an abuse of the right to invoke Article XX environmental exceptions.

Apart from the general relation between discrimination and the environmental objective invoked, the Appellate Body has examined more closely various elements, which may result as such or in their cumulative effects in 'unjustifiable or arbitrary' discrimination. These elements are in particular the lack of transparency, predictability or due process (Sect. 7.3.2.2.1), the inflexibility in the actual PPMs that have to be adopted by exporting WTO Members (Sect. 7.3.2.2.2) and discrimination in the application of the measure, in particular as regards the conduct of international negotiations (Sect. 7.3.2.2.3).

7.3.2.2.1 Transparency, Predictability, Due Process and Basic Fairness

One of the elements that led the Appellate Body to conclude that the United States' measure in the *US – Shrimp* case was applied in a manner resulting in unjustifiable or arbitrary discrimination was that the United States did not meet certain minimum standards set up by the GATT for transparency and procedural fairness in the administration of trade regulations.[293]

These due process requirements ensue from GATT Article X, which concerns the application of all laws, regulations, judicial decisions or administrative rulings relating to trade in goods.[294] These rules apply logically to restrictive trade measures that may be justified under Article XX since they are applicable also to measures that comply with WTO obligations.[295]

To avoid that a measure be inconsistent with Article X and the chapeau of Article XX, WTO Members must set up transparent rules regarding certification procedure and must guarantee fairness and due process to applicant countries during that procedure.[296] At the start, the regulation must express clearly what

---

[293]See *US – Shrimp*, Appellate Body Report, para. 183.

[294]Article X:1 requires WTO Members to publish them promptly in such a manner as to enable governments and traders to become acquainted with them. Article X:3 states in particular that '(a) each Member shall administer in a uniform, impartial and reasonable manner all its laws, regulations, decision and rulings of the kind described in paragraph 1 of this Article. (b) Each Member shall maintain, or institute as soon as practicable, judicial, arbitral or administrative tribunals or procedures for the purpose, *inter alia*, of the prompt review and correction of administrative action relating to customs matters.'

[295]See *US – Shrimp*, Appellate Body Report, para. 182 ('[i]nasmuch as there are due process requirements generally for measures that are otherwise imposed in compliance with WTO obligations, it is only reasonable that rigorous compliance with the fundamental requirements of due process should be required in the application and administration of a measure which purports to be an exception to the treaty obligations of the Member imposing the measure and which effectively results in a suspension *pro hac vice* of the treaty rights of other Members').

[296]See *US – Shrimp*, Appellate Body Report, para. 181. They were missing in the case of the measure at issue in the *US – Shrimp* case, in which the Appellate Body held that there was no 'transparent and predictable certification process' (*US – Shrimp*, Appellate Body Report, para. 180).

actions the exporting countries have to make to obtain certification, in particular whether or not they have to apply for it. In the course of the certification procedure, certain due process requirements must be respected, such as the right to be heard and the possibility to respond to arguments made against the applicant country. When a decision is about to be made, the importing country must set up a reasoned written decision. The applicant countries must then receive a formal notice of the decisions and the reasons of a possible denial. Finally, the importing country must provide for a formal legal procedure for review of, or appeal from, a denial of an application.[297]

In the view of the Appellate Body, since the United States measure in the *US – Shrimp* case did not contain any of these elements, the certification process was 'singularly informal and casual', which could result in the negation of WTO Members' rights, insofar as there was no way that exporting Members could be certain that the terms of the US measure was being applied in a fair and just manner by the appropriate governmental agencies of the United States. Thus, the Appellate Body considered that 'exporting Members applying for certification whose applications are rejected are denied basic fairness and due process, and are discriminated against, *vis-à-vis* those Members which are granted certification'.[298]

These requirements apply generally to all trade regulations and are an important aspect of the multilateral trading system, playing also a role to avoid new trade disputes between WTO Members. However, there may be certain specificities relating to PPM measures and the way the regulation has to be drafted for such measures. In order to ensure a transparent procedure, as well as procedural fairness, in the administration of PPM regulations, it is necessary to determine precisely, for instance, the criteria to be met by exporting countries, the objectives in terms of environmental protection that they should achieve or the circumstances in the producing country that might result in the denial of certification. In general, process regulations probably need to be more detailed than product regulations since the former have to be flexible enough and to take into account differing conditions that may occur abroad.

Moreover, the application of most PPM measures requires the use of *verification mechanisms* to ensure compliance with the prescribed standards. The regulating country should be cautious with respect to verification mechanisms, offer similar procedure to its different partners and be transparent on how these verifications would be carried out.

---

[297]The Appellate Body noted that '[w]ith respect to both types of certification, there is no formal opportunity for an applicant country to be heard, or to respond to any arguments that may be made against it, in the course of the certification process before a decision to grant or to deny certification is made. Moreover, no formal written, reasoned decision, whether of acceptance or rejection, is rendered on applications for either type of certification (. . .). No procedure for review of, or appeal from, a denial of an application is provided' (*US – Shrimp*, Appellate Body Report, para. 180).

[298]*US – Shrimp*, Appellate Body Report, para. 181.

7.3.2.2.2 Flexibility

It has been shown that the 'coercive' nature of PPM measures requiring the adoption of policies unilaterally prescribed by the importing Member has been one of the main arguments invoked, in particular, by developing countries against the use of PPM measures.[299] Usually, this argument is raised so as to deny the justifiability of PPM measures in the context of Article XX. For instance, in the *US – Shrimp* report, the fact that the measure had been unilaterally imposed by the United States and required the adoption of particular turtle protection policies in exporting countries was viewed as sufficient by the complainants to deny justifiability under Article XX.

A particularity of the US measure in the *US – Shrimp* case was that it did not only prescribe the adoption of particular policies in the exporting Members; it required as well the adoption of a turtle protection programme that was 'essentially the same' as the one enacted by the United States.

Examining this issue, the Appellate Body held that perhaps the 'most conspicuous flaw' in the measure's application related to its 'intended and actual coercive effect' on the specific policy decisions made by other Members of the WTO.[300] Because the United States measure amounted to an economic embargo, which required other WTO Members to adopt essentially the same policy and enforcement programmes as those applied by the United States,[301] and because the adoption of a programme comparable to that of the United States would not be taken into consideration, the Appellate Body considered that it was a 'single, rigid and unbending requirement'.[302] The measure specified the only way that a harvesting country's regulatory programme could be deemed to be 'comparable' to that of the United States.[303] The Appellate Body emphasised that such a measure did not take into account other specific policies and measures that an exporting country might have adopted for the protection and conservation of sea turtles and did not take into consideration different conditions that might prevail in the territories of exporting countries.[304] In the view of the Appellate Body, this 'rigidity and inflexibility' constituted 'arbitrary discrimination' within the meaning of the chapeau.[305]

Following the *US – Shrimp* Appellate Body report, the United States modified its measure and allowed certification to exporting Members having programmes 'comparable in effectiveness' to that of the US programme. Malaysia complained in the following *US – Shrimp 21.5* report, arguing in particular that the United States measure still constituted unjustifiable or arbitrary discrimination, because it

---

[299] See in particular *supra*, Chap. 2.

[300] See *US – Shrimp*, Appellate Body Report, para. 161.

[301] *Ibid.*

[302] *Ibid.*, para. 163.

[303] *Ibid.*, para. 162.

[304] *Ibid.*, para. 163 f.

[305] *Ibid.*, para. 177.

conditioned the importation of shrimp into the United States on compliance by the exporting Members with policies and standards 'unilaterally' prescribed by the importing country.[306] In other words, in Malaysia's view, the 'unilateral' character of the US measure prevented as such any justifiability under Article XX.

The Appellate Body rejected this argument. It considered that a measure that required the adoption in the exporting country of a programme 'comparable in effectiveness' to that of the importing country allowed *sufficient flexibility* in the application of the measure so as to avoid 'arbitrary and unjustifiable discrimination'. It allowed exporting Members to take into consideration, in the adoption of their own regulatory scheme, the specific conditions prevailing in their territory.[307]

Hence, even though the revised US measure allowed the adoption of programmes that were only 'comparable in effectiveness' to US legislation, the exporting countries still had to achieve the level of effectiveness unilaterally prescribed by the United States. In other words, the Appellate Body adopted the view that an importing Member can decide the level of effectiveness to be achieved by exporting Members, as long as they are granted sufficient latitude with respect to the programmes they adopt to achieve this level, so that they can adapt them to the specific conditions prevailing in their territory.[308]

The consequence of these findings is that some form of unilateralism has been upheld by the Appellate Body despite the 'coercive effects' of unilaterally prescribed PPMs: as long as sufficient flexibility is left to exporting Members to implement in domestic law the prescribed environmental policies, the importing country can unilaterally impose an environmental protection objective and the required level of effectiveness.

7.3.2.2.3   Discrimination and International Negotiations of a Multilateral Solution

In the *US – Shrimp* report, the Appellate Body referred to differential treatment among countries desiring certification, which contributed to the finding that the US measure amounted to 'unjustifiable discrimination'. In particular, it noted that the 'phase-in' *periods* during which the respective shrimp trawling sectors of these different countries could adjust to the use of the required PPM (the use of turtles, excluding devices or TEDs) were not the same for the different exporting Members concerned. Whereas the countries of the Caribbean and western Atlantic region had phase-in periods of three years, all other countries had four months to implement the requirement of compulsory use of TEDs. The Appellate Body stated that the length of these phase-in periods directly related to the onerousness of the burdens of complying with the requisites of certification and the practical feasibility of locating

---

[306]See *US – Shrimp 21.5*, Appellate Body Report, para. 135.

[307]*Ibid.*, para. 144.

[308]*Ibid.*

and developing alternative export markets for shrimp. It pointed out that the shorter the period is, the heavier were the burden of compliance, in particular where the exporting countries had a large number of trawler vessels, and thus the heavier was the influence of the import ban.[309] The Appellate Body further noted that differing treatment of different countries desiring certification was also observable in the differences in the levels of efforts made by the United States in *transferring the required TED technology* to specific countries. It held that 'far greater' efforts to successfully transfer this technology were made for the Caribbean and western Atlantic countries than for other countries.[310]

But one of the most important issues that were raised in the *US – Shrimp* case in the context of the 'arbitrary or unjustifiable discrimination' condition was the way the United States had conducted with its trading partners *negotiations for the conclusion of an international agreement* for the protection of sea turtles. The approaches adopted by the two panels (initial Panel report and DSU Article 21.5 Panel report) were quite restrictive on this issue, while the two Appellate Body reports (initial report and DSU Article 21.5 report) seem more deferent to the regulating Member.

7.3.2.2.3.1   The US – Shrimp *Reports*

When it comes to the initial Panel report, the United States had argued that Article XX did not require a Member to seek to negotiate an international agreement instead of, or before, adopting unilateral measures.[311] The Panel disagreed, on the one hand, because it considered that the WTO multilateral trading system would be undermined if Members were allowed to adopt measures making access to their market conditional upon the adoption by the exporting Members of certain conservation policies, which could lead to conflicting requirements.[312] The Panel stated that the policies at stake, according to various international environmental agreements, implied that a Member seeking to promote such environmental concerns should engage in international negotiations.[313] It noted that the United States did not undertake negotiations with the complainants on a turtle conservation agreement before the imposition of the import ban, even though it had been negotiating the Inter-American Convention at the same time with several other countries. The Panel added that Article XX did not imply that recourse to unilateral measures was always excluded, particularly after 'serious attempts' had been made to negotiate an international environmental agreement.[314] It concluded that the contested measure was not within the scope of measures permitted under the chapeau of Article XX.[315]

---

[309]See *US – Shrimp*, Appellate Body Report, para. 174.

[310]*Ibid.*, para. 175.

[311]See *US – Shrimp*, Panel Report, para. 7.54.

[312]*Ibid.*, para. 7.55.

[313]*Ibid.*

[314]*Ibid.*, para. 7.61.

[315]*Ibid.*, para. 7.62.

As it has already been mentioned, the Appellate Body upheld the conclusion that the measure constituted 'unjustifiable discrimination' for various reasons,[316] among which discrimination in the way international negotiations of an MEA had been conducted by the United States. The conclusion that the measure amounted to 'unjustifiable discrimination' was thus based not solely on the lack of cooperative efforts but also on a variety of the measure's features.

When it comes to the issue of whether WTO Members have the duty to negotiate an international environmental agreement before adopting a unilateral trade measure, the Appellate Body stated:

> Another aspect of the application of Section 609 that bears heavily in any appraisal of justifiable or unjustifiable discrimination is the failure of the United States to engage the appellees, as well as other Members exporting shrimp to the United States, in serious, across-the-board negotiations with the objective of concluding bilateral or multilateral agreements for the protection and conservation of sea turtles, before enforcing the import prohibition against the shrimp exports of those other Members.[317]

The Appellate Body added:

> Clearly, the United States negotiated seriously with some, but not with other Members (including the appellees), that export shrimp to the United States. The effect is plainly discriminatory and, in our view, unjustifiable.[318]

The Appellate Body report emphasised that different treatment granted to the complaining Members in the negotiations amounted to 'unjustifiable discrimination'. It did not, however, state that a self-standing duty to negotiate an international environmental agreement before applying a restrictive trade measure was implied by Article XX of the GATT.[319]

The *US – Shrimp 21.5* Panel had to interpret these Appellate Body's findings. It took a much more restrictive view on the negotiations obligations of WTO Members. It held:

> [I]n a context such as this one where a multilateral agreement is clearly to be preferred and where measures such as that taken by the United States in this case may only be accepted under Article XX if they were allowed under an international agreement, or if they were taken further to the completion of serious good faith efforts to reach a multilateral agreement, the possibility to impose a unilateral measure to protect sea turtles under Section 609 is more to be seen, for the purposes of Article XX, as the possibility to adopt

---

[316]These reasons where the following: inflexibility of the measure (para. 161–165), the fact that the measure itself directed the Secretary of State to negotiate with shrimp exporting countries (para. 167), the need for 'concerted and cooperative efforts' on the part of the different countries concerned in order to achieve protection of migratory species (para. 168), the fact that the United States did negotiate and conclude a regional international agreement with some WTO members but not others (para. 169), the fact that other differential treatment occurred among the various countries desiring certification, such as the length of the phase-in periods or the efforts to transfer technologies (para. 173–175).

[317]*US – Shrimp*, Appellate Body Report, para. 166.

[318]*Ibid.*, para. 172.

[319]See Howse (2002), pp. 507 f.; Chang (2005), p. 48.

a provisional measure allowed for emergency reasons than as a definitive 'right' to take a permanent measure. The extent to which serious good faith efforts continue to be made may be reassessed at any time. For instance, steps which constituted good faith efforts at the beginning of a negotiation may fail to meet that test at a later stage.[320]

The Panel thus interpreted the report of the Appellate Body as meaning that (1) WTO Members have an obligation to undertake serious good faith efforts to negotiate a multilateral agreement with all interested trading partners; (2) these efforts have to take place before the enforcement of a unilaterally designed import prohibition;[321] (3) Article XX only allows the adoption of a 'provisional' measure, which means that the importing Member has to guarantee a 'continuity of efforts' to negotiate,[322] which can be reassessed at any time; (4) these provisional measures are only allowed for emergency reasons and should not be seen as a right to take 'permanent measures'. These findings seem to introduce several additional condi tions, compared to the initial Appellate Body report, to the possibility of WTO Members to enact a unilateral trade measure if multilateral negotiations to conclude an environmental agreement fail.

The Panel also held that the importing Member had no obligation to *conclude* an international environmental agreement in order to comply with Article XX.[323] However, in the view of the Panel, the good faith efforts to negotiate an interna- tional agreement had to be a 'continuous process', including once a unilateral measure had been adopted pending the conclusion of an agreement. The Appellate Body confirmed that there was no obligation to conclude an international agreement since it would otherwise imply that any country that is a party to the negotiations with the importing Member would have a *veto* over whether that Member could fulfil its WTO obligations.[324]

Since only this issue was appealed by Malaysia, the Appellate Body did not have the opportunity to examine the Panel findings relating to the extent of the negoti- ation efforts expected from an importing Member. It did, however, remind that its initial report in this case resulted in a finding of 'unjustifiable discrimination' in part because the United States treated WTO Members differently in the negotiations of an international environmental agreement.[325] It thus emphasised that in order to comply with the chapeau, the United States had to provide all exporting countries 'similar opportunities to negotiate' an international agreement.[326] It did not confirm that WTO Members had a self-standing duty to negotiate before the application of a restrictive trade measure, nor did it make any comments on the extent of such possible duty.

---

[320]*US – Shrimp 21.5*, Panel Report, para. 5.88.

[321]See *US – Shrimp 21.5*, Panel Report, para. 5.66.

[322]*Ibid.*, para. 5.60.

[323]*Ibid.*, para. 5.67.

[324]See *US – Shrimp 21.5*, Appellate Body Report, para. 123.

[325]*Ibid.*, para. 119.

[326]*Ibid.*, para. 122.

The Appellate Body's *EC – Seal Products* report briefly mentions the issue of non-discrimination in the negotiations with trading partners. The seal product import ban concerned in this case provided for an exception for recognised Inuit community hunts (the 'IC exception'). In this report, the Appellate Body expressed the view that the European Union had not made 'comparable efforts' to facilitate the access of the Canadian Inuits to the IC exception as it did with respect to Greenlandic Inuits.[327] This aspect represented one of the elements on the basis of which the Appellate Body concluded that the EU measure did not meet the requirements of the chapeau.[328]

Thus, it is clear from these reports that an importing Member is required to avoid discrimination in international negotiations and that it is not required to conclude an international agreement before the application of a restrictive trade measure. It remains, however, unclear if Members necessarily have to negotiate *before* imposing a restrictive trade measure and, in that case, what the *extent* is of the negotiation efforts that the importing Member is expected to make. These issues have a considerable importance to determine the extent to which the conditions of the chapeau may restrict the ability of WTO Members to enact environmental trade measures addressing international environmental issues. They will be examined further below.[329]

7.3.2.2.3.2   *Critical Analysis of the* US – Shrimp *Reports*

The *US – Shrimp 21.5* Panel had the opportunity to interpret the findings of the Appellate Body concerning the international negotiations issue. The Appellate Body never stated explicitly in its initial report that the chapeau implied an independent duty to negotiate. Its main concern was the discrimination caused by the fact that the United States had negotiated with certain Members and not with others. As to the *US – Shrimp 21.5* Panel, it focused on the extent of the cooperation efforts that were required from the importing Member. It reminded that, in the view of the Appellate Body, the chapeau of Article XX referred to the doctrine of *abus de droit* and that the task of interpreting and applying the chapeau was essentially the one of locating and marking out a line of equilibrium between the right of a Member to invoke an exception under Article XX and the rights of other Members under the substantive provisions of the GATT.[330] It also referred to the statement that this line of equilibrium was not fixed and unchanging but moved depending on the kind and shape of the measures imposed and on the particular circumstances of the case.

The Panel then recalled that various international environmental agreements, as well as different WTO documents, recognised the need to find multilateral solutions based on international consensus to deal with international environmental

---

[327]See *EC – Seal Products*, Appellate Body Report, para. 5.337.

[328]*Ibid.*, para. 5.338.

[329]See *infra*, 7.3.4.1.

[330]See *US – Shrimp 21.5*, Panel Report, para. 5.51.

problems. In its view, 'undoubtedly, these elements move the line of equilibrium towards multilateral solutions and non trade-restrictive measures'.[331]

More precisely, the Panel considered that the negotiations had to be initiated by the importing country, with all interested parties, and that serious good faith efforts to negotiate had to be made *before* the enforcement of a unilaterally designed measure.[332] The need to address successfully the issue of conservation of sea turtles implied, moreover, a 'continuity of efforts' to find a cooperative solution, including once a unilateral measure had been adopted.[333] Finally, it expressed the view that, in any case, unilateral measures imposed to address an international environmental issue were to be seen as *provisional* measures, allowed for *emergency* reasons; it seemed to deny that WTO Members had a 'definitive right' to take a 'permanent' measure.[334]

These findings imply a narrow interpretation of the chapeau of Article XX, which would only *exceptionally* allow unilateral measures, if efforts to find a cooperative solution have failed, if an urgent need for intervention exists and if the unilateral trade measure is only adopted on a provisional basis.

It is doubtful that this narrow interpretation is implied by the Appellate Body's report and even more that this interpretation is justified from a legal viewpoint. As mentioned, the *US – Shrimp 21.5* Panel reasoning is mainly based on the concept of the 'line of equilibrium' between the right of an importing Member to adopt a restrictive measure under Article XX and the substantive rights of other Members under the GATT. The Panel considered that the need for cooperation in the field of international environmental problems moved this line of equilibrium closer to multilateral solutions, away from unilateral ones. Such statement seems to imply that WTO adjudicating bodies should proceed to a balance of interests (which has been critically commented above),[335] which would lean towards multilateral solutions. In itself, a balance of interests is already more demanding than a simple control that the regulating Member has not abused of its right to invoke Article XX. But implying that it would only exceptionally lean towards unilateral measures moves the applicable test even further, to a logic that has arguably nothing to do with the notion of abuse of right.

Moreover, it has been shown that the initial Panel in the *US – Shrimp* case had expressed the view that the chapeau of Article XX did not allow WTO Members to adopt measures making access to their market conditional upon the adoption by the exporting country of certain conservation policies. It had thus considered that all measures that 'threatened the multilateral system', by the risks of conflicting requirements, were not within the scope of measures permitted under Article XX. Even if the Panel claimed that its findings did not imply that unilateral

---

[331] *US – Shrimp 21.5*, Panel Report, para. 5.58.

[332] See *US – Shrimp 21.5*, Panel Report, para. 5.67.

[333] *Ibid.*, para. 5.60 and 5.67.

[334] *Ibid.*, para. 5.88.

[335] See *supra*, 7.3.1.

measures were always excluded, particularly after serious attempts have been made to negotiate, it seems difficult to imagine many measures that could potentially pass the test applied by the Panel.

The Appellate Body overturned these findings and held that conditioning market access to the adoption of policies unilaterally prescribed by the importing Member might be a common aspect of measures falling under the scope of Article XX. It thus expressly rejected the restrictive approach applied by the Panel under the chapeau in relation to unilateral measures.

When it comes to the relevant findings of the *US – Shrimp 21.5* Panel commented above, they would in practice imply that the justification of unilateral measures under the chapeau of Article XX would be exceptional. The reasoning of the *US – Shrimp 21.5* Panel may not be quite as far-reaching as that of the initial *US – Shrimp* Panel report. But, in practice, it would also restrict to a very large extent the possibility of WTO Members to impose unilateral trade measures since it implies that in the absence of any emergency, no unilateral measure could be applied. In that respect, some commentators have argued that in fact WTO adjudicating bodies have led a genuine 'crusade' against unilateralism and sought implicitly to exclude in practice almost all unilateral measures.[336]

It is submitted by the present author that it is doubtful that the Appellate Body made, on the one hand, a strong statement that measures falling under the scope of Article XX may all share a certain unilateral character while on the other hand introducing conditions on the possibility to impose unilateral measures that are so restrictive that this statement would be emptied of most of its substance.

Certain commentators also argue that Article XX contains no textual basis that could justify a general duty to negotiate.[337] The text of the chapeau even provides that 'any contracting party' may adopt measures that otherwise violate the GATT if they comply with Article XX, which tends to show that WTO members can act unilaterally.[338] The drafters of the GATT could have referred to measures adopted 'by *the* contracting parties' instead to signal that unilateral measures were excluded.[339] In the light of the importance given to the ordinary meaning of the text by the Appellate Body, and given the lack of any explicit statement in the Appellate Body's *US – Shrimp* report of the existence of an independent duty to negotiate, some consider that it should not be assumed that the Appellate Body derogated in its report from its usual interpretative approach.[340]

---

[336]See Prost (2005), pp. 168 ff.

[337]See Gaines (2001), p. 807 ('[n]othing in the lettered paragraphs or the chapeau constrains a member government's choice among multilateral, regional, bilateral, or unilateral approaches'); Howse (2002), pp. 517 f.; Chang (2005), p. 47.

[338]See Chang (2005), p. 45; Prost (2005), p. 173.

[339]See Prost (2005), p. 173.

[340]See Howse (2002), p. 507; Chang (2005), pp. 47 f. (in particular, p. 47: '[m]ost important, once we recall the Appellate Body's focus on the ordinary meaning of the text of Article XX, we cannot reasonably read in the Appellate Body's rulings to impose a duty to negotiate in the absence of any "discrimination between countries where the same conditions prevail"'); Trebilcock et al. (2013), p. 678.

On the other hand, the Appellate Body's examination in the *US – Shrimp* case of the United States negotiation efforts focused on non-discrimination and differential treatment among different WTO Members. The Appellate Body analysed whether the failure of the United States to negotiate with certain of its trading partners amounted to 'unjustifiable discrimination'. It logically held that for the application of a measure to result in 'unjustifiable discrimination', some form of discrimination had to have occurred in the first place.[341] Stating that a failure to negotiate would result in 'unjustifiable discrimination', regardless of whether actual discrimination in the negotiations occurred, would contradict this approach and would not respect the text of the chapeau.

It is thus submitted here that it cannot be inferred from the *US – Shrimp* Appellate Body's report that the 'unjustifiable discrimination' condition implies a general duty to negotiate. In the *US – Shrimp* case, if the United States had not discriminated between Members in the way it conducted international negotiations to conclude a multilateral agreement, the Appellate Body would probably not have adopted the view that the United States efforts amounted 'unjustifiable discrimination'. In that respect, the relevance of the interpretation of this report made by the *US – Shrimp 21.5* Panel is subject to doubts.

However, the efforts made by a Member to negotiate an international agreement before imposing a unilateral measure are not irrelevant in the examination of the conditions of the chapeau, including the disguised restriction on international trade criterion. The Appellate Body acknowledged that the need for, and appropriateness of, cooperative efforts to tackle international environmental problems have been recognised in the WTO itself and in various other international instruments and declarations.[342] This debate and the way the international negotiations issue may be taken into account in the examination of Article XX are further examined below.[343]

7.3.2.3 Arbitrary or Unjustifiable Discrimination 'Between the Countries Where the Same Conditions Prevail'

The third element of the discrimination condition of the chapeau is that the measure results in unjustifiable or arbitrary discrimination *between the countries where the same conditions prevail*.

Case law brought mainly two important precisions. In *US – Gasoline*, the Appellate Body accepted the assumption of the participants that the chapeau of

---

[341]*US – Shrimp*, Appellate Body Report, para. 150. Thus if there is no 'discrimination', no 'unjustifiable' discrimination can occur. The Panel in the *US – Shrimp 21.5* case seemed unaware of that contradiction, since it stated explicitly that to avoid unjustifiable discrimination, WTO Members had *inter alia* to negotiate with all their trading partners before adopting a unilateral measure (*US – Shrimp 21.5*, Panel Report, para. 5.66).

[342]See *US – Shrimp*, Appellate Body Report, para. 168. See also *US – Shrimp 21.5*, Appellate Body Report, para. 124.

[343]See *infra*, 7.3.4.1.

Article XX referred to discrimination not only between different exporting WTO Members but also between exporting states and the importing country concerned.[344]

In the *US – Shrimp* case, as it has been explained, the Appellate Body objected to the decision of the United States to apply a rigid standard, which required the adoption of essentially the same policy and enforcement programme as that applicable to US domestic shrimp trawlers and which implied that shrimp from non-certified countries could not be imported in the United States, even if they had been harvested in a way that was harmless to sea turtles. The Appellate Body took the following view:

> This suggests to us that this measure, in its application, is more concerned with effectively influencing WTO Members to adopt essentially the same comprehensive regulatory regime as that applied in the United States to its domestic shrimp trawlers, even though many of those countries may be differently situated. We believe that discrimination results not only when countries in which the same conditions prevail are differently treated, but also when the application of the measure at issue does not allow for any inquiry into the appropriateness of the regulatory program for the conditions prevailing in those exporting countries.[345]

This finding has important consequences for environmental trade measures and PPM measures, more particularly, since an importing country must design its measure in a way that takes into consideration the differences in the conditions prevailing abroad.[346] That could include differences in the characteristics of the environment (sink capacities in case of restriction on pollution emissions; abundance of natural resources stocks; lower environmental threat in the particular country, which could, for instance, have been the case in the circumstances of the *US – Shrimp* in the absence of sea turtles in the territorial waters of a particular Member; etc.) or differences in the level of development (exemption for LLDCs and others) or even possibly differences in the level of responsibility in the environmental harm addressed.

Therefore, this requirement may be central in taking into account, to a certain extent, the concerns of developing countries with respect to the imposition of PPM standards, to which they may object for a number of reasons. This would be particularly important in the field of measures to combat climate change, in the light of the principle of common but differentiated responsibilities. This issue is examined further below.[347]

---

[344]See *US – Gasoline*, Appellate Body Report, pp. 23 f.; *US – Shrimp*, Appellate Body Report, para. 150.

[345]*US – Shrimp*, Appellate Body Report, para. 165 (emphasis added).

[346]See also Bartels (2015), pp. 112 ff.

[347]See *infra*, 7.3.4.2.

7.3.3 Disguised Restriction on International Trade

As the Panel in the *EC – Asbestos* case noted, the actual scope of the words 'disguised restriction on international trade' has not yet been clearly defined in case law.[348] However, past reports did suggest certain interpretation elements that will be examined here.

Contrary to what certain GATT 1947 panels had held,[349] the Appellate Body has indicated that '*concealed* or *unannounced* restriction or discrimination does *not* exhaust the meaning of "disguised restriction"'.[350] In other words, it is not a mere transparency requirement,[351] even if it seems to imply that a measure that was not published would not comply with that requirement.[352]

Case law has also clarified that while there may be some overlap between 'arbitrary or unjustifiable discrimination' and 'disguised restriction on international trade', since the same considerations can be used in both contexts, the former may also cover other requirements.[353] In other words, the application of a measure provisionally justified under the sub-paragraphs of Article XX could violate one of these conditions, both or none of them. The Appellate Body reminded that both tests had 'the object and purpose of avoiding abuse or illegitimate use of the exceptions to the substantive rules available in Article XX'.[354]

When it comes to the definition of the terms 'disguised restriction on international trade', one Panel held that the facts that would be decisive in deciding whether a measure has complied with this condition would vary from case to case.[355] However, two panel reports considered more particularly the *intention* to pursue trade-restrictive objectives and indirectly the actual protectionist *effects* of the measure.

About the intent of the measure, the *EC – Asbestos* Panel suggested:

---

[348]See *EC – Asbestos*, Panel Report, para. 8.233. See also Bartels (2015), pp. 123 ff., describing the terms 'disguised restriction on international trade' as the 'much overlooked' condition of the chapeau.

[349]The *EC – Asbestos* Panel Report noted in para. 8.233 that '[u]nder the GATT 1947, Panels seem mainly to have considered that a disguised restriction on international trade was a restriction that had not been taken in the form of a trade measure or had not been announced beforehand or formed the subject of a publication, or even had not been the subject of an investigation'. See *US – Canadian Tuna*, Panel Report, para. 4.8; *US – Automotive Springs*, Panel Report, para. 56.

[350]*US – Gasoline*, Appellate Body Report, p. 25 (original emphasis).

[351]See Mavroidis (2008b), p. 274.

[352]See *EC – Asbestos*, Panel Report, para. 8.234.

[353]See *US – Gasoline*, Appellate Body Report, p. 25; *EC – Asbestos*, Panel Report, para. 8.235.

[354]*US – Gasoline*, Appellate Body Report, p. 25.

[355]See *Brazil – Tyres*, Panel Report, para. 7.322: '[b]earing in mind our earlier observations and the Appellate Body's ruling as cited above, we agree that no single element will necessarily be determinative in each and every case, and that a range of factors may be relevant to our determination'.

(...) we consider that the key to understanding what is covered by 'disguised restriction on international trade' is not so much the word 'restriction', inasmuch as, in essence, any measure falling within Article XX is a restriction on international trade, but the word 'disguised'. In accordance with the approach defined in Article 31 of the Vienna Convention, we note that, as ordinarily understood, the verb 'to disguise' implies an *intention*. Thus, 'to disguise' *(déguiser)* means, in particular, 'conceal beneath deceptive appearances', counterfeit', 'alter so as to deceive', 'misrepresent', 'dissimulate'. Accordingly, a restriction which formally meets the requirements of Article XX(b) will constitute an abuse if such compliance is in fact only a disguise to conceal the pursuit of trade-restrictive objectives.[356]

When it comes to the way the actual *intent* of the measure should be determined, two panels applied a principle developed by the Appellate Body in the context of the national treatment obligation, under which 'the protective application of a measure can most often be discerned from its design, architecture and revealing structure'.[357] The fact that this principle had been developed in the context of national treatment did not bother the *EC – Asbestos* Panel, which was of the view that there was no reason why this approach should not be applicable in other circumstances, where it is necessary to determine whether a measure is being applied for protective purposes.[358] The *US – Shrimp 21.5* Panel report noted that these findings were neither reversed nor modified by the Appellate Body.[359]

In relation to the possible protectionist *effects* of the measure, the *EC – Asbestos* Panel held:

Admittedly, there is always the possibility that measures such as those contained in the Decree might have *the effect of favouring the domestic substitute product manufacturers*. This is a natural consequence of prohibiting a given product and in itself cannot justify the conclusion that the measure has a protectionist aim, as long as it remains *within certain limits*. In fact, the information made available to the Panel does not suggest that the import ban has benefited the French substitute fibre industry, to the detriment of third country producers, *to such an extent* as to lead to the conclusion that the Decree has been so applied as to constitute a disguised restriction on international trade.[360]

As for the *US – Shrimp 21.5* Panel, it considered the following:

Even though, when the application of Section 609 was extended to the whole world, US fishermen were probably in favour of a measure imposing the same requirements on foreign fishermen, *they are likely to incur little commercial gain from a ban* since the Revised Guidelines make it easier to export shrimp to the United States under Section 609, compared with the situation under the 1996 Guidelines.[361]

---

[356]*EC – Asbestos*, Panel Report, para. 8.236 (original emphasis). The *US – Shrimp 21.5* Panel Report relied on these findings in para. 5.142: '[t]he Panel is of the view that there would be an abuse of Article XX(g) 'if [the compliance with Article XX(g) was] in fact only a disguise to conceal the pursuit of trade-restrictive objectives'.

[357]See *EC – Asbestos*, Appellate Body Report, para. 8.236; *US – Shrimp 21.5*, Panel Report, para. 5.142.

[358]See *EC – Asbestos*, Panel Report, note 199, p. 449.

[359]See *US – Shrimp 21.5*, Panel Report, note 250, p. 100.

[360]*EC – Asbestos*, Panel Report, para. 8.239 (emphasis added).

[361]*US – Shrimp 21.5*, Panel Report, para. 5.143 (emphasis added).

Thus, the protectionist effects do have a role to play in examining whether the application of a measure results in a disguised restriction on international trade. Both protectionist *intent* and *effects* are relevant to determine if the measure results in a restriction that is 'disguised' to conceal the protection of the domestic industry under a public policy goal of one of the sub-paragraphs. The Panel suggested that some comparison should be made between the extent of the protectionist effects of the measure and the conclusion that the measure has a protectionist aim.

If this approach were confirmed by the Appellate Body, it would imply some restrictions to the principle under which the design of a measure is to be examined under Article XX sub-paragraphs, while the chapeau only relates to the way the measure is applied.[362] More importantly, it would certainly allow some form of convergence between the necessity test of Article XX(b) and the 'relating to' test of Article XX(g), combined with the disguised restriction on international trade conditions of the chapeau, as will be further argued below.[363]

7.3.4   Critique

The previous sections have shown that the chapeau of Article XX disciplines the use of trade measures justified under the sub-paragraphs, in particular PPM measures. This section makes a critical assessment of three particularly important issues for the analysis of PPM measures under the chapeau. It starts by the debate on unilateralism and the question of whether the introductory clause of Article XX contains a duty to negotiate an international agreement before imposing a unilateral PPM measure (Sect. 7.3.4.1). It examines then how the interests of developing countries can be taken into account under the general exceptions clause (Sect. 7.3.4.2). Finally, it focuses on the means-ends relationship and on the possible overlap between the sub-paragraphs of Article XX and its introductory clause (Sect. 7.3.4.3).

7.3.4.1   A Duty to Negotiate a Multilateral Environmental Agreement (MEA) Under the Chapeau of Article XX?

7.3.4.1.1   The Debate on Unilateralism

It has been shown above that the *US – Shrimp* reports have established clearly that the conditions of the chapeau implied that a Member wishing to address an

---

[362] See *US – Gasoline*, Appellate Body Report, p. 22; *US – Shrimp*, Appellate Body Report, para. 115; *Brazil – Tyres*, Appellate Body Report, para. 215; *EC – Seal Products*, Appellate Body Report, para. 5.302. See also *supra*, 7.3.1.

[363] See *infra*, 7.3.4.3.

environmental issue requiring the adoption of certain practices or policies in the exporting country must negotiate with the relevant trading partners in a *non-discriminatory manner* with the objective of concluding a multilateral environmental agreement. It is also clear that the legality of a trade measure under Article XX does *not* depend on whether an international agreement is actually *concluded*.

It remains, however, unclear if WTO Members have the obligation to negotiate *before* the imposition of a trade measure. The extent of the negotiation efforts that have to be undertaken by the importing Member remains also uncertain. The answer to these questions can have a considerable importance on the extent of the ability of WTO Members to enact environmental trade measures, in the absence of a relevant MEA.

The interpretation of the *US – Shrimp* report findings relating to the issue of international cooperation must be viewed in the larger context of the debate on unilateralism, in which the principle of state sovereignty may be seen as conflicting with international duties to cooperate, in particular those set out in MEAs. As it has been shown in Chap. 4, many international treaties refer to cooperation obligations. This does not mean, however, that unilateral actions are prohibited per se.

In the general debate about unilateral measures, it should be pointed out that they might have gradually acquired a negative connotation.[364] When an importing state adopts unilateral environmental trade measures, exporting countries may perceive that it imposes its choices or values on others.[365] The unilateral character of a trade measure tends thus to reinforce the perception that such measures are 'extraterritorial' or 'coercive',[366] even though it has been shown above that such argument is not legally correct. Measures that are viewed as 'unilateral' are sometimes adopted in a field in which there is no international consensus or negotiations pertaining to the desirability of the objective concerned.[367] The imposition of unilateral measures in these circumstances may appear to conflict with states' duty to cooperate pursuant to general or environmental international law.

From a legal viewpoint, unilateralism is forbidden neither by WTO law nor by public international law. But both of them have recognised a preference for multilateral and cooperative solutions.

In the WTO context, as it has been reminded in the previous section, the Appellate Body has stated that measures falling within the ambit of Article XX shared to a certain extent a unilateral character. A preference of WTO Members for multilateral solutions has at the same time been recognised. For instance, the CTE expressed the view that WTO Members supported that multilateral solutions based

---

[364]See Esty (1994), p. 143 ('ugly word'); Bodansky (2000), p. 339 (speaking of 'dirty word'); Boisson de Chazourne (2000), pp. 318 f. ('negative connotation'); Dupuy (2000), p. 20 ('strong pejorative connotation').

[365]See Bodansky (2000), p. 342.

[366]See Boisson de Chazourne (2000), p. 325; Luff (2004), p. 192.

[367]Even though there is a variety of degree of 'unilateralism' and 'multilateralism' as Bodansky has shown. See Bodansky (2000), pp. 342 f.

on cooperation and consensus are the 'best and most effective way for governments to tackle environmental problems of a transboundary or global nature'.[368]

As far as general international law is concerned, cooperation among states plays a fundamental role. The very general duty to cooperate laid down in Article 1 of the UN Charter, as well as numerous international agreements referring to the principle of cooperation, illustrate the wide recognition of this obligation.[369] This general duty to negotiate is, however, too vague to establish any specific obligations in relation to the way states should act or measures that they should adopt.[370] It is through the adoption of international treaties that states have translated that general principle into specific commitments.[371]

Most multilateral environmental agreements refer to the principle of cooperation, and some of them introduce specific commitments,[372] which constrain state sovereignty to varying degrees.[373] Some MEAs also assert a corollary duty, that unilateral environmental measures should be avoided,[374] in particular Principle 12 of the Rio Declaration, which states:

> Unilateral actions to deal with environmental challenges outside the jurisdiction of the importing state should be avoided. Environmental measures addressing transboundary or global environmental problems should, as far as possible, be based on an international consensus.

The relevant question for the present concern is whether this duty of states to cooperate to achieve protection of the global environment and the principle that unilateral measures should be avoided mean that, in international law, 'unilateral' measures can be adopted only if international negotiations to conclude an environmental agreement have been attempted and have eventually failed.[375] In other

---

[368] *US – Shrimp*, Appellate Body Report, para. 168, referring to the Report of the CTE forming part of the Report of the General Council to Ministers on the occasion of the Singapore Ministerial Conference.

[369] See Dupuy (2000), p. 22 (arguing that the principle of cooperation has a customary nature); Perrez (2000), p. 271, with further references (concluding that cooperation as a general duty of international law is well accepted). See also *supra*, 4.1.4.

[370] See *supra*, 4.1.4.

[371] *Idem.*

[372] For instance, the Appellate Body referred to Principle 12 of the Rio Convention, to paragraph 2.22(i) of Agenda 21, to Article 5 of the Convention on Biological Diversity and to Annex I of the Convention of Migratory Species of Wild Animals (See the *US – Shrimp* Appellate Body Report, para 168). One could also mention Principle 24 of the Stockholm Declaration or Principle 21 of the World Nature Charter.

[373] See *supra*, 4.1.4.

[374] See e.g. Rio Declaration, Principle 12; Agenda 21, para. 39.3(d); WSSD Plan of Implementation, para. 101.

[375] Which seems to be the view of Dupuy. He wrote that international law implied that 'no state may have recourse to the taking of unilateral measures before first exhausting means of international negotiation' and that this rule was 'very close to what the Appellate Body recently posited in the *Shrimp/Turtle* case'. See Dupuy (2000), p. 25.

words, one should examine the extent to which it restricts states' sovereignty over their import policies.

The Rio Declaration is non-binding, even though it has been suggested that it represents at present 'the most significant universally endorsed statement of general rights and obligations of states affecting the environment'.[376] The text of Principle 12 does not prohibit unilateral measures *per se*; it merely states that these actions 'should be avoided'.[377] A prohibition of unilateral measures would result in a major restriction to the principle of state sovereignty as far as trade measures are concerned since they are currently only limited by the prohibition of coercion.[378] Moreover, Principle 12 specifies the circumstances under which unilateral measures may be taken. They need to be based 'as far as possible on an international consensus'. This requirement highlights that first-best solutions are interventions at the source, which require concerted actions achieved through international negotiations.[379] But as such, the language of Principe 12 indicates that international consensus is desirable but not a prerequisite.[380] More specifically, the wording 'as far as possible' shows that there might be situations where it would not be possible to avoid unilateralism. This aspect evokes the view expressed by some that, in many cases, because effective multilateral environmental action is impossible, the alternative to unilateralism is inaction and not multilateralism.[381]

In brief, Principle 12 shows that unilateral measures are supposed to be the exception, while multilateral actions should be the rule.[382] But it does not *prohibit* unilateral measures.[383] This means that the Rio Declaration—independently from its soft law nature—does not introduce a *general duty to negotiate* before having the right to resort to unilateral measures. They should be avoided, but depending on the circumstances, it might not be possible to do so. Such issues cannot be governed by

---

[376]Birnie et al. (2009), p. 112.

[377]See Sands (2000), pp. 295 f. See also Sands (2012), p. 807.

[378]Cf. the Nicaragua case (*Military and Paramilitary Activities in and against Nicaragua*, Nicaragua v. United States, Merits, Judgment, ICJ Reports 1986). See *supra*, 5.2.

[379]See *supra*, 3.4.1.

[380]As the use of the word 'should' shows. See Prost (2005), p. 174; Sands (2000), p. 296.

[381]See Charnovitz (1994b), p. 805; Bodansky (2000), p. 346 (in his view, the choice is between unilateralism and doing nothing, rather than between unilateralism and multilateralism); Prost (2005), p. 177.

[382]See Dupuy (2000), p. 25; Vranes (2009), pp. 176 f. *Contra*: Prost (2005), p. 175 who argues that because MEAs usually recommend cooperation 'as far as possible', unilateralism is the rule and multilateralism the exception. This may not necessarily be in line with international practice (he also asserts that obligations stemming from Principle 12 of the Rio Declaration are merely duties to consult and inform trading partners). Similarly, Bodansky (2000), p. 345 notes that 'although international law often seems to contain a presumption in favour of multilateralism, it is good to remember that, in general, unilateral action (sovereignty) remains the norm in environmental policy and international action the exception, requiring special justification'.

[383]Reference to the principle *in dubio mitius* could be made here, since the question is whether Principle 12 restricts the sovereignty of the importing state.

rigid abstract rules. The regulating state should be able to show that the adoption of unilateral measures was justified.[384, 385]

This study submits that a further argument militates against the interpretation of Principle 12 of the Rio Declaration as implying a general duty to negotiate before having the right to enact trade-related environmental measures. Prohibiting all unilateral environmental measures because of the principle of cooperation would defeat the primary goal (*ratio legis*) of the duty to cooperate. One of the main challenges of environmental protection that the international community has to address is the free rider problem, which may undermine any significant result and give rise to risks of cooperation failures.[386] The duty to cooperate is a way to preclude the possibility of free riding and to limit the situations of 'prisoner's dilemma'.[387] Many specific provisions of MEAs introducing duties to cooperate refer clearly to that objective.[388] In other words, the cooperation obligation is laid down in the Rio Declaration in order to achieve efficient protection and conservation at a global level. The focus of the Rio Declaration and other MEAs is primarily on effective protection of transboundary or global environmental goods and *not* on the restriction of the possibility of states to take action to protect resources located beyond their territory.

These considerations must be taken into account when it comes to the interpretation of the scope of duty to negotiate laid down in Principle 12. Reading a general duty to exhaust the means of international negotiations before having the right to resort to unilateral measures would give states unwilling to participate in international efforts a *right to free ride*, at least until it can be held that good faith efforts to reach a negotiated solution have been undertaken.[389] It could also encourage

---

[384]See Vranes (2009), p. 177.

[385]This reflects the risk of cooperation failure leading to a 'tragedy of the commons', implied by prisoner's dilemma situations that characterise the management of global environmental issues. See *supra*, 3.4.

[386]See *supra*, 3.4.

[387]See Perrez (2000), p. 300, who asserts in relation to shared resources that '[*t*]*he reason for the obligation to cooperate* concerning the use of shared resources lies in the fact that non-cooperation might lead to the classical situation of a tragedy of the commons: while each state has an interest in using the shared resource as much as possible, no state has an interest in adopting measures to protect the shared resource from over-exploitation' (emphasis added).

[388]For instance, Principle 7 of the Rio Declaration expresses that states 'shall cooperate in a spirit of global partnership *to conserve, protect and restore* the health and integrity of the Earth's ecosystem' (emphasis added). Art. 118 UNCLOS provides that states 'shall cooperate with each other in the conservation and management of living resources in the areas of the high seas. States whose nationals exploit identical living resources, or different living resources in the same area, shall enter into negotiations wi*th a view to taking the measures necessary for the conservation of the living resources concerned*' (emphasis added).

[389]See Esty (1994), p. 152: 'permitting non-parties to environmental agreements to assert their GATT rights while in contravention of internationally determined environmental requirements (. . .) encourages free riding on the environmental efforts of others and creates a disincentive to join international agreements. Not only does this nonparticipation diminish the effectiveness of the environmental accord, it gives free riders an opportunity to enjoy a competitive advantage in the

strategic delays in order to obtain more concessions from the regulating country in the form of side payments or less restrictive regulations.[390] Should this view prevail, Principle 12 of the Rio Declaration would in fact reinforce the risks of cooperation failures and the problems caused by the prisoner's dilemma, because they would reduce the costs of defect, and thus increase the incentives not to cooperate, at least for the duration of the negotiations.

It is clear, therefore, that this interpretation that would undermine or defeat the objective of Principle 7 of the Rio Declaration cannot be upheld and that Principle 12 does not imply any general *duty* to have recourse in all cases to diplomacy before applying a trade measure. There may be circumstances in which unilateralism cannot be avoided and in which consensus cannot be achieved.

In the reality of international relations, unilateral measures may sometimes be useful or even necessary to protect the environment. Achieving international cooperation may be difficult, in particular when it comes to achieving broad membership treaties.[391] The tremendous difficulties of the international community to agree on a post-Kyoto agreement on climate change are a good example of the challenges involved. In this context, unilateral measures may be viewed as an instrument to accelerate international cooperation.[392] There may be cases in which unilateral measures may create new state practice that may eventually be recognised as international custom (creative unilateralism).[393] A state may also act alone to try and shape a given legal regime in a way that is more congruent with the interest it defends ('policy-forging' unilateralism).[394] In the field of environmental protection, these unilateral acts may be helpful to secure multilateral coopera-tion.[395] In addition, multilateral enforcement mechanisms may be inexistent or ineffective, which means that requiring multilateral measures may often lead in fact to inaction.[396]

---

global marketplace by carrying on environmentally harmful (and likely cost-reducing) practices others have forsworn, creating both environmental and competitiveness tensions.'

[390]See McGinnis and Movsesian (2000), p. 593.

[391]See Charnovitz (2002), p. 71 with further references.

[392]See Charnovitz (1994c), pp. 493 ff.; Appleton (1997a), pp. 100 ff.; Schoenbaum (1997), p. 300 (noting that the United States had tried during twenty years to obtain an agreement on reduction of dolphin mortality caused by tuna fishing but that it succeeded only shortly after the adoption of its unilateral measure examined in the *US – Tuna I* case). See also Dunoff (1992), pp. 1407 ff.; who retraces the history of dolphin mortality reduction in the United States since the 1960s.

[393]See Schoenbaum (1997), pp. 299 ff. See also Hakimi (2014), who argues in the general context of public international law that even acts of 'unfriendly unilateralism', including sometimes unlawful unilateral acts, help generate international law.

[394]See Boisson de Chazourne (2000), pp. 317 and 325 ff.

[395]See Charnovitz (1994c), pp. 493 ff.; Gaines (2001), pp. 809 ff.; Prost (2005), p. 178.

[396]See Bodansky (2000), p. 346 (in his view, the choice is between unilateralism and doing nothing, rather than between unilateralism and multilateralism); Charnovitz (1994b), p. 805; Prost (2005), p. 177.

In brief, unilateral measures may be controversial to a certain extent and give rise to the opposition of certain exporting countries. A clear preference exists both in international environmental law and in WTO law for concerted solutions, which are in principle the most effective means to achieve conservation outcomes, insofar as they allow interventions at the source. But, on the other hand, there is no legal basis—be it in WTO law or in international law—for a general duty to necessarily exhaust all means of negotiations before adopting a trade measure.

This general framework should provide some guidance to determine the manner in which international negotiations aimed at finding a collaborative solution can influence the interpretation of the chapeau of Article XX.

Certain commentators argue that Article XX should not be interpreted as restricting too broadly the ability of states to take unilateral measures because they may be necessary in the light of the difficulties to conclude multilateral environmental agreements or to guarantee state compliance with international obligations.[397] Others have suggested that Article XX should only justify trade restrictions provided for in an MEA because unilateral measures are often imposed by larger importing nations against smaller trading nations, which thus cannot choose their own environmental policies[398] and have to 'bow' to standards unilaterally determined by importing states.[399] But the most largely shared view in academic writings is that the objective should be to find some middle-term solution that would enable an examination of whether unilateralism is *justified*.[400]

---

[397]See Gaines (2001), pp. 804 ff.; Howse (2002), pp. 504 ff.; Pauwelyn (2004) p. 587; Prost (2005), pp. 176 ff.; Chang (2005), pp. 44 ff.

[398]See Bierman (2001), p. 434 *et passim*.

[399]See e.g. the argument of Malaysia and the EC in the *US – Shrimp 21.5* case, para. 4.44 ('Malaysia argues that it cannot be compelled to submit its own conservation measures to scrutiny of their equivalence with the US standards because that would mean that it has to bow to standards unilaterally determined by the United States. The European Communities shares Malaysia's concern regarding the unilateral application of domestic standards outside the territory of the state that originally developed them'). See also Boisson de Chazourne (2000), p. 325.

[400]See Bodansky (2000), p. 346 ('[t]he question is, when is it appropriate for a state to act on its own, rather in concert with other states, in order to promote an interest of the international community?'); Charnovitz (2002), p. 108 ('[p]rior efforts to negotiate a treaty can be relevant to Article XX review in order to see whether unilateralism is justified'); Pauwelyn (2004), p. 587 ('in some situations unilateral action with extraterritorial effects will have to be tolerated, albeit as a last resort to the collective action problem of protecting a global environment'); Prost (2005), p. 178 ('le role du GATT serait finalement de rationaliser le recours aux mesures environnementales, de minimiser les dommages collatéraux des efforts de libéralisation des échanges, et de contribuer à la légitimation des mesures unilatérales appropriées, tout en mettant en lumière les abus protectionnistes. En conclusion, la question ne devrait pas être de savoir *si* les mesures unilatérales sont justifiables mais *quand* elles sont justifiées'); Stern (2006), pp. 141 ff.; 143 ('between exhausting all possible lines of action, or requiring agreement, on the one hand, and adopting unilateral measures without any negotiations, on the other hand, there are undoubtedly a variety of possible levels of duty to conduct negotiations in good faith'); Vranes (2009), p. 177 (suggesting that a proportionality test be applied to examine if unilateralism was justified).

An important question is therefore how it is possible to reconcile WTO Members' preferences for multilateral and concerted solutions with the text of the chapeau.

Some have suggested that a necessity test could be applied.[401] It could be used in that opinion to determine if the adoption of a trade restriction in the absence of negotiations was the mildest means available to achieve the environmental purpose. Such an approach seems, however, not consistent with the view that the chapeau of Article XX is an application of the concept of *abus de droit*. Applying a necessity test would indeed be much more restrictive than examining whether a Member has abused of its right to invoke Article XX.

7.3.4.1.2 Suggested Approach

7.3.4.1.2.1 *Assessment of Cooperation Efforts Under the Conditions of the Chapeau*

It has been shown that the 'unjustifiable discrimination' condition cannot be interpreted as requiring WTO Members to make negotiation efforts before imposing trade-restrictive measures but can only require that negotiations be undertaken in a non-discriminatory manner. On the other hand, WTO Members have recognised a preference for multilateral solutions, without prohibiting unilateral measures.

In the absence of any discrimination in the conduct of international negotiations, there can be no 'unjustifiable discrimination' within the meaning of chapeau. However, it is submitted that the failure to engage in international negotiations before imposing a unilateral trade measure could amount in certain cases to a 'disguised restriction on international trade'.

In the environmental field, the most efficient measures are those addressing the source of the problem, through international cooperation. Import restrictions are only second-best instruments.[402] If an importing state does not even try to achieve first-best solutions, it could be an indication that its primary motivation is rather to protect its domestic producers by applying the same standards to imported products, i.e. that the application of the measure results in a 'disguised restriction to trade'.

The importing state should, however, have the opportunity to explain why recourse to a unilateral measure before negotiating with its trading partners, or before the completion of 'good faith efforts' to conclude an international agreement, is nonetheless justified from an environmental viewpoint. It could, for instance, show that, in the light of the urgency of the situation, it was not justified to wait till the end of the negotiations.[403]

---

[401]See Bodansky (2000), pp. 346 f.; Vranes (2009), p. 280.

[402]See *supra*, 3.4.

[403]See Luff (2004), p. 194. Cf. also Charnovitz (2002), p. 108 (stating that prior efforts to negotiate a treaty can be relevant to Article XX review in order to see whether unilateralism was justified).

The Appellate Body did not examine the disguised restriction on international trade criterion in the *US – Shrimp* case for reasons of judicial economy. However, it held that the 'line of equilibrium' between the obligations of WTO Members under the GATT and the general exceptions was not 'fixed or unchanging'[404] but that it moved 'as the kind and the shape of the measures at stake vary and as the facts making up specific cases differ'.[405] Applying the disguised restriction on international trade criterion would be in line with the idea that 'the position of the line itself depends on the type of measure imposed and on the particular circumstances of the case'.[406] The *US – Shrimp 21.5* Panel held that the facts of that case moved the line of equilibrium 'towards multilateral solutions and non-restrictive measures'.[407]

Depending on the facts of the case, the imposition of a unilateral measure without any negotiations might appear to be unjustified, i.e. a disguised restriction on international trade, or it might appear that there were good reasons to choose this course of action, for instance in case of emergency or when particular important issues are at stake.[408]

It should be kept in mind, however, in this examination, that the chapeau of Article XX is an application of the doctrine of *abus de droit*. The function of the different conditions of the introductory clause is to control that the importing Member does not abuse of its right to take restrictive measure violating the substantive obligations of the GATT, including unilateral measures. An 'abuse' of such right implies a *clear* imbalance between the right of the importing Member to take unilateral measures and the substantive right of exporting Members under the GATT.

In brief, the extent of the negotiation efforts that should be carried out before a possible imposition of a unilateral measure should depend on the importance of the environmental interests at issue and on the urgency of intervention.[409]

It is submitted that this approach would remain faithful to the ordinary meaning of the text of the chapeau, which does not contain any reference to a *general* duty to negotiate, but without ignoring the preference expressed in international environmental law and in the context of the WTO for multilateral solutions.

7.3.4.1.2.2 Controlling the Existence of 'Good Faith Efforts' to Negotiate a Treaty

A further question is how it is possible to assess if a state has made genuine good faith efforts to negotiate an international agreement. It is sometimes argued that WTO adjudicating bodies lack the legitimacy to examine the content of the

---

[404]*US – Shrimp*, Appellate Body Report, para. 159.

[405]*Ibid.*

[406]*US – Shrimp 21.5*, Panel Report, para. 5.51.

[407]*Ibid.*, para. 5.58.

[408]For further details on the suggested approach, see also *infra*, 9.4.1.

[409]See also *infra*, 9.4.

proposals made by the negotiating parties in international negotiations. Some have contended that the Appellate Body should not attempt to second-guess the manner in which WTO Members conduct treaty negotiations.[410] The main risk if the Appellate Body were to examine the substance of treaty negotiations is that it would in effect start shaping international standards.[411] This would clearly exceed its mandate. A duty to negotiate could also encourage strategic delays until the importing state agrees to side payments or comparatively lax regulations.[412] But at the same time, not examining the content of the proposals made would entail a risk that it would be enough for an importing state, so as to comply with the negotiation requirement arising from the chapeau of Article XX, to ask for concessions that the trading partners would never accept.[413]

Finding a solution to both of these sets of arguments is certainly challenging. A solution that would reduce the risks that the Appellate Body could overstep its authority would be to assess the negotiation efforts primarily in a *formal way*. That is basically what the *US – Shrimp 21.5* Panel did. It did not in fact analyse the 'substance' of the proposals made but rather considered the formal efforts made by the United States. The Panel examined in particular the documents sent to the exporting countries containing possible elements of a regional convention, the participation to international conferences or symposiums and the adoption of common declarations or resolutions.[414] The Panel also assessed the efforts made to provide technical assistance or to transfer technologies.[415] The formal efforts to conclude a treaty are arguably a less sensitive basis than the actual substance of the negotiations, and they should constitute the main focus of WTO adjudicating bodies.

The substance of the negotiations should not be completely ignored, but it should be analysed with a deferential standard of review since it is not the mandate of the Appellate Body to shape international standards. The question should be whether the regulating country has *abused* of its right to pursue unilaterally defined policies. A state would be deemed to have negotiated in bad faith when elements exists showing that this state has clearly no intent to conclude a treaty, in the light of the proposals that it has formulated or its general behaviour (contradictory conduct;

---

[410]Charnovitz (2002), note 279.

[411]See McGinnis and Movsesian (2000), p. 593: 'the Appellate Body could assure itself that members had negotiated 'seriously' only by evaluating the substance of proposals that members had made and rejected in the course of their consultations. Otherwise, nations could fulfil the duty to negotiate by offering proposals that no other nation would accept. As a result, the duty would require the Appellate Body to make sensitive judgments about the desirability of various regulatory options and thereby inexorably move it towards shaping international standards.'

[412]*Ibid.*

[413]*Ibid.*

[414]See *US – Shrimp 21.5*, Panel Report, para. 2.4 and 5.79.

[415]*Ibid.*, para. 5.118. The Panel reviewed the efforts made by the US to negotiate a treaty with the Asian countries involved and compared these efforts to those made to conclude the Inter-American Convention, in which context the US had made efforts to transfer technologies.

inflexible approach; unbending standards specifying the design to be adopted rather than performance, while the design is inappropriate for the conditions occurring in the exporting country; etc.).

One may argue that this solution would be problematic as regards legal predictability. It is certainly difficult to say when an importing state would have sufficiently negotiated to be able to adopt unilateral trade measures. But this assertion is, however, also true with respect to the approach of the *US – Shrimp 21.5* Panel that seeks to derive a general duty to negotiate from the unjustifiable discrimination criterion.

Furthermore, it should be remembered that the role of the chapeau of Article XX is to prevent *abuses* of the general exceptions and that therefore panels and the Appellate Body should pay some deference to the regulating country in the determination of the negotiation efforts that are appropriate in a particular case, in the light of the importance of the goal. The text of Article XX implies that a measure should be invalidated only when the negotiation efforts suggest that the environmental goal is only a pretext and that therefore the measure is applied in a manner that results in a disguised restriction on international trade.

In the absence of any particular emergency, it seems that there should be at least enough exchanges of views between the parties for them to know precisely their respective positions in relation to the objective to be achieved and the means that could be appropriate. At some point, these elements may be clear, and parties may fail to conclude a treaty because of irreconcilable divergences of views.

7.3.4.2 Consideration of Specific Interests of Developing Countries

7.3.4.2.1 The Specific Interests of Developing Countries

Chapter 3 showed that PPM measures could be a useful tool, in particular, to assist in the effectiveness of international regimes to protect the global environment. PPM measures may appear to be necessary, for instance when the same externality is caused by the production processes used in the importing country and abroad or when international cooperation is unable to achieve any effective results in the management of an international or global environmental problem.

At the same time, trade restrictions based on PPM requirements can cause specific difficulties for developing countries, which usually vehemently oppose such measures. They often argue that such trade restrictions conflict with their economic and developmental priorities. They also point out that many of the current global environmental problems have been caused primarily by developed countries, which should thus bear the costs of addressing these problems. Trade barriers in the form of PPM regulations are also problematic for LDCs insofar as access to large markets of industrialised countries is fundamental to achieve economic development, which should eventually enable developing countries to devote more financial resources to environmental protection, as the Rio Declaration has acknowledged.[416] Several MEAs have also emphasised that standards applied by developed countries may be inappropriate and of unwarranted economic cost for developing countries.[417] Moreover, the principle of common but differentiated responsibilities has recognised that states have contributed differently in causing global environmental harm and have different capabilities to address these threats.[418] The application of the same process standards for developed and developing countries may thus appear inappropriate.[419]

The Preamble of the Marrakesh Agreement establishing the WTO also recognises that there is a 'need for positive efforts designed to ensure that developing countries, and especially the least developed among them, secure a share in the growth in international trade commensurate with the needs of their economic development'. These different considerations highlight that Article XX may have to be interpreted in a way that takes into account these specific interests of developing countries in the context of PPM measures.

It should be pointed out that it is difficult to generalise what the interests of developing countries are. Like any generalisation, it may overlook the specificities of particular developing countries, or groups of countries. For instance, in the field of climate change, the situation of China or other emerging powers may be quite different, both with respect to their financial and technical means and to their current responsibility for CO_2 emissions, from that of LLDCs such as Bangladesh. Regardless of such differences, both are likely to oppose the use of PPM measures, in particular those aimed at greenhouse gas reductions.

This opposition has been translated, in particular, into the support of developing countries for approaches that forbid or restrict considerably the legality of process-based restrictions, such as a strict product-process distinction, or arguments that PPM measures should not be allowed because they are extraterritorial or unilateral or interfere in the internal affairs of foreign states.[420] In a way, these arguments may be seen in part as a conflict between large developed markets of the North and the

---

[416]Rio Declaration, Principle 12 ('States should cooperate to promote a supportive and open international economic system that would lead to economic growth and sustainable development in all countries, to better address the problems of environmental degradation'). Likewise, the Preamble of the WTO Agreement states that the WTO Members seek to enhance the means for protecting and preserving the environment 'in a manner consistent with their respective needs and concerns at different levels of economic development'. See also *US – Shrimp 21.5*, Appellate Body, para. 5.55: 'recourse to trade-related measures not based on international consensus is generally not the most appropriate means of enforcing environmental measures, since it leads to the imposition of unwanted constraints on the multilateral trading system and may affect sustainable development'.

[417]Stockholm Declaration, Principle 23; Rio Declaration, Principle 11; WSSD Plan of Implementation, para. 15(a).

[418]Rio Declaration, Principle 7.

[419]See also Cooreman (2017), pp. 276 ff., stating that developed countries should 'take the needs of developing countries into account to the extent possible when designing their policy'.

[420]See *supra*, Chap. 2.

smaller WTO Members of the developing world.[421] However, as the last chapters have shown, such arguments are largely unfounded from a legal viewpoint. Moreover, simply prohibiting the use of PPM measures would deprive WTO Members of the main instrument that they have in order to protect the global environment and deal with the free rider problem when international cooperation fails or is inefficient.

However, as it has been mentioned above, the chapeau of Article XX could provide a more reliable basis on which particular interests of developing countries could be taken into account. It is submitted that two conditions of the chapeau could potentially be relevant to take into account the interests of developing countries: the question of whether the 'same conditions prevail' in the countries concerned (Sect. 7.3.4.2.2) and the disguised restriction on international trade criterion (Sect. 7.3.4.2.3).

7.3.4.2.2   Countries Where the 'Same Conditions Prevail'

The chapeau refers to unjustifiable or arbitrary discrimination between countries *where the same conditions prevail*. In the *US – Shrimp* case, the Appellate Body took the view that discrimination resulted not only when countries in which the same conditions prevail were differently treated but also when the application of the measure at issue did not allow for any inquiry into the appropriateness of the regulatory programme for the conditions prevailing in the exporting countries.[422] In that context, it meant that the United States could not require the adoption of 'essentially the same' regulatory programme to avoid the incidental killing of sea turtles in shrimp trawling, *without* taking into account other specific policies and measures adopted by the exporting countries concerned to achieve the environmental goal pursued. In other words, discrimination can occur not only when countries where the same conditions prevail are treated differently but also when countries where *different* conditions prevail are treated the *same*.[423]

In *US – Shrimp*, the requirement to consider whether the 'same conditions prevail' arguably allowed to consider the interests of developing countries only partially. The United States measure was eventually upheld by the Appellate Body, after it was modified so as to allow foreign regulatory programmes that were 'comparable in effectiveness' to the US scheme. As a result, the United States was eventually authorised to unilaterally determine the level of protection that exporting countries had to achieve by these programmes. It should be noted, though, that the objective of the measure was the prevention of incidental killings of endangered sea turtles. Differentiation in the level of efforts required by the

---

[421]See Bierman (2001), p. 421.

[422]See *US – Shrimp*, Appellate Body Report, para. 165.

[423]See Pauwelyn (2007), p. 39; Cosbey (2008), p. 4; O'Brien (2009), p. 1111; Hertel (2011), pp. 676 f.

different countries concerned could have defeated the goal pursued by the United States because the threatened turtles constituted a shared stock of a highly migratory species. Failure to internalise the externalities in one country could have potentially ruined the efforts of the other countries to preserve these shared resources.

However, there are other cases in which the contributions to the achievement of an environmental objective by the different states concerned could or should be more flexible, such as in the case of climate change mitigation efforts. The climate international regime expressly provides different obligations for developed and developing countries with respect to greenhouse gas reductions. From a factual viewpoint, there is also a possibility in this case to compensate less demanding obligations regarding greenhouse gases, which seem appropriate for LLDCs, with more important efforts by developed countries, which was not possible in a case similar to that of the *US – Shrimp* report.

In such cases, differences in the characteristics of the environment (sink capacities of ecosystems, abundance of natural resource stocks, share of the costs for providing a global public good, etc.), economic development, technical and financial means, as well as differences in the respective responsibilities for the environmental harm caused could be regarded as 'differing conditions' that should be taken into consideration in the examination of the conditions of the chapeau.

This would result in three main consequences. First, importing Members might have to provide technical and financial assistance, or to transfer environmentally sound technologies, to LDCs so as to take into consideration the differing conditions occurring in exporting Members.

Second, there might be cases in which the importing state would have to *compensate* exporting countries, in particular when the importing Member's measure addresses the loss of global public goods. This study has submitted that the loss of global positive externalities must be considered as a legitimate interest in the sense of the sub-paragraphs.[424] However, it does not imply that it would necessarily be legitimate to *require* foreign states to provide global uncompensated benefits and sanction their reduction through trade restrictions.[425] In the view of the Appellate Body, discrimination can occur not only between different exporting countries but also between exporting Members and the importing Member concerned.[426] This means that it is necessary to examine the conditions that prevail both in the exporting and importing countries.[427] Arguably, the enjoyment of global benefits and the share of the costs between the importing and the exporting states are part of

---

[424]See *supra*, 7.2.1.2.2 (iv).

[425]See Esty (1994), p. 126 referring to the 'weak moral position of those wishing to coerce others into providing uncompensated global benefits'. He contends that 'trade restrictions or sanction should be invoked in these cases only on a multilateral basis, after fair compensation has been offered, and in the face of ongoing intransigence on the part of the nation whose resources are at issue'.

[426]See *US – Shrimp*, Appellate Body Report, para. 150.

[427]See *US – Gasoline*, Appellate Body Report, p. 23.

the conditions prevailing in the different countries. Consequently, if an importing country indirectly requires an exporting country to provide global benefits without bearing part of the costs of this global public good or without offering to bear part of the costs, it could be viewed as failure to treat differently Members in which different conditions occur, which could amount to a violation of the chapeau.

Third, taking into consideration the different conditions that prevail in the different Members concerned also means that an importing country should not only accept that different *means* could be used by an exporting state to achieve the *same* level of protection[428] but also that, in certain circumstances, the importing country has to accept that exporting states might have to achieve *lower* level of protection, if the high environmental standards of the developed importing country appeared to be inappropriate for developing exporting countries.

Providing for different efforts from certain exporting Members based on the level of development and their technical or financial means would also be a way to apply the principle of common but differentiated responsibilities (CBDR) in the interpretation of the chapeau of Article XX. The CBDR principle can be seen as one of the principles that stem from sustainable development, as the Rio Declaration Principle 7 explicitly recognises.[429] The Preamble of the WTO Agreement explicitly refers to sustainable development as an objective of the world trading system. The Preamble also mentions the 'need for positive efforts designed to ensure that developing countries, and especially the least developed among them, secure a share in the growth in international trade commensurate with the needs of their economic development'. The specific needs of LDCs and LLDCs are also recognised by international environmental law, for instance in Principle 6 of the Rio Declaration. In the view of the Appellate Body, the Preamble of the WTO Agreement 'informs all the covered agreements including the GATT 1994'[430] and add 'colour, texture and shading' to the Appellate Body's interpretation of the covered agreements.[431] The Preamble is thus relevant for the interpretation of Article XX.[432]

---

[428]As the Appellate Body required in the *US – Shrimp* case.

[429]Principle 7, third sentence, states that '[t]he developed countries acknowledge the responsibility that they bear in the international pursuit to sustainable development in view of the pressures their societies place on the global environment and of the technologies and financial resources they command'. See also ILA New Dehli Declaration of Principles of International Law Relating to Sustainable Development, Principle 3 (which includes the CBDR principle in 'principles of international law relevant to the activities of all actors involved [which] would be instrumental in pursuing the objective of sustainable development in an effective way'); Honkonen (2009), pp. 5 f. ('the principle of CBDR has many similarities and connections with the concept of sustainable development. [...] Actually, it could be conceived that the CBDR principle assists on its own part if realized in a reasonable manner, in the implementation of sustainable development at the international, regional and local levels').

[430]*EC – Tariff Preferences*, Appellate Body Report, para. 161.

[431]*US – Shrimp*, Appellate Body Report, para. 153.

[432]See also Condon (2006), p. 218.

Chapter 4 showed, however, that although the CBDR has been introduced in several agreements with near universal acceptance, its legal status and consequences remain unclear. Since it cannot be regarded as a customary international rule, it is necessary to examine how the specific conventional regime has implemented this 'framework principle'.[433]

One of the most important MEAs that include the CBDR principle is the UNFCCC. This example will be analysed here in more detail.

Non-WTO law could be examined on the basis of Article 7 DSU, which provides that panels must examine the matter before them 'in the light of the relevant provisions' of the relevant covered agreements and that they 'shall address the relevant provisions in any covered agreement or agreements cited by the parties to the dispute'. The interpretation of this Article is still debated.[434] However, the Appellate Body made it clear that WTO agreements should not be read 'in clinical isolation' from public international law.[435] It further held that its task was to interpret the language of the chapeau, seeking additional interpretative guidance from the general principles of international law, referring to Article 31(3)(c) of the Vienna Convention.[436] Under this provision, any relevant rules of international law applicable in the relations between the parties can be used as a means to interpret a treaty. The *EC – Biotech* Panel took a restrictive view in its interpretation of what amounted to 'relevant rules of international law applicable between the parties'. In its view, the only international rule that was covered by Article 31(3)(c) were those that all WTO Members had signed.[437] This report was never appealed to the Appellate Body. It is, however, not sure that the Appellate Body would have confirmed that interpretation, in the light of the approach adopted in the *US – Shrimp* case.[438] In that case, the Appellate Body examined international treaties that had not been signed by all WTO Members and some that were not even entered into force to interpret the meaning of 'exhaustible' natural resources.

In any case, the arguments developed here are directly based on the chapeau of Article XX and not on MEAs. International treaties acknowledging the CBDR principle, such as the UNFCCC, could, however, provide useful guidance for the interpretation of the chapeau, in the light of the objective of sustainable development of the WTO.

---

[433]See *supra*, 4.1.3.

[434]See Pauwelyn (2003b), p. 1001 (arguing that panels can apply relevant non-WTO rules); Hertel (2011), pp. 659 f.; *contra*: Trachtman (1999), p. 342 (who considers that Article 7 DSU implies that panels can only refer to WTO rules).

[435]See *US – Gasoline*, Appellate Body Report, p. 17.

[436]See *US – Shrimp*, Appellate Body Report, para. 158 *in fine*.

[437]*EC – Biotech*, Panel Report, para. 7.68 ('[t]his understanding of the term "the parties" leads logically to the view that the rules of international law to be taken into account in interpreting the WTO agreements at issue in this dispute are those which are applicable in the relations between the WTO Members').

[438]See Hertel (2011), p. 661.

In the UNFCCC, the CBDR principle is mentioned both in the Preamble[439] and in Article 3, which states in relevant parts as follows:

1. The Parties should protect the climate system for the benefit of present and future generations of humankind, on the basis of equity and in accordance with their common but differentiated responsibilities and respective capabilities.

2. The specific needs and special circumstances of developing country Parties, especially those that are particularly vulnerable to the adverse effects of climate change, and of those Parties, especially developing country Parties, that would have to bear a disproportionate or abnormal burden under the Convention, should be given full consideration.

The actual formulation of this provision is the result of a long negotiation process mostly between developed and developing countries. While the former sought to include recognition on the historical responsibility of industrialised states for the current concentration of greenhouse gases in the atmosphere, the latter feared that such recognition would imply a legal obligation to finance efforts to combat climate change[440] and wanted to avoid giving the CBDR principle a customary international law status.[441] The final formulation refers to the CBDR in a specific provision of the convention, yet in a watered-down form, since it does not contain any imperative language and only provides guidance to the parties.[442] On the other hand, the developed nations succeeded in including also a reference to the 'respective capabilities' of states, which means that the burden sharing must be arranged not only on the basis of the historical responsibility but also on the basis of the capability to take action.[443]

In the event of a WTO dispute relating to carbon measures, interpreting Article XX in a way compatible with Article 3 UNFCCC could require a differentiation in the requirements applicable to imported products depending on the respective responsibilities and capabilities of the countries in which these products were produced.[444] When it comes to a carbon tax applied on imports, this could mean that a developed country may be obliged to have lower or even no carbon restrictions on imports from developing countries, especially the very poor ones.[445] However, the reference to states' 'respective capabilities' would arguably not prevent a differentiation in the standards applicable between different developing

---

[439]In the Preamble, the Parties recognised that 'the global nature of climate change calls for the widest possible cooperation by all countries and their participation in an effective and appropriate international response, in accordance with their common but differentiated responsibilities and respective capabilities and their social and economic conditions'.

[440]See Hertel (2011), p. 666.

[441]See Honkonen (2009), p. 123, with further references.

[442]*Ibid.*

[443]See Honkonen (2009), p. 123.

[444]See Hertel (2011), p. 677 (who posits that the CBDR principle 'would require unilateral trade measures to be "graded" in accordance with countries' mitigation responsibilities under the International Climate Change Regime [ICCR] to be a permissible use of coercion and compliant with the *chapeau*').

[445]See Pauwelyn (2007), pp. 39 f.

countries. For instance, the respective 'capabilities' of China and Bangladesh in terms of financial and technical means could be taken into consideration.

Developing countries would, however, be likely to oppose the imposition of carbon import restrictions, in particular by arguing that the Kyoto Protocol subjects only developed states to emission reduction objectives, whereas developing countries are exempted. Because of this, it could be argued that the CBDR principle prevents developed country signatories of the Kyoto Protocol to adopt unilateral trade measures by which the carbon requirements of the developed countries would be imposed to developing nations.[446] Under this interpretation, as far as carbon trade measures are concerned, the chapeau requirement to take into account different conditions occurring in exporting countries could result in the illegality of any trade measure adopted by an Annex I country against a non-Annex I country.

However, it is questionable whether such far-reaching interpretation would be compatible with the principles of CBDR and of sustainable development. In the climate context, developed states have similarly recognised that the largest share of historical and current global emissions of greenhouse gases has originated in their countries[447] and that they should take the lead in combating climate change.[448] This represents a particular case of the more general developed countries' acknowledgement of the responsibility they bear in the international pursuit of sustainable development, in view of the pressures that their societies place on the global environment.[449] The pursuit of sustainable development has been given more concrete expression in the 'overarching objective' of the elimination of unsustainable consumption and production patterns,[450] which can be achieved *inter alia* through the polluter-pays principle and the internalisation of externalities.[451]

In this context, in order to achieve sustainable consumption and production patterns, it is essential to internalise the externalities caused by greenhouse gas emissions, in conformity with the polluter-pays principle, by putting a price on carbon.[452] In the light of the objective of stabilisation of greenhouse gases in the

---

[446]See Pauwelyn (2007), p. 39, n. 119 (the fact that the EU 'ratified the Kyoto Protocol could force the EU to exclude those developing countries from its carbon tax' because it would be held by the 'concession that developing countries should not cut emissions at all'); O'Brien (2009), p. 1111 ('taking into account the principle of "common but differentiated responsibilities" and the differing carbon reduction commitments made by different countries also indicated that it would not be appropriate for an importing country to effectively impose its own carbon reduction standard on other countries').

[447]See the Preamble of the UNFCCC.

[448]See Article 3(1) of the UNFCCC.

[449]See Principle 7 of the Rio Declaration.

[450]See Johannesburg Declaration on Sustainable Development, para. 11 ('[w]e recognize that poverty eradication, changing consumption and production patterns and protecting and managing the natural resource base for economic and social development are overarching objectives of and essential requirements for sustainable development').

[451]See WSSD Plan of Implementation, para. 15(b), which refers to the Rio Declaration Principle 16 (polluter-pays principle and internalisation of externalities).

[452]See Stern (2007), Executive Summary, p. xviii.

atmosphere[453] and of the interdependent nature of the global atmosphere, the responsibility of developed states to take the lead in efforts to combat climate change means that they should take action addressing both their domestic production and the environmental impact of the products sold on their territory, based on a full life-cycle analysis. To ignore the latter objective would ignore part of the problem caused by the pressure that developed countries' societies place on the global environment because goods produced abroad for the consumers of developed countries cause the same externality as those produced domestically. From an economic and environmental viewpoint, all products on the internal market should be sold at a price that includes the costs of greenhouse gas emissions.

In that respect, denying or restricting the possibility of states with the largest markets to take measures to internalise the costs of CO_2 emissions of all the products sold domestically on their internal market would contradict the objective of the elimination of unsustainable consumption and production patterns, which is itself one of the objectives of sustainable development.

There is no doubt that finding an appropriate balance in the way the particular interests of LDCs should be taken into account in 'trade and climate change' context is particularly challenging. However, it is submitted that these challenges cannot be resolved simply by considering that Annex I countries are prohibited to impose carbon-related trade measures against non-Annex I countries. Neither can the very general rules of the chapeau of Article XX provide a comprehensive solution to this kind of issues. In the absence of more specific rules negotiated between the parties, it can, however, provide some minimal requirements in the way WTO Members should take into consideration the conditions prevailing in other Members, in particular developing countries.

WTO law and international law more generally do recognise the need to take account of the special interests and needs of developing countries, especially the poorest ones. In the context of the chapeau Article XX, it is submitted that the situations of the different countries concerned should be done on a case-by-case analysis. WTO adjudicating bodies should examine in particular the different conditions that prevail in the different developing countries concerned, such as, in the case of climate change, their historic contributions to the accumulation of greenhouse gases in the atmosphere (past stock), their current emissions (flow)[454] and their respective capabilities in terms of financial and technical means.

It should be pointed out that if such examination seems to be coherent with the approach of the Appellate Body in the *US – Shrimp* case and seems more generally to be appropriate in order to take the interests of developing countries into account in the examination of the chapeau of Article XX, there would be important difficulties in establishing the relevant factual circumstances. In particular, evaluating the respective contributions of states to climate change is a challenging task, *inter alia*, because of the lack of objective criteria defined in the Kyoto Protocol for

---

[453]See Article 2 UNFCCC.

[454]On the distinction between stock and flow and how they could influence a global climate deal, see Bhagwati (2004), pp. 158 ff.

differentiating responsibilities.[455] In addition, calculating the amount of greenhouse gases emitted during the production processes would probably give rise to considerable implementation difficulties in developing countries, in particular because of the Appellate Body's requirement to differentiate between foreign producers (shipment-by-shipment requirement).[456]

7.3.4.2.3   Disguised Restriction on International Trade

Apart from the issue of whether 'different conditions' prevail in the different countries concerned, it is submitted that the 'disguised restriction to international trade' criterion could also provide to a certain extent a textual basis to take the interests of developing countries into account in Article XX.

As already explained, the adoption of PPM standards in exporting countries can give rise to implementation difficulties, such as the unavailability or the costs of the required technologies. Besides, because npr-PPMs do not physically affect products, they usually require not only changes in the production practices abroad but also the implementation certification schemes and control mechanisms to ensure that producers comply with the process regulations. These difficulties have been recognised in several MEAs, which encourage the transfer of environmentally sound technologies.[457]

In the context of the GATT, when a developed Member wants to enact a PPM measure applied to developing Members, it could take these difficulties into account by providing technical and financial assistance or by proceeding to transfers of technology to help developing countries to comply with a PPM standard. For instance, the United States did provide technical assistance and transfers of technology to exporting countries in the *US – Shrimp* case. Such assistance is certainly desirable and may reduce the hostility of developing countries towards unilateral PPM measures and be profitable to the objective of sustainable development. Economists have shown that a combination of 'carrots' and 'sticks' is often the most efficient way to protect common resources and the global environment.[458]

However, there is no general obligation in the GATT to provide assistance or technology transfers, by contrast to the TBT Agreement, which contains detailed provisions on technical assistance to LDCs (TBT Art. 11). The chapeau of Article XX does not seem to be a sufficient basis for a general *duty* to provide technical assistance or to transfer technologies. The Preamble of the WTO mentions the

---

[455]See on that issue in particular Machado Filho (2008), pp. 352, 356 *et passim* (discussing inter alia the 'Brazilian Proposal', which suggests the use of scientific instruments to calculate the historical contributions of states in the concentration of greenhouse gases in the atmosphere).

[456]See Cosbey (2008), pp. 4 ff.

[457]See e.g. Principle 20 of the Stockholm Declaration or Chapter 34 of Agenda 21.

[458]See Barrett (2003), pp. 324 ff.

needs of developing countries but does not refer to any positive obligation for developed countries.

However, it is submitted that the provision by an importing state of technical or financial assistance, or of technology transfers, could be relevant in the examination of the 'disguised restriction to international trade' in certain circumstances. First-best solutions from an environmental viewpoint are interventions at the source. On the other hand, exporting countries may lack the ability or the necessary technologies to comply with the prescribed process standards, whereas the importing state may have successfully implemented these requirements and may possess the necessary technologies. For instance, an exporting Member could be denied access to the importing Member's market because of the lack of verifiable data on greenhouse gas emissions due to technical difficulties in the implementation of certification mechanisms. In such conditions, a failure of the importing country to provide possible assistance or transfers of technology could be one element showing that the main motivation of the importing country is protectionism rather than environmental protection.

It should be kept in mind, however, that, in the view of the present author, the chapeau sanctions only clear abuses or disproportions. The factual circumstances should thus show that the primary goal of the importing country is *clearly* protectionism and not environmental protection for a failure to provide assistance or transfers of technology to be considered as a disguised restriction on international trade or, in other words, for this failure to amount to an abuse of right.

7.3.4.3 The Means-Ends Relationship: The Possible Role of the Disguised Restriction on International Trade Criterion

As it has been shown, an important difference between Article XX(b) and Article XX(g) is the means-ends relationship required under these two sub-paragraphs: a 'relating to' test for the latter and a necessity test for the former. As a result, it may be easier to justify a measure to conserve exhaustible natural resources than to protect life and health, which seems rather odd.[459] The evolution of the necessity test into a 'weighing and balancing' test allows greater flexibility under Article XX(b) and may have reduced the difference between the two sub-paragraphs, at least when the objective pursued is important. But still, a necessity test logically requires a more intense means-ends relationship than a 'relating to' test.

As it has been mentioned above, some have argued that the Appellate Body is in the process of harmonising the means-ends tests applicable in sub-paragraphs (b) and (g), through the application of a proportionality test, in both cases.[460] It has been shown that it is, however, doubtful that the necessity test of Article

---

[459]See e.g. Appleton (1999), p. 483; Condon (2009), p. 918.
[460]See Schoenbaum (1998), p. 37; Prost (2005), pp. 54 f.

XX(b) amounts to a proportionality test.[461] Applying a more restrictive test in sub-paragraph (g) than in sub-paragraph (b), by introducing in the former a pro-portionality test, which the latter does not contain, would not seem coherent with the wording of Article XX.

Therefore, the Appellate Body could seemingly not adopt a similar test in Article XX(b) and (g). On the other hand, the prospect of achieving some convergence between the means-ends relationship through combined effects of Article XX(g) and of the conditions of the chapeau seems more promising. Different solutions have been suggested to reduce these differences between the two sub-paragraphs. Condon has suggested that if it might be easier to comply with the 'relating to' test, it might be at the same time more difficult to comply with the conditions of the chapeau when a Member invokes sub-paragraph (g) because this sub-paragraph implies a duty to negotiate equally with all trading partners concerned before having the right to take a restrictive trade measure. Thus, the burden of sub-paragraphs (b) and (g) might in fact evolve till a point where they would in fact converge.[462] His view is, however, based on the controversial assumption that Article XX(b) can only be invoked to protect life or health domestically, which should be rejected.[463] Moreover, this argument is also based on the assumption that WTO Members have a generally applicable duty to nego-tiate before resorting to unilateral measures, which is controversial as well, as it has been shown above.[464] This view should thus be rejected.

It has also been argued that the Appellate Body had introduced elements of the necessity test in the 'unjustifiable discrimination' test. The view is based on the Appellate Body's statements, in the *US – Shrimp* report, that the contested measure was a countrywide import ban, whereas import prohibitions on certain products would have been sufficient to achieve the goal pursued, and that the promotion of sea turtle conservation demanded concerted and cooperative efforts.[465] However, introducing a necessity test in the 'unjustifiable discrimination' seems difficult to reconcile with the nature of the latter concept.[466] Moreover, it would not be coherent with the view that the chapeau is an expression of the principle of abuse of right, which requires the application of a lower degree of scrutiny than a necessity test.[467] It would also be incoherent for the interpretation of Article XX as a whole since the chapeau applies to all sub-paragraphs, including those that contain a necessity test. Thus, introducing a necessity test in the 'unjustifiable discrimination' test would result in some form of double testing, in particular for Article XX(b).

---

[461]See *supra*, 7.2.1.2.1.

[462]See Condon (2009), p. 919 (attributing this idea to Professor Matsushita).

[463]See *supra*, 7.3.2.

[464]See *supra*, 7.3.2.2.3.

[465]See Vranes (2009), p. 280.

[466]See *supra*, 7.3.1.

[467]*Idem.*

It is submitted that another possibility to apply the conditions of the chapeau in a more restrictive manner for measures examined under Article XX(g) is the 'disguised restriction on international trade' criterion. The analysis of this condition entails the consideration of both the intent and the effects of the measure at stake, as it has been shown above.[468] A measure provisionally justified under Article XX(g), which results in protectionist effects but is clearly not necessary, could thus be held to be a 'disguise' to conceal the pursuit of trade-restrictive objectives.

It would therefore seem more coherent to examine the protectionist or trade-restrictive effects of the measure, as well as the possible alternatives to the chosen measure, in the context of the 'disguised restriction on international trade' criterion rather than under the 'unjustifiable and arbitrary discrimination' condition. The former test would certainly be more difficult to meet for measures provisionally justified under Article XX(g) than under XX(b) since a measure that is both necessary and non-discriminatory is unlikely to be found to fail the 'disguised restriction on international trade' requirement.[469]

This condition seems to be a more reliable basis to allow some convergence in the means-ends relationship for measures falling under Article XX(b) and (g). Convergence could also be achieved more easily if the 'line of equilibrium' is understood as a reference to the degree of scrutiny applicable in each case, which varies depending on the importance of the goal pursued, as it has been suggested above.[470] The more important the goal is, the more protectionist effects should be tolerated and the more difficult it should be to conclude that the actual objective of the measure is 'concealed beneath deceptive appearances', i.e. that the invocation of the general exceptions provision is abusive. Thus, some of the considerations made in relation to the criterion of the 'importance of the goal' used by case law in the assessment of whether a measure has complied with the necessity test might also be relevant to a certain extent in the context of measures justified by sub-paragraph (g), through the criterion on the 'disguised restriction on international trade'.

However, the conditions of the chapeau have to be examined with a low degree of scrutiny since they only sanction abuses of right.[471] In that respect, it might not be possible through the interpretation of the chapeau to have complete convergence between the respective means-ends relationship of Article XX(b) and (g). At least, what is possible is to make the margin of manoeuvre of the importing state vary in a similar way in both contexts, depending on the importance of the goal pursued.

---

[468] See *supra*, 7.3.3.

[469] See Mavroidis (2008b), p. 276.

[470] See *supra*, 7.3.1.

[471] *Idem.*

Chapter 8
The Technical Barriers to Trade (TBT) Agreement

8.1 Coverage of PPM Measures Under the TBT Agreement

The Agreement on Technical Barriers to Trade (TBT) contains particular disciplines applicable to technical regulations and standards.

The TBT Agreement gives the following definition of a technical regulation:

> Document which lays down product characteristics or their related processes and production methods, including the applicable administrative provisions, with which compliance is mandatory. It may also include or deal exclusively with terminology, symbols, packaging, marking or labelling requirements as they apply to a product, process or production method.

The first sentence refers to technical requirements, whereas the second sentence applies to mandatory labelling requirements.

It is generally recognised that product-related PPMs (i.e., PPMs that leave a physical trace in the product) are subject to the rules of the TBT Agreement, both for technical regulations and mandatory labelling requirements. It is, however, more debated whether non-product-related PPMs (i.e., PPMs that leave no trace in the final product) are also covered by the TBT Agreement.

As far as *labelling requirements* are concerned, the Appellate Body has recently held in the *US – Tuna II (Mexico)* case that labels relating to non-product-related PPMs are covered by the TBT Agreement. The measure at issue required the use of a label on tuna products indicating whether tuna had been harvested using a method that harmed dolphins. The Panel considered that the dolphin-safe labelling requirements fell under the TBT Agreement because they applied to an identifiable product, in that case tuna products.[1] It did not even discuss the fact that the labelling

---

[1] See *US – Tuna II (Mexico)*, Panel Report, para. 7.78. The Panel held that it was 'satisfied that the measures at issue lay down labelling requirements, as they apply to a product, process or production method and that the subject-matter of the measure therefore falls within the scope of the second sentence of Annex 1.1'.

© Springer International Publishing AG 2018
D. Sifonios, *Environmental Process and Production Methods (PPMs) in WTO Law*,
European Yearbook of International Economic Law 3,
DOI 10.1007/978-3-319-65726-4_8

requirements at hand concerned the way tuna was caught, i.e. a non-product-related PPM characteristic. Hence, all mandatory labelling requirements, including those applying to differences in production methods, whether or not such methods leave a physical trace in the product, seem to be covered by the TBT Agreement.

It has been more been debated whether *technical requirements* concerning npr-PPMs also fall within the TBT. The prevailing view rejects it, mainly on the basis of a textual and historical interpretation. A textual difference exists indeed between the first and the second sentences of the definition of technical regulations. While the first sentence refers to *technical requirements* applying to product characteristics 'or their related' PPMs, the second sentence covers mandatory *labelling requirements* applying to a 'product, process or production method'.

Grammatically, the term 'their' in the first sentence refers to product *character-istics* and not to the word 'product'.[2] The 'characteristics' of a product have usually been construed as *physical* characteristics, as opposed to those that have no physical impact on the final product (non-product-related PPMs), even though this interpre-tation is not self-evident (in a large sense, the environmental impact of the PPM of a product *might* also be viewed as some form of product characteristics). This restrictive interpretation, which would exclude technical requirements based on npr-PPMs from the TBT Agreement, is also based on the textual difference between the two sentences. The second sentence does not refer to 'product characteristics' or to their 'related' PPMs but simply refers to labelling requirements applying to a 'product, process or production methods'. The terms used in the second sentence are thus wider than those of the first sentence. The principle of effective treaty interpretation, which requires that each term be given a proper meaning, could thus imply that while the TBT Agreement applies to all labelling requirements, regard-less of whether they apply to a PPM that leaves a physical trace in the final product, technical requirements based on differences in PPMs are only covered by the TBT Agreement if they have an impact on the product's physical characteristics.

It should nonetheless be conceded that product characteristics do not clearly refer to 'physical' characteristics. It could also mean that technical regulations only refer to PPMs that *sufficiently relate* to the production of the particular products concerned, including those that have no physical impact on the product, as opposed to general policy considerations that are not specifically related to the production of these goods, such as general labour standards or family allowance programmes.[3]

Yet the *travaux préparatoires* confirm that technical requirements concerning npr-PPMs were not intended by the drafters to be covered by the TBT Agreement.[4] During the negotiations, the United States had proposed that TBT disciplines

---

[2]See also the French version '[d]ocument qui énonce les caractéristiques d'un produit ou les procédés et méthodes de production s'y rapportant'. In this phrase, process and production methods 'se rapportent', i.e. relate to, product characteristics.

[3]See Marceau and Trachtman (2002), p. 862; Vranes (2009), p. 342; Marceau (2014), pp. 327 f.

[4]See Rege (1994), p. 110; Schlagenhof (1995), p. 131; Appleton (1997a), p. 122; Puth (2004), p. 211; Joshi (2004), p. 79; Vranes (2009), p. 340; Conrad (2011), pp. 378 ff.

should be extended to technical specifications based on PPMs because lack of full coverage of PPMs seriously weakened in its view the effectiveness of the agreement.[5] Support was originally expressed among negotiators.[6] In the final phase of the negotiations, however, Mexico proposed to clarify the coverage of PPM-based measures in the definition of 'technical regulations' and 'standards', by inserting the words 'or related' PPMs in several places in the text of the agreement. Mexico made it clear that the intent was to exclude PPMs unrelated to the characteristics of a product from the coverage of the agreement.[7] The proposed wording was integrated in the final text of the TBT Agreement. Thus, it seems that at least a majority of negotiators intended to exclude technical regulations and standards based on differences in npr-PPMs from the TBT Agreement.

If npr-PPMs' technical requirements are not subject to the TBT Agreement, it means that they fall within the scope of the GATT, more particularly Articles III:4 and XX.[8] Based on a teleological interpretation, some have thus criticised such result, in which pr-PPMs are subject to the stricter rules of the TBT Agreement, while npr-PPMs are only covered by the GATT disciplines. It has been contended that npr-PPM measures are 'less transparent' and that it would be coherent to subject both product-related and non-product-related PPMs to the stricter TBT disciplines.[9] It seems also curious that labelling requirements concerning npr-PPMs would be covered by the TBT Agreement, while technical regulations based on the same differences in npr-PPMs would be subject to the GATT.[10]

It could be further noted that while WTO adjudicating bodies have not to date held that particular npr-PPM technical requirements laying down product characteristics or their related PPMs are covered by the TBT Agreement, the findings of the Panel in the *US – Tuna II (Mexico)* case in relation to labelling requirements could possibly influence future panels when it comes to technical requirements. The *US – Tuna II (Mexico)* Panel expressed the view that the dolphin-safe labelling requirements were covered by the TBT Agreement because they applied to identifiable products. The issue of whether PPMs covered by the second sentence had to be related to the *physical* characteristics of the product was not even examined by the Appellate Body.[11] A similar reasoning, based on whether a technical regulation is 'applied to a product', could *potentially* be applied in the context of technical regulations as well, which would mean that npr-PPM technical regulations could be covered by the TBT Agreement.[12]

---

[5]See WTO, Note by the Secretariat (1995), para. 121.

[6]See WTO, Note by the Secretariat (1995), para. 122.

[7]*Ibid.*, para. 146.

[8]See Marceau and Trachtman (2002), p. 861.

[9]*Ibid.*; Vranes (2009), pp. 339 ff. See also Crowley and Howse (2014), p. 327.

[10]See Marceau and Trachtman (2002), p. 861.

[11]See Howse and Levy (2013), p. 359; Crowley and Howse (2014), p. 326. See also Conconi and Voon (2016), pp. 216 f.

[12]See Crowley and Howse (2014), pp. 325 ff., who argue that the *US – Tuna II (Mexico)* Appellate Body Report implies that both pr- and npr-PPMs are covered by the TBT Agreement.

Moreover, there are some indications in the 2014 *EC – Seal Products* that the Appellate Body would consider that npr-PPMs could amount to a 'technical regulation' covered by the TBT Agreement. The Panel noted that under the challenged measure, only certain seal products were allowed. They had to meet different criteria relating to seal hunts from which the seals used as their input were derived. These criteria were the identity of the hunter (Inuit or indigenous), the type of hunt (traditional Inuit hunts), the purpose of the hunt (subsistence or marine resource management) and the way the products were marketed (non-systematically and on a non-profit basis).[13] In the view of the Panel, these criteria constituted 'objectively definable features' of the seal products that were allowed to be placed on the EU market and consequently '[laid] down particular "characteristics" of the final products'.[14] In other words, the Panel considered that an npr-PPM measure, based on differences in the producer's characteristics and in the hunting methods used, fell under the TBT Agreement because these differences could be viewed as product characteristics.

However, the Appellate Body reversed these findings, by holding as follows:

> A plain reading of Annexe 1.1 thus suggests that a 'related' PPM is one that is 'connected' or 'has a relation' to the characteristics of a product. The word 'their', which immediately precedes the words 'related processes and production methods', refers back to 'product characteristics'. Thus, in the context of the first sentence of Annex 1.1, we understand the reference to 'or their related processes and production methods' to indicate that the subject matter of a technical regulation may consist of a process or production method that is related to product characteristics. In order to determine whether a measure lays down related PPMs, a panel thus will have to examine whether the processes and production methods prescribed by the measure have a sufficient nexus to the characteristics of a product in order to be considered related to those characteristics.[15]

Thus, the Appellate Body reversed the findings that the contested measure laid down 'product characteristics'. Logically, the next step was then to examine whether that measure fell under the second criterion of the definition of technical regulations, i.e. whether it laid down 'related process and production methods'. Yet, because the Panel had made no findings on whether the contested measure fell under that second criterion, the Appellate Body refused to further examine this issue, although it noted that it raised 'important systemic issues'.[16] As a result, it remains unsettled whether an npr-PPM is covered by the TBT Agreement.

However, by holding that, in order to be covered by the TBT Agreement, a PPM measure must lay down PPMs that have a 'sufficient nexus' with the characteristics of a product, the Appellate Body seems to indicate that such 'nexus' does not necessarily need to be a physical one.[17] It remains to be seen if the Appellate Body

---

[13]See *EC – Seal Products*, Panel Report, para. 7.109.

[14]*EC – Seal Products*, Panel Report, para. 7.110.

[15]*EC – Seal Products*, Appellate Body Report, para. 5.12.

[16]*Ibid.*, para. 5.69.

[17]See Marceau (2014), pp. 327 f. (who also notes that *EC – Seal Product* Appellate Body report seems to open the door for a broader meaning of pr-PPM than has been understood in the literature thus far); Mavroidis (2016b), pp. 413 and 416.

will confirm this evolution in future cases. Many commentators interpret, however, these findings as an indication that case law is evolving towards the recognition that the TBT Agreement covers technical regulations applying to product-related and non-product-related PPMs alike.[18]

Moreover, it is submitted that the view considering that npr-PPMs are not covered by the TBT rules on technical regulations should be rejected, in particular, for reasons of global coherence. If such measures are not covered by the TBT Agreement (which contains a necessity test, even for non-discriminatory measures), they fall under the GATT, in particular its Article III (which contains no necessity test); it would be illogical that (the generally less trade-restrictive) labelling requirements, which must comply with the necessity test of TBT Article 2.2, be subject to stricter rules than npr-PPM technical regulations, which would fall in this view under the GATT non-discrimination obligations.[19] In the same vein, it would not be logical that pr-PPMs would, generally speaking, be subject to the stricter (TBT) rules than npr-PPMs. Indeed, pr-PPMs are generally viewed as less controversial than npr-PPMs.[20] It seems therefore much more coherent that technical regulations falling under the TBT Agreement may cover npr-PPMs.

From a practical viewpoint, it could nonetheless be pointed out that the differences in the disciplines of the TBT Agreement and the GATT, as they are interpreted by WTO adjudicating bodies, should not be overstated.[21] If GATT Article III contains no necessity test, it has been shown that most PPM measures are likely to infringe Article III and would require justification under Article XX, which has proved challenging. In other words, the practical differences, in terms of WTO Members' autonomy, between the rules of the TBT Agreement and those of GATT Articles III and XX, as they are interpreted by WTO adjudicating bodies, would probably not be quite significant in practice, even if they may exist.

In brief, the prevailing view among commentators has long been that npr-PPM technical requirements (i.e., PPMs that leave no physical trace in the final product) are not covered by the TBT Agreement, which means that they fall within the scope of the GATT. However, the text of the TBT Agreement does not clearly rule out any other interpretation, and the *travaux préparatoires* may not be entirely conclusive, insofar as the negotiators may have assumed that npr-PPMs were not justifiable under the GATT, following the *US – Tuna* reports. On the other hand, there is no particular reason that would justify that npr-PPMs be subject to the GATT, while pr-PPMs would fall under the scope of the TBT Agreement, especially since npr-PPM labelling requirements are subject to the TBT disciplines. Finally, the

---

[18]See Howse and Levy (2013), p. 359; Crowley and Howse (2014), p. 326; Marceau (2014), pp. 327 f.; Conconi and Voon (2016), pp. 216 f.; Herwig (2016), p. 117.

[19]It is true that in the light of the Appellate Body interpretation of the conditions of Article III, many PPM measures would in practice have to be justified under Article XX. Yet not all sub-paragraphs contain a necessity test; for instance, Article XX(g) only contains a more lenient 'relating to' test.

[20]See e.g. Marceau and Trachtman (2002), p. 861.

[21]See Conrad (2011), pp. 380 f.

findings of the Appellate Body in the *EC – Seal Products* report tend to indicate that npr-PPMs could be covered by the TBT Agreement.

8.2   No Less Favourable Treatment to Like Products (TBT Art. 2.1)

TBT Article 2.1 states that 'Members shall ensure that in respect of technical regulations, products imported from the territory of any Member shall be accorded treatment no less favourable than that accorded to like products of national origin and to like products originating in any other country'.

The application of this provision requires three elements: (1) the measure at issue constitutes a technical regulation within the meaning of Annex 1.1, (2) the imported products must be 'like' the domestic products and the products of other origins, (3) the treatment accorded to imported products must be less favourable than that accorded to like domestic products and like products from other countries.[22] Article 2.1 thus contains at the same time a national treatment obligation and a most favoured nation clause. This gives rise to the issue of the relationship between TBT Article 2.1 and GATT Articles I, III and XX.

The Appellate Body examined this issue in the *US – Clove Cigarettes* case. Based on the second recital of the TBT Agreement Preamble, which states that the signatories desire to further the objectives of the GATT 1994, the Appellate Body expressed the view that the two agreements 'overlap in scope and have similar objectives' and that the TBT Agreement 'expands on pre-existing GATT disciplines and emphasises that the two Agreements should be interpreted in a coherent and consistent manner'.[23]

TBT Article 2.1 refers to 'like products' and 'less favourable treatment', like GATT Article III:4. An important difference between the two agreements is, however, that the TBT Agreement has no equivalent to GATT Article XX, i.e. no general exceptions clause, providing justification for a violation of substantive obligations under certain conditions. It has thus been debated in academic writings whether the absence of equivalent to GATT Article XX in the TBT Agreement meant that discriminatory measures in the sense of TBT Article 2.1 could not be justified and were illegal per se.[24] Various theories have been suggested as a response to the absence of a general exceptions clause in the TBT Agreement. It has been suggested, for instance, that the scope of like products might be narrower

---

[22]See *US – Tuna II (Mexico)*, Appellate Body Report, para. 229; *US – Clove Cigarettes*, Appellate Body Report, para. 87.

[23]*US – Clove Cigarettes*, Appellate Body Report, para. 91.

[24]See e.g. Vranes (2009), pp. 302 f. with further references.

in TBT Article 2.1 than in GATT Article III:4[25] or that GATT Article XX might provide a justification for a violation of the TBT Agreement.[26] Others have contended that the possibility of justification provided in TBT Article 2.2 should also be applicable to infringements of TBT Article 2.1.[27]

The Appellate Body has adopted a different approach based on a systematic and teleological interpretation of both the TBT Agreement and the GATT. It analysed the TBT Preamble and noted that it contained both a trade-liberalisation objective (fifth recital) and recognition that Members have the right to regulate in order to fulfil legitimate policy objectives (sixth recital). For the Appellate Body, this right counterbalances the trade-liberalisation objective,[28] in a similar way as the balance that exists between GATT Articles III and XX.

It held:

> [T]he balance that the preamble of the TBT Agreement strikes between, on the one hand, the pursuit of trade liberalization and, on the other hand, Members' right to regulate, is not, in principle, different from the balance that exists between the national treatment obligation of Article III and the general exceptions provided under Article XX of the GATT 1994. The second recital of the preamble links the two Agreements by expressing the 'desire' 'to further the objectives of the GATT 1994', while the 'recognition' of a Member's right to regulate in the sixth recital is balanced by the 'desire' expressed in the fifth recital to ensure that technical regulations, standards, and conformity assessment procedures do not create unnecessary obstacles to international trade. We note, however, that in the GATT 1994 this balance is expressed by the national treatment rule in Article III:4 as qualified by the exceptions in Article XX, while, in the TBT Agreement, this balance is to be found in Article 2.1 itself, read in the light of its context and of its object and purpose.[29]

These findings mean that, in the view of the Appellate Body, the regulatory purpose underlying the contested measure is examined in principle under GATT Article XX and not GATT Article III,[30] while the regulatory purpose must be taken into account directly in the discrimination analysis in TBT Article 2.1. It has been shown extensively that in the GATT Article III context, it has been debated, among those who argue that the regulatory purpose is relevant in the national treatment analysis, whether the objective of the measure should be examined under the 'like products' or the 'less favourable treatment' condition.

---

[25]See Marceau and Trachtman (2002), p. 822. See also Mavroidis (2013), pp. 519 f. and (2016b), pp. 426 f., who argues that likeness in the TBT context should be understood as policy-likeness (i.e. based on a regulatory purpose approach) and not as market-likeness. With the same view, see Houston McMillan (2016), p. 551.

[26]*Ibid.*, p. 874 (these authors consider however that such approach requires a 'rather heroic approach to interpretation').

[27]See Vranes (2009), pp. 304 f.

[28]See *US – Clove Cigarettes*, Appellate Body Report, para. 95.

[29]*US – Clove Cigarettes*, Appellate Body Report, para. 109.

[30]The relevance of the regulatory purpose is not completely excluded from Article III, since it may have an influence on the analysis of the traditional criteria, in particular on consumers' tastes and habits (see *US – Clove Cigarettes*, Appellate Body Report, para. 117 ff.; *EC – Asbestos*, Appellate Body Report, para. 122 and *supra*, 6.3).

Not surprisingly, similar issues arose in the context of the TBT Article 2.1.[31] In the *US – Clove Cigarettes* case, the Panel applied a subjective approach to the definition of *like products*. It expressed doubts that the economic definition of like products, based on an analysis of the competitive relation between products on the market, was justified in the context of the TBT Agreement,[32] in particular because of the absence in the TBT Agreement of language such as that in GATT Article III:1, which influenced the economic definition of like products applied for the national treatment obligation of GATT Article III:4. The Panel applied a subjective approach to the definition of likeness, in which the traditional criteria of the likeness analysis are relevant but are evaluated in the light of the objective of the measure.[33] In other words, in the view of the Panel, the regulatory purpose influenced the relevance for the likeness analysis of different characteristics that two products may or may not share. In that case, the Panel focused on shared characteristics of clove cigarettes and menthol cigarettes that related to the public health objective of the measure, i.e. reducing youth smoking, and disregarded differences that did not relate to that objective.[34]

The Appellate Body overturned the Panel findings and rejected the view that the text and the context of the TBT Agreement supported an interpretation of the concept of likeness in Article 2.1 that focused on the legitimate objective of the measure, rather than on the competitive relationship between and among products.[35] The Appellate Body considered that the concept of like products served to define the scope of products that should be compared to establish whether less favourable treatment was being accorded to imported products. In its view, the 'less favourable treatment' analysis implied a comparison between all imported and domestic products that are in a sufficiently strong competitive relationship to be considered 'like'. A more narrow definition of like products, based on the relevance of certain product characteristics for the objective pursued, would in its view 'distort the less favourable treatment comparison, as it would refer to a "market place" that would include some like products, but not others'.[36]

Hence, the Appellate Body concluded that the likeness analysis in TBT Article 2.1, like in GATT Article III:4, 'is a determination about the nature and extent of a competitive relationship between and among products at issue'. Such relationship is analysed on the basis of the traditional four likeness criteria. Referring to its *EC – Asbestos* report, the Appellate Body added that the regulatory purpose might have

---

[31] See e.g. Broude and Levy (2014); Mavroidis (2016b), pp. 451 f. (who critically comments the Appellate Body case law on Article 2.1 of the TBT Agreement and argues that the likeness test in this provision should not be whether two products are marketlike but whether they are policylike); Houston-McMillan (2016), pp. 550 ff.

[32] See *US – Clove Cigarettes*, Panel Report, para. 7.99 and 7.119.

[33] *Ibid.*, para. 7.109 and 7.119.

[34] See *US – Clove Cigarettes*, Panel Report, para. 7.116, 7.247 *et passim*.

[35] See *US – Clove Cigarettes*, Appellate Body Report, para. 112 and 116.

[36] *US – Clove Cigarettes*, Appellate Body Report, para. 116.

at least an indirect role in this analysis. It held that 'to the extent that they are relevant to the examination of certain "likeness" criteria and are reflected in the products' competitive relationship, regulatory concerns underlying technical regulations may play a role in the determination of likeness'.[37] This means that two products with different PPMs may be considered as unlike under Article 2.1 if consumers treat them as unlike.

In brief, the Appellate Body rejected the subjective approach to likeness suggested by the Panel and applied the same economic definition of likeness in Article 2.1 of the TBT Agreement as that adopted in the context of GATT Article III:4.

But as it has been shown above, the Appellate Body considered that the regulatory purpose underlying the measure had to be taken into account in the examination of the conditions of Article 2.1 because of the absence of an equivalent of GATT Article XX in the TBT Agreement. In its view, it is in the 'less favourable treatment' condition that the regulatory purpose of the measure should be examined. The Appellate Body reminded that the object and purpose of the TBT Agreement was to strike a balance between the objective of trade liberalisation and Members' right to regulate. It expressed the view that this object and purpose suggested that Article 2.1 should not be interpreted as prohibiting any detrimental impact on competitive opportunities for imports, in cases where such detrimental impact on imports stems exclusively from legitimate regulatory distinctions.[38] In other words, the Appellate Body considered that while Article 2.1 prohibits both *de jure* and *de facto* discrimination against imported products, this provision permits detrimental impact on competitive opportunities for imports that stems exclusively from legitimate regulatory distinctions.[39]

The Appellate Body held:

[W]here the technical regulation at issue does not *de jure* discriminate against imports, the existence of a detrimental impact on competitive opportunities for the group of imported vis-à-vis the group of domestic like products is not dispositive of less favourable treatment under Article 2.1. Instead, a panel must further analyze whether the detrimental impact on imports stems exclusively from a legitimate regulatory distinction rather than reflecting discrimination against the group of imported products. In making this determination, a panel must carefully scrutinize the particular circumstances of the case, that is, the design, architecture, revealing structure, operation, and application of the technical regulation at issue, and, in particular, whether that technical regulation is even-handed, in order to determine whether it discriminates against the group of imported products.[40]

---

[37]*Ibid.*, para. 120 (see also para. 119, in which the Appellate Body stated that the regulatory purpose could be relevant in the analysis of the likeness criteria 'to the extent they have an impact on the competitive relationship between and among the products concerned').

[38]See *US – Clove Cigarettes*, Appellate Body Report, para. 174. See also para. 181; *US – Tuna II (Mexico)*, Appellate Body Report, para. 216.

[39]See *US – Clove Cigarettes*, Appellate Body Report, para. 175.

[40]*US – Clove Cigarettes*, Appellate Body Report, para. 182.

These findings were subsequently confirmed in the *US – Tuna II (Mexico)* and *US – COOL* Appellate Body reports.[41]

They show that, as proponents of the subjective approach to less favourable treatment have argued in the context of GATT Article III, a finding of *de facto* discrimination in the analysis of Article 2.1 requires (i) a detrimental impact on the competitive opportunities of the group of imported products compared to the group of domestic like products (i.e., *discriminatory effect*)[42] and (ii) the absence of justification of this detrimental impact based on a legitimate regulatory distinction (which would suggest the existence of a *discriminatory purpose*). The Appellate Body also suggests that this second step is relevant only in cases of *de facto* discrimination, while the first step is sufficient in cases of *de jure* discrimination.[43]

When it comes to the burden of proof, the complaining party has to make a *prima facie* case showing that treatment accorded to imported products is less favourable than that accorded to like domestic products,[44] for instance by adducing evidence showing that the measure is not even-handed. If the complaining party succeeds in doing so, then the responding party may rebut that showing by establishing that the detrimental impact on imported products stems exclusively from a legitimate regulatory distinction.[45] For instance, in the *US – Tuna II (Mexico)* case, Mexico had shown that the contested measure resulted in a detrimental impact on Mexican tuna products because most Mexican tuna products contained tuna caught in the Eastern Tropical Pacific Ocean (ETP) by setting on dolphins and were thus not eligible for a dolphin-safe label, while most tuna products from the United States and other countries that were sold in the US market contained tuna caught outside the ETP using other fishing methods and were therefore eligible for a dolphin-safe label. Since Mexico had made a *prima facie* case that the measure resulted in 'less favourable treatment', it was for the United States to show that the US labelling provisions were 'calibrated' to the risks to dolphins that the measure aimed to address.[46]

---

[41]See *US – Tuna II (Mexico)*, Appellate Body Report, para. 215; *US – COOL*, Appellate Body Report, para. 271.

[42]See *US – Clove Cigarettes*, Appellate Body Report, para. 193, in which the Appellate Body rejected the applicability of the Most Favoured Product rule and endorsed the discriminatory impact view ('the national treatment obligation of Article 2.1 does not require Members to accord no less favourable treatment to each and every imported product as compared to each and every domestic like product. Article 2.1 does not preclude any regulatory distinctions between products that are found to be like, as long as treatment accorded to the group of imported products is no less favourable than that accorded to the group of like domestic products'). See also *US – COOL*, Appellate Body Report, para. 270 ('in every case, it is *the effect of the measure on competitive opportunities in the market* that is relevant to an assessment of whether a challenged measure has a detrimental impact on imported products'; original emphasis).

[43]See also *US – Clove Cigarettes*, Appellate Body Report, para. 215.

[44]In this examination, the Appellate Body does not seem to require the quantification of trade effects; see Mavroidis (2016b), p. 427.

[45]See *US – Tuna II (Mexico)*, Appellate Body Report, para. 216.

[46]*Ibid.*, para. 283 f.

In order to show that the detrimental impact of the competitive conditions stems exclusively from a legitimate regulatory distinction, the Appellate Body's recent reports seem to imply that the defending Member must show in particular that its *regulatory distinction* is legitimate and not necessarily its regulatory purpose as such. For instance, in the *US – Tuna II (Mexico)* case, the United States had to show that the difference in labelling conditions for tuna caught on setting on dolphins in the ETP and for tuna caught by other fishing methods outside the ETP was legitimate (the issue was not whether avoiding dolphin bycatch in tuna fishing was legitimate).[47] In the *US – Clove Cigarettes*, the United States had to show why the regulatory distinction between clove cigarettes and menthol cigarettes, which gave rise to similar youth health concerns, was legitimate (the issue was not whether protecting youth health was legitimate).[48]

Provided that the regulatory distinction is legitimate, the complaining Member must then show that its measure is *even-handed*, which means that the measure must be 'calibrated' to the risks it aims to address.[49] In the *US – Tuna II (Mexico)* case, the Appellate Body concluded that the US measure was not even-handed in the way it addressed the risks to dolphins arising from different fishing techniques in different areas of the ocean. The measure 'fully addressed' the adverse effects on dolphins resulting from setting on dolphins in the ETP but, in the view of the Appellate Body, did not address dolphin bycatch arising from the use of other fishing methods outside the ETP.[50] Therefore, the United States failed to rebut the *prima facie* case of less favourable treatment by showing that the detrimental impact of its measure on Mexican tuna stemmed exclusively from a legitimate regulatory distinction.[51]

Arguably, this report may be explained by the requirement that the detrimental effect on imported products stemmed *exclusively* from a legitimate regulatory distinction. The fact that the US measure provided for stringent requirements for tuna caught in the ETP was not in itself problematic; the problem was rather that other situations, which gave rise to similar, albeit less strong, dolphin protection concerns, were not subject to any requirements. It is possible that the Appellate Body considered that the detrimental impact on Mexican tuna was hence not

---

[47] *Ibid.*, Appellate Body Report, para. 284.

[48] See *US – Clove Cigarettes*, Appellate Body Report, para. 225 f. The Appellate Body rejected the United States' argument that its regulatory distinction was justified on the basis of concerns relating to the need to treat millions of menthol cigarettes smokers affected by withdrawal symptoms in case of menthol cigarettes ban. The Appellate Body noted that the addictive ingredient was nicotine and not menthol. Since it seemed unlikely that the risks that the United States claimed to minimise by allowing menthol cigarettes to remain in the market would materialise, the Appellate Body concluded that the United States had not demonstrated that detrimental effects on imported clove cigarettes stemmed from a legitimate regulatory distinction.

[49] See *US – Tuna II (Mexico)*, Appellate Body Report, para. 297.

[50] *Ibid.*, para. 297 f.

[51] See *US – Tuna II (Mexico)*, Appellate Body Report, para. 298.

exclusively explained by the need for more stringent requirements in the ETP, and these requirements were thus, at least partly, discriminatory.

Yet the term 'exclusively' seems to represent a form of overstatement, insofar as various circumstances and motivations may underlie a particular measure. It would probably be more correct to require that the detrimental impact be 'primarily' explained by the legitimate regulatory distinction. The *US – Tuna II (Mexico) 21.5* Panel report has attempted to define more precisely what amounted to a detrimental impact that stemmed exclusively from a legitimate regulatory distinction.[52] It stated *inter alia* that the Panel could consider 'whether the detrimental impact [could] be reconciled with, or is rationally related to, the policy pursued by the measure at issue'. In that case, the Panel seemed to consider that the eligibility requirement for the dolphin-safe label outside the ETP could not be reconciled with the dolphin protection policy.[53]

The Panel also expressed the view that the requirement of even-handedness was 'closely related' to the question whether the detrimental impact stemmed exclusively from a legitimate regulatory distinction.[54] It stated:

> [A]sking whether a measure is even-handed can help a panel to determine whether the identified detrimental treatment is fully explainable as a consequence of a legitimate regulatory distinction—in which case it could be said to stem exclusively from that distinction—or whether the detrimental treatment, while perhaps connected to or broadly based on a legitimate regulatory distinction, is nevertheless not fully or precisely accounted for, in terms of both its nature and its scope, by the regulatory distinction that the responding Member seeks to pursue—in which case it could not be concluded that the detrimental treatment stems exclusively from the distinction pursued.[55]

Examining whether the detrimental impact is 'fully' explainable as a consequence of a regulatory distinction seems a more realistic test than asking whether the detrimental impact stems 'exclusively' from that distinction. In the former test, there may be circumstances *unrelated* to the legitimate regulatory distinction, which *also* explain the detrimental impact; it would yet be sufficient that the regulatory distinction 'fully' explains the detrimental impact. In the latter test, it might be argued that even if the legitimate regulatory distinction fully explains the detrimental impact, if other circumstances unrelated to that legitimate distinction *also* explain this impact, it could be claimed that the detrimental impact does *not*

---

[52]See *US – Tuna II (Mexico) 21.5*, Panel Report, para. 7.91 ff.

[53]See *US – Tuna II (Mexico) 21.5*, Panel Report, para. 7.263, in which the Panel insisted on the less stringent requirements for tuna caught outside the ETP and held that the United States 'has not provided sufficient explanation as to why this aspect of the amended tuna measure is structured in this way, or how it relates to the objectives pursued by the labelling regime'. See also the comments made by the Panel about the *US – Clove Cigarettes* Appellate Body's report. The Panel noted that a central element of the Appellate Body's findings in this case was the fact that the 'detrimental impact at issue in that case could not be reconciled with or justified by reference to the policy objective' of discouraging youth smoking (see para. 7.92).

[54]For a critical analysis of the 'even-handness' criterion, see Houston-McMillan (2016), p. 556 ff.

[55]*US – Tuna II (Mexico) 21.5*, Panel Report, para. 7.93.

stem 'exclusively' from the legitimate distinction.[56] It is submitted by the present author that such view would be too restrictive and that it must be sufficient for a defending Member to establish that its legitimate regulatory distinction 'fully explains' the detrimental impact. Thus, it would be more appropriate to consider that the test is whether this impact stems 'primarily', and not 'exclusively', from a legitimate regulatory distinction.

Concerning the result of the *US – Tuna II (Mexico)* case, it is interesting to note that even if the United States lost this case on the basis of Article 2.1 of the TBT Agreement, the outcome of this case does not necessarily result in the reduction of obstacles to trade.[57] In order to comply with TBT Article 2.1, the United States was not obliged to adapt the labelling requirements so as to allow tuna caught in the ETP by setting on dolphins to be eligible. It could simply apply more stringent requirements for tuna caught in other oceans using other fishing methods.

The Appellate Body's interpretation of TBT Article 2.1 may be seen as an application of general principles applicable to discrimination cases. The Appellate Body examines, in a way similar to all discrimination cases, if the regulatory distinction is based on a legitimate regulatory purpose (such as minimising bycatch in fishing activities) or, rather, on the prohibited criterion of origin. More generally, the Appellate Body seems to apply the general principle that non-discrimination means that similar situations must be treated in a similar fashion, while different situations must be treated differently. If a Member chooses to adopt a measure that reduces certain environmental risks through a regulatory distinction, it must not discriminate between the different categories distinguished in this measure. For instance, tuna caught in the ETP by setting on dolphins gives rise to high dolphin bycatches and may justify an exclusion from the 'dolphin-safe' label. But the use of other methods in other oceans also gives rise to similar risks, albeit not as strong. It would be discriminatory to address only the former and not the latter. In other words, the regulatory distinction is legitimate only insofar as it is not based on discriminatory criteria.

In the *US – COOL* report, the Appellate Body seemed to introduce additional conditions in the examination of whether the detrimental effect stems exclusively from a legitimate regulatory distinction, not clearly related to non-discrimination but rather to proportionality. The Appellate Body held that the regulatory distinctions imposed by the contested measure amounted to *arbitrary and unjustifiable discrimination* against imported products and that they could not be said to be

---

[56]See also Mavroidis (2016b), p. 427, arguing that it is 'simply untenable' to state that 'the TBT Agreement, on the one hand, does not require efficient, first-best interventions, but on the other, it requires the absence of negative external effects from whatever interventions WTO Members have privileged'; see also his further discussion of this test in pp. 447 ff. in which he describes it as an 'error' and argues that either the Appellate Body will have to backtrack on this requirement or it will have to interpret it in future case law in a very lenient manner. See also Houston-McMillan (2016), pp. 554 f., who points out that the interpretation of the word 'exclusively' raises many unanswered questions.

[57]See e.g. Kelly (2014), p. 523, with further references.

applied in an even-handed manner.[58] But more surprisingly, the Appellate Body had also stated in the same report that the record-keeping and verification requirements of the measure at issue imposed 'a disproportionate burden on upstream producers and processors'.[59] It seems clear that a measure that results in 'arbitrary or unjustifiable discrimination' should be viewed as discriminatory in the sense of Article 2.1 of the TBT Agreement. Nevertheless, applying an additional proportionality test, which compares the environmental benefits of the measure (or more generally its non-economic benefits) with its trade costs, does not seem justified. Indeed, Article 2.1 does not contain any textual basis for a proportionality test, and it does not seem self-evident that such test is implied by any non-discrimination analysis. Moreover, Article 2.2, which is applicable even to measures that comply with Article 2.1, contains a necessity test. Reading a proportionality test in Article 2.1 would lead to some form of double testing and would overly restrict the scope of Article 2.2. In brief, textual, teleological and systematic arguments exist to reject the introduction of a proportionality test in Article 2.1.

In sum, in the Appellate Body's case law, a technical regulation containing a regulatory distinction based on differences in PPMs may comply with Article 2.1 of the TBT Agreement if

- consumers do not consider products with different PPMs as like products; or
- products are regarded as like, but

  - there is no detrimental effects on the group of imported products compared to the group of domestic like products; or
  - there is no genuine relationship between the measure at issue and the adverse impact on competitive opportunities for imported products (i.e., factual circumstances unrelated to the measure explain this detrimental impact); or

- products are regarded as like and there is a genuine relationship between the measure at issue and the adverse impact on competitive opportunities for imported products, but this adverse impact on imports stems exclusively from a legitimate regulatory distinction.

---

[58] See *US – COOL*, Appellate Body Report, para. 349.

[59] *Ibid*. In the *US – Tuna 21.5* reports, both the Panel and the Appellate Body referred to this paragraph of the *US –COOL* report and referred to the question whether the impact of the measure were 'disproportionate'; See *US – Tuna II (Mexico) 21.5*, Panel Report, para. 7.95 ('even if a measure were based on a legitimate regulatory distinction, the measure would nonetheless not stem exclusively from that legitimate regulatory distinction if the detrimental impact were disproportionate, or if the measure otherwise reflected, for example, protectionism, and thus was not clearly justifiable by reference only to the legitimate regulatory distinctions invoked'); *US – Tuna II (Mexico)*, Appellate Body Report, para. 7.97 ('While an examination of whether a technical regulation constitutes a means of arbitrary or unjustifiable discrimination and thus is not even-handed must be conducted in the light of the "particular circumstances of the case", it is likely that this assessment involves consideration of the nexus between the regulatory distinctions found in the measure and the measure's policy objectives, including by examining whether the requirements imposed by the measure are disproportionate in the light of the objectives pursued'); see also para. 7.153 in the same report.

In Chap. 6, it has been explained that a central aspect of the debates on the interpretation of Articles III and XX of the GATT was the appropriate place to examine the regulatory purpose: in the concept of likeness (Article III), in the discriminatory treatment conditions (Article III) or in the general exceptions provision (Article XX).[60] In the GATT context, since the Appellate Body refused to examine the regulatory purpose in the analysis of Article III, it is in practice the interpretation of the conditions of Article XX that determines the restrictiveness of the GATT towards internal measures.

In the context of the TBT Agreement, there is no provision equivalent to Article XX that could justify a violation of the non-discrimination obligation embodied in Article 2.1. As a result, it is the scope given to the conditions of Article 2.1 that determine the restrictiveness of the TBT Agreement. It has been shown that the Appellate Body has used the same (large) market-based definition of like products to define likeness in the context of TBT Article 2.1. Thus, the regulatory purpose is examined under the less favourable treatment standard, which becomes the crucial condition to successfully defend a measure under this provision. Yet it has been shown in this section that the Appellate Body has applied a very demanding test as far as the less favourable treatment is concerned since a detrimental effect on imported products must stem 'exclusively' from the legitimate regulatory distinction. The restrictiveness of this test has been criticised by commentators.[61]

It is submitted here that the crucial aspect to remember is that a non-discrimination test must establish whether the measure at issue distinguishes between products based on a legitimate objective or rather on their foreign origin. It seems excessive to require that any detrimental effects on imported products should be 'exclusively' explained by the legitimate objective pursued. The threshold set by this test should thus be lowered. One possibility would be to require that the detrimental impact would be 'primarily' explained by the legitimate regulatory distinction; such test would seem sufficient to verify that the measure does not distinguish between products based on the prohibited criterion of origin.

8.3   Necessity (TBT Art. 2.2)

Article 2.2 of the TBT Agreement provides in relevant parts as follows:

---

[60]See *supra*, 6.2.

[61]Mavroidis has in particular argued that the Appellate Body less favourable treatment test was wrong (Mavroidis [2016b] p. 447) but also that the methodology applied by the Appellate Body should be modified. In his view, the approach of the Appellate Body is not in line with the negative integration nature of the TBT Agreement, which means that WTO Members are free to intervene in the market, provided that the pursue a legitimate objective and that the chosen measure is necessary and non-discriminatory. He has thus suggested that Article 2.2 should be examined before Article 2.1 (Mavroidis 2013, pp. 524 ff.; Mavroidis and Saggi 2014, pp. 315 ff.; Mavroidis 2016b, p. 451). See also Houston McMillan (2016), pp. 551 f.

Members shall ensure that technical regulations are not prepared, adopted or applied with a view to or with the effect of creating unnecessary obstacles to international trade. For this purpose, technical regulations shall not be more trade-restrictive than necessary to fulfil a legitimate objective, taking account of the risks non-fulfilment would create. Such legitimate objectives are, *inter alia*: national security requirements; the prevention of deceptive practices; protection of human health or safety, animal or plant life or health, or the environment.

The obligations laid down in TBT Article 2.2 are similar to those contained in GATT Article XX, including those mentioned in the chapeau. But certain differences exist. In particular, the obligation to adopt measures that do not create unnecessary obstacles to trade is laid down as a *positive* obligation in TBT Article 2.2 and not as an exception.[62] In other words, this obligation is also applicable to non-discriminatory measures,[63] by contrast to the GATT, in which necessity needs to be established only for measures found to be in violation of the non-discrimination provisions.

Moreover, while under GATT Article XX the respondent must prove that the relevant conditions are met, the burden of proof lies with the complainant under TBT Article 2.2.[64] More precisely, the complainant must make a *prima facie* case to establish that the challenged measure is more trade restrictive than necessary. It may seek to identify a possible alternative measure, which is less trade restrictive, makes an equivalent contribution to the achievement of the objective and is reasonably available. It is then for the respondent to rebut the complainant's *prima facie* case, by showing that the measure is not more trade restrictive than necessary and by demonstrating that the alternative measure identified does not meet the relevant conditions.[65]

Article 2.2 of the TBT Agreement, unlike GATT Article XX, does not set out a closed list of legitimate objectives, but rather lists of several examples of legitimate objectives.[66] The elaboration of legitimate objectives is the prerogative of the Member establishing a measure. But a panel is not bound by the Member's characterisation of the purposes of its own measures and must make its own independent and objective assessment.[67] In doing so, 'it may take into account the texts of statutes, legislative history, and other evidence regarding the structure and operation of the measure'.[68]

---

[62] See *US – Tuna II (Mexico)*, Panel Report, para. 7.458.

[63] See Marceau and Trachtman (2014), p. 368; Vranes (2009), pp. 305 f. with further references.

[64] See *US – Tuna II (Mexico)*, Appellate Body Report, para. 323; Marceau and Trachtman (2014), p. 378.

[65] See *US – Tuna II (Mexico)*, Appellate Body Report, para. 323.

[66] *Ibid.*, para. 313.

[67] See *US – Tuna II (Mexico)*, Panel Report, para. 7.405; *US – Tuna II (Mexico)*, Appellate Body Report, para. 314.

[68] *US – Tuna II (Mexico)*, Appellate Body Report, para. 314.

As already noted above,[69] it is interesting to point out that, in the context of TBT Article 2.2, the issue of 'extraterritoriality' did not arise, in particular in the *US – Tuna II (Mexico)* reports. Yet this case concerned the protection of dolphins living outside the jurisdiction of the importing Member. It could thus have been claimed that this measure was 'extraterritorial', like the measures concerned in the two unadopted *US – Tuna I* and *II* reports. In *US – Tuna II (Mexico)*, the United States had explained that one of its objectives for the dolphin-safe label was

> contributing to the protection of dolphins, by ensuring that the US market is not used to encourage fishing fleets to catch tuna in a manner that adversely affects dolphins.[70]

The Panel and the Appellate Body recognised that the objective of the US dolphin-safe provisions was 'legitimate' within the meaning of Article 2.2 of the TBT Agreement.[71] By focusing on whether the importing Member wishes to ensure that its internal market is not used to encourage environmentally harmful PPMs abroad, the measure was arguably viewed by the Panel and the Appellate Body as *territorial* in nature. This approach could influence the interpretation of GATT Article XX, as mentioned above,[72] since the Appellate Body seeks to interpret the TBT Agreement and the GATT in a coherent and consistent manner.[73]

Article 2.2 contains a necessity test, which analyses whether the *trade restrictiveness* of the measure is necessary, unlike in GATT Article XX, in which the necessity of the *measure* for the achievement of the objective is relevant.[74] The Appellate Body has applied a similar 'weighing and balancing' approach to the definition of necessity in TBT Article 2.2 as that endorsed under GATT Article XX. It held that the necessity analysis involves the evaluation of different factors that include (1) the degree of contribution made by the measure to the legitimate objective at issue, (2) the trade restrictiveness of the measure and (3) the nature of the risks at issue and the gravity of consequences that would arise from the non-fulfilment of the objective(s) pursued by the Member through the measure.[75] When it comes to the comparison with possible alternatives to the challenged measure, the Appellate Body examines whether that alternative is less trade restrictive, makes an equivalent contribution to the relevant legitimate objective taking account of the risks that non-fulfilment would create and is reasonably available.[76] Since a less trade-restrictive and equally efficient alternative measure must be 'reasonably available' in order to hold that the necessity has not been complied

---

[69] See *supra*, 7.1.2.1.3.

[70] *US – Tuna II (Mexico)*, Panel Report, para. 7.401 and 7.426 (emphasis added).

[71] See *US – Tuna II (Mexico)*, Panel Report, para. 7.444; Appellate Body Report, para. 338.

[72] See *supra*, 7.1.2.2.1.

[73] See *US – Clove Cigarettes*, Appellate Body Report, para. 91.

[74] See *US – Tuna II (Mexico)*, Panel Report, para. 7.460; *US – Tuna II (Mexico)*, Appellate Body Report, para. 319.

[75] See *US – Tuna II (Mexico)*, Appellate Body Report, para. 322.

[76] *Ibid.*

with, it can be noted that, compared to the strict definition of necessity that prevailed during the GATT era,[77] case law has thus evolved towards a more deferential approach, in which some 'benefit of the doubt' works in favour of the regulating state.[78]

8.4   International Standards

The TBT Agreement gives an important role to international standards.[79] First, TBT Article 2.4 provides:

> Where technical regulations are required and relevant international standards exist or their completion is imminent, Members shall use them, or the relevant parts of them, as a basis for their technical regulations except when such international standards or relevant parts would be ineffective or inappropriate means for the fulfilment of the legitimate objectives pursued.

This provision mentions that international standards might be ineffective or inappropriate, for instance because of fundamental climatic or geographical factors or fundamental technological problems.

The choice of a WTO Member to rely or not on an existing international standard also has consequences in the context of Article 2.2 necessity analysis. Under TBT Article 2.5, a technical regulation based on international standards is 'rebuttably presumed not to create an unnecessary obstacle to international trade' and thus to comply with Article 2.2.

The Appellate Body has interpreted the notion of 'international standards' broadly. They do not need to be adopted by an international 'organization'. It is sufficient that they were adopted by an international standardising 'body',[80] which does not need to have been active in the development of more than one standard.[81] What is, however, fundamental is, first, that this 'international standardising body' be 'recognised', both 'factually' (acknowledgement of the existence of the relevant body) and 'normatively' (acknowledgement of the validity and legality of the relevant body).[82] Second, its membership must be open to all WTO Members.[83] In the *US – Tuna II (Mexico)* case, the Appellate Body considered that the Agreement on the International Dolphin Conservation Programme (AICDP) did not represent an 'international standardising body' for the purpose of the TBT

---

[77]See *supra*, 7.2.1.1.1.

[78]Mavoidis (2016b), p. 422.

[79]See e.g. Crowley and Howse (2014), pp. 338 f. and their analysis of the Appellate Body report concerning international standards in the *US – Tuna II (Mexico)* case.

[80]See *US – Tuna II (Mexico)*, Appellate Body Report, para. 356.

[81]*Ibid.*, para. 360.

[82]*Ibid.*, para. 361.

[83]*Ibid.*

Agreement because it was not open to all WTO Members since an invitation to accede to the AIDCP required a decision, which itself required consensus.[84] Since the AIDCP was not deemed to be an 'international standardising body', the AIDCP 'dolphin-safe' definition and certification was not recognised as an 'international standard'.

An international standard is not necessarily a standard adopted by consensus.[85] As a result, it has been argued that standards developed by a subgroup of WTO Members, for instance in the area of climate change, could be qualified as 'international standards' and thus benefit from the Article 2.5 presumption of WTO compatibility, even if they may not appear to be appropriate for developing countries.[86]

The requirement that exporting countries comply with international standards may give rise to particular difficulties for developing countries. Article 12.4 of the TBT Agreement provides that developing countries should not be expected to use international standards as a basis for their technical regulations or standards, including test methods, which are not appropriate to their development, financial and trade needs.

In relation to the PPM debate, the importance given to international standards in the context of the TBT Agreement can be seen as a response to the particular concerns that exist when a PPM measure is imposed *unilaterally* by the importing state. Under the TBT Agreement, when an international standard exists in a particular field, a WTO Member that would have decided to impose different standards would need to establish that the existing international standards would be an 'ineffective or inappropriate means for the fulfilment of the legitimate objectives pursued' (TBT Article 2.4). Particular circumstances would thus have to exist in in this situation to justify a 'unilateral' technical regulation. On the other hand, when such standards do exist, the importing country benefits from the presumption that it does not constitute an unnecessary obstacle to trade, even if that international standard might have been adopted without consensus among Members of the relevant international standardisation body.

8.5 Special and Differential Treatment

The TBT Agreement contains several provisions concerning special and differential treatment for developing countries, in particular in cases involving PPM measures. These provisions concern, in particular:

---

[84]*Ibid.*, para. 398.

[85]See *EC – Sardines*, Appellate Body Report, para. 222.

[86]See Low et al. (2012), pp. 525 f.; Holzer (2014), p. 190.

– Additional adaptation periods: they relate to the interval between the publication of technical regulations and their entry into force, to allow time for producers in exporting Members, and particularly in developing country Members, to adapt their products or methods of production to the relevant requirements (Arts. 2.12, 5.9).
– Technical assistance and advice: if requested, Members shall provide advice to other Members, especially developing countries, and grant them technical assistance (Arts. 11.4 to 11.7); the Secretariat shall draw the attention of developing country Members to any notifications relating to products of particular interest to them (Art. 10.6).
– Provision of more favourable treatment: Members shall provide differential and more favourable treatment to developing countries (Art. 12.1), in particular through additional adaptation periods and technical assistance, and in the implementation of the TBT Agreement (Art. 12.2), the preparation and application of technical regulations (Art. 12.3) or the representation of developing countries in international standardising bodies (Art. 12.5).

The most important provision relating to more favourable treatment is Article 12.8, which allows deviations from the substantive provisions when developing countries face 'special problems' in the field of preparation and application of technical regulations, standards and conformity assessment procedures. The TBT Committee is enabled under this provision to grant upon request specified and time-limited 'exceptions in whole or in part from obligations under the TBT Agreement'.

This exception plays an important role with respect to technical regulations and standards adopted or applied by developing countries. It is, however, not designed to address the ability of developing countries to meet technical regulations or standards applied by developed countries, which might be viewed as developing countries' main concern.[87] The approach adopted in the TBT Agreement is thus to favour assistance and the provision of additional adaptation periods to enable developing countries to comply with the relevant requirements but not to accept that developing countries may be exempted per se from compliance with those requirements.

If the TBT Agreement expressly and extensively recognises the special needs and interests of developing countries, it should also be noted that the provisions concerning developing countries, in the way they are drafted, are not enforceable rights. They mainly remain soft law.[88] It seems, however, clear that taking the interests of developing countries into account is an important objective of the TBT Agreement and arguably of the WTO system as a whole. One of the objectives mentioned in the Marrakesh Agreement is indeed to enter into 'reciprocal and mutually advantageous arrangements'. Taking interests of developing countries

---

[87] See Conrad (2011), p. 417.
[88] Ibid.

into account is probably a fundamental element for ensuring the continuous support to the WTO by many of its Members.

Even though the TBT Agreement contains specific provisions concerning developing countries, it remains open if their interests may not in fact be taken into account more extensively in the context of GATT Article XX. Indeed, GATT general exceptions provision requires the importing Member to take into account the differing conditions that occur between the different countries concerned, which may include in particular differences in the level of development or in the historical responsibilities in the environmental risks at issue. In practice, it may be asked whether the obligation to take the interests of developing countries into account in the context of GATT Article XX is thus not more extensive than the obligations existing under the TBT Agreement, despite their being more detailed.

8.6   Link Between the TBT Agreement and the GATT

It has been shown that the TBT Agreement covers, in particular, mandatory labelling requirements based on differences in PPMs, whether or not they are incorporated in the final product, as well as technical regulations based on incorporated PPMs. The TBT Agreement covers neither technical regulations designed in terms of unincorporated PPMs (at least in the prevailing view) nor measures that deny market access to certain products, on the basis of their PPMs (whether or not they are incorporated in the final product), which are thus subject to the GATT.

With respect to technical regulations that fall under the TBT Agreement, the relation between the TBT and the GATT is not addressed specifically in the WTO Agreements. The *General interpretative note to Annex 1A of the Marrakesh Agreement establishing the WTO* simply provides that in the event of a conflict between a provision of the GATT and a provision of another Agreement of Annex 1A (including the TBT Agreement), 'the provision of the other agreement shall prevail to the extent of the conflict'. But this interpretative note does not specify if the TBT Agreement is a *lex specialis*, whether a measure that violates the TBT Agreement could be justified on the basis of GATT Article XX or, conversely, if a measure that complies with the conditions of the TBT Agreement could still be found to be inconsistent with WTO law on the basis of GATT Article XX.

More precisely, this rule does not define what amounts to a 'conflict' between the GATT and the TBT Agreement. A strict definition would mean that a conflict occurs when compliance with one obligation would lead to a violation of another obligation.[89] In such a case, one could argue that if a measure complies with the TBT Agreement but not with the GATT, there is no 'conflict' between two obligations but only a conflict between an obligation (compliance with the

---

[89]See Pauwelyn (2002), pp. 74 f. (referring to *Guatemala – Cement*, Appellate Body Report, para. 65).

GATT) and a right (adoption of a measure consistent with the TBT). In the absence of a relevant conflict, the *Interpretative note* would not apply, and the strictest obligation would prevail.[90]

On the other hand, it could also be contended that a conflict situation encompasses the cases in which one agreement allows what another agreement prohibits.[91] The Panel in the case *EC – Bananas III* had held that a conflict included 'the situation where a rule in one agreement prohibits what a rule in another agreement explicitly permits'.[92]

In the first view, a WTO Member would have to comply with both the conditions of the TBT Agreement and the GATT, while in the second one, a measure that complies with the TBT Agreement could not be found inconsistent with the GATT.

In the *EC – Asbestos* report, the Appellate Body held:

> [A]lthough the TBT Agreement is intended to 'further the objectives of GATT 1994', it does so through a specialized legal regime that applies solely to a limited class of measures. For these measures, the TBT Agreement imposes obligations on Members that seem to be different from, and additional to, the obligations imposed on Members under the GATT 1994.[93]

The first sentence might indicate that the TBT Agreement is a *lex specialis*, but the Appellate Body declined to examine its measure under the TBT Agreement and analysed its compliance with the GATT.[94] The second sentence, on the other hand, which refers to 'additional' obligations imposed on Members, does not exclude that a measure consistent with the TBT Agreement could still be found in violation of the GATT.

In the *US – Clove Cigarettes* report, the Appellate Body further stated that the GATT and the TBT 'overlap in scope and have similar objectives' and that they 'should be interpreted in a coherent and consistent manner'.[95] One of the differences between the TBT Agreement and the GATT is that, contrary to the latter, the former does not contain a closed list of legitimate objectives that can be pursued by the regulating country. When a Member enacts a measure pursuing a purpose recognised as legitimate under TBT Article 2.2 but that is not mentioned in the list of Article XX, should it be held to be inconsistent with the GATT?[96] This interpretation would deprive part of the intended scope of the TBT Agreement since it would mean in practice that the closed list of Article XX would be applicable to the TBT Agreement. Such result is clearly not intended and would be inconsistent with the rule of effective treaty interpretation. It would, in other words, not lead to 'coherent and consistent' interpretation and must be rejected.

---

[90]See Pauwelyn (2002), p. 76; Conrad (2011), p. 415.

[91]See Pauwelyn (2002), p. 78; Conrad (2011), p. 415.

[92]*EC – Bananas III*, Panel Report, para. 7.159.

[93]*EC – Asbestos*, Appellate Body Report, para. 80.

[94]See Marceau and Trachtment (2014), p. 424.

[95]See *US – Clove Cigarettes*, Appellate Body Report, para. 91.

[96]Cf. Conrad (2011), p. 414, who mentions this possible interpretation but rejects it.

The Panel and the Appellate Body in the *US – Tuna 21.5* reports examined the contested measure both under the TBT Agreement and the GATT. They did not expressly discuss the issue of conflict rules between these two agreements. It should be noted, however, that the conclusion they reached under each of them were compatible: for instance, the Panel upheld the eligibility criteria for the dolphin-safe label both under TBT Article 2.1 and GATT Article XX(g), while the certification requirements and tracking and verification requirements were both deemed to be in violation of TBT Article 2.1 and GATT Article XX(g).[97]

In brief, it is argued by the present author that the conflict rule of the *General interpretative note* must be interpreted as applying to cases in which one agreement allows what the other does not. In such a case, the TBT prevails. Thus, a measure is in principle still consistent with WTO law if it complies with the TBT Agreement but not with the GATT. Conversely, a measure is in violation of WTO law if it fulfils the conditions of the GATT but not those of the TBT Agreement.[98]

8.7 Conclusions

This chapter has shown that certain PPM measures are subject to the TBT Agreement, namely pr-PPM technical regulations and npr-PPM labelling requirements, while the other PPM measures are covered by the GATT. Some uncertainties remain concerning npr-PPM technical regulations, but it is likely that they would not fall within the ambit of the TBT Agreement.

The substantive disciplines of the TBT Agreement and the GATT are formally different but are certainly similar, if all the different conditions laid down in the TBT Agreement, on the on hand, and in the GATT, on the other hand, are examined as a whole. One important theoretical difference is the fact that only the TBT Agreement contains a necessity test for non-discriminatory measures, by contrast to the GATT. This would seem to imply that the TBT regime is more restrictive than the GATT regime. However, the economic interpretation of GATT Article III endorsed by the Appellate Body implies that most PPM measures would be subject, in practice, to the conditions of GATT Article XX, which reduces the practical differences between the two different regimes.

When it comes to the main problematic characteristics of PPM measures, namely their possible 'extraterritorial' and 'unilateral' character, as well as the particular difficulties that they may cause to developing countries,[99] it has been

---

[97] See *US – Tuna II (Mexico) 21.5*, Panel Report, para. 8. Note that the Appellate Body reversed the Panel findings and held that the amended measure was inconsistent with TBT Article 2.1 and GATT Articles I:1 and III:4 and was not justified under GATT Article XX.

[98] See also Pauwelyn (2002), p. 78; Conrad (2011), p. 415.

[99] See *supra*, Chap. 2.

shown that the Appellate Body has adopted a view that makes the 'extraterritoriality' issue irrelevant.

Unilateralism concerns are addressed in the TBT Agreement context by the importance given to international standards, which should be used when they exist in a particular field, except when the importing Member may show that they represent an ineffective or inappropriate means to fulfil the objective pursued.

The interests of developing countries are taken into account by various provisions of the TBT Agreement. These provisions do not justify, however, that developing countries be exempted from compliance with particular requirements. They mainly provide for additional adaptation periods and the provision of technical assistance. In this sense, the interests of developing countries are not taken as extensively in the TBT Agreement as in GATT Article XX, in which a textual basis exists to require that the importing Member take into account the differing conditions occurring in the different Members concerned, which arguably includes the level of development or the historical responsibility in the environmental risks at issue.

Chapter 9
Conclusions: A Critical Analysis of the PPM Measures' Legal Regime *De Lege Lata* and *De Lege Ferenda*

9.1 What Is Left of the Product-Process Distinction?

The product-process distinction, in the form it was expressed mainly in the *US – Tuna* GATT Panel reports, has been largely undermined by different evolutions of case law.[1] It might thus be asked what is left of this doctrine in the current Appellate Body's practice. The product-process distinction was mainly based on the following assumptions:

(i) *PPM measures are not covered by Article III but are subject to Articles II (tariffs) and XI (prohibition of quantitative restrictions)*[2];

(ii) *In any event, differences in PPMs cannot render two products unlike and thus cannot be justified under Article III*[3];

(iii) *Unincorporated PPM measures are extraterritorial in nature and thus cannot in principle be justified by Article XX*[4];

(iv) *PPM measures that unilaterally prescribe the adoption of a particular conduct abroad threaten the multilateral trading system and are thus unjustifiable*[5];

---

[1]See *supra*, Chaps. 6 and 7.

[2]Concerning regulatory measures, see *US – Tuna I*, Panel Report, para. 5.11–5.18; *US – Tuna II*, Panel Report, para. 5.9 and 5.10. See also *supra*, 6.1.

[3]See *US – Tuna I*, Panel Report, para. 5.9 ff. *US – Tuna II*, Panel Report, para. 5.9. See also *supra*, 6.3.1.2.2.

[4]See *US – Tuna I*, Panel Report, para. 5.28; *US – Tuna II*, Panel Report, para. 5.17 ff. See also *supra*, 7.1.2.1.1.

[5]See *US – Tuna II*, Panel Report, para. 5.26; *US – Shrimp*, Panel Report, para. 7.45. See also *supra*, 7.1.2.1.1.

© Springer International Publishing AG 2018
D. Sifonios, *Environmental Process and Production Methods (PPMs) in WTO Law*,
European Yearbook of International Economic Law 3,
DOI 10.1007/978-3-319-65726-4_9

(v) *When it comes to technical barriers to trade, the TBT Agreement only applies to incorporated PPMs and does not cover unincorporated PPMs.*[6]

These different elements that constituted the product-process distinction are examined in turn, in order to see the extent to which they remain relevant.

(i) PPM measures are not covered by Article III but are subject to Articles II (tariffs) and XI (prohibition of quantitative restrictions): the Appellate Body has applied a broad approach of the coverage of national treatment, through its interpretation of the concept of taxes 'indirectly applied on products' in the sense of Article III:2, and of the interpretation of the notion of internal regulatory measures 'affecting the internal sale' of products on the importing state's market, in the sense of Article III:4.[7] PPM regulations are indeed capable of affecting the sale, i.e. of adversely modifying the conditions of competition between domestic and imported products, and the economic framework underlying the Appellate Body's interpretation of national treatment logically implies that such measures must be subject to Article III disciplines. This view is largely supported in academic writings.[8]

(ii) In any event, differences in PPMs cannot render two products unlike: no Panel or Appellate Body reports have specifically stated that differences in PPMs were an independent criterion relevant in the likeness analysis. Still, it has been clearly implied by case law that two physically identical products may be regarded as unlike if consumers treat them as unlike.[9] Because likeness is examined on the marketplace, it is not relevant as such to distinguish between measures addressing product standards or process standards. What matters is the competitive relationship between products, which may be influenced by both kinds of standards. Moreover, a measure that distinguishes between two products on the basis of differences in PPMs may still comply with the conditions of Article III, even if the products are considered to be like, if there is no detrimental impact on the group of imported products compared to the group of domestic like products.[10] In other words, not only PPM measures are covered by Article III, but they may also comply with the conditions laid down in the national treatment provision.

(iii) Unincorporated PPM measures are extraterritorial in nature and thus cannot in principle be justified by Article XX: the Appellate Body mentioned the issue of a possible 'implied jurisdictional limitation' in Article XX but did not have to clarify this issue in the *US – Shrimp* case because a 'sufficient nexus' existed in this case since the protected sea turtles at issue were migratory animals, and some of them were present at some moment of their lives in the United States territorial waters.[11] However, in the context of the TBT Agreement, the Appellate Body did

---

[6]See *supra*, 8.1.

[7]See *supra*, 6.1.

[8]See *supra*, 6.1.

[9]See *supra*, 6.3.1.4.4.

[10]See *supra*, 6.4.

[11]See *supra*, 7.1.2.1.2.

not examine at all in its *US – Tuna II (Mexico)* report the 'implied jurisdictional limitation' issue, even though the protected dolphins were not present in United States territorial waters.[12] It was sufficient in its view that the measure aimed at ensuring that the US market was not used to encourage fishing fleets to harvest tuna in a manner that adversely affected dolphins.[13] The *US – Tuna II (Mexico) 21.5* Panel applied a similar reasoning in the context of GATT Article XX(g).[14] Thus, while this measure would have been qualified as extraterritorial under the reasoning of the *US – Tuna I and II* Panels,[15] the Appellate Body considered the measure as territorial in the *US – Tuna II (Mexico)* report. In order to guarantee a 'coherent and consistent' interpretation of the GATT and the TBT Agreement,[16] it is likely that the Appellate Body would apply a similar interpretation for both agreements. It is thus unlikely that the 'extraterritoriality' issue will play a significant role in future cases in the context of Article XX either.[17] In any case, such requirement would not be legally justified, as it has been explained in Chap. 7.[18]

(iv) PPM measures that unilaterally prescribe the adoption of a particular conduct abroad threaten the multilateral trading system and are thus unjustifiable: the Appellate Body clearly rejected this view, stating that conditioning access to a Member's domestic market on whether exporting Members adopt policies unilaterally prescribed by the importing state may be a common aspect of measures falling within the scope of the Article XX exceptions.[19] Negotiation efforts may be necessary in certain circumstances,[20] but the unilateral character of a PPM measure is not, as such, sufficient to render such measure unjustifiable.

(v) The TBT Agreement only applies to incorporated PPMs and does not cover unincorporated PPMs: it is clear after the *US – Tuna II (Mexico)* case that the TBT Agreement does apply at least to labelling requirements based on differences in non-product-related PPMs.[21] Moreover, it seems, after the *EC – Seal Products* report, that the case law of the Appellate Body is evolving towards the recognition that technical regulations include differentiations based on npr-PPMs, even though the Appellate Body made no definitive findings on this issue in this case.[22]

---

[12]See *supra*, 8.3.

[13]See *US – Tuna II (Mexico)*, Panel Report, para. 7.401 and 7.425; *US – Tuna II (Mexico)*, Appellate Body Report, para. 337. See *supra*, 8.3.

[14]See *US – Tuna II (Mexico) 21.5*, Panel Report, para. 7.522 ff. See also *supra*, 7.1.2.1.1.

[15]See *supra*, 7.1.2.1.1.

[16]See *US – Clove Cigarettes*, Appellate Body Report, para. 91 (stating that the GATT and the TBT 'should be interpreted in a coherent and consistent manner').

[17]See *supra*, 7.1.2.1.2.

[18]See *supra*, 7.1.2.2.

[19]See *US – Shrimp*, Appellate Body Report, para. 121. See also *supra*, 7.1.2.1.1 and 7.1.2.1.2.

[20]See *supra*, 7.3.2.2.3.

[21]See *US – Tuna II (Mexico)*, Panel Report, para. 7.78. See *supra*, 8.1.

[22]See *supra*, 8.1.

In sum, under the strict product-process distinction, it was considered that npr-PPM measures were not covered by GATT Article III (or probably by the TBT Agreement), that these measures violated GATT Article XI (and GATT Article II in cases of fiscal measures)[23] and that they were usually unjustifiable under GATT Article XX.[24]

In current case law, as interpreted in this study at least, npr-PPMs fall under the TBT Agreement in cases of labelling requirements, and possibly in cases of technical regulations, and under the GATT non-discrimination provisions in other cases.[25] They may comply with the non-discrimination provisions of these agreements, if consumers treat products with different PPMs as unlike or if the measure does not result in less favourable treatment for the group of imported products compared to the group of domestic like products.[26] If PPM measures infringe GATT Articles I or III, they may be justified under Article XX. The fact that they are 'extraterritorial' (i.e., apply to a situation that has no territorial link with the importing state) or consists in the imposition of a policy unilaterally prescribed by the importing Member, does not, per se, render the measure unjustifiable.[27]

In brief, not much is left of the product-process distinction as such.[28] The only issue that remains open is whether a difference exists between npr-PPMs and product standards (or pr-PPM) as far as the coverage of the TBT Agreement is concerned since it has been traditionally considered in academic writings that npr-PPM technical requirements (to the exclusion of *labelling* requirements) fall under the GATT and not the TBT Agreement.[29] But it seems unsure that the Appellate Body will confirm this view, and in any case this distinction does not mean that some PPM measures are unjustifiable, only that they are subject to different rules.

Moreover, when it comes to the substantive conditions applicable to npr-PPMs and other trade measures, there is arguably no rigid dichotomy left between permissible and impermissible measures. The fact that a measure deals with npr-PPMs does not render such a measure illegal under WTO law. It only means that compliance with the relevant conditions may be more demanding or require particular efforts. For instance, it may be more difficult to show that products that differ only by their PPMs are unlike under the non-discrimination provisions,[30] or the conditions of the chapeau of GATT Article XX may imply that the regulating Member has to pay particular attention, to justify a PPM measure, to the differing

---

[23]See *supra*, 6.1.1.

[24]See *supra*, 7.1.2.1.1.

[25]See *supra*, 8.1.

[26]See *supra*, 6.4 and 8.2.

[27]See *supra*, 7.1.2.

[28]See also Matsushita et al. (2015), p. 724, stating that '[m]uch of the reasoning in the *Tuna Dolphin* cases has been effectively overruled'.

[29]See *supra*, 8.1.

[30]See *supra*, 6.3.1.4.4.

conditions that prevail in the exporting Member, to the flexibility of its measure or to the need for international cooperation to achieve a multilateral solution.[31]

9.2 The Need for a Flexible System

The strict product-process distinction, applied in particular by the *US – Tuna I* and *II* Panels, represented a form of rigid dichotomy between permitted measures (product standards) and prohibited ones (most PPM measures).[32]

It is doubtful that this approach was legally justified on the basis of the international law principles of treaty interpretation. Neither the text of the GATT nor its object and purpose clearly reject the legality of PPM measures.[33] Moreover, the prohibition of PPM measures denied importing Members the ability to address many environmental situations, even those that they might have been genuinely and legitimately concerned about, such as climate change caused by greenhouse gas emissions.[34] This rigid product-process distinction also contradicted many principles of international environmental law,[35] such as the principle of the internalisation of externalities or the reduction of unsustainable consumption and production practices, which form a part of the principle of sustainable development,[36] which itself represents one of the objectives mentioned in the WTO Agreement. From the viewpoint of international relations, prohibiting PPM measures was also likely to reinforce risks of cooperation failures in international efforts to address transboundary and global environmental issues since trade measures could not serve as an instrument to sanction refusal to participate in such international efforts, through free riding or non-compliance with international commitments.[37]

Therefore, it is argued in this study that it is in principle a positive evolution that the Appellate Body never endorsed as such the product-process distinction and that it adopted an interpretation of the relevant provisions that implicitly rejected it almost completely.[38]

---

[31] See *supra*, 7.3.2.2.

[32] See *supra*, 6.1 and 6.3.1.2.2. See also 7.1.2.1.1.

[33] See Hudec (2000), pp. 187 ff.; Howse and Regan (2000), pp. 249 ff.; Vranes (2009), p. 322. See also *supra*, 6.3.1.2.2.

[34] See *supra*, 7.1.2.2.

[35] *Idem.*

[36] See *supra*, 4.1.

[37] See *supra*, 3.4.

[38] See also Matsushita et al. (2015), p. 747, stating that the fact that under the WTO, the hard line against all PPM restrictions that are not based on product characteristics has been modified is 'one of the most important aspect of WTO jurisprudence'. See also Cosbey and Mavroidis (2014), p. 300, stating that the dominant trend in the treatment of environmental trade measures by WTO adjudicating bodies has been towards deference to the regulating WTO Member. It has allowed in their view to correct the 'clear mistake' committed in the two original Tuna-Dolphin GATT reports.

Nevertheless, the rejection of the 'bright line rule' that some saw in the product-process distinction[39] does not alter the fact that the use of PPM measures is controversial, especially because competing and various interests are particularly likely to be entangled in this type of measures.[40] This means, on the one hand, that PPM measures may potentially be used abusively to achieve protectionist purposes, disguised under environmental motives. It has often been pointed out that risks of 'slippery slope' existed if any aspect of the production processes used in other countries could justify restrictive import measures.[41] On the other hand, process standards are often adopted by powerful industrialised nations. Developing countries may have significant implementation difficulties, which can result in practice in the impossibility to comply with these standards.[42] Multiplication of such barriers to trade could thus undermine the reciprocal and mutually advantageous nature that WTO agreements are supposed to have.[43] In brief, if PPM measures can be a means to achieve the objective of the 'optimal use of the world's resources in accordance with the objective of sustainable development', a widespread and unregulated use of PPM regulations could also potentially undermine other objectives of the WTO, namely expanding trade in goods and ensuring the mutually advantageous nature of WTO agreements.

One of the fundamental challenges is thus to determine the criteria that can be used to distinguish between legitimate and illegitimate PPM measures. The implicit rejection of the product-process distinction means that no black and white distinctions can be made but that the legitimacy of a PPM measure depends rather on a series of different factors.

The basic objectives of the WTO system may provide some guidance. Trade liberalisation is a means to achieve the main objectives of the WTO, in particular raising the standards of living through an expansion of international trade. Reduction of barriers to trade allows the market to function more efficiently and to increase benefits from comparative advantages. The benefits of trade liberalisation are thus based on the optimal functioning of the market. In practice, different factors imply that the market does not function optimally, in particular because of the existence of externalities. Economic theory recognises that state interventions are sometimes required to internalise externalities, in order for the market to function in an optimal way.[44] Trade liberalisation, in itself, does not address or offer a solution to the problem of the correction of market failures. It cannot thus be assumed that WTO Members have committed to refrain from internalising

---

[39]See Jackson (2000), p. 303.

[40]See e.g. *supra*, Chaps. 2–4.

[41]See e.g. Jackson (2000), p. 306.

[42]See *supra*, 2.1.

[43]See the Preamble of the Marrakesh Agreement Establishing the WTO, which refers to the objective of 'entering into reciprocal and mutually advantageous arrangements directed to the substantial reduction of tariffs and other trade barriers to trade'.

[44]See *supra*, 3.1.

externalities affecting them when they adopted the GATT.[45] On the other hand, the Preamble of the WTO Agreement explicitly refers to the objective of allowing the optimal use of the world's resources in accordance with the objective of sustainable development. The internalisation of externalities and the application of the polluter-pays principle may contribute to the achievement of sustainable development.[46] Therefore, WTO law should allow, in principle, state interventions aimed at the internalisation of externalities affecting the importing country.[47]

This general principle needs, however, to be refined with additional and more precise criteria. Indeed, an externality can affect the importing country in more or less intense ways, which means that the proximity of interests varies accordingly, as it has been described in detail in Chap. 7.[48] Multilateral trade rules must thus provide the necessary tools to allow in principle measures addressing externalities affecting the importing state, in a way that takes into account the proximity of interests between this country and the environmental situation concerned. In addition, trade rules must be able to take into consideration competing trade and developmental interests in order to find some balance between possibly conflicting interests.

In other words, it is submitted by this study that the international trade regime has to provide for a *flexible* system, which allows consideration of the particular circumstances and underlying interests.

It is debatable whether such objective should be achieved through the interpretation of the existing trade rules or if it would be more appropriate to amend them. Chapters 6 and 7 have shown that impressively diverse theories have been developed regarding the interpretation of the applicable GATT rules.[49] Likewise, the evolutions and fluctuations of case law illustrate that the same text has led to very different interpretations, which have very different consequences on the legal regime applicable to PPM measures,[50] some of which were strict prohibitions of particular measures (such as process standards in general, as well as extraterritorial or unilateral measures) rather than flexible approaches.

These intense debates were caused in particular by the vague character of some of the main relevant concepts, which have been extensively discussed in Chaps. 6 and 7. It has been hence often suggested that this regime could be clarified, either through a modification of the relevant agreements or through the adoption of an authoritative interpretation of the relevant WTO law provisions.[51]

---

[45]See Horn and Mavroidis (2008), p. 1132.

[46]See *supra*, 4.1.1.

[47]See Conrad (2011), p. 473.

[48]See *supra*, 7.1.2.2.2.

[49]See in particular *supra*, 6.5.1 and 7.1.2.

[50]See e.g. theories and fluctuations in case law relating to the conditions of Article III in Chap. 6 (see in particular *supra*, 6.5.1).

[51]See Bierman (2001), pp. 434 ff.; Conrad (2011), pp. 438 ff., with further references.

However, there are no doubts that it is quite unlikely that any of these two possibilities could be realised in any foreseeable future. Indeed, on the one hand, WTO Members already have considerable difficulty in successfully getting through the current round of multilateral trade negotiations. But in any event, given the considerable variety of different and competing interests that arise in the PPM debate,[52] it seems quite unlikely that a consensus could be reached between WTO Members on more precise terms, which would more likely favour certain interests to the detriment of others. It is submitted that the vagueness of the current terms might be viewed as a form of lowest common denominator, sufficiently vague to allow Members to interpret them in way favourable to their own interests or priorities.

In other words, the current provisions of the relevant WTO agreements are likely to remain in their current form. The downside of this result is some form of legal uncertainty. Clarification of the legal regime applicable to PPM measures will mainly come from the Appellate Body case law, through cases that will gradually be brought to the dispute settlement system.

Since case law is likely to have a very important role to play in the clarification of the legal regime applicable to PPM measures, the rules of treaty interpretation and the way they are applied by the Appellate Body have also an obvious importance.

Under Article 3.2 DSU, the dispute settlement system of the WTO serves *inter alia* to clarify the existing provisions of the covered agreements 'in accordance with customary rules of interpretation of public international law'. Within the Vienna Convention on the Law of Treaties, Articles 31 and 32 address the interpretation of treaties. They provide in particular that a treaty shall be interpreted in good faith in accordance with the ordinary meaning to be given to the terms of the treaty in their context and in the light of its object and purpose (Art. 31(1) VCLT).

The rules of treaty interpretation have given rise to many doctrinal disputes,[53] and their detailed analysis is beyond the scope of this study. What can be noted is the manner in which the Appellate Body has taken these rules into consideration. It has, in particular, expressed the view that customary rules of interpretation of public international law

> call for an examination of the ordinary meaning of the words of a treaty, read in their context, and in the light of the object and purpose of the treaty involved. A treaty interpreter must begin with, and focus upon, the text of the particular provision to be interpreted. It is in the words constituting that provision, read in their context, that the object and purpose of the states parties to the treaty must first be sought. Where the meaning imparted by the text itself is equivocal or inconclusive, or where confirmation of the correctness of the reading of the text itself is desired, light from the object and purpose of the treaty as a whole may usefully be sought.[54]

---

[52] See e.g. *supra*, Chaps. 2–4.

[53] See e.g. Sinclair (1984), p. 114; Shaw (2014), pp. 675 f.

[54] *US – Shrimp*, Appellate Body Report, para. 114.

Therefore, the Appellate Body seems to start with the search for the ordinary meaning of the text in the light of the object and purpose of the provision at issue. If this approach does not yield clear results, it is then necessary, in its view, to examine in a second step the object and purpose of the treaty as a whole. The Appellate Body refers thus both to textual and teleological interpretations. Moreover, the Appellate Body interestingly distinguishes between a narrow form of teleological interpretation—in which the relevant object and purpose is that of the applicable provision—and broad form of teleological interpretation, in which the object and purpose is that of the treaty as a whole. The latter should be used if the former gives equivocal or inconclusive results.

When it comes to the main provisions of the GATT and the TBT Agreement examined in this study, it seems obvious that the ordinary meaning of the text, examined in the context of the specific provisions at issue, gives equivocal and inconclusive results.[55] Therefore, a broad form of teleological interpretation is justified.

The GATT and the TBT Agreement are part of Annex 1 of the Marrakesh Agreement and are integral parts of this Agreement.[56] As a result, it logically means, in the view of the present author, that it should be possible, when a broad form of teleological interpretation is relevant, to examine the purpose of the covered agreements as a whole. More specifically, it should mean that in the interpretation of a provision of the GATT or the TBT Agreement, the treaty interpreter should take into account the general context of the rest of these agreements and their object and purpose.

In some cases, the Appellate Body has considered the global context of the covered agreements in its interpretation, for instance when it stated that the TBT Agreement and the GATT had to be interpreted in a 'coherent and consistent manner'.[57] However, despite the findings referred to above, in most of the cases, the Appellate Body has given, in practice, a clear prominent importance in its interpretation of the WTO agreements to the ordinary meaning of the text,[58] without consideration of the broader context of the treaty itself. This constant focus on the textual interpretation, usually based on dictionary definitions, has been criticised.[59]

Unsurprisingly, dictionary definitions and the ordinary meaning of the text are insufficient to achieve a conclusive result, for a number of reasons. First, the concepts used in the relevant provisions of the GATT and the TBT Agreement,

---

[55]The most obvious example is the notion of like products in the GATT and the TBT Agreement, which is examined in details in this book.

[56]See Article II(2) of the Marrakesh Agreement Establishing the WTO.

[57]See *US – Clove Cigarettes*, Appellate Body Report, para. 91.

[58]See e.g. Mavroidis (2008a), p. 446 ff.; Distefano and Mavroidis (2011), p. 755. See also e.g. *US – Shrimp*, Appellate Body Report, para. 115; Weiler (2001), p. 206; Chang (2005), pp. 28 f.

[59]See e.g. Distefano and Mavroidis (2011), p. 757 with further references. See also Mavroidis (2008a), p. 446 ff.

such as the notion of 'like' products, are vague and have no clear 'ordinary' meaning, without sufficient consideration of the context.[60] Second, the differences in the structure of the GATT and the TBT Agreement, in particular the fact that the TBT Agreement does not contain any general exceptions provision,[61] cannot be taken into account simply by relying on the ordinary meaning of the text. Third, the outdated text of Article XX, such as the fact that environmental protection is not mentioned as such in the list of policy goals of the sub-paragraphs,[62] means that the text itself cannot have a decisive role.

Reliance on the text may probably be explained by an effort to guarantee the legitimacy of case law and to avoid appearances of 'judicial activism'.[63] But, in practice, it eventually jeopardises the transparency of the Appellate Body's reasoning and probably the overall legitimacy of case law.

Therefore, it is submitted here that a coherent interpretation of the covered agreements requires the use of a broad teleological approach, in which, in particular, the TBT Agreement and the GATT are viewed as parts of a global set of rules, which needs to be interpreted in a coherent manner. Such an approach could lead to the results developed in the next sections.

9.3   Applying the Existing Provisions While Ensuring Coherence, Legal Predictability and Legitimacy of Case Law: Squaring the Circle

The challenge of defining a coherent regulatory framework for PPM measures on the basis of the relevant rules as they are currently drafted is that the different objectives that the Appellate Body should achieve in its analyses of cases dealing with PPM measures are, at least potentially, partly incompatible. These objectives are, among others, the following:

- ensuring legal predictability;
- finding some balance in the respective interests at stake in a way that undermines neither the internal nor the external legitimacy of the WTO;
- interpreting the existing trade rules in a way that achieves a coherent global regulatory framework for PPM measures, both under the GATT and the TBT Agreement.

A first incompatibility stems from the desire to ensure legal predictability on the one hand and both the 'internal' and 'external' legitimacy of the WTO

---

[60]See Distefano and Mavroidis (2011), p. 759.

[61]See *supra*, 8.2.

[62]See *supra*, 7.3.1.

[63]Of the same view, see Distefano and Mavroidis (2011), p. 758.

on the other.[64] As already pointed out, the vagueness of the relevant provisions opens the door to quite different interpretations,[65] which may schematically be favourable either to WTO Members' regulatory autonomy or to trade liberalisation. Adopting an interpretation that clearly favours one or the other increases legal predictability but may reduce the internal or external legitimacy of the WTO. For instance, the adoption of an exclusively economic approach of like products in GATT Article III may increase legal predictability, and possibly the internal legitimacy of the WTO, but could reduce its external legitimacy since critics could then argue that the Appellate Body is impervious to any public policy considerations in its examination of one of the most important provisions of the GATT.[66]

The objective of ensuring a coherent global framework for PPM measures both under the TBT Agreement and the GATT may represent a difficult challenge since the Appellate Body can only make recommendations on the cases brought before it, without necessarily being able to ensure a global coherence between the relevant provisions of the WTO agreements. Even more importantly, a decision on a particular issue can have consequences on other aspects that are not relevant to the case concerned but that are relevant for the PPM regulatory framework as a whole.

More specifically, one of the most debated issues examined in this book is whether the regulatory purpose should be examined under the GATT non-discrimination provisions or if it is only relevant under GATT Article XX.[67] Depending on whether one focuses on a narrow or large context, a narrow or a broad teleological interpretation results in quite different possible outcomes.

If one focuses on the context of Article III itself, it may be argued that any non-discrimination analysis requires the examination of the regulatory purpose, in order to determine if the contested measure is based on the forbidden criterion of origin or on any other criteria, even though the Appellate Body seems to reject this view.[68] But that would lead to the odd result that WTO Members would have less constraints for, say, an internal sale prohibition based on npr-PPMs applicable to domestic and imported products (subject to GATT Article III:4) than for a labelling requirement based on npr-PPMs, or possibly a technical regulation based on npr-PPMs (subject to the TBT Agreement). Even though the former may generally be considered as more trade restrictive than the latter, measures covered by the TBT Agreement have to comply with a necessity test, even if they are non-discriminatory, whereas there is no such test in Article III of the GATT.

---

[64]On the notions of 'internal legitimacy' (legitimacy *vis-à-vis* trade officials, Secretariat employees, etc.) and 'external legitimacy' (legitimacy *vis-à-vis* constituencies outside the WTO, such as national parliaments, governments, multinational corporations, NGO, citizens, etc.), see Weiler (2001), pp. 191 ff.

[65]See in particular *supra*, 6.5.1 and 7.1.2.

[66]See in particular the arguments made by the *US – Tuna* reports' opponents (*supra* 2.3).

[67]See in particular *supra*, 6.2, 6.3.1.3, 6.4.3.3 and 7.1.

[68]See in particular *supra*, 6.4.3.3.

Hence, the rules applicable to incorporated and unincorporated PPMs should logically be at least similar and not more favourable to the latter. In other words, a result that may seem justified under a narrow teleological approach focusing on the purpose of non-discrimination (examination of the regulatory purpose in Article III) may result in undesired consequences in a broad teleological perspective (more stringent regime for the most trade-restrictive npr-PPMs such as internal sale prohibitions).

In practice, it has been shown that the Appellate Body has rather endorsed an economic definition of the conditions of Article III, without direct consideration of the regulatory purpose,[69] which is mainly examined under Article XX. This view means that many PPM measures must in practice be justified under the conditions of Article XX (when they concern 'like products' and result in less favourable treatment for the group of imported products compared to the group of like domestic products). Such interpretation reduces the differences between the legal regime applicable to PPM measures covered by the TBT Agreement and the GATT since Article XX contains a necessity test and various other conditions in its introductory clause. In this sense, an economic definition of the conditions of Article III may seem justified under a broad teleological interpretation.

Nevertheless, in the view of the present author, if the economic approach applied in Article III arguably enhances the overall coherence of the PPM regime, at the same time it arguably also entails unwarranted consequences: the conditions of Article XX are then applicable to many internal measures regulating the sale of products, which may be viewed as non-discriminatory under a classical non-discrimination test (because they are based not on the foreign origin of the product but on a legitimate criterion). Yet, under an economic analysis of Article III, most of these 'non-discriminatory' measures are subject to the conditions of Article XX, even though it is only in the TBT Agreement that the WTO Members have decided that both discriminatory and non-discriminatory measures must be necessary, while the GATT contains no such rule.[70]

In other words, a broad teleological interpretation could justify both an examination of the regulatory purpose in Article III (in order to respect the fact that non-discriminatory measures do not have to be necessary under the GATT, by contrast to the TBT Agreement) and a rejection of such examination (because otherwise it would mean that the legal regime applicable to PPM requirements falling under the GATT would be more demanding than that applicable to those covered by the TBT Agreement).

It may be tempting for the Appellate Body to keep some legal imprecision in order to avoid clearly favouring one of these alternatives. This may thus explain the hesitation of the Appellate Body in the endorsement of a purely economic approach in Article III.[71] But, in turn, these hesitations reduce legal predictability. It is thus

---

[69]See *supra*, 6.3.1.4.

[70]See *supra*, 6.5.2.2.

[71]See *supra*, 6.3.1.4.

difficult to achieve at the same time coherence (which would suggest that similar regimes should be applicable to PPM measures falling under the TBT Agreement and the GATT), legitimacy (which requires *inter alia* that differences between the relevant provisions must not be ignored) and legal predictability (which implies that the respective legal regimes for PPM measures falling under the TBT Agreement and the GATT should be clear).

Another example of the difficulty to achieve coherence in the way the provisions of the WTO agreements treat PPM measures concerns the relation between Article GATT XX(b) and (g). The evolutionary interpretation applied by the Appellate Body to Article XX(g) means that this sub-paragraph is applicable to living natural resources.[72] But this conversely means that the more lenient 'relating to' test is applicable to the conservation of exhaustible natural resources, while the more demanding necessity test is applicable to the protection of human, animal or plant life or health, which does not seem coherent.[73] If one can be stricter in the examination of the conditions of the chapeau for cases falling under Article XX(g) than for those covered by Article XX(b), it may also result in undesirable results. The chapeau is indeed applicable to all sub-paragraphs, and a strict interpretation of its conditions, for cases examined under Article XX(g), could lead to the same restrictive interpretation for the other sub-paragraphs.[74]

These examples show the difficulty to achieve a coherent regulatory framework for PPM measures and other internal measures in WTO law, without amending the text of the relevant provisions, while ensuring at the same time legal predictability and internal and external legitimacy of the WTO.

9.4   A Regulatory Framework for PPM Measures in WTO Law

9.4.1   The Need for a Flexible Interpretation of Article XX

In brief, it has been shown that distinguishing between legitimate and illegitimate efforts to internalise environmental externalities required a flexible system in order to take into consideration, *inter alia*, the proximity of interests between the regulating country and the environmental situation at stake, as well as the importance of the relevant risks concerned.

On the other hand, the existing text of the relevant WTO provisions is unlikely to be modified or amended in a foreseeable future. Yet they do not always integrate in a coherent fashion. Trade-offs must thus be achieved between overall coherence of the applicable WTO rules, legal predictability and legitimacy.[75]

---

[72]See *supra*, 7.1.1.2.

[73]See *supra*, 7.3.4.3.

[74]See *supra*, 7.3.1.

[75]See *supra*, 9.3.

When it comes to the examination of the regulatory purpose, it has been shown extensively that three different possibilities exist. It may first be taken into account in the context of the national treatment condition examination, either in the 'like products' or in the discriminatory treatment condition analyses, or it may be examined exclusively in the context of the general exceptions of Article XX.[76]

Arguably, taking into consideration that the national treatment clause is a non-discrimination obligation, the most logical place to examine the regulatory purpose is the second option, i.e. in the national treatment discriminatory conditions. It would allow WTO adjudicating bodies to examine if a measure has a discriminatory effect on imported products because of their foreign origin or because of, for instance, their environmental impact.[77]

Such subjective definition of discriminatory treatment has been endorsed by the Appellate Body in the context of Article 2.1 of the TBT Agreement. Yet no equivalent to GATT Article XX exists in the TBT Agreement. The endorsement of a similar definition of discrimination in the context of GATT Article III would raise delicate questions. If the regulatory purpose could justify a discriminatory effect under the national treatment analysis, would Article XX still be available in case of an Article III violation? In that case, what would be the difference in the examination of the regulatory purpose in Article III and in Article XX? It seems difficult to have a coherent system in which the regulatory purpose could be examined both under the non-discrimination clauses and the general exceptions provision.

Some have suggested thus that the examination of the measure's aim should be done in Article III only, without any possibility to invoke Article XX in case of national treatment infringement.[78] But in that case, it would mean that the GATT regime would probably be significantly less burdensome than the TBT rules. All technical regulations, including those based on differences in pr-PPMs, would have to comply with the TBT Article 2.2 necessity test, even when they are non-discriminatory. On the other hand, all internal measures falling under the GATT, including those based on differences in npr-PPMs, would be subject to GATT Article III and could comply with GATT rules even if they are not necessary.[79] The rules of treaty interpretation suggest that the treaty interpreter should not ignore differences in the text of the relevant provisions, including the fact that the GATT national treatment clause does not contain a necessity test. But on the other hand, under a broad teleological interpretation, taking into consideration the aim of overall coherence of the WTO rules,[80] it may also appear inappropriate to

---

[76]See *supra*, 6.2, 6.3.1.3, 6.4.3.3 and 7.1.

[77]See e.g. Horn and Mavroidis (2004), pp. 60 ff.; Pauwelyn (2008), pp. 358 f. and *supra*, 6.4.3.3 (concerning the examination of the regulatory purpose in Article III discriminatory treatment conditions). See also *supra*, 6.3.2.1 (concerning the examination of the regulatory purpose in the likeness analysis).

[78]See Mavroidis (2008b), pp. 249 ff.

[79]See *supra*, 8.1.

[80]See e.g. *US – Clove Cigarettes*, Appellate Body Report, para. 91, in which the Appellate Body stated that the GATT and the TBT Agreement 'should be interpreted in a coherent and consistent manner'.

interpret the GATT rules in a way that implies that WTO Members could adopt measures subject to national treatment more easily than measures falling under the TBT Agreement. It would, for instance, be surprising if WTO Members would have less constraints for an internal sale prohibition applicable to domestic and imported products (subject to GATT Article III:4) than for a labelling requirement (subject to the TBT Agreement).[81] Similarly, it would not seem logical that pr-PPM measures would be subject to more stringent conditions than npr-PPM standards.[82]

In brief, certain aspects of both approaches—examining the regulatory purpose under Article III or under Article XX—are open to criticism. It is, however, difficult to assume in the view of this author that the WTO rules should be interpreted in a way that would result in more burdensome disciplines for less trade-restrictive measures. The substantial reduction of barriers to trade is indeed one of the objectives of the WTO mentioned in the Marrakesh Agreement.

The endorsement of the view that the regulatory purpose must be examined under Article XX and not under Article III has thus, in the view of the present author, the advantage of ensuring a better coherence between the TBT Agreement and the GATT and of avoiding that npr-PPM measures be subject to more lenient rules than pr-PPM standards.

Yet the concept of national treatment should not be extended too much by this interpretation, which may result in overly strict scrutiny for cases of *de facto* discrimination.[83] The fact that the GATT does not require non-discriminatory measures to be necessary should be taken into account. In other words, the search for coherence between the GATT and TBT regimes should not lead to an overly broad definition of discriminatory measures under Article III. A trade-off should be found between safeguarding the essence of the principle of non-discrimination (and the absence of a necessity test under Article III) and ensuring the global coherence of PPM regimes of the TBT Agreement and the GATT.

It is submitted by the present author that this trade-off could be achieved through particular interpretation of all three relevant steps of the analysis of internal regulatory measures.

First, under the 'like products' analysis, the degree of likeness should vary according to the importance of the non-economic interests underlying the measure. The more important these interests are, the closer the competitive relationship between products should be.[84] This would be consistent with the view of the Appellate Body that there are different degrees of likeness and that the width of the 'accordion' of likeness depends in particular on the context and the circumstances that prevail in any given case.[85] However, reliance on the market in the

---

[81]Since the reduction of barriers to trade is an objective of the WTO (See the Preamble of the Marrakesh Agreement).

[82]Cf. e.g. Marceau and Trachtman (2002), p. 861.

[83]See *supra*, 6.4.4.

[84]See *supra*, 6.5.2.1.

[85]See *Japan – Alcohol II*, Appellate Body Report, p. 21.

likeness analysis would mean, in particular in cases of market failures, that in practice it would be difficult for a Member to show that two products with different PPMs would not be 'like'.

Second, in the discriminatory condition analysis, it is submitted that WTO adjudicating bodies should not only examine a possible disparate impact against the group of imported products compared to the group of domestic like products. Evidence showing that the measure has potential or actual protectionist effects should be relevant as well. This analysis should include, as it has been suggested in Chap. 6, a comparison of the actual and potential proportion of domestic and imported goods within, respectively, the disfavoured and favoured categories, the actual and potential respective size of the groups of domestic and imported products and the actual and potential imports from other third-party Members.[86]

Third, since the exclusion of the relevance of the regulatory purpose from the analysis of the conditions of Article III means that many internal measures would have to be justified under Article XX, the present author considers that the conditions of the general exceptions clause themselves should be interpreted in a flexible manner. The objective is to avoid that the GATT as a whole unduly restricts WTO Members' regulatory autonomy, in particular in cases of *de facto* discrimination. Applying the conditions of Article XX in a flexible manner could represent a form of trade-off between the need to take into account intended differences in the GATT and TBT regimes and to ensure minimal coherence between them. It would recognise that the Appellate Body has endorsed a particularly broad definition of discrimination,[87] which subjects to the conditions of Article XX certain origin-neutral measures, which could have been found to be non-discriminatory if a more traditional non-discrimination analysis had been applied.

It is argued here that the flexibility in the application of the conditions of Article XX should be achieved through the application of a varying degree of deference to the regulating Member (i.e., a varying standard of review), depending on the importance of the goal pursued, determined *inter alia* in the light of the proximity of interests, the international recognition of the legitimacy of the regulatory purpose and the importance of the environmental risks at stake.[88]

Several conditions of the relevant provisions could thus be interpreted in the light of the importance of the goal pursued, allowing more regulatory autonomy to WTO Members when the underlying non-economic interests are particularly important and stricter trade disciplines when the proximity of interests is more distant or when the environmental risks at issue are less important.

First, it has already been suggested that the importance of the goal pursued could influence the degree of likeness required under Article III. Second, in the context of Article XX(a) and (b) necessity test, the Appellate Body has endorsed a 'weighing and balancing' approach, under which the more important the interests and values

---

[86]See *supra*, 6.5.2.2.

[87]See *supra*, 6.4.

[88]See *supra*, 7.1.2.2.2.

underlying a measure are, the easier it would be to accept a measure as necessary.[89] As it has been explained in detail above, the reference to the importance of the interests and values at stake should be interpreted as a reference to the applicable standard of review, i.e. the degree of deference shown by the Appellate Body to the regulating Member, which varies depending on the importance of the goal pursued by the measure at issue.[90]

Third, it is argued here that one could build on the case law relating to the necessity test and adopt a similar flexible approach based on the importance of the goal, in the analysis of the introductory clause of Article XX. The conditions of the chapeau, in the view of the Appellate Body, represent an expression of the principle of abuse of right.[91] Logically, whether invoking the general exceptions provision is abusive in a particular case depends, *inter alia*, on the importance of the goal pursued by the contested measure. An abuse of right occurs in particular if a specific right is invoked to achieve other objectives than those that this right aims to protect. In the context of Article XX, relying on the general exceptions provision would be abusive if the main goal pursued by the regulating Member were protectionism, disguised under one of the legitimate objectives listed in this provision. In practice, a measure that achieves a legitimate objective recognised in Article XX may have at the same time some protectionist effects. Whether the invocation of Article XX is abusive in such a case depends *inter alia* on the importance of the legitimate values and interests at stake. The more important the goal is, the higher the threshold at which a measure is qualified as abusive should be set. In other words, the degree to which the conditions of the chapeau are intrusive should depend, *inter alia*, on the importance of the values and interests underlying the contested measure.[92]

Thus, it is submitted that the application of a flexible standard of review depending on the importance of the interests at stake could also be applied to the conditions of the chapeau of Article XX. This would be consistent with the view that these conditions represent a 'line of equilibrium' between the right to invoke an exception under Article XX and the rights of other Members under the different substantive provisions.[93] The importance of the interests and values at stake should thus, in any given case, influence the location of this 'line of equilibrium'. It would be consistent with the view of the Appellate Body that 'the position of the line itself depends on the type of measure imposed and on the particular circumstances of the case'.[94] It should nonetheless be kept in mind, as explained in Chap. 7, that the conditions of the chapeau must not be interpreted as a form of proportionality test. They should merely be viewed as a safeguard against *clear* disequilibrium between the right to invoke the general exceptions provision and the GATT substantive

---

[89] See *Korea – Beef*, Appellate Body Report, para. 162 f. See also *supra*, 7.2.1.1.1.

[90] See *supra*, 7.2.1.2.1.

[91] See *supra*, 7.3.1.

[92] *Idem.*

[93] See *US – Shrimp*, Appellate Body Report, para. 159. See also *supra*, 7.3.1.

[94] *US – Shrimp 21.5*, Panel Report, para. 5.51.

rights since the concept of abuse of right and the terms used in the chapeau clearly refer to *gross* imbalances rather than to a form of balancing.[95]

In brief, WTO adjudicating bodies should admit more or less easily that the application of a measure results in 'arbitrary' or 'unjustifiable' discrimination or in a 'disguised' restriction on international trade, depending on the importance of the goal pursued by the regulating Member.

In the specific context of PPM measures, the importance of the interests and values at stake could in particular be relevant in the examination of the cooperation efforts made by the regulating Member, for the purpose of concluding a multilateral environmental agreement. The importance of these interests and the intensity of the environmental risks at stake should be considered in the examination of whether, for instance, the imposition of a unilateral measure was abusive or seemed justified in the light of these circumstances.[96]

In brief, it is submitted that because the Appellate Body's case law on national treatment subjects most PPM measures to Article XX, a flexible approach of the conditions of these provisions is required. Indeed, under this approach, cases of *de jure* and *de facto* discrimination are both examined under the same conditions. A restrictive approach of the conditions of Article XX may appear to be justified for the former, while a more deferent interpretation may be needed for the latter. The flexibility that must be achieved could stem from the rule that the more important the goal is, the more deferent WTO adjudicating bodies should be in the examination of the conditions of Article XX. That way, Members would have a larger margin for manoeuvre in the design of their facially neutral internal measures pursuing important objectives.

It has been pointed out that the exclusion of any regulatory purpose analysis in the examination of the GATT non-discrimination provision is, as such, criticisable.[97] However, endorsing a coherent discrimination analysis would conversely lead to incoherencies in the overall PPM regime under the GATT and the TBT Agreement.[98] The approach consisting in analysing the regulatory purpose only under Article XX is not problem-free but might seem justifiable in the view of the present author, provided that Article XX is interpreted in a flexible enough manner, depending on the nature of discrimination (*de jure* or *de facto* discrimination) and on the importance of the values and interests underlying the contested measure. It would thus represent a trade-off between legitimacy (avoid an overly broad restrictive interpretation of the GATT in cases of 'mere' *de facto* discrimination) and coherence (avoid important differences in the legal regime applicable to pr-PPMs under the TBT Agreement and to npr-PPMs under the GATT).

It might be objected that such approach would lead to legal unpredictability since evaluating the importance of the goal implies inevitably some subjectivity and

---

[95]See *supra*, 7.3.1.

[96]See *supra*, 7.3.4.1.2.

[97]See *supra*, 6.5.2.

[98]See *supra*, 9.3.

since it might be difficult to determine precisely, in advance, how the importance of the goal pursued would influence WTO adjudicating bodies' analysis of the conditions of Article XX. One would also be quite far from the 'bright-line rule' that the product-process distinction represented in the view of some.[99]

It should, however, be pointed out that this 'bright-line rule' has already been largely blurred by current case law since the dichotomy between forbidden process standards and permitted product standards has not been endorsed by the Appellate Body.[100] Moreover, the suggested approach is not a 'rule of thumb'. Indeed, it builds on the one hand on existing case law and tries to apply more generally an approach that has already been endorsed by the Appellate Body in the context of the necessity test.[101] Flexibility also stems naturally from the concept of necessity and abuse of right. Furthermore, the existing framework formed by the criteria of Article XX would still be applicable. Adopting a flexible approach simply means that the verification that a measure is justified under Article XX may be more or less intense depending on the circumstances of the case, but the same conditions would still be applicable. In that respect, there is probably a greater legal predictability with such approach than with a subjective approach to the conditions of Article III.[102]

In any event, the need for a flexible approach to the analysis of Article XX conditions is, in the view of the present author, a direct consequence of the rejection of the subjective approach to the conditions of Article III, which means that both cases of *de facto* and *de jure* discrimination have to be examined under the same conditions, and which is itself justified to guarantee some minimal coherence in the global regime of the GATT and TBT Agreement. The ideal solution in terms of legal predictability, and perhaps in terms of legitimacy, would probably be to modify the texts of the WTO agreements. It could, for instance, be clearly indicated that the existence of discriminatory effects is sufficient for an Article III violation. It would thus be clear that the regulatory purpose is only relevant in the context of general exceptions provision, which would also clearly confirm that Article XX can be viewed not as a narrowly defined set of exceptions but rather as the last step of internal measures' review. This would arguably enhance the recognition of the importance of Article XX in finding an appropriate balance between GATT obligations and WTO Members' regulatory autonomy. It could also be agreed in a revised treaty that the TBT Agreement covers all PPM technical regulations, including those based on differences in npr-PPMs.

But as it has been pointed out, it seems quite unlikely for the time being that WTO Members could find a consensus to modify the relevant provisions.[103]

---

[99]See Jackson (2000), p. 303.

[100]See e.g. *supra*, 9.1.

[101]See *supra*, 7.2.1.

[102]See the arguments made by the opponents to the subjective definition of likeness, *supra*, 6.3.2.1.2.

[103]See *supra*, 9.2.

The improvement of the PPM regime will thus mainly depend on the interpretation of the relevant provisions by WTO adjudicating bodies.

The flexible approach suggested here certainly has drawbacks. Certain of its aspects are open to criticism. In particular, it must be conceded that it cannot fully guarantee legal predictability and legitimacy of case law. But in the light of the existing rules of the GATT and the TBT Agreement, this approach is probably the next best thing to reconcile the different conflicting objectives that the WTO adjudicating bodies should try and achieve. Because of the vagueness of the texts and of the lack of coherence between the different applicable provisions of the WTO agreements, it seems essential to give some margin for manoeuvre to WTO adjudicating bodies in the analysis of the conditions of Article XX to be able to apply the same conditions to all the degrees of discrimination severity that may occur, without unduly favouring either trade liberalisation or WTO Members' regulatory autonomy.

9.4.2   The Importance of the Conditions of the Chapeau

Within the flexible approach suggested in the previous subsection, it must be pointed out that the conditions of the chapeau will in practice play an essential role, in the light of the Appellate Body's case law.

Even if it has been shown that PPM measures could in theory comply with the conditions of Article III, most PPM measures will have, in practice, to be justified under Article XX. Two physically identical products could, in theory, be regarded as 'unlike' if consumers treat them as 'unlike'. Yet if state intervention in the form of a trade measure is required, it probably means that consumers consider that such products are 'like'.[104] Moreover, the discriminatory treatment conditions of Article III have been given a broad definition by the Appellate Body,[105] which increases the likelihood that internal measures be regarded as discriminatory under the national treatment clause.

Article XX will thus often be applied in practice in cases of PPM trade measures. When it comes to Article XX's two-tiered analysis, the reports concerning environmental trade measures have shown that the Appellate Body tends to show deference to the regulating Member under the sub-paragraphs and to apply a stricter scrutiny under the chapeau. Indeed, in most disputes relating to environmental trade measures in which the defendant has lost, the Appellate Body held that the measure had complied with the sub-paragraphs but not with the conditions of the chapeau.

For instance, in the *US – Shrimp* case, the core of the measure was upheld, and the United States only had to make certain modifications so as to comply with the chapeau (in particular, the adoption by the exporting Member of measures

---

[104]See e.g. *supra*, 6.3.1.4.4.

[105]See *supra*, 6.4.4.

comparable in effectiveness had to be allowed; similar negotiation efforts with all the importing Member's trading partners had to be made).[106] In the *Brazil – Tyres* case, one of the main flaws of the contested measure under the chapeau analysis was the MERCOSUR exemption, i.e. an exception to the import ban that allowed imports of retreated tyres from MERCOSUR countries.[107] The Appellate Body accepted, on the other hand, the necessity of the import ban and its life and health protection objective. Likewise, in the *EC – Seal Products* report, the import ban was considered as necessary to protect public morals. The Appellate Body held, however, that the exception to the import ban, i.e. the Inuit communities' hunts exemption, did not comply with the conditions of the chapeau.[108] Finally, in the *US – Tuna II (Mexico)* case, the main problem with the contested measure was not that it denied the dolphin-safe label to tuna caught in the ETP by setting on dolphins but rather that the US measure could not guarantee that tuna caught outside the ETP did not result in any harmed or killed dolphin.[109]

In all these cases, WTO adjudicating bodies did not require changes that would deny any possibilities for the importing Member to pursue its environmental objective as such. Rather, they required the elimination of certain specific aspects of the measure that were in its view discriminatory or not in line with the environmental objective sought.

In theory, the Appellate Body has held that the chapeau is an application of the principle of *abus de droit* and that it had to achieve a line of equilibrium between the right to invoke Article XX and the substantive rights under the GATT.[110] In the light of the structure and the text of Article XX, and if one focuses on the idea of a possible *abuse* of right, it would appear logical to hold that a measure that complies with the sub-paragraphs is *in principle* justified under Article XX but that it may *exceptionally* be nonetheless considered as abusive under the chapeau in the light of certain specific circumstances. In this view, a situation in which a measure complies with the sub-paragraphs but not with the chapeau should be the exception rather than the norm and not the other way round.

In practice, however, the Appellate Body has shown generally some deference towards the regulating state under the sub-paragraphs for the choice of the environmental goal pursued and for that of the appropriate measure to achieve this goal. On the other hand, the interests of exporting Members, and of trade liberalisation

---

[106]See *US – Shrimp*, Appellate Body Report, para. 161 ff. See also *supra*, 7.3.2.2.

[107]See *Brazil – Tyres*, Appellate Body Report, para. 217 ff.

[108]See *EC – Seal Products*, Appellate Body Report, para. 5.316 ff.

[109]See e.g. *US – Tuna II (Mexico)*, Appellate Body Report, para. 297. See also *US – Tuna II (Mexico) 21.5*, Panel Report, para. 7.591 f. and *US – Tuna II (Mexico) 21.5*, Appellate Body Report, para. 7.359 (in which the Appellate Body indicated that the crucial aspect of the assessment of the contested measure was to determine if the regulatory distinctions applicable to the different fisheries could be explained by the differences in the relative risks associated with different methods of fishing for tuna in different areas of the ocean).

[110]See *supra*, 7.3.1.

more generally, have been taken into account mainly through the application of the conditions of the chapeau.

Moreover, the different cases mentioned above seem to show that in practice, under the chapeau, the Appellate Body does not really examine the way the measure is applied[111] but focuses rather on certain specific discriminatory aspects of a measure that is provisionally justified under the sub-paragraphs. As a consequence, it seems in the view of the present author that the chapeau has more a role of 'fine tuning' of the design of the measure rather than a role of defence against clear abuses of the way the measure is applied.

So why has the Appellate Body given such importance to the conditions of the chapeau? Is such approach justified?

In the context of the PPM debate, it has been argued shortly after the Appellate Body's *US – Shrimp* report that the 'real question' was 'if one abandons the product/process doctrine, how does one draw an appropriate line to prevent abuses?'[112] Part of the answer is that under current jurisprudence, most PPM measures require a justification under Article XX. But more precisely, the main instrument by which PPM measures are disciplined in practice is the chapeau of Article XX.

In this context, WTO adjudicating bodies will tend to show some deference to the regulating Member in the choice of the environmental goal pursued, and possibly in the means-ends relationship between this goal and the measure chosen to achieve it. This explains why a measure perceived as 'extraterritorial' or as 'unilateral' may still comply with the sub-paragraphs.[113] The main disciplines are thus in general those of the chapeau. It seems that, in this second step of Article XX's two-tiered analysis, WTO adjudicating bodies will examine whether the different aspects of the measure, including its possible 'anomalies' (exceptions to the main trade restriction such as those of the *Brazil – Tyres* and *EC – Seal Products* cases, differential treatment such as that of the *US – Tuna II (Mexico)* case, etc.), are justifiable.

This approach may be seen as the way that enables the Appellate Body to find a balance, in particular in cases of PPM measures, between the right of a Member to invoke the general exceptions (deferent interpretation of the sub-paragraph) and the protection of certain competing interests of other Members (strict application of the conditions of the chapeau). Instead of prohibiting all PPM measures, the Appellate Body applies a flexible approach that enables a much more precise analysis of the justifiability of the measure and that takes into account a much wider spectrum of competing interests. It is submitted by the present author that this approach has

---

[111]In the Appellate Body's view, the sub-paragraphs are concerned with the design of the measure, whereas the chapeau concerns the way the measure is applied. See *US – Gasoline*, Appellate Body Report, p. 22; *US – Shrimp*, Appellate Body Report, para. 118. See also *supra*, 7.3.1.

[112]Jackson (2000), p. 304.

[113]See *supra*, 7.1.2.

introduced the main disciplines that replace, in practice, those that stemmed from the product-process distinction.

If this jurisprudence certainly represents a more balanced approach to the examination of PPM measures, and other trade measures more generally, it should be pointed out that it is not entirely faithful to the text of the chapeau. As already indicated, the conditions of the introductory clause of Article XX, which refer to the notion of *abus de droit*, are drafted in a way that refers to clear excess or abuses, by using the words 'unjustifiable' or 'arbitrary' discrimination and 'disguised' restriction on international trade. As a result, it could be argued that the structure of Article XX should mean that the main test is that of the sub-paragraphs and that the chapeau is only a rather exceptional protection against clear abuses in the application of the measure. It may thus seem questionable whether Article XX and the chapeau, more specifically, are really conceived so as to make the chapeau the main and crucial step in the analysis of the general exceptions provision.

Yet, in the view of this author, the Appellate Body's approach to the conditions of the chapeau must be viewed as another form of trade-off that had to be found between the text of the GATT (and more specifically of its chapeau, which suggest that Article XX's main test is that of the sub-paragraphs), the outdated wording of the sub-paragraphs (the problem of the overlap between sub-paragraphs [b] and [g], which contain different means-ends relationship)[114] and the need to guarantee a flexible approach and to ensure the legitimacy of case law (avoid prohibiting all PPM measures while guaranteeing certain protection against protectionist abuses).[115] Hence, in the view of the present author, this approach represents another instance in which the Appellate Body had to 'square the circle'. If this approach may not be entirely convincing from a strict legal viewpoint, it may be seen as a trade-off between competing objectives that WTO adjudicating bodies have to achieve, in the absence of any real perspectives to modify the text of the agreements.

The risk of this approach is, however, to transform the search for a 'line of equilibrium' in an 'appropriateness' test, in which WTO adjudicating bodies would substitute their assessment of the policy choices made by the regulating Member for all the aspects of the measure. Such result would, in the view of the present author, be clearly inconsistent with the text of the chapeau. The question should not be whether the regulating Member could have taken another policy option that would have been more consistent with the goal pursued or that would have taken competing interests into account in a better way. It should be rather whether the discriminatory aspects of the measure examined under the chapeau are so questionable that they result in 'unjustifiable' or 'arbitrary' discrimination.[116]

For instance, in the *US – Tuna II (Mexico)* case, the real question was not, in the view of this author, whether it would have been more appropriate to avoid all

---

[114]See e.g. *supra*, 7.3.4.3. See also 7.3.1.

[115]See *supra*, 9.3.

[116]See also *supra*, 7.3.1.

incidental killings of dolphins caused by fishing methods used to capture tuna both within and outside the ETP,[117] i.e. if the contested measure was the most appropriate way to achieve the environmental objective. Under the chapeau, the test should rather be whether the difference in the requirements applicable within and outside the ETP resulted in a qualified form of discrimination ('arbitrary' or 'unjustifiable'), which could clearly not be explained by the difference in the probabilities of dolphin injury or mortality.

In the context of the *EC – Seal Products* case, it could be wondered if the Inuit communities' hunts exemptions really resulted in 'unjustifiable' or 'arbitrary' discrimination. The absence of this exemption could have been viewed as a more consistent way to apply the import ban so as to protect public morals. Yet it is questionable whether providing for certain limited exceptions to safeguard certain very specific interests, in that case those of certain small communities that were particularly dependent on the products concerned and thus vulnerable to the import ban, clearly resulted in an 'unjustifiable' or 'arbitrary' discrimination.

There should be thus some restraint in the way the conditions of the chapeau are applied so as to be consistent with the terms of the chapeau. The chapeau should only reject the aspects of a measure that result in a qualified form of discrimination, but not all the aspects that may have a discriminatory dimension.

9.4.3   Applying the Conditions of Article XX: Particularities for PPM Measures

The flexible approach suggested above would constitute a general framework that could guide the analysis of PPM measures. On a more specific level, the nature and characteristics of these measures would also imply various particular factors that would be relevant in the examination of Article XX's conditions.

The restrictive approach for PPM measures applied by some GATT and WTO panels was based in particular on the exclusion of 'extraterritorial' and 'unilateral' PPM measures, which had the effects of rejecting probably all controversial PPM measures (i.e., those in which there was no territorial link between the importing country and the environmental situation at issue and those that were not based on a multilateral environmental agreement). These clear categories of 'illegal' PPM measures have not been endorsed by the Appellate Body, which has applied a much more flexible approach.[118]

---

[117]In this case, the Panel considered in its *US – Tuna 21.5* report that the less stringent certification requirements for tuna caught outside the ETP (certification could be made by the captain of the ship, while within the ETP, an independent observer had to be present on the ship) could not guarantee that no dolphin had been harmed or killed (see Panel Report, para. 7.586 ff).

[118]See *supra*, 7.1.2.1.

If case law does not contain any basis for the exclusion *per se* of the justifiability of PPM measures, the application of the conditions of Article XX does result in certain particularities for PPM measures.

(i) The nexus between the importing Member and the environmental risk at stake: what is left of the 'extraterritoriality' issue in current case law is that a 'sufficient nexus' should exist between the importing state and the environmental situation harmed by the PPM at stake.[119] The Appellate Body has not explicitly defined this 'sufficient nexus'. But in the context of the TBT Agreement, it accepted that an importing country could choose to avoid that the products sold in its territory encourage the use of environmental-unfriendly PPMs in the exporting country, even though no territorial nexus existed in this case.[120] The clear tendency is thus that the 'sufficient nexus' issue should not represent a significant hurdle for PPM measures in the future.[121]

Nonetheless, in the view of the present author, while PPM measures are not subject to the rules on extraterritorial jurisdiction, not all environmental externalities should necessarily justify restrictive import measures.[122] The proximity of interests between the importing state and the environmental situation concerned should have some influence in the analysis of the justifiability of PPM measures.[123] In other words, the intensity of the nexus should be taken into account in the assessment of the importance of the interests and values at stake, which influences in turn the applicable standard of review.[124]

It should be pointed out as well that it may not be possible to exclude in principle that an importing Member could have a legitimate interest in environmental goods located wholly in the exporting country, even when no transboundary physical externalities occur. Nonetheless, the risk of disguised protectionism is higher in such cases, and the potentially less intense proximity of interests should be taken into account in the examination of the conditions of Article XX.[125]

(ii) The nexus between the products concerned and the environmental risks at stake: a second aspect that subsists in case law and that may be viewed as a component of the 'extraterritoriality' issue in a large sense is the fact that PPM measures, since they target foreign activities without any direct application of the process standards prescribed, may have a varying degree of efficiency in the achievement of the environmental goal pursued and may require changes in the practices of foreign producers, which has been viewed by some as 'coercive' effects.[126]

---

[119]See *US – Shrimp*, Appellate Body Report, para. 133 and *supra*, 7.1.2.1.2.

[120]See *US – Tuna II (Mexico)*, Panel Report, para. 7.401 and 7.425 and *supra*, 8.2.

[121]See *supra*, 7.1.2.1.

[122]See *supra*, 7.1.2.2.

[123]*Idem.*

[124]See *supra*, 9.4.1. See also *supra*, 7.1.2.2.

[125]See *supra*, 7.1.2.2.

[126]See *supra*, 5.2 and 7.1.2.2.

Even though an importing country cannot directly intervene to modify environmentally harmful practices in the exporting country, the Appellate Body has recognised in the *EC – Seal Products* case that the imposition of an import ban on seals killed in a cruel way could contribute to global demand reduction in seal products.[127] In this case, there was a direct nexus between the banned products and the morally objectionable externality, which means that reduction of demand in the importing country could indeed result, all other things being equal, to a reduction of global demand and thus to a decrease in the number of inhumanly killed seals. Similarly, a close nexus exists, for instance, between an imported product and greenhouse gases emitted during its manufacturing process (how-produced standard).[128]

This nexus can also be more indirect. For example, in the *US – Shrimp* case, the United States had initially prohibited the importation of shrimp from countries that had not adopted essentially the same turtle protection scheme than the United States (country-by-country restriction), which could be referred to as a 'government-policy standard'.[129] As a result, even shrimps caught in a way that did not harm turtles could not be exported to the United States if they had been harvested in a country that did not require all its producers to use turtle-friendly shrimp harvesting methods.[130] For these products, the only nexus between them and the environmental harm concerned was that these shrimps had been harvested in such country. This nexus is thus much less intense, and the possible efficiency of the measure is more doubtful since it affects all the shrimp products of that country, even those harvested with the desired PPMs.

The absence of a close nexus between the products to which the measure applies and the environmental externalities at stake may have an influence on the examination of the conditions of Article XX. First, it may be questionable whether such measure may comply with the necessity test, which requires at least some contribution of the measure to the achievement of the goal. It might be at least more difficult to comply with the necessity test since the Appellate Body considers that the greater is the contribution of the measure to the achievement of the goal pursued, the more easily a measure might be considered to be necessary.[131]

Second, the absence of a close nexus between the products and the environmental harm at issue may be relevant in the context of the chapeau as a form of unjustifiable or arbitrary discrimination. For instance, in the *US – Shrimp* case, one of the main elements on which the findings of unjustifiable or arbitrary discrimination were based was precisely the fact that the United States had only allowed the importation of shrimp from countries that had adopted essentially the

---

[127]See *EC – Seal Products,* Panel Report, para. 7.459; Appellate Body Report, para. 5.225. See also *supra,* 7.2.1.1.3.

[128]See Charnovitz (2002), p. 67.

[129]*Ibid.*

[130]See *supra,* 7.3.2.2.2.

[131]See *Korea – Beef,* Appellate Body Report, para. 162 f. See also *supra,* 7.2.1.1.1.

same turtle protection regulatory scheme.[132] Such 'rigid and unbending' require-ment, which did not examine the policies in place in the exporting countries for the protection of sea turtles, was deemed to constitute arbitrary discrimination.

(iii) Unilateralism and international negotiations: when it comes to the possible 'unilateral' character of PPM measures, it may not, as such, justify a conclusion that such measures are unjustifiable. The Appellate Body has indeed acknowledged that many measures falling under Article XX could be unilateral measures.[133] This does not mean that the 'unilateralism' issue does not have any relevance in the exami-nation of the conditions of Article XX. In the *US – Shrimp* case, the Appellate Body focused, in the unjustifiable or arbitrary discrimination analysis, on the way in which the importing Member had conducted international negotiations to conclude a multilateral environmental agreement.[134]

It remains more debated whether Article XX implies a self-standing duty to negotiate before adopting a unilateral PPM trade measure.[135] As such, the text of the introductory clause of Article XX does not contain any clear basis for such duty. But this study submits that one should keep in mind that trade measures are only indirect instruments to achieve the desired changes in foreign production practices, i.e. second-best instruments. Thus, the absence of any negotiation efforts prior to the adoption of a restrictive environmental trade measure might be viewed, except in cases of environmental emergency, as a sign that the measure may not be motivated exclusively by environmental objectives but also by protectionist goals. In such cases, it may be difficult to comply with the 'disguised restriction on international trade' criterion.[136]

(iv) Flexibility: a further requirement that may have particular implications for PPM measures is the need to leave enough flexibility to the exporting Members in the choice of the instruments adopted in order to achieve the environmental goal set by the importing Member. This requirement may influence first the necessity test. It has been shown that, in the *Brazil – Tyres* case, the Appellate Body applied a deferent standard of review and considered that only the measures that could achieve Brazil's tyres non-generation objective were deemed to be relevant alter-natives, even if other types of measures, such as improved tyre disposal techniques, could achieve the same level of health protection.[137] In other words, in that case, the Appellate Body expressed the view that the importing Member could choose its goal *lato sensu* (choice of environmental or health policy) and not only its goal *stricto sensu* (protection of health to a certain level).[138]

---

[132]See *supra*, 7.3.2.2.2.
[133]See *US – Shrimp*, Appellate Body Report, para. 121. See *supra*, 7.1.2.1.2.
[134]See *supra*, 7.3.2.2.3.
[135]See *supra*, 7.3.4.1.1.
[136]See *supra*, 7.3.4.1.2.
[137]See *supra*, 7.2.1.1.2.
[138]*Idem.*

Similarly, in the *US – Shrimp* case, the importing Member had initially required that the exporting Members had to achieve the same *lato sensu* goal, i.e. they had to adopt essentially the same regulatory scheme than that of the United States, even if other measures could have achieved the same level of turtle protection. However, in that case, the Appellate Body held that this feature of the measure bore heavily on its conclusion that the application of the measure resulted in unjustifiable or arbitrary discrimination.[139]

Thus, it seems clear that when it comes to PPM measures, the importing Member may prescribe only the level to which its environmental protection objective has to be attained but not the particular measures that have to be adopted to achieve it. Otherwise, the measure could fail the necessity test, if other less trade-restrictive instruments exist to achieve the same level of protection, and would probably not comply with the conditions of the chapeau.

(v) The interests of developing countries: the last main particularity that the conditions of Article XX may imply for PPM measures is the way in which the importing Member may have to take the interests of developing countries into consideration. One of the main arguments invoked by developing countries against PPM measures was their 'extraterritorial' character, which made them, in their view, unjustifiable.[140] The Appellate Body has arguably largely rejected this argument, at least as a sole basis for invalidating a PPM measure.[141]

Therefore, the interests of developing countries must be taken into consideration through special and differential treatment rather than through an exclusion of PPM measures. The numerous references to special and differential treatment for developing countries in the TBT Agreement illustrate this trend.[142]

In the context of GATT Article XX, the chapeau of this provision expressly mentions the need to examine the differing conditions that may occur between the different countries concerned.[143] The importance for the legitimacy of the WTO system of considering the needs of developing countries in cases of PPM measures should not be underestimated. Yet it seems more logical and legally justified to take these needs into account through special and differential treatment rather than to warrant an exclusion of a whole category of measures, without any clear textual or teleological basis to do so.

---

[139]See *supra*, 7.3.2.2.2.

[140]See in particular *supra*, 2.1.

[141]See *supra*, 7.1.2.1.2.

[142]See *supra*, 8.5.

[143]See *supra*, 7.3.4.2.

Chapter 10
Summary

After a brief introduction in *Chapter 1*, the main traditional arguments that have been invoked against the use of PPM measures are presented in *Chapter 2*.

The first argument is the principle of states' sovereignty in a large sense. In this context, it includes prescriptive jurisdiction and the principle of permanent sovereignty over natural resources. It has been argued that PPM measures conflict with the sovereignty of the exporting state to regulate activities in its own jurisdiction, i.e. that PPM measures require a justification on the basis of the rules on extraterritorial jurisdiction. It has also been contended that process standards represent a form of interference in the internal affairs of the exporting state and that they conflict with the principle of permanent sovereignty over natural resources.

A second frequent argument against PPM measures is the incompatibility with the world trading system. It has been claimed that authorising trade restrictions based on differences in PPMs would represent a 'slippery slope', which could lead to proliferation of trade barriers without restraint. In that view, the use of PPM measures entails the risk of impeding the proper functioning of the world trading system, which is based on the theory of comparative advantages, which itself relies on differences in the regulation of factors of production, including environmental regulations.

Chapter 3 focuses on the reasons based on economic theory to justify the regulation of production methods. It explains that state intervention is justified in particular to correct market failures. A first form of market failure is externalities. When it comes to international ecosystems, externalities may take the form of physical transborder spillovers, non-physical externalities and moral externalities. A state cannot take measures to address directly the sources of environmental externalities located beyond its jurisdiction. The internalisation of these externalities requires thus either international cooperation or the adoption of trade restrictions.

A second form of externalities is public goods, which are non-excludable and have non-rivalrous consumption. Certain public goods have impacts indivisibly

© Springer International Publishing AG 2018
D. Sifonios, *Environmental Process and Production Methods (PPMs) in WTO Law*,
European Yearbook of International Economic Law 3,
DOI 10.1007/978-3-319-65726-4_10

spread across the entire globe (global public goods), such as a stable climate or biodiversity. Other goods shared by all states are non-excludable but have a rivalrous consumption (common pool resources), such as fish stocks of the high seas. The non-excludable nature of these goods means that all states can free ride on the efforts of others to protect a global public good or to preserve common pool resources, without any possibility to be denied by other countries the enjoyment of those goods (the so-called free rider problem). The dominant strategy of states is thus non-cooperation, which is a classical prisoner's dilemma situation. Cooperation failures may in turn lead eventually to the 'tragedy of the commons', i.e. to the destruction of common pool resources or to the loss of global public goods. When international cooperation fails, the sole possibility for the states willing to avoid environmental damage is to adopt trade restrictions against the products of non-complying countries.

Since trade measures represent in certain cases the only available instrument to sanction free-riding or non-complying states, the prohibition of environmental PPM measures would increase the risks of cooperation failures in the management of international environmental issues, insofar as it would deprive states of any solution to address the free rider problem.

Chapter 4 analyses different principles and concepts of international environmental law relevant to the PPM debate. Sustainable development is one of the objectives mentioned in the Preamble of the WTO Agreement. It is usually recognised that sustainable development is based on the objective of integrating economic, social and environmental policies. Various principles are generally considered to be part of sustainable development, such as the principle of sustainable use, the elimination of unsustainable patterns of production and consumption, the principle of common but differentiated responsibilities and cooperation. These principles show that PPM measures may be necessary to eliminate unsustainable production methods. Nevertheless, international environmental law encourages states to take the particular interests of developing countries into account and to favour international cooperation over unilateral measures to address these problems.

On the other hand, international environmental law acknowledges the principle of permanent sovereignty over natural resources, which is sometimes invoked as an argument against the use of PPM measures. However, various principles and concepts of international environmental law have emerged, which increasingly restrict the unfettered nature of permanent sovereignty over natural resources. They tend to impose limits on the possibilities of states to exploit their natural resources without any constraints. One can refer in particular to the principles of transboundary harm prevention, equitable use and common concern. These principles show that foreign states may have a legitimate interest in the consequences of the internal environmental policies of a particular country, even in the absence of transboundary physical effects.

Chapter 5 addresses the customary international law rules on prescriptive jurisdiction so as to determine the extent to which these rules are relevant in the PPM debate. The Permanent Court of International Justice held in the *Lotus* case that states could exercise jurisdiction as long as no rule of international law forbade it. This view has been largely debated, and it has often been argued that international law as it currently stands requires rather that a state must be able to rely on a particular jurisdictional basis, such as territoriality or nationality, in order to exercise prescriptive jurisdiction.

In the context of PPM measures, this debate would only be relevant if one admits that trade measures must be categorised as an exercise of extraterritorial jurisdiction. It has been argued by the present author that this view should be rejected since PPM measures do not directly regulate a foreign conduct but merely prescribe the conditions on the entry of products produced abroad into the importing state. Moreover, there is no right to trade in international law, which means that a state is entitled to adopt an embargo to prohibit all imports from a particular country. If a state has the right to prohibit the importation of all goods of a particular origin, it can *a fortiori* restrict the importation of some of those goods only. A trade measure may nonetheless be unlawful if it interferes with a right of the exporting state, granted in an international agreement, such as the WTO agreements.

A related issue is whether PPM measures can amount to a violation of the principle of non-interference in internal affairs. Since the 1960s, developing countries have sought to obtain, mainly through UN General Assembly Resolutions, international recognition that economic coercion constituted a breach of the principle of non-intervention. These resolutions are, however, non-binding. In the *Nicaragua* case, the ICJ held that the complete economic embargo adopted by the United States against Nicaragua, aimed explicitly at putting pressure on the Sandinista government in order to achieve political changes in Nicaragua, did not represent a breach of the principle of non-intervention, i.e. an illegal form of coercion. States have, in other words, the right to use their import policies to put pressure on foreign governments to adopt political changes in their countries. Thus, in principle, PPM measures do not amount to coercion in a legal sense and do not represent violations of the principle of non-interference.

Chapter 6 examines the possibilities for PPM measures to comply with the national treatment clause of GATT Article III. It has been debated whether PPM measures fall within the ambit of Article III or whether they are rather covered by the more restrictive conditions of Articles II and XI. It was concluded that case law has favoured a broad interpretation of the coverage of the national treatment clause, which should be endorsed. The disciplines set out in Article III apply thus in principle to PPM measures. It has been much debated in academic writings whether PPM measures could comply with the conditions of Article III or whether they might only be justified on the basis of Article XX. These debates have focused, in particular, on whether two physically identical products could be considered as unlike on the basis of differences in their production methods. They have also, to a lesser degree, addressed the question of whether the legitimate objective of a measure could be relevant in the examination of the discriminatory treatment conditions of Article III.

The definition of like products has fluctuated in case law. A first approach applied by GATT 1947 panels is the objective approach, which focuses in particular on products' physical characteristics and has eventually resulted in the product-process distinction applied in the first two *US – Tuna* reports. At the end of the GATT era, two panel reports applied a completely different theory, known as the *aim-and-effects* test, which resulted in a much more narrow definition of like products. Under the WTO Dispute Settlement Body, the Appellate Body rejected the *aim-and-effects* test and endorsed a third approach. It gave an economic definition to the concept of 'like products', which essentially consists in determining the nature and extent of the competitive relationship between and among products in the marketplace. However, this approach does not represent a pure economic definition of like products since the elasticity of demand, determined on the basis of econometric instruments, is not the decisive criterion. The Appellate Body has also relied on assumptions about how a reasonable and informed consumer would behave.

The definition of likeness has given rise to intense debates in academic writings. Despite the Appellate Body's rejection of the *aim-and-effects* test, some scholars continue to argue that the 'like products' analysis should comprise an analysis of the regulatory purpose underlying the measure. Their objective is to examine if two products are accorded differing treatment because they have different national origin or because they differ from the viewpoint of a legitimate regulatory objective, such as regulating the sale of environmentally harmful products. Other scholars, who maintain that this subjective definition of likeness would unduly restrict the scope of the national treatment clause and implies legal unpredictability, have opposed this theory.

Among those who support the economic approach endorsed by the Appellate Body, some have argued in favour of a pure economic definition of likeness, in which like products would be assessed mainly by an analysis of the elasticity of demand, established through econometric instruments. Proponents of this approach argue that it would allow a more objective assessment of likeness. These arguments have not remained uncontested. It has been pointed out that data on the elasticity of demand could be missing or contradictory and that consumers could in certain cases distinguish products for reasons incompatible with the GATT objectives.

The consequences of the different definitions of like products for the legality of PPM measures have then been examined in Chap. 6. It was shown that the objective definition of likeness excluded the possibility that differences in PPMs could render two products unlike. The *aim-and-effects* test, on the other hand, would justify such differentiation. Finally, under the economic approach endorsed by the Appellate Body, it is in theory possible that physically identical products with different PPMs be considered as unlike, if consumers treat them as unlike. It is, however, likely that in most cases in which state intervention seems necessary, a market failure exists, which means that consumers do consider two products that ought to be distinguished as 'like'.

When it comes to the discriminatory conditions of Article III, the cases that have given rise to the most intense debates are instances of *de facto* discrimination. It is usually recognised that discriminatory treatment is determined through the application of a discriminatory impact test, which compares the treatment of the group of imported products to that of the group of domestic like products. The Appellate Body does not require, however, an examination of actual trade effects of the measure, which has been criticised. It is sufficient that the measure results in a detrimental impact on the competitive conditions among products. It has been debated whether, once such detrimental impact is established, a regulating Member may still show that these effects are explained not by the foreign origin of imported products but by a legitimate criterion, such as environmental impact. The Appellate Body has recently rejected this view, which results in a very large definition of discrimination, since neither protectionist effects nor protectionist intent is relevant for the Appellate Body.

It has been argued that the ideal consumer test lacks transparency. It may probably be explained by the will of the Appellate Body to show deference to the regulating Member when the non-economic objective of the measure is particularly important. However, in such cases, it would be more coherent to recognise explicitly that health or environmental concerns could be part of the relevant evidence that panels have to examine in the likeness analysis. The importance of the values underlying the goal pursued could also influence the intensity of the competitive relationship between products that is required for two products to be considered as like. More generally, when it comes to whether or not likeness should be defined as a pure economic notion, it seems necessary to apply not only a narrow teleological approach but also broad one.

As regards discriminatory treatment, the exclusion of any trade effects test may result in a too large scope to national treatment, which remains a non-discrimination obligation. This is especially true if like products are given a pure economic definition. It has been argued that all circumstances showing that the measure has actual or potential protectionist effects should be examined. The non-discrimination nature of national treatment should also imply that the regulatory purpose should be examined in the discriminatory conditions analysis. The Appellate Body has rejected this view because the regulatory purpose is examined under Article XX.

The extent to which the GATT represents a significant restriction to WTO Members' regulatory autonomy thus depends also on the interpretation of the conditions of Article XX. The definition of the conditions of national treatment *de lege ferenda* cannot be examined in isolation from the context of the GATT as a whole.

The general exceptions provision, GATT Article XX, has been analysed in detail in *Chapter 7*. To justify a measure under Article XX, the regulating Member must show that the contested measure falls within one of the policy goals listed in the sub-paragraphs and complies with the means-ends relationship specified therein. As far as environmental trade measures are concerned, sub-paragraphs (b) and (g) are particularly relevant. Under Article XX(b), which concerns protection of human, animal or plant life or health, the defending Member must show the existence of a risk to human, animal or plant life or health and establish that the objective of the measure is to reduce such risk. Under Article XX(g), the defending Member must demonstrate that the objective of the measure is the conservation of exhaustible natural resources. Based on an evolutionary interpretation of this concept, the

Appellate Body has held that this provision covers both living and non-living resources. Even though Article XX does not refer to measures aimed at the protection of the 'environment', the combined scope of XX(b) and (g) may in principle cover most environmental trade measures.

In the *US – Shrimp* case, the Appellate Body referred to a possible 'implied jurisdictional limitation' in Article XX. It did not elaborate, for reasons of judicial economy, since there was in this case, in its view, a sufficient nexus between the sea turtles and the United States, insofar as sea turtles were migratory animals and were present at some moment of their lives in US territorial waters. It is debatable whether this 'sufficient nexus' was a reference to the rules on extraterritorial jurisdiction. Recent evolution of case law in the context of GATT Article XX(a) and TBT Article 2.2 seems to reject this view. It has been further argued in this book that the commitments made by WTO Members in the GATT do not make the rules on extraterritorial jurisdiction applicable to trade measures. Any possible 'implied jurisdictional limitations' are those resulting from the GATT commitments themselves.

WTO Members have accepted, in principle, to conduct trade with their trading partners on the basis of differences in internal regulations, as long as they are based on relevant comparative advantages but not when the cost advantages are based on the production of negative externalities affecting the importing country, shared resources, global ecosystems or global public goods. Each of these categories has been examined in detail. It has been shown that, in all of these cases, the importing country may have a sufficient legitimate interest in the environmental situation at stake to justify, in principle, the adoption of a restrictive trade measure. There seems to be a trend in case law to reduce the importance of the extraterritoriality issue. It has been argued in Chap. 7 that the attention could shift towards an analysis of the proximity of interests between the regulating Member and the environmental situation at stake. It has been submitted by this study that this proximity of interest may influence in turn the degree of deference showed by WTO adjudicating bodies in the examination of the conditions of Article XX.

When it comes to the means-ends relationship required by Article XX(b), i.e. that the measure be 'necessary' to protect human, animal or plant life or health, the Appellate Body has endorsed a 'weighing and balancing' test, which takes into account the importance of the interests and values protected by the measure, the contribution of the measure to the achievement of its objective and its trade restrictiveness. Certain elements of case law could be interpreted as meaning that this weighing and balancing test amounts to some form of proportionality test. However, the Appellate Body also confirmed that WTO Members have the right to choose the level of health protection they consider appropriate. This right is not compatible with a proportionality test since the least trade-restrictive measure to achieve the chosen level of protection could in theory be considered as disproportionate.

It was argued that when the Appellate Body has held that a contested measure had to make a 'material' contribution to the achievement of the goal pursued, it did not mean that the health or environmental benefits of the measure had to outweigh the trade costs, i.e. that a proportionality test had to be applied. It rather meant that the measure must first pass a 'suitability' test to be necessary. The 'weighing and balancing' test should not be viewed as a proportionality test. It was further submitted in Chap. 7 that the Appellate Body has applied a more deferent approach in the different elements of the necessity analysis, when the interests and values underlying the measure were particularly important. This may influence the examination of the efficiency of the measure, its suitability to achieve the environmental goal pursued, the definition of the level of protection, the assessment of existing alternatives, the analysis of whether these alternatives are less trade restrictive and achieve the same level of protection, etc. The application of a varying degree of scrutiny depending on the importance of the goal pursued could introduce desirable flexibility in the examination of the necessity test.

The assessment of the importance of the goal pursued should focus not on the importance of the protected values as such but on the intensity of the health or environmental risks at stake. The analysis should include a consideration of the extent of environmental damage, the intensity of the threat, the importance of the ecosystem or species at issue, the rate at which degradation occurs, the urgency of intervention, etc. This flexibility contrasts with the narrow interpretation of Article XX applied by certain GATT 1947 panels and may compensate the strict interpretation of the national treatment obligation.

When it comes to PPM measures, the proximity of interests between the regulating country and the environmental situation at issue is one of the elements that may be taken into account in the assessment of the importance of the goal pursued. Even if PPM measures are only second-best instruments to address the source of environmental harm located abroad, the Appellate Body has recognised in the context of Article XX(a) that a restrictive measure could reduce the domestic and global demand for harmful products and thus contribute to the achievement of the objective pursued, which is a required element of the necessity test. A similar reasoning may arguably be applied in the context of Article XX(b).

As regards the 'relating to' test in Article XX(g), pre-WTO panel practice has applied a strict approach, in which it was interpreted as meaning 'primarily aimed at' conservation of exhaustible natural resources. The Appellate Body has applied a less strict rational connection standard, which assesses whether the means are directly and reasonably connected to the aim pursued. The 'relating to' test requires a less intense means-ends relationship than the necessity test, which indicates that it might be easier to comply with sub-paragraph (g) than with sub-paragraph (b). However, it can be argued that the test of the two respective provisions might actually converge, if one considers the cumulative effects of the sub-paragraphs and the chapeau of Article XX.

Chapter 7 also analyses in detail the conditions of the chapeau of Article XX. The function of the chapeau is to prevent the abuse of a Member's right to invoke an exception to the GATT substantive rules. In the view of the Appellate Body, the chapeau should allow the determination of a line of equilibrium between the right of a Member to invoke an exception and the rights of the other Members under the other provisions of the GATT. It was contended by the present author that the concept of the 'line of equilibrium' must not be interpreted as a reference to a proportionality test. Indeed, the chapeau only sanctions clear abuses of the right to invoke the general exceptions provision. The importance of the values and interests at stake may be part of the relevant elements for locating the line of equilibrium in a specific case, i.e. for assessing whether the invocation of Article XX appears to be abusive under the relevant circumstances.

The chapeau refers to the existence of a form of 'discrimination'. When a regulating Member seeks to justify a measure that infringes the non-discrimination provisions of Articles I and III, the Appellate Body has considered that different discrimination standards apply. The chapeau addresses situations in which some additional discriminatory characteristics exist, such as the presence of discriminatory intent.

The Appellate Body has taken various elements into account in its examination of whether a measure results in 'unjustifiable or arbitrary' discrimination. It must comply with requirements of transparency, predictability, due process and basic fairness. It is also necessary to provide enough flexibility to the exporting country, in the way it may implement domestically the PPM standard to be adopted. An importing Member cannot require exporting countries to enact essentially the same regulatory scheme as that in force in the importing Member. It is, however, possible to require the adoption of a regulatory programme comparable in effectiveness. An importing Member may thus, in certain circumstances, *unilaterally* impose an environmental objective to exporting states. It is, however, debated whether WTO Members have the duty to negotiate with their trading partners an international environmental agreement before enforcing a unilateral trade restriction. The Appellate Body has clearly held that WTO Members had to comply with the principle of non-discrimination in the way they conduct such international negotiations. But it has not specified if unilateral measures are prohibited in the absence of prior negotiation efforts.

Under the chapeau, trade measures must not be applied in a manner that would constitute a means of unjustifiable or arbitrary discrimination 'between countries were the same conditions prevail'. The importing state must take into consideration differing conditions between the importing and the exporting Members and between different exporting Members. As far as environmental trade measures are concerned, differing conditions possibly include, in particular, differences in the characteristics of the local environment, differences in the level of development and differences in the historical responsibility for the environmental problems at issue.

The last criterion of the chapeau, the 'disguised restriction on international trade', refers, in the view of several panel reports, both to the intention to pursue trade-restrictive objectives and to the actual protectionist effects. These criteria may serve to determine if the measure results in a trade restriction that is disguised to conceal the protection of the domestic industry under a legitimate objective of one of the sub-paragraphs.

Chapter 7 then makes a critical analysis of three main issues. It remains unsettled if the chapeau contains a self-standing duty to negotiate a multilateral environmental agreement before resorting to unilateral trade restrictions. A preference exists both in international environmental law and in WTO law for multilateral solutions. Yet unilateral measures are not prohibited in any of these fields. Prohibition of unilateral measures would also entail risks of increasing cooperation failures in the management of global environmental issues, leading to the 'tragedy of the commons'. As far as the conditions of the chapeau of Article XX are concerned, the 'unjustifiable or arbitrary discrimination' cannot be interpreted as a basis for a general duty to negotiate. It can only apply when some form of discrimination in the conduct of negotiations occurred. It was submitted that the failure to engage in international negotiations before imposing a unilateral trade measure could, however, amount, in certain cases, to a 'disguised restriction to international trade'. The most efficient measures are those addressing the source of the problem, through cooperation. If the importing state does not attempt to achieve first-best solutions, it might be an indication that its primary motivation is the protection of its domestic producers. But it should be still possible to show that unilateralism was nonetheless justified in the particular circumstances of the case, for instance when intervention is urgent.

A second issue that was discussed is the manner in which specific interests of developing countries may be taken into consideration in the analysis of Article XX. Developing countries have often strongly opposed the use of PPM measures, arguing that such measures conflict with their economic and developmental priorities, that they do not have the same responsibility in the current global environmental problems than developed states and that they do not have the same technical and financial means to address these problems. The Preamble of the WTO, as well as various provisions of the covered agreements, refers to the need to take into account the specific needs of developing countries.

In the context of Article XX, the chapeau refers to unjustifiable or arbitrary discrimination *between countries where the same conditions prevail*. Discrimination can occur not only when countries where the same conditions prevail are treated differently but also when countries where *different* conditions prevail are treated the *same*. These requirements may imply that the importing state has to take into consideration differences in the characteristics of the environment of the different countries concerned (sink capacities of ecosystems, abundance of natural resource stocks, share of the costs for providing a global public good, etc.), economic development, technical and financial means, as well as differences in the respective responsibilities for the environmental harm caused. Taking these circumstances into account may require to accept that certain countries, in particular the poorest ones, may not have to achieve the same level of environmental protection than the importing country. It may also mean that, in certain cases, the importing country should provide technical and financial assistance. The provision of rules adapted in particular to the level of development of different countries would be a way to implement the principle of common but differentiated responsibilities, which is usually seen as being part of sustainable development.

This study has submitted that the 'disguised restriction on international trade' criterion could also be a textual basis allowing, in the analysis of Article XX, the consideration of developing countries' interests. It was argued that the failure to take into account differing conditions that prevail in exporting countries and the difficulties that the implementation of PPM standards may cause, in particular in developing countries, could be seen as an indication that the importing state's primary motivation is to achieve not environmental conservation but protection of its domestic producers. Although there is no duty to provide assistance to developing countries under Article XX, failure to do so, in particular when it leads to major compliance or implementation difficulties for developing countries, could appear as an element to take into account in the analysis of the disguised restriction on international trade criterion.

Finally, regarding the differences in the means-ends relationship in Article XX(b) and (g), it was argued that the 'disguised restriction on international trade' condition could allow some convergence in the applicable disciplines, through the cumulative effects of the sub-paragraphs and the chapeau. The analysis of whether a measure results in disguised restriction on international trade requires consideration of protectionist intent and effects. On the other hand, the function of the chapeau is to draw a line of equilibrium between the right to invoke Article XX and the substantive rights under the GATT. It was submitted by the present author that the concept of the 'line of equilibrium' could be understood as a reference to the degree of scrutiny applicable in each case, which varies according to the importance of the goal. Thus, the more important is the goal, the more protectionist effects should be tolerated and the more difficult it should be to conclude that the actual objective of the measure is 'concealed beneath deceptive appearances', i.e. that the invocation of the general exceptions provision is abusive. Thus, some of the considerations made in relation to the criterion of the 'importance of the goal' used by case law in the assessment of whether a measure has complied with the necessity test might also be relevant to a certain extent in the context of measures justified by sub-paragraph (g), through the criterion of the 'disguised restriction on international trade'.

Chapter 8 analyses the Technical Barriers to Trade (TBT) Agreement. This agreement covers pr-PPMs, both for technical regulations and mandatory labelling requirements. It covers as well npr-PPM labelling requirements. It has been debated whether technical requirements relating to npr-PPM requirements also fall within the TBT Agreement. It was concluded that it was not the case and that such measures are subject to the disciplines of the GATT.

TBT Article 2.1, which is a non-discrimination obligation, has given rise to similar debates as those that have prevailed in the context of the GATT national treatment obligation. With respect to the definition of *like products*, the Appellate Body rejected the subjective definition of like products applied by the *US – Tuna II (Mexico)* Panel. It endorsed an economic definition of likeness based on the examination of the four traditional likeness criteria. The Appellate Body pointed out, however, that the regulatory purpose of the measure could have an indirect role in the like products analysis, to the extent that it was reflected in the products competitive relationship.

When it comes to the definition of *less favourable treatment*, the Appellate Body has endorsed a subjective approach, which is different from that applicable to GATT Article III:4. It has noted that in the TBT Agreement, there is no general exceptions clause equivalent to GATT Article XX. Yet, in both contexts, it is necessary to strike a balance between trade liberalisation and WTO Members' regulatory autonomy. While this balance is found through the combined application of Articles III and XX in the context of the GATT, it has to be achieved through the application of Article 2.1 itself, in the context of the TBT Agreement. Therefore, a finding of violation of TBT Article 2.1 requires that (i) a *detrimental effect* on the group of imported products compared to the group of domestic like products exists, (ii) there is a *genuine relationship* between the measure at issue and the adverse impact on competitive opportunities for imported products, (iii) this detrimental impact on imports *stems exclusively from a legitimate regulatory distinction.*

TBT Article 2.2 introduces a generally applicable necessity test, applicable both to discriminatory and non-discriminatory measures, by contrast to the GATT regime, in which Article XX(b) necessity test is not applicable to non-discriminatory measures. TBT Article 2.2 does not set out a closed list of legitimate objectives but only refers to several examples of legitimate objectives. The Appellate Body has applied a similar 'weighing and balancing' approach as that endorsed under GATT Article XX, which consists in evaluating different factors that include (i) the degree of contribution made by the measure to the legitimate objective at issue, (ii) the trade restrictiveness of the measure and (iii) the nature of the risks at issue and the gravity of consequences that would arise from non-fulfilment of the objective(s) pursued by the Member through the measure.

In the context of the TBT Agreement, the extraterritoriality issue was not addressed by the Panel or the Appellate Body in the *US – Tuna II (Mexico)* case, even though there was no territorial nexus between the regulating Member (the United States) and the environmental situation at issue. It was accepted that it was legitimate to make efforts to ensure that the United States' market was not used to encourage fishing fleets to catch tuna in a manner that adversely affected dolphins. Thus, the measure was arguably seen as territorial in nature.

The TBT Agreement gives an important role to international standards. Where technical regulations are required and international standards exist, Members have to use them, except when they are ineffective or inappropriate (Art. 2.4 TBT). Moreover, a technical regulations based on international standards is rebuttably presumed not to create any unnecessary obstacle to international trade (Art. 2.5 TBT). In the context of the PPM debate, the importance given to international standards can be seen as a response to the particular concerns that exist when a PPM measure is imposed unilaterally by the importing state. Particular circumstances would have to exist to justify a 'unilateral' technical regulation, such as the fact that existing international standards are ineffective or inappropriate.

The interests of developing countries are taken into account in the context of the TBT Agreement through different provisions that set out special and differential treatment for developing countries. These provisions introduce, in particular, adaptation periods, requirements of technical assistance and advice and, in some cases, obligations of more favourable treatment. The TBT Committee has the ability to grant upon request specified and time-limited exceptions for obligation under the TBT Agreement. These exceptions do not allow, however, developing countries not to comply with the relevant standards and thus do not address the difficulties that developing countries might have in meeting technical standards applied by developed countries. Moreover, the TBT Agreement clauses concerning special and differential treatment remain primarily soft law. By contrast, GATT Article XX requires the importing Member to take into account differing conditions that occur between the different countries concerned, which may represent a more extensive obligation to take the particular situation of developing countries into account.

When it comes to the relation between the TBT Agreement and the GATT, and the question whether the obligation laid down in these two agreements might be cumulative, it was argued in Chap. 8 that if a measure complies with the TBT Agreement but not with the GATT, the TBT Agreement should prevail. Conversely, a measure is in violation of WTO law if it fulfils the conditions of the GATT but not those of the TBT Agreement.

Chapter 9 contains a critical analysis of the PPM legal regime *de lege lata* and *de lege ferenda*. Due to the various evolutions of case law, one may ask what remains of the product-process distinction. It has been shown that the main bases of the product-process distinction have been rejected by WTO adjudicating bodies. *First*, the Appellate Body has implicitly accepted that PPM measures are covered by Article III and that they are not exclusively subject to the more stringent disciplines of Articles II and XI. *Second*, the Appellate Body has shown that differences in PPMs are not necessarily excluded from the likeness analysis, as long as they are reflected in consumers' preferences. *Third*, a strict exclusion of 'extraterritorial' PPM measures under Article XX has been rejected. It is enough if a 'sufficient nexus' exists between the importing state and the environmental situation at stake. It has been accepted, in the context of the TBT Agreement, that the absence of any territorial nexus between the importing Member and the environmental resources at issue was not necessarily relevant, as long as it could be recognised that it was legitimate for the importing state to ensure that its market was not used to encourage environmentally harmful practices. *Fourth*, unilateral PPM measures that prescribe the adoption of a particular conduct abroad are not per se GATT inconsistent. In the view of the Appellate Body, conditioning access to a Member's domestic market on whether exporting Members adopt policies unilaterally prescribed by the importing Member may be a common aspect of measures falling within the scope of the Article XX exceptions. Negotiation efforts may be necessary in certain circumstances, but the unilateral character of a PPM measure is not, as such, sufficient to render a measure unjustifiable. *Fifth*, it has been established that the TBT Agreement covers pr-PPM technical regulations but also certain unincorporated PPM measures, i.e. mandatory labelling requirements based on differences in npr-PPMs.

Thus, not much remains of the product-process distinction. There are no rigid dichotomies left between permissible product standards (or pr-PPMs) and impermissible process standards. The fact that a measure deals with npr-PPMs does not render such measure illegal under WTO law. It only means that compliance with the relevant conditions (likeness analysis, conditions of the chapeau of Article XX, etc.) may be more demanding or require particular efforts.

It was further argued in Chap. 9 that the strict dichotomy between permissible products standards and impermissible process standards was not justified, both under textual and teleological interpretations. On the other hand, the unconstrained use of PPM measures should be avoided since process standards are likely to conflict with competing trade and developmental interests. It is thus necessary to define criteria that can be used to distinguish between legitimate and illegitimate PPMs. WTO law should at least allow, in principle, state interventions aimed at the internalisation of externalities affecting the importing country. Disciplining PPM measures requires a flexible system, which may allow some form of balancing between these different interests and takes into consideration the proximity of interests between the importing Member and the environmental situation at stake. This objective could be achieved through an amendment of trade rules, aimed at clarifying the criteria disciplining the use of PPM measures. Since it is quite unlikely that WTO Members may agree on any modification of existing trade rules, clarification of the legal regime applicable to PPM measures will probably come mainly from the practice of WTO adjudicating bodies.

One may, however, ask if the role of WTO adjudicating bodies does not amount to trying to square the circle. They indeed have to achieve multiple and partly competing objectives, such as ensuring coherence of the PPM legal regime, legal predictability, as well as the internal and external legitimacy of case law. Clarification of the legal regime applicable to PPM measures may enhance legal predictability. But if it clearly favours either trade liberalisation or WTO Members' regulatory autonomy, the adoption of clear interpretation may reduce either the internal or external legitimacy of the WTO. Moreover, ensuring a coherent global regime for PPM measures falling under the GATT, on the one hand, and under the TBT Agreement, on the other, requires certain interpretations of the relevant provisions that seem questionable, when they are examined as such. For instance, dismissing the relevance of the regulatory purpose in a non-discrimination analysis such as GATT Article III seems, as such, open to criticism. Yet by subjecting thus many regulatory measures to the conditions of GATT Article XX, such interpretation reduces the differences between the legal regime applicable to PPM measures falling under the TBT Agreement and that applicable to the measures subject to the GATT. In brief, on the basis of existing rules, which do not always integrate in a coherent fashion, WTO adjudicating bodies need to make some trade-offs between coherence of the global legal regime applicable to PPM measures (consistency of the respective GATT and TBT regimes), legal predictability and legitimacy.

These trade-offs could be made through the adoption of a flexible approach to the interpretation of the relevant provisions of the GATT. This flexibility could be achieved through the application of a varying degree of deference to the regulating Member (i.e., a varying standard of review), depending on the proximity of interests and on the importance of the environmental risks at stake. This approach could build on the necessity test case law, in which the Appellate Body has held that the more important the goal is, the easier it is to accept that it is necessary. Several conditions of the relevant provisions could thus be interpreted in the light of the importance of the goal pursued, namely the concept of 'like products' (intensity of the competitive relationship between products), the necessity test of Article XX and the conditions of the chapeau (line of equilibrium, 'arbitrary' or 'unjustifiable' character of discrimination, 'disguised' restriction on international trade, extent of cooperation efforts to conclude a multilateral environmental agreement, etc.). This approach could allow more regulatory autonomy to WTO Members when the underlying non-economic interests are particularly important and stricter trade disciplines when the proximity of interests is less intense or when the environmental risks at issue are less important.

This flexible approach would be a first general way to find the balance between legitimate and illegitimate PPM measures. The specificities of PPM measures would also mean that the relevant conditions of Article XX imply that additional elements discipline the use of PPM measures. *First*, a 'sufficient nexus' between the importing Member and the environmental situation at stake should exist. Recent case law suggests that this criterion should often not be a sufficient reason to deny any justifiability to a PPM measure. It may, however, be one of the crucial elements in the determination of the proximity of interests and thus in the applicable standard of review. *Second*, a nexus should also exist between the products at issue and the environmental risks at stake. Hence, it might be difficult to justify a trade restriction based on a 'government policy standard' when it results in a trade restriction that is also applicable to products that comply with the PPM standard. *Third*, WTO Members should in principle make cooperation efforts in view of concluding a multilateral environmental agreement before applying unilateral environmental trade measures. The absence of any prior negotiation efforts could amount, in the light of the specific circumstances of the case, to a disguised restriction on international trade. *Fourth*, PPM measures must be designed in a way that leaves sufficient flexibility to exporting countries in the way they wish to implement the environmental objective to be achieved. WTO Members may decide the level of protection to be attained in producing countries but, in principle, cannot impose the means to achieve it. *Fifth*, WTO Members must take into account the different conditions that may prevail in exporting countries. The particular interests of developing countries may be particularly relevant in this respect. It might be necessary to consider the respective means and responsibilities of the developed and developing Members concerned.

Bibliography

Afilalo, Ari/Foster, Sheila, "The World Trade Organization's Anti-Discrimination Jurisprudence: Free Trade, National Sovereignty, and Environmental Health in the Balance", 15 *Georgetown International Environmental Law Review* (2003) 633-676

Akehurst, Michael, "Jurisdiction in International Law", 46 *British Yearbook of International Law* (1972/1973) 145-257

American Law Institute, *Restatement of the Law, Third, Foreign Relations of the United States*, American Law Institute, St Paul Minn. 1987

Anderson, Belina, "Unilateral Trade Measures and Environmental Protection Policy", 66 *Temple Law Review* (1993) 751-784

Appleton, Arthur E., *Environmental Labelling Programs: Limitations pursuant to General International Law, the UNCED Instruments, and the WTO*, PhD thesis, The Graduate Institute, Geneva 1997 [cit. Appleton (1997a)]

Appleton, Arthur E., "GATT Article XX's Chapeau: A Disguised 'Necessary' Test ?: The WTO Appellate Body's Ruling in *United States – Standards for Reformulated and Conventional Gasoline*", 6(2) *RECIEL* (1997) 131-138 [cit. Appleton (1997b)]

Appleton, Arthur E., "Shrimp/Turtle: Untangling the Nets", 2(3) *Journal of International Economic Law* (1999) 477-496

Appleton, Arthur E., "Private Standards and Labelling Schemes and the TBT", in Thomas Cottier *et al.* (eds), *International Trade Regulation and the Mitigation of Climate Change: World Trade Forum*, Cambridge University Press, Cambridge 2009, 131-151

Atapattu, Sumudu A., *Emerging Principles of International Environmental Law*, Transnational Publishers, New York 2006

Axelrod, Robert M., *The Evolution of Cooperation*, Basic Books, New York 1984

Bagwell, Kyle/Mavroidis, Petros C./Staiger, Robert W., "It's a Question of Market Access", 96 (1) *The American Journal of International* Law (2002) 56-76

Barrett, Scott, "The Strategy of Trade Sanctions in International Environmental Agreements", 19 (4) *Resources and Energy Economics* (1997) 345-361

Barrett, Scott, *Environment and Statecraft: The Strategy of Environmental Treaty-Making*, Oxford University Press, Oxford/New York 2003

Barrett, Scott, *Why Cooperate? The Incentive to Supply Global Public Goods*, Oxford University Press, Oxford 2007

Barstow Magraw, Daniel/Hawke, Lisa D., "Sustainable Development", in Daniel Bodansky *et al.* (eds), *The Oxford Handbook of International Environmental Law*, Oxford University Press, Oxford 2007, 613-638

© Springer International Publishing AG 2018
D. Sifonios, *Environmental Process and Production Methods (PPMs) in WTO Law*,
European Yearbook of International Economic Law 3,
DOI 10.1007/978-3-319-65726-4

Bartels, Lorand, "Article XX of GATT and the Problem of Extraterritorial Jurisdiction", 36 (2) *Journal of World Trade* (2002) 353-403

Bartels, Lorand, " The Chapeau of the General Exceptions in the WTO, GATT and GATS Agreements: a Reconstruction", 109 *American Journal of International Law* (2015) 95-125

Baslar, Kemal, *The Concept of the Common Heritage of Mankind in International Law*, Kluwer Law International, The Hague 1998

Beyerlin, Ulrich, "Different Types of Norms in International Environmental Law: Policies, Principles and Rules", in Daniel Bodansky *et al.* (eds), *The Oxford Handbook of International Environmental Law*, Oxford University Press, Oxford 2007, 425-448

Bhagwati, Jagdish, "Trade and the Environment: The False Conflict?" in Durwood Zaelke *et al.* (eds), *Trade and the Environment: Law, Economics, and Policy*, Vol. 1, Island Press, Washington D.C. 1993, 159-223

Bhagwati, Jagdish, *In Defense of Globalization*, Oxford University Press, Oxford 2004

Bhagwati, Jagdish/Mavroidis, Petros C., "Is Action against US Exports for Failure to Sign the Kyoto Protocol WTO-legal?", 6(2) *World Trade Review* (2007) 299-310

Biermann, Frank, "Common Concern of Humankind": The Emergence of a New Concept of International Environmental Law, 34(4) *Archiv des Völkerrechts* (1996) 426-481

Bierman, Frank, "The Rising Tide of Green Unilateralism in World Trade Law, Options for Reconciling the Emerging North-South Conflict", 35(3) *Journal of World Trade* (2001) 421-448

Birnie, Patricia/Boyle, Alan/Redgwell, Catherine, *International Law and the Environment*, 3rd ed., Oxford University Press, Oxford 2009

Bodansky, Daniel, "What's So Bad about Unilateral Action to Protect the Environment?", 11 (2) *European Journal of International Law* (2000) 339-347

Bodansky, Daniel, "Legitimacy", in Daniel Bodansky *et al.* (eds), *The Oxford Handbook of International Environmental Law*, Oxford University Press, Oxford 2007, 704-723

Bodansky, Daniel/Brunnée, Jutta/Hey, Ellen, *The Oxford Handbook of International Environmental Law*, Oxford University Press, Oxford 2007

Böhringer, Christoph, *Controlling Global Warming: Perspectives from Economics, Game Theory and Public Choice*, Edward Elgar, Cheltenham 2002

Boisson de Chazournes, Laurence, "Unilateralism and Environmental Protection: Issues of Perception and Reality of Issues", 11(2) *European Journal of International Law* (2000) 315-338

Bowles, Samuel, *Microeconomics: Behaviour, Institutions, and Evolution*, Princeton University Press, New York 2004

Bowman, Michael, "Environmental Protection and the Concept of Common Concern of Mankind", in Malgosia Fitzmaurice *et al.* (eds), *Research Handbook on International Environmental Law*, Edward Elgar, Cheltenham 2010, 493-518

Bown, Chad P./Trachtman, Joel P., "*Brazil – Measures Affecting Imports of Retreated Tyres*: A Balancing Act", 8(1) *World Trade Review* (2009) 85-135

Bronckers, Marco/McNelis, Natalie, "Rethinking the 'Like Product' Definition in GATT 1994: Anti-Dumping and Environmental Protection", in Thomas Cottier and Petros C. Mavroidis (eds), *Regulatory Barriers and the Principle of Non-Discrimination in Trade Law*, University of Michigan Press, Ann Arbor 2000, 345-385

Broude, Tomer/Levy, Philip I., "Do You Mind if I Don't Smoke? Products, Purpose and Indeterminacy in *US – Measures Affecting the Production and Sale of Clove Cigarettes*", 13(2) *World Trade Review* (2014) 357-392

Brown Weiss, Edith, "The Rise and Fall of International Law", 69 *Fordham Law Review* (2000) 345-372

Brownlie, Ian, "Legal Status of Natural Resources in International Law (Some Aspects)", 162 *Recueil des Cours* (1979) 245-318

Brownlie, Ian (ed. by James Crawford), *Brownlie's Principles of Public International Law*, 8th ed., Oxford University Press, Oxford 2012

Brunée, Jutta, "International Environmental Law: Rising to the Challenge of Common Concern?", 100 *ASIL Proceedings* (2006) 307-310

Brunnée, Jutta, "Common Areas, Common Heritage, and Common Concern", in Daniel Bodansky *et al.* (eds), *The Oxford Handbook of International Environmental Law*, Oxford University Press, Oxford 2007, 550-573

Bürgenmeier, Beat, *Economie du développement durable*, De Boeck, Bruxelles 2005

Carreau, Dominique/Juillard, Patrick, *Droit international économique*, 5th ed., Dalloz, Paris 2013

Cassese, Antonio, *International Law*, 2nd ed., Oxford University Press, Oxford 2005

Center for International Environmental Law (CIEL) *et al.*, *Amicus Brief to the Appellate Body on United States – Import Prohibition of Certain Shrimp and Shrimp Products*, Center for International Environmental Law, 1999

Chambers, Paul/Kohn, Robert, "Environmental Barriers to Trade: The Case of Endangered Sea Turtles", 9(1) *Review of International Economics* (2001) 123-132

Chang, Howard F., "An Economic Analysis of Trade Measures to Protect the Global Environment", 83 *Georgetown Law Journal* (1995) 2131-2213

Chang, Howard F., "Towards a Greener GATT: Environmental Trade Measures and the Shrimp-Turtle Case", 74 *Southern California Law Review* (2000) 31-48

Chang, Howard F., "Environmental Trade Measures, the Shrimp – Turtle Rulings and the Ordinary Meaning of the Text of the GATT", 8 *Chapman Law Review* (2005) 25-51

Charnovitz, Steve, "Encouraging Environmental Cooperation Through the Pelly Amendment", 3 (1) *Journal of Environment and Development* (1994) 3-28 [cit. Charnovitz (1994a)]

Charnovitz, Steve, "Environmental Trade Sanctions and the GATT: An analysis of the Pelly Amendment on Foreign Environmental Practices", 9(3) *American University Journal of International Law and Policy* (1994) 751-807 [cit. Charnovitz (1994b)]

Charnovitz, Steve, "Free Trade, Fair Trade, Green Trade: Defogging the Debate", 27 *Cornell International Law Journal* (1994) 459-525 [cit. Charnovitz (1994c)]

Charnovitz, Steve, "The Moral Exception in Trade Policy", 38 *Virginia Journal of International Law* (1998) 689-745

Charnovitz, Steve, "The Law of Environmental 'PPMs' in the WTO: Debunking the Myth of Illegality", 27(1) *Yale Journal of International Law* (2002) 59-110

Charnovitz, Steve, "The WTO's Environmental Progress", 10(3) *Journal of International Economic Law* (2007) 685-706

Chi, Manjiao, "'Exhaustible Natural Resource' in WTO Law: GATT Article XX(g) Disputes and Their Implications", 48(5) *Journal of World Trade* (2014) 939-966

Choi, Won Mog, *"'Like Products' in International Trade Law: Towards a Consistent GATT/WTO Jurisprudence*, Oxford University Press, Oxford 2003

Condon, Bradly J., "GATT Article XX and Proximity-of-Interest: Determining the Subject Matter of Paragraphs b and g", 9 *UCLA Journal of International Law and Foreign Affairs* (2004) 137-162

Condon, Bradly J., *Environmental Sovereignty and the WTO: Trade Sanctions and International Law*, Transnational Publishers, Ardsley 2006

Condon, Bradly J., "Climate Change and Unresolved Issues in WTO Law", 12(4) *Journal of International Economic Law* (2009) 895-926

Conrad, Christiane R., *Processes and Production Methods (PPMs) in WTO law: Interfacing Trade and Social Goals*, Cambridge University Press, Cambridge 2011

Cooter, Robert/Ulen, Thomas, *Law and Economics*, Pearson/Addison-Wesley, Boston 2008

Cooreman, Barbara, *Global Environmental Protection Through Trade: A Systematic Approach to Extraterritoriality*, Edward Elgar, Cheltenham 2017

Common, Mick/Stagl, Sigrid, *Ecological Economics: An Introduction*, Cambridge University Press, Cambridge 2005

Conconi, Paola/Voon, Tania, "*EC – Seal Products*: The Tension between Public Morals and International Trade Agreements" 15(2) *World Trade Review* (2016) 211-234

Cosbey, Aaron, *Border Carbon Adjustment*, Trade and Climate Change Seminar, June 18-20 June 2008, Copenhagen, Denmark (https://www.iisd.org/pdf/2008/cph_trade_climate_border_car bon.pdf)

Cosbey, Aaron, "The Trade, Investment and Environment Interface", in Shahrukh Rafi Khan (ed.), *Trade and Environment: Difficult Choices at the Interface*, Zed Books, London/New York 2002, 7-16

Cosbey, Aaron/Mavroidis, Petros C., "Heavy Fuel: Trade and Environment in the GATT/WTO Case Law", 23(3) *RECIEL* (2014) 288-301

Cottier, Thomas/Matteotti-Berkutova, Sofya, "International Environmental Law and the Evolving Concept of 'Common Concern of Mankind'", in Thomas Cottier *et al.* (eds), *International Trade Regulation and the Mitigation of Climate Change: World Trade Forum*, Cambridge University Press, Cambridge 2009, 21-47

Cottier, Thomas/Mavroidis, Petros C., "Regulatory Barriers and the Principle of Non-Discrimination in WTO Law: An Overview", in Thomas Cottier and Petros C. Mavroidis (eds), *Regulatory Barriers and the Principle of Non-Discrimination in World Trade Law*, The University of Michigan Press, Ann Arbor 2000, 3-10

Cottier, Thomas/Oesch, Matthias, *International Trade Regulation*, Staempfli/Cameron May, Bern/London 2005

Crowley, Meredith A./Howse, Robert, "*Tuna – Dolphin II*: a Legal and Economic Analysis of the Appellate Body Report" 13(2) *World Trade Review* (2014) 321-355

Cullet, Philippe, "Differential Treatment in International Law: Towards a New Paradigm of Inter-State Relations", 10(3) *European Journal of International Law* (1999) 549-582

Cullet, Philippe, "Common but Differentiated Responsibilities", in Malgosia Fitzmaurice *et al.* (eds), *Research Handbook on International Environmental Law*, Edward Elgar, Cheltenham 2010, 161-181

Davey, William J., "Dispute Settlement in GATT", 11(1) *Fordham International Law Journal* (1987) 52-109

Davey, William J./Pauwelyn, Joost, "MFN Unconditionality: A Legal Analysis of the Concept in View of its Evolution in the GATT/WTO Jurisprudence with Particular Reference to the Issue of 'Like Product'", in Thomas Cottier and Petros C. Mavroidis (eds), *Regulatory Barriers and the Principle of Non-Discrimination in World Trade Law*, The University of Michigan Press, Ann Arbor 2000, 13-50

Daillier, Patrick/Forteau, Mathias/Pellet, Alain, *Droit international public*, 8th ed., L.G.D.J., Paris 2009

Desmedt, Axel, "Proportionnality in WTO Law", 4(3) *Journal of International Economic Law* (2001) 441-480

Diebold, Nicolas F., *Non-Discrimination in International Trade in Services: "Likeness" in WTO/GATS*, Cambridge University Press, Cambridge 2010

DiMaschio, Nicolas/Pauwelyn, Joost, "Non-Discrimination in Trade and Investment Treaties: Worlds Apart or Two Sides of the Same Coin?", 102 *American Journal of International Law* (2008) 48-89

Distefano, Giovanni/Mavroidis, Petros C., "L'interprétation systémique: le liant de l'ordre inter-national", in *Mélanges en l'honneur de Pierre Wessner*, Helbing & Lichtenhahn, Basel 2011, 743-759

Du, Ming, "'Treatment No Less Favourable' and the Future of National Treatment Obligation in GATT Article III:4 after *EC – Seal Products*", 15(1) *World Trade Review* (2016) 139-163

Dunoff, Jeffrey L., "Reconciling International Trade with Preservation of the Global Commons: Can We Prosper and Protect?", 49 *Washington & Lee Law Review* (1992) 1407-1454

Dupuy, Pierre-Marie, "International Law: Torn between Coexistence, Cooperation and Globali-zation", 9(2) *European Journal of International Law* (1998) 278-286

Dupuy, Pierre-Marie, "The Place and Role of Unilateralism in Contemporary International Law", 11(1) *European Journal of International Law* (2000) 19-29

Ehring, Lothar, "*De Facto* Discrimination in World Trade Law: National and Most-Favoured-Nation Treatment – or Equal Treatment?", 36(5) *Journal of World Trade* (2002) 921-977

Ehring, Lothar, "National Treatment under the GATT 1994: Jurisprudential Developments on *De Facto* Discrimination", in Anselm Kamperman Sanders (ed.), *The Principle of National Treatment in International Economic Law*, Edward Elgar, Cheltenham/Northampton 2014, 34-54

Esty, Daniel, *Greening the GATT: Trade, Environment and the Future*, Institute for International Economics, Washington DC 1994

Farber, Daniel A., "Stretching the Margins: The Geographic Nexus in Environmental Law", 48 *Stanford Law Review* (1996) 1247-1278

Freeman, A. Myrick III, *The Measurement of Environmental and Resource Values: Theory and Methods*, 2nd ed., Resources for the Future, Washington D.C. 2003

French, Duncan, "Developing States and International Environmental Law: The Importance of Differentiated Responsibilities", 49 *International and Comparative Law Quarterly* (2000) 35-60

French, Duncan, "Sustainable Development", in Malgosia Fitzmaurice *et al.* (eds), *Research Handbook on International Environmental Law*, Edward Elgar, Cheltenham 2010, 51-68

Friedman, Wolfgang Gaston, *The Changing Structure of International Law*, Stevens & Sons, London 1964

Gathii, James Thuo, "Neoliberalism, Colonialism and International Governance: Decentering the International Law of Governmental Legitimacy", 98(6) *Michigan Law Review* (2000) 1996-2055

Gaines, Sanford, "The WTO's Reading of GATT Article XX Chapeau: A Disguised Restriction on Environmental Measures", 22 *University of Pennsylvania Journal of International Economic Law* (2001), 739-862

Gaines, Sanford, "Processes and Production Methods: How to Produce Sound Policy for Environmental PPM-Based Trade Measures?", 27 *Columbia Journal of Environmental Law* (2002) 383-432

GATT Secretariat, "Trade and the Environment", in *International Trade 1990-1991*, Vol. 1, Geneva 1992

Green, Andrew, "Climate Change, Regulatory Policy and the WTO: How Constraining are Trade Rules?", 8(1) *Journal of International Economic Law* (2005) 143-189

Grossman, Gene M./Horn, Henrik/Mavroidis Petros C., "National Treatment", in *Legal and Economic Principles of World Trade Law*, Cambridge University Press, Cambridge 2013, 205-345

Guzman, Andrew T., "Trade, Labor, Legitimacy", 91 *California Law Review* (2003) 885-902

Guzman, Andrew T., "Global Governance and the WTO", 45 *Harvard International Law Journal* (2004) 303-351

Guzman, Andew T./Pauwelyn, Joost, *International Trade Law*, 3rd ed., Wolters Kluwer Law & Business, New York 2016

Hakimi, Monica, "Unfriendly Unilateralism", 55(1) *Harvard International Law Journal* (2014) 105-150

Hardin, Russel, *Collective Action*, The Johns Hopkins University Press, Baltimore/London 1982

Hardin, Garett, "The Tragedy of the Commons", 162 *Science* (13 December 1968) 1243-1248

Hertel, Michael, "Climate-Change-Related Trade Measures and Article XX: Defining Discrimination in Light of the Principle of Common but Differentiated Responsibilities", 45(3) *Journal of World Trade* (2011) 653-678

Herwig, Alexia, "Too Much Zeal on Seals? Animal Welfare, Public Morals, and Consumer Ethics at the Bar of the WTO" 15(1) *World Trade Review* (2016) 109-137

Hilf, Meinhard, "Power, Rules and Principles – Which Orientation for WTO/GATT Law", 4 (1) *Journal of International Economic Law* (2001) 111-130

Holzer, Kateryna, *Carbon-Related Border Adjustment and WTO Law*, E. Elgar, Northampton 2014

Honkonen, Tuula, *The Common but Differentiated Responsibility Principle in Multilateral Environmental Agreements: Regulatory and Policy Aspects*, Kluwer Law International, Alphen aan den Rijn 2009

Horn, Henrik/Mavroidis, Petros C., "Still Hazy after all these Years: The Interpretation of National Treatment in the GATT/WTO Case-Law on Tax Discrimination", 15(1) *European Journal of International Law* (2004) 39-69

Horn, Henrik/Mavroidis, Petros C., "The Permissible Reach of National Environmental Policies", 42(6) *Journal of World Trade* (2008) 1107-1178

Horn, Henrik/Weiler, Joseph H. H., "EC – Asbestos", *in* H. Horn and P. Mavroidis (eds), *The WTO Case Law of 2001: The American Law Institute Reporters' Studies,* Cambridge University Press, Cambridge 2003, 14-40

Houston-McMillan, Jason, "The Legitimate Regulatory Distinction Test: Incomplete and Inadequate for the Particular Purposes of the TBT Agreement", 15(4) *World Trade Review* (2016) 543-562

Howse, Robert, "The Appellate Body Rulings in the Shrimp/Turtle Case: A New Legal Baseline for the Trade and Environment Debate", 27 *Columbia Journal of Environmental Law* (2002) 491-521

Howse, Robert, "The World Trade Organization and the Protection of Workers' Rights", 3 *The Journal of Small and Emerging Business Law* (1999) 131-172

Howse, Robert/Langille, Joanna/Sykes, Katie, "Sealing the Deal: the WTO Appellate Body's Report in *EC–Seal Products'*, 18(12) ASIL Insights, June 2014

Howse, Robert/Levy, Philip, "The TBT Panels: *US – Cloves, US – Tuna, US – COOL*", 12 (2) *World Trade Review* (2013) 327-375

Howse, Robert/Regan, Donald, "The Product/Process Distinction – An Illusory Basis for Disciplining 'Unilateralism' in Trade Policy", 11(2) *European Journal of International Law* (2000) 249-289

Howse, Robert/Tuerk, Elisabeth, "The WTO Impact on Internal Regulations – A Case Study of the Canada – EC Asbestos Dispute", in Grainne De Burca and Joanne Scott (eds), *The EU and the WTO: Legal and Constitutional Issues*, Hart Publishing, Oxford 2001

Hudec, Robert E., "GATT/WTO Constraints on National Regulation: Requiem for an 'Aim and Effects' Test", 32 *The International Lawyer* (1998) 619-649

Hudec, Robert E., "The Product-Process Distinction in GATT/WTO Jurisprudence", in Marco Bronckers and Reinhard Quick (eds), *New Directions in International Economic Law: Essays in Honour of John H. Jackson*, Kluwer Law International, The Hague 2000, 187-217

Hufbauer, Gary Clyde/Charnovitz, Steve/Kim, Jisun, *Global Warming and the World Trading System*, Peterson Institute for International Economics, Washington D.C. 2009

Jackson, John, "World Trade Rules and Environmental Policies: Congruence or Conflict?", 49 *Washington & Lee Law Review* (1992) 1227-1278

Jackson, John, *The World Trading System*, The MIT Press, Cambridge Mass./London 1997

Jackson, John, "Comments on *Shrimp/Turtle* and the Product/Process Distinction", 11(2) *European Journal of International Law* (2000) 303-307

Jansen, Bernhard, "The Limits of Unilateralism from a European Perspective", 11(2) *European Journal of International Law* (2000) 309-313

Jansen, Bernhard/Lugard, Maurits, "Some Considerations on Trade Barriers Erected for Non-Economic Reasons and WTO Obligations", 2(3) *Journal of International Economic Law* (1999) 530-536

Joshi, Manoj, "Are Eco-Labels Consistent with World Trade Organization Agreements?" 38 (1) *Journal of World Trade* (2004) 69-92

Kaul, Inge/Grunberg, Isabelle/Stern, Marc A., *Global Public Goods: International Cooperation in the 21ˢᵗ Century*, Oxford University Press, New York/Oxford 1999

Kelleher, Kieran, *Discards in the World's Marine Fisheries, An Update*, FAO Fisheries Technical Paper 470, Rome 2005

Kelly, Trish, "Tuna-Dolphin Revisited", 48(3) *Journal of World Trade* (2014) 501-524

Kirgis, Frederic L., "Standing to Challenge Endeavors that Could Change the Climate", 84 (2) *American Journal of International Law* (1990) 525-530

Kiss, Alexandre, "The Protection of Environmental Interests of the World Community Through International Environmental Law", in Rüdiger Wolfrum (ed.), *Enforcing Environmental Standards: Economic Mechanisms as Viable Means?*, Springer, Berlin 1996

Kiss, Alexandre/Beurier, Jean-Pierre, *Droit international de l'environnement*, 4th ed., A. Pedrone, Paris 2010

Leroux, Eric H., "Eleven Years of GATS Case Law: What Have We Learned?", 10(4) *Journal of International Economic Law* (2007) 749-793

Lester, Simon, *World Trade Law : Text, Materials and Commentary*, 2nd ed., Hart Publishing, Oxford 2012

Levy, Philip/Regan, Donald, *"EC – Seal Products*: Seals and Sensibilities (TBT Aspects of the Panel and Appellate Body Reports)", 14(2) *World Trade Review* (2015) 337-379

Low, Patrick/Marceau, Gabrielle/Reinaud, Julia, "The Interface between the Trade and Climate Change Regimes: Scoping the Issues", 46(3) *Journal of World Trade* (2012) 485-544

Lowe, Vaughan, "Sustainable Development and Unsustainable Arguments", in Alan E. Boyle and David Freestone (eds), *International Law and Sustainable Development: Past Achievements and Future Challenges*, Oxford University Press, New York 1999

Luff, David, *Le droit de l'organisation mondiale du commerce: analyse critique*, Bruylant/L.G.D. J., Bruxelles/Paris 2004

Machado Filho, Haroldo, *The Principle of Common But Differentiated Responsibilities and the Climate Change Regime*, PhD Thesis, Geneva 2008

Mann, Frederick A., "The Doctrine of Jurisdiction in International Law", 111 *Recueil des cours* (1964) 1-162

Mann, Frederick A., "The Doctrine of International Jurisdiction Revisited After Twenty Years", 186 *Recueil des cours* (1984) 9-116

Marceau, Gabrielle, "A Call for Coherence in International Law – Praises for the Prohibition Against 'Clinical Isolation' in WTO Dispute Settlement", 33(5) *Journal of World Trade* (1999) 87-152

Marceau, Gabrielle, "WTO Dispute Settlement and Human Rights", 13(4) *European Journal of International Law* (2002) 753-814

Marceau, Gabrielle, "A Comment on the Appellate Body Report in *EC – Seal Products* in the Context of the Trade and Environment Debate", 23(3) *RECIEL* (2014) 318-328

Marceau, Gabrielle/Trachtman, Joel P., "The Technical Barriers to Trade Agreement, the Sanitary and Phytosanitary Measures Agreement, and the General Agreement on Tariffs and Trade: A Map of the World Trade Organization Law of Domestic Regulation of Goods", 36(5) *Journal of World Trade* (2002) 811-881

Marceau, Gabrielle/Trachtman, Joel P., "A Map of the World Trade Organization Law of Domestic Regulation of Goods The Technical Barriers to Trade Agreement, the Sanitary and Phytosanitary Measures Agreement, and the General Agreement on Tariffs and Trade", 48 (2) *Journal of World Trade* (2014) 351-432

Marín Durán, Gracia, "Measures with Multiple Competing Purposes after *EC – Seal Products*: Avoiding a Conflict between GATT Article XX-Chapeau and Article 2.1 TBT Agreement", 19 *Journal of International Economic Law* (2016) 467-495

Matsushita, Mitsuo/Schoenbaum, Thomas J./Mavroidis, Petros C./Michael Hahn, *The World Trade Organization : Law, Practice, and Policy*, 3rd ed., Oxford University Press, Oxford 2015

Mavroidis, Petros C., "Driftin' too far from shore – why the test for compliance with the TBT Agreement developed by the Appellate Body is wrong, and what should the AB have done instead", 12(3) *World Trade Review* (2013) 509-531

Mavroidis, Petros C., "'Like Products': Some Thoughts at the Positive and Normative Level", in Thomas Cottier and Petros C. Mavroidis (eds), *Regulatory Barriers and the Principle of Non-Discrimination in World Trade Law*, The University of Michigan Press, Ann Arbor 2000, 125-135

Mavroidis, Petros C., "No Outsourcing of Law? WTO Law as Practiced by WTO Courts", 102 *American Journal of International Law* (2008) 421-474 (cit. Mavroidis [2008a])

Mavroidis, Petros C., *The Regulation of International Trade, Volume 1: GATT*, The MIT Press, Cambridge, MA/London 2016 (cit. Mavroidis [2016a])

Mavroidis, Petros C., *The Regulation of International Trade, Volume 2: The WTO Agreements on Trade in Goods*, The MIT Press, Cambridge, MA/London 2016 (cit. Mavroidis [2016b])

Mavroidis, Petros C., *Trade in Goods: The GATT and the Other Agreements Regulating Trade in Goods*, Oxford University Press, 2008 (cit. Mavroidis [2008b])

Mavroidis, Petros C., *Trade in Goods: The GATT and the Other Agreements Regulating Trade in Goods*, 2nd edition, Oxford University Press, Oxford 2012

Mavroidis, Petros C./Bermann, George A./Wu, Mark, *The Law of the World Trade Organization (WTO)*, West, St-Paul 2010

Mavroidis, Petros C./Saggi, Kamal, "What is not so Cool about *US – COOL* Regulations? A Critical Analysis of the Appellate Body's Ruling on *US – COOL*" 13(2) *World Trade Review* (2014) 299-320

McGinnis, John O./Movsesian, Mark L., "The World Trade Constitution", 45 *Harvard Law Review* (2000) 511-605

McGinnis, John O./Movsesian, Mark L., "Against Global Governance in the WTO", 45 *Harvard Law Review* (2004) 353-365

Murase, Shinya, "Perspectives from International Economic Law on Transnational Environmental Issues", 253 *Recueil des cours* (1995) 283-431

Nadakavukaren Schefer, Krista, *Social Regulation in the WTO: Trade Policy and International Legal Development*, Edward Elgar, Cheltenham/Northampton 2010

Neumann, Jan/Tuerk, Elisabeth, "Necessity Revisited: Proportionality in World Trade Organization Law After *Korea – Beef*, *EC – Asbestos* and *EC – Sardines*", 37(1) *Journal of World Trade* (2003) 199-233

Nielsen, Laura, *The WTO, Animals and PPMs*, Martinus Nijhoff Publishers, Leiden/Boston 2007

Nollkaemper, André, "Rethinking States' Rights to Promote Extra-Territorial Environmental Values", in Friedl Weiss *et al.* (eds), *International Economic Law with a Human Face*, Kluwer Law International, The Hague 1998

Nordhaus, William D., "Paul Samuelson and Global Public Goods", in Michael Szenberg *et al.* (eds), *Samuelsonian Economics and the Twenty-First Century*, Oxford University Press, Oxford 2006

O'Brien, Julia, "The Equity of Levelling the Playing Field in the Climate Change Context", 43 (5) *Journal of World Trade* (2009) 1093-1114

Organization for Economic Cooperation and Development (OECD), *Eco-Labelling: Actual Effects of Selected Programmes*, OCDE/GD(97)105 (cit. OECD [1997a])

Organization for Economic Cooperation and Development (OECD), *Process and Production Methods (PPMs): Conceptual Framework and Considerations on Use of PPM-Based Trade Measures*, OCDE/DG(97)137, Paris 1997 (cit. OECD [1997b])

Organization for Economic Cooperation and Development (OECD), *Report on Trade and Environment at the OECD Council at Ministerial Level*, OCDE/GD(95)63

Okubo, Atsuko, "Environmental Labelling Programs and the GATT/WTO Regime", 11 *Georgetown International Law Review* (1999) 599-646

Ortino, Federico, "WTO Jurisprudence on *De Jure* and *De Facto* Discrimination", in Federico Ortino and Ernst-Ulrich Petersmann (eds), *The WTO Dispute Settlement System, 1995-2003*, Kluwer Law International, The Hague 2004, 217-262

Ortino, Federico, "The Principle of Non-Discrimination and its Exceptions in GATS: Selected Legal Issues", in Alexander Kern and Andenas Mads (eds), *The World Trade Organization and Trade in Services*, Cambridge University Press, Cambridge 2008, 173-206

Ostrom, Elinor, *Governing the Commons*, Cambridge University Press, Cambridge 1990

Ostrom, Elinor/Gardner, Roy/Walker, James, *Rules, Games, and Common-Pool Resources*, University of Michigan Press, Ann Arbor 1994

Parker, Richard W., "The Use and Abuse of Trade Leverage to Protect the Global Commons: What We Can Learn from the Tuna – Dolphin Conflict", 12 *Georgetown International Environmental Law Review* (1999) 1-123

Pauwelyn, Joost, "Cross-Agreement Complainants before the Appellate Body: A Case Study of the EC – Asbestos Dispute", 1 *World Trade Review* (2002) 63-87

Pauwelyn, Joost, *Conflict of Norms in Public International Law: How WTO Law Relates to Other Rules of International Law*, Cambridge University Press, Cambridge 2003 [cit. Pauwelyn (2003a)]

Pauwelyn, Joost, "How to Win a World Trade Organization Dispute Based on Non-World Trade Organization Law? Questions of Jurisdiction and Merits", 37(6) *Journal of World Trade* (2003) 997-1030 [cit. Pauwelyn (2003b)]

Pauwelyn, Joost, "Recent Books on Trade an Environment: GATT Phantoms Still Haunt the WTO", 15(3) *European Journal of International Law* (2004) 575-592

Pauwelyn, Joost, *U.S. Federal Climate Policy and Competitiveness Concerns: The Limits and Options of International Trade Law*, Working Paper, Nicolas Institute for Environmental Policy Solutions, Duke University, 2007

Pauwelyn, Joost, "The Unbearable Lightness of Likeness", in Marion Panizzon, Nicole Pohl and Pierre Sauvé (eds), *GATS and the Regulation of International Trade in Services*, Cambridge University Press, Cambridge 2008, 358-369

Petersmann, Ernst-Ulrich, *International and European Trade and Environmental Law after the Uruguay Round*, Kluwer Law International, London 1996

Perrez, Franz Xaver, "The Relationship between 'Permanent Sovereignty' and the Obligation not to Cause Transboundary Environmental Damage", 26 *Environmental Law* (1996) 1187-1212

Perrez, Franz Xaver, *Cooperative Sovereignty: From Independence to Interdependence in the Structure of International Environmental Law*, Kluwer Law International, The Hague 2000

Porges, Amelia/Trachtman, Joel P., "Robert Hudec and Domestic Regulation: The Resurrection of Aim and Effects", 37(4) *Journal of World Trade* (2003) 783-799

Prost, Mario, *D'abord les moyens, les besoins viendront après: commerce et environnement dans la jurisprudence du GATT et de l'OMC*, Bruylant, Bruxelles 2005

Pugel, Thomas A., *International Economics*, Irwin McGraw-Hill, New York 2009

Puth, Sebastian, *WTO und Umwelt: Die Produkt-Prozess Doktrin*, Ducker & Humblot, Berlin 2004

Qin, Julia, "Accomodating Divergent Policy Objectives under WTO Law: Reflecting on *EC – Seal Products*" *AJIL Unbound* 2015

Quick, Reinhard/Lau, Christian, "Environmentally Motivated Tax Distinctions and the WTO: The European Commission's Green Paper on Integrated Product Policy in Light of the 'Like Product' and 'PPM' Debates", 6(2) *Journal of International Economic Law* (2003) 419-458

Qureshi, Asif Hasan/Ziegler, Andreas R., *International Economic Law*, 3rd ed., Sweet & Maxwell, London 2011

Rajamani, Lavanya, *Differential Treatment in International Environmental Law*, Oxford University Press, Oxford 2006

Rao, P. K., *Sustainable Development*, Blackwell, Malden/Oxford 2000

Rao, P. K., *International Environmental Law and Economics*, Blackwell, Malden 2002

Regan, Donald, "Regulatory Purpose and 'Like Products' in Article III:4 of the GATT (With Additional Remarks on Article III:2)", 26(3) *Journal of World Trade* (2002) 443-478

Regan, Donald, "Further Thoughts on the Role of Regulatory Purpose Under Article III of the General Agreement on Tariffs and Trade", 37(4) *Journal of World Trade* (2003) 737-760

Regan, Daniel, "How to Think about PPMs", in Thomas Cottier *et al.* (eds), *International Trade Regulation and the Mitigation of Climate Change: World Trade Forum*, Cambridge University Press, Cambridge 2009, 97-123

Regan, Donald, "Measures with Multiple Purposes: Puzzles from *EC – Seal Products*" *AJIL Unbound* (2015)

Regan, Donald, "The Meaning of 'Necessary' in GATT Article XX and GATS Article XIV: The Myth of Cost-Benefit Balancing, 6(3) *World Trade Review* (2007) 347-369

Rege, Vinod, "GATT Law and Environment-Related Issues Affecting the Trade of Developing Countries", 28(3) *Journal of World Trade* (1994) 95-169

Roessler, Frieder, "Beyond the Ostensible, A Tribute to Professor Robert Hudec's Insights on the Determination of the Likeness of Products Under the National Treatment Provisions of the General Agreement on Tariffs and Trade", 37(4) *Journal of World Trade* (2003) 771-781

Ryngaert, Cedric, *Jurisdiction in International Law*, 2nd ed., Oxford University Press, Oxford/New York 2015

de Sadeleer, Nicolas, *Environmental Principles: From Political Slogans to Legal Rules*, Oxford University Press, Oxford, 2002

Sandler, Todd, *Global Challenges: An Approach to Environmental, Political and Economic Problems*, Cambridge University Press, Cambridge 1997

Sands, Philippe, "'Unilateralism', Values and International Law", 11(2) *European Journal of International Law* (2000) 291-302

Sands, Philippe, "Turtles and Torturers", 33 *New York University Journal of International Law and Politics* (2001) 527-559

Sands, Philippe, *Principles of International Environmental Law*, 3rd ed., Cambridge University Press, Cambridge 2012

Samuelson, Paul Anthony/Nordhaus, William D., *Economics*, 18th ed., McGraw-Hill, Boston 2005

Schlagenhof, Markus, "Trade Measures Based on Enviromental Processes and Production Methods", 29(5) *Journal of World Trade* (1995) 123-155

Schoenbaum, Thomas J., "International Trade and Protection of the Environment: The Continuing Search for Reconciliation", 91(2) *American Journal of International Law* (1997) 268-313

Schoenbaum, Thomas J., "The Decision in the *Shrimp – Turtle* Case", 9(1) *Yearbook of International Environmental Law* (1998), 36-39

Schrijver, Nico, "The Evolution of Sustainable Development in International Law: Inception, Meaning and Status", 329 *Recueil des cours* (2007) 217-412

Schwartz, Priscilla, "The Polluter-Pays Principle", in Malgosia Fitzmaurice, David Ong and Panos Merkouris, *Research Handbook on International Environmental Law*, Edward Elgar, Chelthenham/Northampton Mass. 2010, 243-265

Shaw, Malcolm Nathan, *International Law*, 7th ed., Cambridge University Press, Cambridge 2014

Shelton, Dinah, "Equity", in Daniel Bodansky *et al.* (eds), *The Oxford Handbook of International Environmental Law*, Oxford University Press, Oxford 2007, 639-662

Sinclair, Sir Ian, *The Vienna Convention on the Law of Treaties*, 2nd ed., Manchester University Press, 1984

Strauss, Andrew L., "From GATTzilla to the Green Giant: Winning the Environmental Battle for the Soul of the World Trade Organization", 19 *University of Pennsylvania Journal of International Economic Law* (1998) 769-818

Stern, Brigitte, "Quelques observations sur les règles internationales relatives à l'application extraterritoriale du droit", *Annuaire Français de Droit International* (1986) 7-52

Stern, Brigitte, "L'extraterritorialité revisitée. Où il est question des affaires Alvarez Machain, Pâte de bois et de quelques autres...", *Annuaire Français de Droit International* (1992), 239-312

Stern, Brigitte, "Can the United States Set Rules for the World? A French View", 31(4) *Journal of World Trade* (1997) 5-26

Stern, Brigitte, "Droit international public et sanctions unilatérales", in Habib Gherari and Sandra Szurek (eds), *Sanctions unilatérales, mondialisation du commerce et ordre juridique international*, Montchrestien, Paris 1998, 185-218

Stern, Brigitte, "United States – Import Prohibition of Certain Shrimp and Shrimp Products. Recourse to Article 21.5 of the DSU by Malaysia", in Brigitte Stern and Ruiz Fabri (eds), *La jurisprudence de l'OMC/The Case Law of the WTO, 1998-2*, Martinus Nijhoff Publishers, Leiden/Boston 2006, 106-151

Stern, Nicholas, *The Economics of Climate Change: The Stern Review*, Cambridge University Press, Cambridge 2007

Steward, Richard B., "International Trade and Environment: Lessons from the Federal Experience", 49(4) *Washington & Lee Law Review* (1992) 1329-1372

Steward, Richard B., "Environmental Regulation and International Competitiveness", 102(8) *Yale Law Journal* (1993) 2039-2106

Stiglitz, Joseph E./Walsh, Carl E., *Economics*, 4th ed., W. W. Norton, New York 2006

Stone, Christopher D., "Common but Differentiated Responsibilities in International Law", 98 *American Journal of International Law* (2004) 276

Sykes, Alan, "Regulatory Protectionism and the Law of International Trade", 66(1) *University of Chicago Law Review* (1999) 1-46

Sykes, Alan, "The Least Restrictive Means", 70(1) *University of Chicago Law Review* (2003), 403-419

Tomuschat, Christian, "International Law: Obligations Arising for States Without or Against Their Will", 241 *Recueil des Cours* (1993) 195

Trachtman, Joel, "The Domain of Dispute Resolution", 40(2) *Harvard International Law Journal* (1999) 333-377

Trebilcock, Michael J./Giri, Shiva K., *The National Treatment Principle in International Trade Law*, American Law and Economics Association Annual Meeting, Working Paper n° 8, 2004 (http://law.bepress.com/cgi/viewcontent.cgi?article=1007&context=alea)

Trebilcock, Michael/Howse, Robert, "Trade Liberalization and Regulatory Diversity: Reconciling Competitive Markets with Competitive Politics", 6 *European Journal of Law and Economics* (1998) 5-37 [cit. Trebilcock/Howse (1998)]

Trebilcock, Michael/Howse, Robert/Eliason, Antonia, *The Regulation of International Trade*, 4th ed., Routledge, London, New York, 2013 [cit. Trebilcock/Howse (2013)]

Vogler, John, *The Global Commons: Environmental and Technological Governance*, 2nd ed., John Wiley & Sons, Chichester 2000

Vogel, David, *Trading Up: Consumer and Environmental Regulation in a Global Economy*, Harvard University Press, Cambridge Mass. 1995

Voon, Tania, "Exploring the Meaning of Trade-Restrictiveness in the WTO", 14(3) *World Trade Review* (2015) 451-477

Vranes, Erich, *Trade and the Environment: Fundamental Issues in International Law, WTO Law and Legal Theory*, Oxford University Press, Oxford 2009

Weiler, Joseph H. H., "The Rule of Lawyers and the Ethos of Diplomats: Reflections on the Internal and External Legitimacy of the WTO Dispute Settlement", 35(2) *Journal of World Trade* (2001) 191-207

Wiers, Jochem-Jurrian Derk, *Trade and Environment in the EC and the WTO: A Legal Analysis*, Europa Law Publishing, Groningen 2002

Will, Ulrike, "The Extra-Jurisdictional Effects of Environmental Measures in the WTO Law Balancing Process", 50(4) *Journal of World Trade* (2016) 611-640

World Bank, *World Development Report 1992: Development and the Environment*, Oxford University Press, Oxford 1992

World Commission on Environment and Development, *Our Common Future*, Oxford University Press, Oxford/New York 1987

WTO, *Negotiating History of the Coverage of the Agreement on Technical Barriers to Trade with Regard to Labelling Requirements, Voluntary Standards, and Processes and Production Methods Unrelated to Product Characteristics*, Note by the Secretariat, WT/CTE/W/10, G/TBT/W/11, 29 August 1995

Young, Margaret, "Trade Measures to Address Environmental Concerns in Faraway Places: Jurisdictional Issues" 23(3) *RECIEL* (2014) 302-317

Zeitler, Helge Elisabeth, *Einseitige Handelbescränkungen zum Schutz extraterritorialer Rechtsgüter: eine Untersuchung zum GATT, Gemeinschaftsrecht und allgemeinen Völkerrecht*, Nomos, Baden-Baden 2000

Ziegler, Andreas R./Sifonios, David, "The Assessment of Environmental Risks and Process and Production Methods (PPMs) in International Trade Law", in Monika Ambrus, Rosemary Rayfuse and Wouter Werner (eds), *Risk and the Regulation of Uncertainty in International Law*, Oxford University Press, Oxford/New York 2017

Table of Cases

Argentina – Bovine Hides and Leather: Panel Report, *Argentina – Measures Affecting the Export of Bovine Hides and the Import of Finished Leather*, WT/DS155/R, adopted 16 February 2001

Australia – Ammonium Sulphate: Working Party Report, *The Australian Subsidy on Ammomium Sulphate*, GATT/CP.4/39, adopted 3 April 1950

Belgium – Family Allowances: GATT Panel Report, *Belgian Family Allowances*, G/32, adopted 7 November 1952

Brazilian Internal Taxes: Working Party Report, *Brazilian Internal Taxes*, GATT/CP.3/42 (First Report), adopted 2 December 1949; GATT/CP.5/37 (Second Report), adopted 13 December 1950

Brazil – Tyres: Panel Report, *Brazil – Measures Affecting Imports of Retreaded Tyres*, WT/DS332/R, adopted 17 December 2007

Appellate Body Report, *Brazil – Measures Affecting Imports of Retreaded Tyres*, WT/DS332/AB/R, adopted 17 December 2007

Canada – FIRA: GATT Panel Report, *Canada – Administration of the Foreign Investment Review Act*, L/5504, adopted 7 February 1984

Canada – Autos: Panel Report, *Canada – Certain Measures Affecting the Automotive Industry*, WT/DS139/R, WT/DS142/R, adopted 19 June 2000

Canada – Herring and Salmon: GATT Panel Report, *Canada – Measures Affecting Exports of Unprocessed Herring and Salmon*, L/6268, adopted 22 March 1988

Canada – Periodicals: Panel Report, *Canada – Certain Measures Concerning Periodicals*, WT/DS31/R, adopted 14 March 1997

Appellate Body Report, *Canada – Certain Measures Concerning Periodicals*, WT/DS31/AB/R, adopted 30 July 1997

Chile – Alcoholic Beverages: Panel Report, *Chile – Taxes on Alcoholic Beverages*, WT/DS87/R, WT/DS110/R, adopted 12 January 2000

Appellate Body Report, *Chile – Taxes on Alcoholic Beverages*, WT/DS87/AB/R, WT/DS110/AB/R, adopted 12 January 2000

China – Auto Parts: Panel Reports, *China – Measures Affecting Imports of Automobile Parts*, WT/DS339 /R, WT/DS340/R, WT/DS342/R and Add.1 and Add.2, adopted 12 January 2009

Appellate Body Reports, *China – Measures Affecting Imports of Automobile Parts*, WT/DS339/AB/R / WT/DS340/AB/R / WT/DS342/AB/R, adopted 12 January 2009

China – Publications and Audiovisual Products: Panel Report, *China – Measures Affecting Trading Rights and Distribution Services for Certain Publications and Audiovisual Entertainment Products*, WT/DS363/R, adopted 19 January 2010

Appellate Body Report, *China – Measures Affecting Trading Rights and Distribution Services for Certain Publications and Audiovisual Entertainment Products*, WT/DS363/AB/R, adopted 19 January 2010

Dominican Republic – Cigarettes: Panel Report, *Dominican Republic – Measures Affecting the Importation and Internal Sale of Cigarettes*, WT/DS302/R, 26 November 2004

Appellate Body Report, *Dominican Republic – Measures Affecting the Importation and Internal Sale of Cigarettes*, WT/DS302/AB/R, adopted 19 May 2005

EC – Asbestos: Panel Report, *European Communities – Measures Affecting Asbestos and Asbestos-Containing Products*, WT/DS135/R and Add.1, adopted 5 April 2001

Appellate Body Report, *European Communities – Measures Affecting Asbestos and Asbestos-Containing Products*, WT/DS135/AB/R, adopted 5 April 2001

EC – Banana III: Panel Report, *European Communities – Regime for the Importation, Sale and Distribution of Bananas*, WT/DS27/R, adopted 25 September 1997

Appellate Body Report, *European Communities – Regime for the Importation, Sale and Distribution of Bananas*, WT/DS27/AB/R, adopted 25 September 1997

EC – Biotech: Panel Report, *European Communities – Measures Affecting the Approval and Marketing of Biotech Products*, WT/DS291/R/Corr.1, WT/292/R/Corr.1, WT/293/R/Corr.1, adopted 21 November 2006

EC – Hormones: Panel Report, *European Communities – Measures Concerning Meat and Meat Products (Hormones)*, WT/DS26/R, WT/DS48/R, adopted 13 February 1998

Appellate Body Report, *European Communities – Measures Concerning Meat and Meat Products (Hormones)*, WT/DS26/AB/R, WT/DS48/AB/R, adopted 13 February 1998

EC – Sardines: Appellate Body Report, *European Communities – Trade Description of Sardines*, WT/DS231/AB/R, adopted 23 October 2002

EC – Seal Products: Panel Report, *European Communities – Measures Prohibiting the Importation and Marketing of Seal Products*, WT/DS400/R, WT/DS401/R and Add.1, adopted 18 June 2014

Appellate Body Report, *European Communities – Measures Prohibiting the Importation and Marketing of Seal Products*, WT/DS400/R, WT/DS401/R, adopted 18 June 2014

EC – Tariff Preferences: Panel Report, *European Communities – Conditions for the Granting of Tariff Preferences to Developing Countries*, WT/DS246/R, adopted 20 April 2004

Appellate Body Report, *European Communities – Conditions for the Granting of Tariff Preferences to Developing Countries*, WT/DS246/AB/R, adopted 20 April 2004

EEC – Animal Feed Proteins: Panel Report, *EEC – Measures on Animal Feed Proteins*, L/4599, adopted on 14 March 1978

India – Autos: Panel Report, *India – Measures Affecting the Automotive Sector*, WT/DS146/R, WT/DS175/R and Corr.1, adopted 5 April 2002

Italy – Agricultural Machinery: GATT Panel Report, *Italian Discrimination Against Imported Agricultural Machinery*, L/833, adopted 23 October 1958

Japan – Alcohol I: GATT Panel Report, *Japan – Customs Duties, Taxes and Labelling Practices on Imported Wines and Alcoholic Beverages*, L/6216, adopted 10 November 1987

Japan – Alcohol II: Panel Report, *Japan – Taxes on Alcoholic Beverages*, WT/DS8/R, WT/DS10/R, WT/DS11/R, adopted 1 November 1996

Appellate Body Report, *Japan – Taxes on Alcoholic Beverages*, WT/DS8/AB/R, WT/DS10/AB/R, WT/DS11/AB/R, adopted 1 November 1996

Japan – Films: Panel Report, *Japan – Measures Affecting Consumer Photographic Film and Paper*, WT/DS44/R, adopted 22 April 1998

Korea – Alcohol: Panel Report, *Korea – Taxes on Alcoholic Beverages*, WT/DS75/R, WT/DS84/R, adopted 17 February 1999

Appellate Body Report, *Korea – Taxes on Alcoholic Beverages*, WT/DS75/AB/R, WT/DS84/AB/R, adopted 17 February 1999

Korea – Beef: Panel Report, *Korea – Measures Affecting Imports of Fresh, Chilled and Frozen Beef*, WT/DS161/R, WT/DS169/R, adopted 31 July 2000

Appellate Body Report, *Korea – Measures Affecting Imports of Fresh, Chilled and Frozen Beef*, WT/DS161/AB/R, WT/DS169/AB/R, adopted 10 January 2001

Mexico – Soft Drinks: Panel Report, *Mexico – Tax Measures on Soft Drinks and Other Beverages*, WT/DS308/R, adopted 24 March 2006

Appellate Body Report, *Mexico – Tax Measures on Soft Drinks and Other Beverages*, WT/DS308/AB/R, adopted 24 March 2006

Philippines – Distilled Spirits: Appellate Body Report, *Philippines – Taxes on Distilled Spirits*, WT/DS396/AB/R, WT/DS403/AB/R, adopted 20 January 2012

Spain – Unroasted Coffee: GATT Panel Report, *Spain – Tariff Treatment of Unroasted Coffee*, L/5135, adopted 11 June 1981

Thailand – Cigarettes: GATT Panel Report, *Thailand – Restrictions on Importation of and Internal Taxes on Cigarettes*, DS/10/R, adopted 7 November 1990

Thailand – Cigarettes (Philippines): Panel Report, *Thailand – Customs and Fiscal Measures on Cigarettes from the Philippines*, WT/DS371/R, adopted 15 July 2011

Appellate Body Report, *Thailand – Customs and Fiscal Measures on Cigarettes from the Philippines*, WT/DS371/AB/R, adopted 15 July 2011

US – Automotive Springs: GATT Panel Report, *United States – Imports of Certain Automotive Spring Assemblies*, L/5333 – 30S/107, adopted on 26 May 1983

US – Canadian Tuna: GATT Panel Report, *United States – Prohibition of Imports of Tuna and Tuna Products from Canada*, L/5198 – 29S/91, adopted 22 February 1982

US – Clove Cigarettes: Panel Report, *United States – Measures Affecting the Production and Sale of Cigarettes*, WT/DS406/R, adopted 24 April 2012

Appellate Body Report, *United States – Measures Affecting the Production and Sale of Clove Cigarettes*, WT/DS406/AB/R, adopted 24 April 2012

US – COOL: Panel Report, *United States – Certain Country of Origin Labelling (COOL) Requirements*, WT/DS384/R / WT/DS386/R, adopted 23 July 2012

Appellate Body Report, *United States – Certain Country of Origin Labelling (COOL) Requirements*, WT/DS384/AB/R / WT/DS386/AB/R, adopted 23 July 2012

US – FSC 21.5: Appellate Body Report, *United States – Tax Treatment for "Foreign Sales Corporations, Recourse to Article 21.5 of the DSU by the European Communities*, WT/DS108/AB/RW, adopted 29 January 2002

US – Gambling: Panel Report, *United States – Measures Affecting the Cross-Border Supply of Gambling and Betting Services*, WT/DS285/R, adopted 20 April 2005

Appellate Body Report, *United States – Measures Affecting the Cross-Border Supply of Gambling and Betting Services*, WT/DS285/AB/R, adopted 20 April 2005

US – Gasoline: Panel Report, *United States – Standards for Reformulated and Conventional Gasoline*, WT/DS2/R, adopted 20 May 1996

Appellate Body Report, *United States – Standards for Reformulated and Conventional Gasoline*, WT/DS2/AB/R, adopted 20 May 1996

US – Malt Beverages: GATT Panel Report, *United States – Measures Affecting Alcoholic and Malt Beverages*, DS23/R, adopted 19 June 1992

US – Section 337: GATT Panel Report, *United States – Section 337 of the Tariff Act of 1930*, L/6439, adopted 7 November 1989

US – Taxes on Automobiles: GATT Panel Report, *United States – Taxes on Automobiles*, DS31/R, 11 October 1994, unadopted

US – Shrimp: Panel Report, *United States – Import Prohibition of Certain Shrimp and Shrimp Products*, WT/DS58/R, adopted 15 May 1998

Appellate Body Report, *United States – Import Prohibition of Certain Shrimp and Shrimp Products*, WT/DS58/AB/R, adopted 6 November 1998

US – Shrimp 21.5: Panel Report, *United States – Import Prohibition of Certain Shrimp and Shrimp Products – Recourse to Article 21.5 of the DSU by Malaysia*, WT/DS58/RW, adopted 15 June 2001

Appellate Body Report, *United States – Import Prohibition of Certain Shrimp and Shrimp Products – Recourse to Article 21.5 of the DSU by Malaysia*, WT/DS58/AB/RW, adopted 21 November 2001

US – Superfund: GATT Panel Report, *United States – Taxes on Petroleum and Certain Imported Substances*, L/6175, adopted 17 June 1987

US – Tuna I: GATT Panel Report, *United States – Restrictions on Imports of Tuna*, DS21/R, 3 September 1991, unadopted

US – Tuna II: GATT Panel Report, *United States – Restrictions on Imports of Tuna*, DS29/R, 16 June 1994, unadopted

US – Tuna II (Mexico): Panel Report, *United States – Measures Concerning the Importation, Marketing and Sale of Tuna and Tuna Products*, WT/DS381/R, adopted 13 June 2012

Appellate Body Report, *United States – Measures Concerning the Importation, Marketing and Sale of Tuna and Tuna Products*, WT/DS381/AB/R, adopted 13 June 2012

US – Tuna II (Mexico) 21.5: Panel Report, *United States – Measures Concerning the Importation, Marketing and Sale of Tuna and Tuna Products, Recourse to Article 21.5 of the DSU by Mexico*, WT/DS381/RW, adopted 3 December 2015

Appellate Body Report, *United States – Measures Concerning the Importation, Marketing and Sale of Tuna and Tuna Products, Recourse to Article 21.5 of the DSU by Mexico*, WT/DS381/AB/RW, adopted 3 December 2015

Printed by Printforce, the Netherlands